Criminal Law and Procedure

Daniel E. Hall

CENGAGE
Learning·

Australia · Brazil · Japan · Korea · Mexico · Singapore · Spain · United Kingdom · United States

Criminal Law and Procedure

Criminal Law and Procedure
Daniel E. Hall

© 2015 Cengage Learning. All rights reserved.

ALL RIGHTS RESERVED. No part of this work covered by the copyright herein may be reproduced or distributed in any form or by any means, except as permitted by U.S. copyright law, without the prior written permission of the copyright owner.

For product information and technology assistance, contact us at
Cengage Learning Customer & Sales Support, 1-800-354-9706
For permission to use material from this text or product,
submit all requests online at **cengage.com/permissions**
Further permissions questions can be emailed to
permissionrequest@cengage.com

This book contains select works from existing Cengage Learning resources and was produced by Cengage Learning Custom Solutions for collegiate use. As such, those adopting and/or contributing to this work are responsible for editorial content accuracy, continuity and completeness.

Compilation © 2016 Cengage Learning

ISBN: 978-1-337-03473-9

Cengage Learning
20 Channel Center Street
Boston, MA 02210
USA

Cengage Learning is a leading provider of customized learning solutions with office locations around the globe, including Singapore, the United Kingdom, Australia, Mexico, Brazil, and Japan. Locate your local office at:
www.international.cengage.com/region.

Cengage Learning products are represented in Canada by Nelson Education, Ltd.

For your lifelong learning solutions, visit **www.cengage.com/custom.**

Visit our corporate website at **www.cengage.com.**

Brief Contents

Chapter 1	Introduction to the Legal System of the United States	1
Chapter 2	Introduction to Criminal Law	31
Chapter 3	Introduction and Participants	55
Chapter 4	Constitutional Aspects of Criminal Procedure	72
Chapter 5	The Pretrial Process	87
Chapter 6	Trial	114
Chapter 7	Sentencing and Appeal	134
Chapter 8	The Two Essential Elements	162
Chapter 9	Crimes Against the Person	192
Chapter 10	Crimes Against Property and Habitation	225
Chapter 11	Crimes Against the Public	248
Chapter 12	Parties and Inchoate Offenses	298
Chapter 13	Factual and Statutory Defenses	308
Chapter 14	Constitutional Defenses	335
Glossary		355
Index		363

CHAPTER 1

INTRODUCTION TO THE LEGAL SYSTEM OF THE UNITED STATES

Chapter Outline

Federalism
Separation of Powers
The Structure of the Court System
Duties and Powers of the Judicial Branch
Comparing Civil Law and Criminal Law
The Authority of Government to Regulate Behavior
The Purposes of Punishing Criminal Law Violators
  Specific and General Deterrence
  Incapacitation
  Rehabilitation
  Retribution
Ethical Considerations: Basics on Ethics in Criminal Law

Chapter Objectives

After completing this chapter you should be able to:

- describe the basic constitutional structure of state and federal governments with an emphasis on how structure affects criminal law and criminal justice administration.
- compare and contrast federal and state authorities in criminal law.
- describe both civil and criminal law with an emphasis on their differing objectives and procedures.
- describe the third branch of government, the judiciary, including the structure of U.S. courts and the authorities and duties of courts in criminal justice.

FEDERALISM

Before one can undertake learning criminal law or criminal procedure, a basic understanding of the legal system of the United States is necessary. This can be a complex task, as criminal law and procedure are significantly influenced by federal and state constitutional law, the common law, and statutory law at both the federal and state levels. It will be easier to understand how these areas of law affect criminal law if we first explore the basic structure of American government.

The United States is divided into two sovereign forms of government—the government of the **federalism**. It is also common to refer to this division as the vertical division of power, as the national government rests above the state governments in hierarchy in those areas where the constitution grants supremacy to the federal government. The Framers of the Constitution of the United States established these two levels of government in an attempt to prevent the centralization of power, that is, too much power being vested in one group. The belief that "absolute power corrupts absolutely" was the catalyst for the division of governmental power.

In theory, the national government, commonly referred to as the *federal government*, and the state governments each possess authority over citizens, as well as over particular policy areas, free from the interference of the other government (dual sovereignty). Most crimes fall into the jurisdiction of a state court alone, but there are small zones of authority that are exclusively federal as well. In many instances, when the authorities of both a state and the federal government are implicated, the two coordinate their investigations and prosecution. This process, commonly known as cooperative federalism, is discussed more fully later in this chapter.

Determining what powers belong to the national government, as opposed to the states, is not always an easy task. The Framers of the Constitution intended to establish a limited federal government. That is, most governmental powers were to reside in the states, with the federal government being limited to the powers expressly delegated to it by the U.S. Constitution. This principle is found in the Tenth Amendment, which reads: "The powers not delegated to the United States by the Constitution, nor prohibited to it by the States, are reserved to the States respectively, or the people."

federalism

■ A system of political organization with several different levels of government (for example, city, state, and national) coexisting in the same area, with the lower levels having some independent powers.

---

sidebar

At trial, a *sidebar* is a meeting between the judge and the attorneys, at the judge's bench, outside the hearing of the jury. Sidebars are used to discuss issues that the jury is not permitted to hear. In this text, the sidebars will appear periodically. This periodic feature contains information relevant to the legal subject being studied.

What powers are delegated to the United States by the Constitution? There are several, including, but not limited to, the power to take the following actions:

1. Coin money, punish counterfeiters, and fix standards of weights and measures.
2. Establish a post office and post roads.
3. Promote the progress of science and useful arts by providing artists and scientists exclusive rights to their discoveries and writings.
4. Punish piracy and other crimes on the high seas.
5. Declare war and raise armies.
6. Conduct diplomacy and foreign affairs.
7. Regulate interstate and foreign commerce.
8. Make laws necessary and proper for carrying into execution other powers expressly granted in the Constitution.

The last two of these powers—the regulation of interstate commerce and the making of all necessary and proper laws—have proven to be significant sources of federal authority. Also important is the Supremacy Clause of Article VI, which provides that

> This Constitution, and the Laws of the United States which shall be made in Pursuance thereof; and all Treaties made, or which shall be made, under the Authority of the United States, shall be the supreme Law of the Land; and the Judges in every State shall be bound thereby, any Thing in the Constitution or Laws of any State to the Contrary notwithstanding.

The Supremacy Clause declares federal law, if valid, to be a higher form of law than state law. Of course, if the federal government attempts to regulate an area belonging to the states, its law is invalid and the state law is controlling. But if the federal government possesses **jurisdiction** or concurrent state and federal jurisdiction exists, federal law trumps state law. This is true when federal and state laws are in conflict and when the federal government has taken over the area to the exclusion of the states (preemption). This is not a common issue in criminal law, because state and federal laws rarely conflict; rather, they are more likely to be parallel or complementary. In such cases, a state government and the federal government have **concurrent jurisdiction** (see Exhibit 1–1).

Keep in mind that the U.S. Constitution is the highest form of law in the land. It is the federal constitution that establishes the structure of our government. You will learn later the various duties of the judicial branch of government. One duty is the interpretation (determining what written law means) of statutes and constitutions. The highest court in the United States is the United States Supreme Court. (In this text, all references to the *Court* are to the Supreme Court of the United States unless stated otherwise.) As such, that Court is the final word on what powers are exclusively federal or state, or concurrently held. However, once the Supreme Court decides that an issue is exclusively under the control of state governments, each state, through its judiciaries, has the final word on that issue.

jurisdiction

■ The geographical area within which a court (or a public official) has the right and power to operate. Or the persons about whom and the subject matters about which a court has the right and power to make decisions that are legally binding.

concurrent jurisdiction

■ Two or more jurisdictions or courts possessing authority over the same matter.

Exhibit 1-1 FEDERAL AND STATE CRIMINAL JURISDICTION

State Jurisdiction	Concurrent Jurisdiction	National Jurisdiction
1. States may regulate for the health, safety, and morals of their citizens 2. Those acts that involve a state government, its officials and property Examples: Murder; rape; theft; driving under the influence of a drug; gambling	1. Those acts that fall into both federal and state jurisdictions Examples: Bank robbery of a federally insured institution; an act of terrorism against the United States that harms an individual, state property, or individual property	1. Crimes that are interstate in character 2. Crimes involving the government of the United States, including its officials and property Examples: Murder of a federal official or murder on federal land; interstate transportation of illegal item; interstate flight of a felon

During the past 200 years, the Supreme Court has differed in its approach to federalism. Two general models can be identified, though. *Dual federalism* refers to an approach under which the states and federal government are viewed as coequals. Under this approach, the Tenth Amendment is interpreted broadly and the Commerce Clause and the Necessary and Proper Clause are read narrowly. The Tenth Amendment is interpreted as an independent source of state powers, staking out policy areas upon which the national government cannot encroach.

Another model, *hierarchical federalism,* positions the national government as superior to the state governments. Under this approach, the Commerce and Necessary and Proper Clauses are construed broadly. The Tenth Amendment becomes a truism; that is, it reserves to the states only those powers the national government does not possess. Accordingly, state jurisdiction decreases as federal jurisdiction expands.

Cooperative federalism, which is not a third jurisdictional model, but instead, a relational descriptor, is characterized by significant interaction between the states and federal government (and local forms of government) in an effort to effectively regulate and administer laws and programs. Cooperative federalism is a product of the political branches, the executive and legislative, not legal (federalism) mandate. The increased cooperation between state and federal law enforcement agencies to fight the war against drugs in the 1980s and 1990s and the war against terrorism in the 2000s are good examples of cooperative federalism. The Court has vacillated between the two jurisdictional models. The dominant approach in recent decades has been hierarchical federalism. This is not to say that the states are powerless. In fact, one policy area over which the states have maintained considerable control is criminal law. More than 90 percent of all crimes fall within the jurisdiction of the states, not the federal government. However, the sphere of federal government power in criminal law is increasing. This is because more acts are committed in, or are committed using an item that has traveled in, interstate commerce. Acts that have traditionally been state-law crimes may today be federal crimes as well, if there is an interstate component to the act. For example, if carjacking, which is the state crime of robbery, is committed with a gun that has traveled in interstate commerce, it is also a federal crime. An act that harms an individual or property invokes state jurisdiction. If the same act can be characterized as **terroristic,** as defined by federal law, then federal jurisdiction and separate federal criminal liability may exist as well. Drug trafficking, if interstate, is a violation of federal law and possibly multiple state laws. Certain violations of civil liberties also invoke concurrent federal and state jurisdiction. Which government will bring charges in these situations is more a political question than a legal one. It is not a violation of double jeopardy for an individual to be tried and punished by both federal and state governments, even for the same act because the constitutional prohibition of double jeopardy was intended to preclude two trials or punishments by the same jurisdiction, not by multiple jurisdictions.

Regardless of the expansion of federal jurisdiction, most crimes continue to fall within the exclusive jurisdiction of the states. This is because one of the responsibilities of the states is to regulate for the health and safety of its citizens. This is known as the **police power.** Most murders, rapes, and thefts are state-law crimes. A few policy areas belong exclusively to the federal government. Punishing counterfeiters is an example. Although the expansion of federal authority is likely to continue to increase as people and goods become more national and international in character, the Supreme Court has reaffirmed the central role of states in protecting people (police power) and it has conversely made it clear that a genuine connection to interstate commerce or other federal authorities must exist for the federal government to criminalize behavior.

For example, the Supreme Court invalidated the Gun-Free Zone Act of 1990 because it found no genuine connection between guns around schools and interstate commerce. Similarly, the Brady Handgun Violence Protection Act was invalidated in *Printz v. United States*[2] because it required state officials to conduct background checks on gun purchasers. The Court held that Congress was without the authority to direct local enforcement officers in this way. In yet another case favoring state authority *United States v. Morrison*[3] the Supreme Court struck down part of the Violence Against Women Act because it held that it was a state, not federal, authority to provide victims of sex crimes with civil remedies against their attackers. In another 2000 case, *Jones v. United States*[4], the Court invalidated the application of a federal arson statute to the prosecution of a man for firebombing his cousin's home. The Court rejected the United States' theory that it had jurisdiction because the home's mortgage, its insurance, and its natural gas were all purchased in interstate commerce. The Court penned that if it were to accept the government's position, "hardly a building in the land would fall outside the federal statute's domain."

However, a connection was found in the 2005 case *Gonzales v. Raich.*[5] In that case, the federal government's prohibition of the possession of marijuana was upheld, although state law allowed its possession and use for medical purposes. The interstate

terrorism

■ The definition of terrorism is the subject to ongoing debate. However, one federal statute defines it as activities that involve violence or acts dangerous to human life that are violations of law and appear to be intended to intimate or coerce a civilian population, to influence a policy of government by intimidation or coercion, or to affect the conduct of government through mass destruction, assassination, or kidnapping.[1] 18 U.S.C. §2331.

police power

■ The government's right and power to set up and enforce laws to provide for the safety, health, and general welfare of the people.

nature of marijuana production and sales made for an easy case of federal jurisdiction. In fact, the plaintiffs conceded this point. Their theory that California's law permitting limited use of marijuana should trump federal law failed, largely because the federal government had a "rational basis" to believe that the state law would undermine the intention of the federal law by providing a stream through which interstate drug trafficking could occur.

In 2010, the Court affirmed a federal statute that delegated the authority to seek civil commitment of federal sex offenders after their sentences were served to federal prosecutors. Similar state laws were previously upheld, but in the 2010 case *United States v. Comstock*,[6] the defendant complained that civil commitment was a traditional state authority and accordingly, the federal law was invalid. Relying on the Necessary and Proper Clause, the Court rejected the argument. That the statute required the federal government to give the appropriate state officials the first opportunity to file for commitment in state court also reduced the Court's concerns that state autonomy was threatened.

Local governments have not been mentioned so far. This is because the Constitution does not recognize the existence of local governments. However, state constitutions and laws establish local forms of government, such as counties, cities, and districts. These local entities are often empowered by state law with limited authority to create criminal law. These laws, usually in the form of ordinances, are discussed in Chapter 2.

The result of this division of power is that the states (as well as other jurisdictions, such as the District of Columbia), the federal government, and local governments each have a separate set of criminal laws. For this reason, you must keep in mind that the principles you will learn from this book are general in nature. It is both impossible and pointless to teach the specific laws of every jurisdiction of the United States in this textbook.

SEPARATION OF POWERS

separation of powers

■ Division of the federal government (and state governments) into legislative (lawmaking), judicial (law interpreting), and executive (law carrying out) branches.

Another division of governmental power is known as **separation of powers.** This is the division of governmental power into three branches—the executive, legislative, and judicial—making a horizontal division of power, just as federalism is the vertical division (see Exhibit 1–2). Each branch is delegated certain functions that the other two may not encroach upon. The executive branch consists of the president of the United States, the president's staff, and the various administrative agencies that the president oversees. Generally, it is the duty of the executive branch to enforce the laws of the federal government. In criminal law, the executive branch investigates alleged violations of the law, gathers the evidence necessary to prove that a violation has occurred, and brings violators before the judicial branch for disposition. The president does this through the various federal law enforcement and administrative agencies.

statute

■ A law passed by a legislature.

The legislative branch consists of the United States Congress, which creates the laws of the United States. Congressionally created laws are known as **statutes.** Finally, the judicial branch comprises the various federal courts of the land. That branch is

Exhibit 1-2 DIVISION OF GOVERNMENTAL POWER

	Legislative Branch	Executive Branch	Judicial Branch
The Government of the United States (Federal Government)	United States Congress	President of the United States	Federal Courts
State Governments	State Legislatures	Governors	State Courts

charged with the administration of justice. A more comprehensive discussion of the judicial branch follows later in this chapter.

In a further attempt to diffuse governmental power, the framers designed a system of checks and balances that prevents any one branch from exclusively controlling a function. Several checks can be found in the Constitution.

For example, Congress is responsible for making the law. This function is checked by the president, who may veto legislation. The president is then checked by Congress, which may override a veto with a two-thirds majority. The president is responsible for conducting foreign affairs and making treaties and for serving as commander in chief of the military. The Senate, however, must approve the treaties negotiated by the executive branch, and Congress has been delegated the authority to make the rules that regulate the military. In the context of criminal law, this means that Congress, state legislatures, and local councils declare what acts are criminal; for their part, the president, state governors, prosecutors, and law enforcement agencies detect and respond to criminal acts, prosecute violators, and administer judicially ordered punishments. The judicial branch interprets criminal law, oversees criminal adjudications, sentences offenders, and to a limited extent oversees the entire system of adjudication and punishment.

Through the power of judicial review, the judiciary may invalidate actions of the president or Congress that violate the Constitution. In contrast, the political branches select federal judges through the nomination (president) and confirmation (Senate) process. Unpopular judicial decisions may be changed either by statute, if the issue is one of statutory interpretation, or by constitutional amendment, if the issue is one of constitutional interpretation and Congress possess the authority to impeach federal judges.

Keep in mind that two levels of government exist, excluding local entities. Even though the U.S. Constitution does not establish three branches of government for the many states (the U.S. Constitution designs the structure of the federal government only but also demands that states have republican forms of government), all state constitutions do, in varying forms, model the federal constitution. The result is a two-tiered system with each tier split into three parts.

In this form of government, the legislature defines what acts are criminal, what process must be used to assure that a wrongdoer answers for an act, and what punishment should be imposed for the act.

The duty of the executive branch is to enforce and implement the laws created by the legislature, as well as to enforce the orders of courts. For example, if a state legislature prohibits the sale of alcohol on Sundays, it is the duty of the appropriate state law enforcement agencies—the police or the alcohol, tobacco, and firearms agents—to investigate suspected violations and take whatever lawful action is necessary to bring alleged violators to justice. Law enforcement, in the criminal law context, is accomplished through law enforcement agencies and prosecutorial agencies. At the federal level, there are many law enforcement agencies: the Federal Bureau of Investigation, Drug Enforcement Administration, United States Marshal Service, Department of Homeland Security, Immigration and Customs Enforcement, United States Secret Service, United States Coast Guard, Transportation Security Administration (including the Air Marshal Service), and Department of the Treasury are only a few. State law enforcement agencies include state departments of investigation, state police departments, and local police departments. These and other enforcement agencies are responsible for investigating criminal conduct and for gathering evidence to prove that a criminal violation has occurred. When the law enforcement agency has completed its investigation, the case is turned over to a prosecutor. The prosecutor is the attorney responsible for representing the people. The prosecutor files the formal criminal charge, or conducts a grand jury, and then sees the prosecution through to fruition. In the federal system, the prosecutor is called a United States attorney. In the states and localities, prosecutors are known as district attorneys, county attorneys, state attorneys, city attorneys, or, simply, prosecutors.

Finally, the judicial branch is charged with the administration of justice. The courts become involved after the executive branch has arrested or accused an individual of a crime as well as at certain points during criminal investigations. The duties of the judicial branch are explored further in the next section of this chapter. Lawyers, legal assistants, and law enforcement officials are likely to have significant contacts with state and federal courts; therefore, it is important to understand the structure of the court system.

THE STRUCTURE OF THE COURT SYSTEM

Within the federal and state judiciaries, a hierarchy of courts exists. All state court systems, as well as the federal court system, have at least two types of courts: trial courts and appellate courts. However, because each state is free to structure its judiciary in any manner, significant variation is found in the different court systems. What follows are general principles that apply to all states and the federal system.

trial court

■ A court that hears and determines a case initially, as opposed to an appellate court; a court of general jurisdiction.

Trial courts are what most people envision when they think of courts. A case begins at the trial court, where witnesses are heard and evidence is presented—often to a jury as well as a judge—and where verdicts and sentenced are announced. In the federal system, trial courts are known as United States District Courts. The United States is divided into 94 judicial districts, using state boundaries to establish district limits. Each state

> **sidebar**
>
> The court system is actually many court systems composed of the federal system and the many state systems. In 2010, approximately 104 million cases were filed in state and local trial courts, a decline from about 106 million in the two years previous according to the National Center for State Courts. Of these, 54 percent were traffic offenses, 20 percent were criminal cases, 18% were civil cases, 6 percent were domestic cases, and 2 percent were juvenile cases.
>
> *Source of state statistics:* R. LaFountain, R. Schauffler, S. Strickland, and K. Holt, *Examining the Work of State Courts: An Analysis of 2010 State Court Caseloads* (National Center for State Courts 2012).
>
> In 2012 the federal system was composed of 1 Supreme Court, 13 appellate courts, and 94 district courts. The district courts had 372,563 civil and criminal cases, a 5% decline from 2011; 1,261,140 petitions for bankruptcy were filed in federal bankruptcy courts, an astonishing 14% decline in from 2011. The regional courts of appeals didn't experience the declines of the trial courts. Total filings rose by 4% to 57,501. In 2011, 7,082 cases were filed, 79 were heard, and 78 cases terminated in the Supreme Court.
>
> *Source of federal statistics:* 2012 Judicial Business of the United States Courts, Administrative Office of the United States Courts: http://www.uscourts.gov/uscourts/Statistics/JudicialBusiness/2012/JudicialBusinespdfversion.pdf

constitutes at least one district, although larger states are divided into several districts. For example, Kansas has only one district, and the federal trial court located in Kansas is known as the United States District Court for the District of Kansas. California, in contrast, is made up of four districts: the Northern, Eastern, Central, and Southern Districts of California.

State trial courts are known by various names, such as district, superior, county, and circuit courts. Despite variations in name, these courts are very similar.

Appellate courts review the decisions and actions of trial courts (or lower appellate courts, as discussed later) for error. These courts do not conduct trials, but review the **briefs** submitted by the parties and examine the **record** from the trial court for mistakes, known as trial court error. Often, but not always, appellate courts will hear argument from the attorneys involved in the case under review, but witnesses are not heard nor other evidence submitted. After the appellate court has reviewed the record and examined it for error, it renders an opinion. An appellate court can reverse, affirm, or remand the lower court decision. To *reverse* is to determine that the court below has rendered a wrong decision and to change that decision. When an appellate court *affirms* a lower court, it is approving the decision made and leaving it unchanged.

appellate court
■ A higher court that can hear appeals from a lower court.

brief
■ A written document filed with a court through which a party presents a legal claim, legal theory, supporting authorities, and requests some form of relief.

record on appeal
■ A formal, written account of a case, containing the complete formal history of all actions taken, papers filed, rulings made, opinions written, etc.

In some cases, an appellate court will remand the case to the lower court. A *remand* is an order that the case be returned to the lower court and that some action be taken by the judge when the case is returned. Often this will involve conducting a new trial. For example, if an appellate court decides that a judge acted in a manner or made a decision that prevented a criminal defendant from having a fair trial, and the defendant was convicted, an appellate court may reverse the conviction and remand the case to the trial court for a new trial with instructions that the judge not act in a similar manner.

In the federal system and many states, there are two levels of appellate courts, an intermediate and highest level. The intermediate-level courts in the federal system are the United States Courts of Appeal.[7] There are 11 judicial circuits in the United States, with one court of appeal in each circuit. Additionally, there is a court of appeal for Washington, D.C., and for the Federal Circuit. Therefore, there are 13 United States Courts of Appeal in total (see Exhibit 1–3). Appeals from the district courts are taken to the circuit courts. The highest court in the country is the United States Supreme Court. Appeals from the circuit courts are taken to the Supreme Court. Also, appeals of federal issues from state supreme courts are taken to the United States Supreme Court. Although appeal to a circuit court and to a state's first appellate court (and often its second level of appeal as well) is generally a right any litigant has, the Supreme Court is not required to hear most appeals, and it does not. In recent years, the Supreme Court has denied review of approximately 97 percent of the cases appealed. Therefore, the States' Supreme Courts and federal circuit courts are often a defendant's last chance to have his or her case heard.

Many states also have intermediate-level appellate courts, as well as a high court, although a few states have only one appellate court. Most states call the high court the supreme court of that state and the intermediate level court the court of appeals. An example of an exception is New York, which has named its highest court the Court of Appeals of New York and refers to its lower-level courts as supreme courts.

In states that have only one appellate court, appeals are taken directly to that court. New Hampshire is such a state, so appeals from New Hampshire's trial courts are taken directly to the Supreme Court of New Hampshire. Note that in most instances a first appeal is an appeal of right. This means that an individual has a right to appeal, and the appellate court is required to hear the case. However, second appeals are generally not appeals of right, unless state law has provided otherwise. To have a case heard by the United States Supreme Court and most state supreme courts, the person appealing must seek **certiorari,** an order from an appellate court to the lower court requiring the record to be sent to the higher court for review. When "cert." is granted, the appellate court will hear the appeal; and when certiorari is denied, it will not.

Finally, be aware that a number of **inferior courts** exist. These are courts that fall under trial courts in hierarchy. As such, appeals from these courts do not usually go to the intermediate-level appellate courts, as described earlier, but to the trial-level court first. Municipal courts, police courts, and justices of the peace are examples of inferior

certiorari

■ (Latin) "To make sure." A request for certiorari (or "cert." for short) is like an appeal, but one that the higher court is not required to take for decision. It is literally a writ from the higher court asking the lower court for the record of the case.

inferior court

■ A court with special, limited responsibilities, such as a probate court.

Chapter 1: Introduction to the Legal System of the United States 11

Exhibit 1-3 THE 13 FEDERAL JUDICIAL CIRCUITS

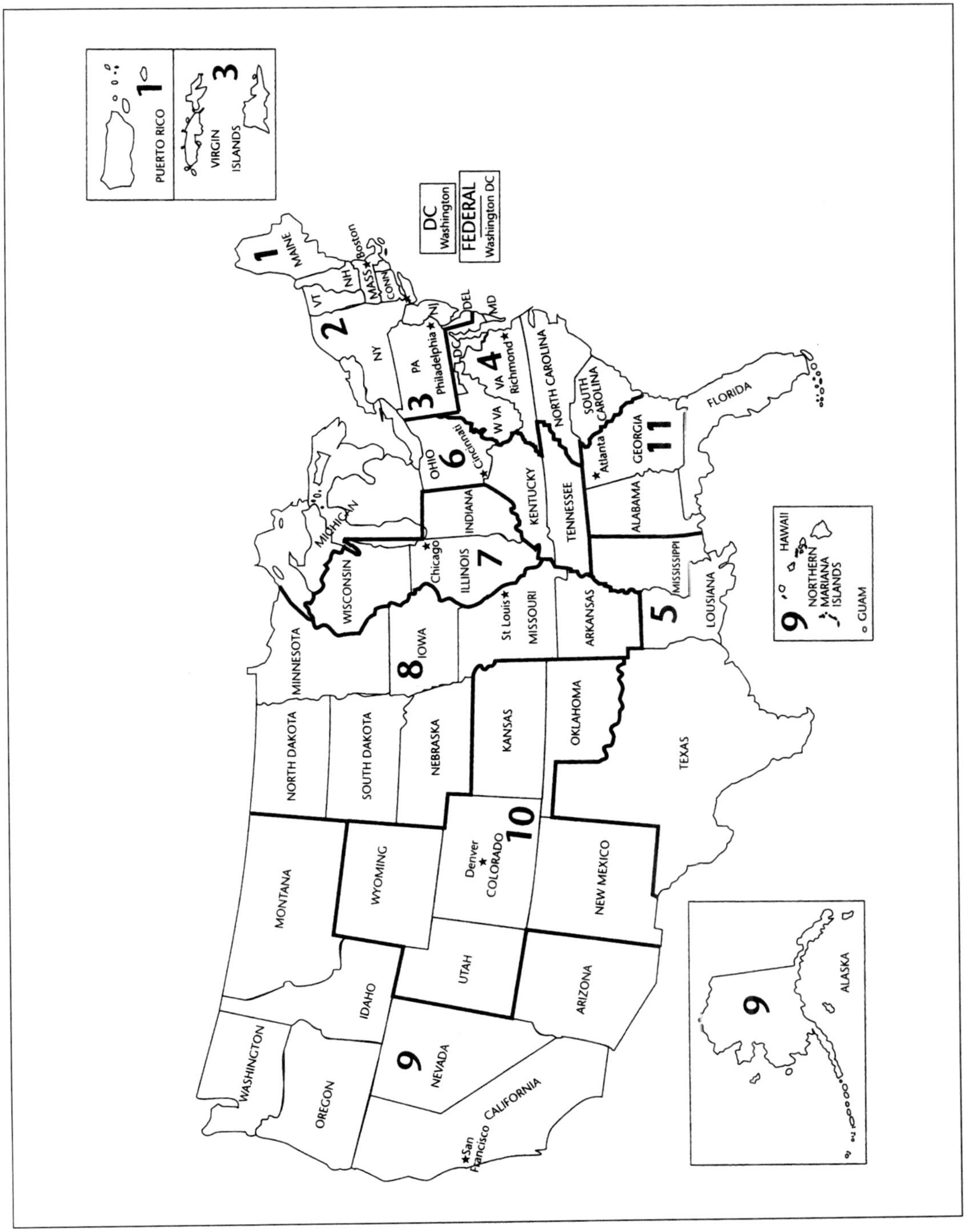

Source: http://www.uscourts.gov/court_locator.aspx

courts. An appeal from one of these courts is initially heard by a state trial-level court before an appeal is taken to a state appellate court. The federal system also has inferior courts. The United States Bankruptcy Courts are inferior courts because appeals from the decisions of these courts go to the district courts, in most cases, and not to the courts of appeals. Only after the trial court has rendered its decision may an appeal be taken to an appellate court.

Many inferior courts in the state system are not **courts of record.** No digital, audio, or stenographic recording of the trial or hearing at the inferior court is made. As such, when an appeal is taken to the trial level court, it is normally **de novo**. This means that the trial-level court conducts a new trial, rather than reviewing a record as most appellate courts do. This is necessary because there is no record to review, because the inferior court is not a court of record. Federal district courts do not conduct new trials, as all federal courts, including bankruptcy courts, are courts of record. State inferior courts have limited jurisdiction; for example, municipal courts usually hear municipal ordinance violations and only minor state law violations. The amount of money that a person may be fined and the amount of time that a defendant may be sentenced to serve in jail are also limited. Generally, no juries are used at the inferior court level.

Exhibit 1–4 is a basic diagram of the federal and state court systems. The appellate routes are indicated by lines drawn from one court to another. Later in this book you will learn how the appeals process works and how the federal and state systems interact in criminal law. Note where this diagram is located so that you may refer to it later.

Most state trial courts are known as **courts of general jurisdiction.** Courts of general jurisdiction possess the authority to hear a broad range of cases, including civil law as well as criminal. In contrast, **courts of limited jurisdiction** hear only specific types of cases. You have already been introduced to one limited jurisdiction court, municipal courts. Inferior courts, such as municipal courts, are always courts of limited jurisdiction. Some states employ systems that have specialized trial courts to handle domestic, civil, or criminal cases. These may be in the form of a separate court (e.g., Criminal Court of Harp County) or may be a division of a trial court (e.g., Superior Court of Harp County, Criminal Division). Appellate courts may also be limited in jurisdiction to a particular area of law, such as the Oklahoma Court of Criminal Appeals.

The federal government also has special courts. As previously mentioned, a nationwide system of bankruptcy courts is administered by the national government. In addition, the United States Claims Court, Tax Court, and Court of International Trade are part of the federal judiciary, and each has a specific area of law over which it may exercise jurisdiction. Often those cases over which they have jurisdiction are exclusive of district courts. However, the jurisdiction of those courts is outside the scope of this book, as they deal only with civil law. Criminal cases in federal court are heard by district courts, and criminal appeals are heard by the United States Courts of Appeals.

court of record
- Generally, another term for trial court.

de novo
- Anew. For a case to be tried again as if there had not been a prior trial.

court of general jurisdiction
- Another term for trial court; that is, a court having jurisdiction to try all classes of civil and criminal cases except those that can be heard only by a court of limited jurisdiction.

court of limited jurisdiction
- A court whose jurisdiction is limited to civil cases of a certain type, or that involve a limited amount of money, or whose jurisdiction in criminal cases is confined to petty offenses and preliminary hearings.

Exhibit 1-4 STATE AND FEDERAL COURT STRUCTURES

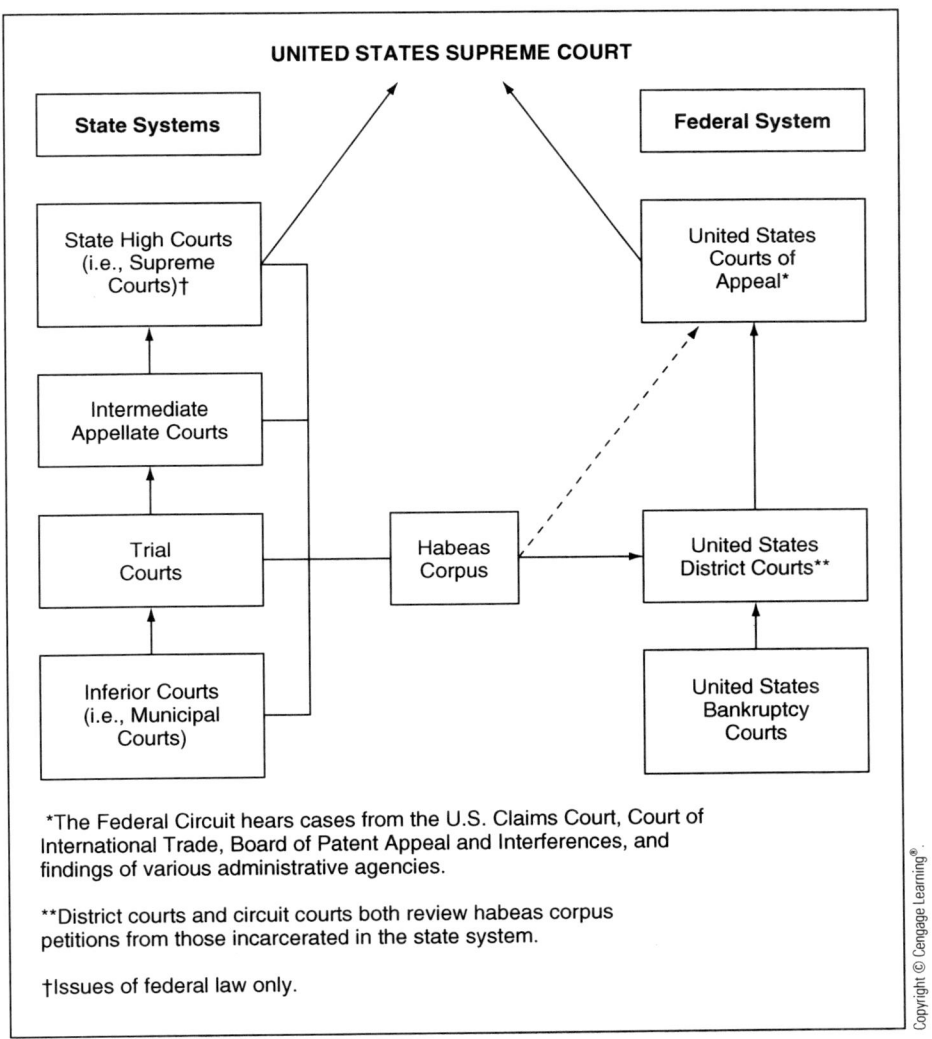

*The Federal Circuit hears cases from the U.S. Claims Court, Court of International Trade, Board of Patent Appeal and Interferences, and findings of various administrative agencies.

**District courts and circuit courts both review habeas corpus petitions from those incarcerated in the state system.

†Issues of federal law only.

DUTIES AND POWERS OF THE JUDICIAL BRANCH

Of the three branches of government, attorneys and other legal professionals have the most interaction with the judicial branch. For that reason, we single out the judicial branch for a more extensive examination of its functions.

First, it must be emphasized that all courts—local, state, and federal—are bound by the U.S. Constitution. Consequently, all courts have a duty to apply federal constitutional law. This duty is important in criminal law because it allows defendants to assert their U.S. constitutional claims and defenses in state court, where most criminal cases are heard. Of course, defendants may assert applicable state laws as well.

As previously stated, the judicial branch is charged with the administration of justice. The courts administer justice by acting as the conduit for dispute resolution. The courts are the place where civil and criminal disputes are resolved, if the parties cannot reach a resolution themselves. In an effort to resolve disputes, courts must apply the laws of the land. To apply the law, judges must **interpret** the legislation and constitutions of the nation. To *interpret* means to read the law in an attempt to understand its meaning. This nation's courts are the final word in declaring the meaning of written law. If a court interprets a statute's meaning contrary to the intent of a legislature, then the legislature may later rewrite the statute to make its intent clearer. This revision has the effect of "reversing" the judicial interpretation of the statute. The process is much more difficult if a legislature desires to change a judicial interpretation of a constitution. At the national level, the Constitution has been amended 26 times. The amendment process is found in Article V of the Constitution and requires action by the federal legislature as well as by the states. Amending a constitution is simply a more cumbersome and time-consuming endeavor than amending legislation.

The judicial branch is independent from the other two branches of government. Often, people think of the courts as enforcers of the law. Though this notion is true in a sense, it is untrue in that the judicial branch does not work with the executive branch in an attempt to achieve criminal convictions. It is the duty of the courts of this nation to remain neutral and apply the laws fairly and impartially. The U.S. Constitution establishes a judiciary system that is shielded from interference from the other two branches. For example, the Constitution prohibits Congress from reducing the pay of federal judges after they are appointed. This prevents Congress from coercing the courts into action under the threat of no pay. The Constitution also provides for lifetime appointments of federal judges, thereby keeping the judicial branch from being influenced by political concerns, which may cause judges to ignore the law and make decisions based on what is best for their political careers. Judicial independence permits courts to make decisions that are disadvantageous to the government, but required by law, without fear of retribution from the other two branches.

The need for an independent judiciary is particularly important when one considers the role courts play as the guardians of constitutional principles, including civil rights. **Judicial review** is a power held by the judicial branch that permits courts to review the actions of the executive and legislative branches, and of the states, and declare acts that are in violation of the Constitution void. Hamilton wrote of the power of judicial review, and of the importance of an independent judiciary, in the *Federalist Papers,* where he stated:

> Permanency in office frees the judges from political pressures and prevents invasions on judicial power by the president and Congress.
>
> * * *
>
> The Constitution imposes certain restrictions on the Congress designed to protect individual liberties, but unless the courts are independent and have the power to declare

interpret

■ Studying a document *and* surrounding circumstances to decide the document's meaning.

judicial review

■ A higher court's examination of a lower court's decision.

the laws in violation of the Constitution null and void these protections amount to nothing. The power of the Supreme Court to declare laws unconstitutional leads some to assume that the judicial branch will be superior to the legislative branch. Let us look at this argument.

Only the Constitution is *fundamental* law; the Constitution establishes the principles and structure of the government. To argue that the Constitution is not superior to the laws suggests that the *representatives of the people* are superior *to the people* and that the Constitution is inferior to the government it gave birth to. The courts are the arbiters between the legislative branch and the people; the courts are to interpret the laws and prevent the legislative branch from exceeding the powers granted it. The courts must not only place the Constitution higher than the laws passed by Congress, they must also place the intentions of the people ahead of the intentions of the representative. . . .

The landmark case dealing with judicial review is *Marbury v. Madison,* 1 Cranch 137, 2 L. Ed. 60 (1803). Chief Justice Marshall wrote the opinion for the Court and determined that, although the Constitution does not contain explicit language providing for the power of judicial review, Article III of the Constitution implicitly endows the judiciary with the authority. Although seldom used by the Supreme Court for over a hundred years following the *Marbury* decision, it is now well established that courts possess the authority to review the actions of the executive and legislative branches and to declare any law, command, or other action void if it violates the U.S. Constitution. The power is held by both state and federal courts. Any state or federal law that violates the U.S. Constitution may be struck down by either federal or state courts. Of course, state laws that violate state constitutions may be stricken for the same reason.

The power to invalidate statutes is rarely used, for two reasons. First, the judiciary is aware of how awesome the power is; consequently, courts invoke the authority sparingly. Second, many rules of statutory construction exist and have the effect of preserving legislation. For example, if two interpretations of a statute are possible, one that violates the Constitution and one that does not, one rule of statutory construction requires that the statute be construed so that it is consistent with the Constitution. Although rarely done, statutes are occasionally determined invalid. In Chapter 13 and 14, on defenses, you will learn many constitutional constraints on government behavior. These defenses often rely on the authority of the judiciary to invalidate statutes or police conduct to give them teeth.[8]

COMPARING CIVIL LAW AND CRIMINAL LAW

Criminal law exists in a larger legal framework than civil law. Understanding the context of any legal subject and its relationship to other legal subjects is important. It is common to distinguish between criminal law and civil law. While important differences exist between the two, there are also many similarities. Exhibit 1–5 compares criminal and civil law.

Exhibit 1-5 CRIMINAL AND CIVIL LAW COMPARED

	Criminal Law	Civil Law
Purposes	Retribution, deterrence, incapacitation, rehabilitation	Compensation and deterrence
Remedies	Fines, restitution, imprisonment, counseling, rehabilitation, injunctions, capital punishment	Damages and equitable relief
Parties	Government and individual defendant	Individual plaintiff and defendant (or government as individual)
Standard of Proof	Beyond a reasonable doubt	Preponderance of evidence
Burdens	Government bears burden of proof and process designed to protect rights of defendant (due process)	Plaintiff bears burden of proof and parties treated equally in process

The source of most of the dissimilarities between criminal law and civil law is the differing objectives of the two. There are many purposes of criminal law. First, it is intended to deter behavior that society has determined to be undesirable. A second purpose of criminal law is to punish those who take the acts deemed undesirable by society, specifically, to give victims and the community at large a sense of retribution. A third purpose is to incapacitate, through imprisonment, electronic monitoring, death, and other methods, offenders. Fourth, the rehabilitation of offenders is also an objective in many cases. Arguably, there is only one purpose, to prevent antisocial behavior. Under this theory, punishment is used as a tool to achieve the primary goal of preventing antisocial behavior. The purposes of punishing individuals who violate criminal laws are discussed in greater detail in Chapter 2.

In contrast, civil law has as its primary purpose the compensation of those injured by someone else's behavior. It is argued that the real purpose of civil law is the same as that of criminal law. By allowing lawsuits against individuals who have behaved in a manner inconsistent with society's rules, civil law actually acts to prevent undesirable behavior. However, prevention of bad behavior may be more the consequence of civil law than the purpose. To understand this you must know something about civil law.

Many definitions of civil law exist. This author prefers a negative definition similar such as, civil law is all law except that which is criminal law. Whatever definition you accept, many areas of law fall under the umbrella of civil law. Two of the largest categories of civil law are contract law and tort law.

Contract law is a branch of civil law that deals with agreements between two or more parties. You probably have already entered into a contract. Apartment leases, credit card agreements, and book-of-the-month club agreements are all contracts.

contract

■ An agreement that affects or creates legal relationships between two or more persons. To be a *contract*, an agreement must involve at least one promise, consideration, persons legally capable of making binding agreements, and a reasonable certainty about the meaning of the terms.

To have a **contract,** two or more people must agree to behave in a specific manner. If you violate your obligation under a contract, you have committed a civil wrong called a breach of contract. The landlord may sue you for your breach and receive **damages.** *Damages* are monetary compensation for loss.

Tort law is a branch of civil law that is concerned with civil wrongs but not contract actions. You have likely seen television ads for personal injury attorneys. These attorneys are practicing in the tort law area. A civil wrong, other than a breach of contract, is known as a **tort.** Torts are different from contracts in that the duty owed another party in contract law is created by the parties through their agreement. In tort law, the duty is imposed by the law. For example, at a party you are struck and injured by a beer bottle heaved by an intoxicated partier: A tort has been committed. The partier is known as a *tortfeasor*, which is the term used to describe one who commits a tort. Yet, why does that partier owe you a duty not to strike you with a flying beer bottle? You have not entered into a contract with the partier whereby he has promised not to harm you in this manner. The answer is that the law imposes the duty to act with caution when it is possible to injure another or cause injury to another's property. This duty is imposed upon all people at all times. The law requires that we all act reasonably when conducting our lives.

When a person fails to act reasonably and unintentionally injures another, that person is responsible for a **negligent** tort. Automobile accidents and medical malpractice are examples of negligent torts. When a person injures another intentionally, an **intentional** tort has occurred. Many intentional torts are also crimes, and this is one zone where criminal and common law coexist. If at that fraternity party you make a partier angry, and as a result he intentionally strikes you with the bottle, then he has committed both a crime and an intentional tort. Although criminal law may impose a jail sentence (or other punitive measures), tort law normally seeks only to compensate you for your injury. So, if you suffered $1,000 in medical bills to repair your broken nose, you would be entitled to that amount; but the partier cannot be sentenced to jail or otherwise be punished within the civil tort action. A separate criminal charge may be filed by the government. Although less common, tort negligence and criminal law also intersect. Extreme negligence, such as driving when drunk, that results in death or injuries can lead to both civil and criminal liabilities.

The final type of tort is the **strict liability** tort. In these situations liability exists even though the tortfeasor acted with extreme caution and did not intend to cause harm. An example of a strict liability tort is blasting. Whenever a mining or demolition company uses blasting, it is liable for any injuries or damages it causes to property, even if the company exercises extreme caution.

Damages that are awarded (won) in a lawsuit to compensate a party for actual loss are **compensatory damages.** Compensatory damages do just what the name states—compensate the injured party. However, another type of damages exists—**punitive damages.** Contrary to what you have learned so far, punitive damages are awarded in civil suits and are intended to prevent undesirable behavior by punishing those who commit outrageous acts. Punitive damages are often requested by plaintiffs in lawsuits but are rarely awarded. Do not worry if the idea of punitive damages confuses you

damages
■ Money that a court orders paid to a person who has suffered damage (a loss or harm) by the person who caused the injury (the violation of the person's rights).

tort
■ A civil (as opposed to a criminal) wrong, other than a breach of contract.

negligence
■ The failure to exercise a reasonable amount of care in a situation that causes harm to someone or something.

intentional
■ Determination to do a certain thing.

strict liability
■ The legal responsibility for damage or injury, even if you are not at fault or negligent.

compensatory damages
■ Damages awarded for the actual loss suffered by a plaintiff.

punitive damages
■ Damages that are awarded over and above compensatory damages or actual damages because of the wanton, reckless, or malicious nature of the wrong done by the plaintiff.

because it appears to be a criminal law concept. Such damages are penal in nature, and many lawyers argue that they should not be allowed because a person can end up punished twice—once when convicted and sentenced by a criminal court and again by a civil court if punitive damages are awarded.

Trial courts have considerable discretion in awarding punitive damages. There is a limit, however. In the 1996 case *BMW v. Gore*,[9] a jury verdict in actual damages of $4,000 accompanied by a punitive damages award of $4,000,000, which was reduced to $2,000,000 by the State Supreme Court, was set aside by the United States Supreme Court because it found that the plaintiff wasn't on notice, a due process requirement, that it could be penalized by such a sum. As such, the judgement was arbitrary. Because it was a civil case, not a criminal case, the court couldn't turn to the Eighth Amendment's bar on excessive fines to review the award. Instead, it held that due process, the basic fairness clause that applies to all governmental conduct and decisions, expects punitive damages awards to be reasonable, considering three factors: (1) the degree of reprehensibility of conduct, (2) the disparity between actual harm and the punitive award, and (3) a comparison of the award to similar civil or criminal penalties. What was Gore's injury? He had not been told that the car he purchased had been repainted to cover damage from acid rain. On remand, the trial court gave the plaintiff the choice between a new trial or accepting $50,000 in punitive damages.

In *State Farm v. Campbell*[10] a plaintiff sued an insurance company over a $50,000 liability policy. The jury awarded the plaintiff $2,600,00 and actual damages of $145,000,000 in punitive damages. The trial judge reduced the punitive award to $1,000,000. The Supreme Court, applying the *BMW* criteria, found the 9:1 ratio of actual to punitive damages excessive and remanded the case to the state court with an order to reduce the award.

In the well-known case involving the massive oil spill in Alaskan waters by one of Exxon's oil tankers, *Exxon Shipping Co. v. Baker*,[11] the jury award of $2.5 billion in punitive damages and $507 million in actual damages, a 5:1 ratio, was found to be excessive. Unlike the earlier cases, *Exxon* was not decided on due process grounds but, rather, upon maritime law. Regardless, the Court's rejection of the 5:1 ratio is instructive in all cases.

The last major case in which the Supreme Court reviewed a punitive damages award was *Phillip Morris U.S.A. v. Williams*.[12] The jury award of $821,485.50 in actual damages and $79.5 million in punitive damages—which had been reduced by the trial judge to $32 million in punitive damages—was reversed and remanded to the trial court to reduce the punitive damages figure. In addition to being excessive, the Court rejected the award because it punished the company for harm caused to third parties, people not involved in the litigation. On remand, the award was reinstated with a different theory. Phillip Morris appealed this decision to the United States Supreme Court, which denied certiorari.

Do not get the concept of punitive damages mixed up with restitution or fines, which are discussed later in this text. Those forms of punishment, which occur in criminal cases, are limited by the Eighth Amendment's prohibition of excessive fines, as well as by due process.

Finally, a few other differences between criminal law and civil law should be mentioned. First, in civil law the person who brings the lawsuit (the plaintiff) is the person who was injured. For example, suppose you are at the grocery store doing your shopping and request the assistance of a checkout person who has recently divorced a spouse who looks very much like you. The checker immediately becomes enraged and vents all of his anger for his ex-wife on you by striking you with a box of cereal, which he was checking. He has committed a possible assault and battery in both tort law (these are intentional torts) and criminal law. However, in tort law, you must sue the checker yourself to recover any losses you suffer.

In criminal law, on the other hand, the government—whether national, state, or local—is always the party that files criminal charges. Often you will hear people say that they have filed criminal charges against someone. This statement is not accurate. What they have usually done is to file a complaint; the government determines whether criminal charges are to be filed. This is because a violation of criminal law is characterized as an attack on the citizens of a state (or the federal government) and, as such, is a violation of public, not private, law. Because it is public, the decision to file—or not to file—is made by a public official, the prosecutor. So, in our example, you have to contact either the police or your local prosecutor to have a criminal action brought against the checker.

Civil cases are entitled *citizen v. citizen;* in criminal law, it is *government* (i.e., *State of Montana*) *v. citizen*. In some jurisdictions, criminal actions are brought under the name of the people. This is done in New York, where criminal cases are entitled *The People of the State of New York v. citizen*.

There is no difference between a criminal action brought in the name of the state and a criminal action brought in the name of the people of a state. All prosecutions at the national level are brought by the United States of America. Note that governments may become involved in civil disputes. For example, if the state of South Dakota enters

---

sidebar

ABOUT CASE NAMES, TITLES, AND CAPTIONS

Cases filed with courts are given a case title, also known as a case name. The title consists of the parties to the action. In civil cases the title is *citizen v. citizen,* for example, *Joe Smith v. Anna Smith.* In criminal actions the title is *the government v. citizen.* For example, *United States of America v. Joe Smith* or *State of New Mexico v. Anna Smith.*

Cases also have captions. The caption appears at the top of the title page of all documents filed with a court and includes the case name, the court name, the case number, and the name of the document being filed with the court. The illustration in Exhibit 1–6 is an example of both a criminal case caption and a civil case caption.

into a contract with a person, and a dispute concerning that contract arises, the suit will be titled either *citizen v. South Dakota* or *South Dakota v. citizen*.

The two fields also differ in what is required to have a successful case. In civil law one must show actual injury to win. If, in our grocery store example, the box of cereal missed your head and you suffered no injury (damages), you would not have a civil suit. However, a criminal action for assault or battery may still be brought, as no injury is required in criminal law. This is because the purpose of criminal law is to prevent this type of conduct, not to compensate for actual injuries.

To turn this idea around, there are many instances in which a person's negligence could be subject to a civil cause of action, but not to a criminal action. If a person accidentally strikes another during a game of golf with a golf ball, causing injury, the injured party may sue for the concussion received; but no purpose would be served by

Exhibit 1–6 SIMPLE CAPTION — CRIMINAL CASE AND CIVIL CASE

```
        IN THE UNITED STATES DISTRICT COURT FOR
                 THE DISTRICT OF MARYLAND
                     NORTHERN DIVISION

UNITED STATES OF AMERICA)     )
_____ Plaintiff,    )
                              )
           v.                 )          Case No. _____
                              )
JOHN D. CRIMINAL,             )
_____ Defendant     )

                              Motion to Suppress Evidence
```

```
        IN THE UNITED STATES DISTRICT COURT FOR
                 THE DISTRICT OF MARYLAND
                     NORTHERN DIVISION

JOHN I. CITIZEN              )
Plaintiff,                   )
                             )
           v.                )          Case No.
                             )
JANE Q. SMITH,               )
Defendant                    )

                          Defendant's Motion for Summary Judgment
```

prosecuting the individual who hit the ball. No deterrent effect is achieved, as there was no intent to cause the injury. In most cases, society has made the determination (through its criminal laws) that a greater amount of **culpability** should be required for criminal liability than for civil. Criminal law is usually more concerned with the immorality of an act than is tort law. This is consistent with the goals of the two disciplines, as it is easier to prevent intentional acts than accidental ones. These concepts will be discussed later in the chapter on mens rea.

culpable

■ Blamable; at fault. A person who has done a wrongful act (whether criminal or civil) is described as "culpable."

THE AUTHORITY OF GOVERNMENT TO REGULATE BEHAVIOR

Freedom and liberty are two concepts that pervade the American political being. Most of us have learned that the longing for freedom of religious thought caused the English Puritan emigration from England to what was to become Plymouth, Massachusetts, in 1620. Later, the desire for freedom from the oppressive crown of England was the catalyst for the Declaration of Independence and the American Revolution. Finally, the fear that all governments tend to abuse their power led to the creation of a constitution that contains specific limits on governmental power and specific protections of individual rights. But what exactly is freedom? Liberty?

Freedom generally means the ability to act without interference. In a political and legal sense, it means the ability to act free from the interference of government. However, even in the freest societies, personal behavior is limited. This is because the actions of every member of society have the potential, at times, to affect other members. The total absence of government is anarchy, and few people believe that freedom results from anarchy. Without government, there would be little control over behavior. No system would exist to punish those who intentionally injure others. No system would exist to allow someone injured by the negligence of another to recover his or her losses. There would be no deterrence to wrongful behavior, other than fear of retribution from the victim. The strong and cunning would prey on the weak and unintelligent; the licentious on the decent. Although it is true that to live in such a world would be living free from government interference, it would not be a life free of oppression and arbitrary harm. Fear of sexual and other assault, fear that the strong will freely take property from others, the inability to obtain compensation for injuries, and so forth, all reduce an individual's freedom. To prevent anarchy and thereby increase freedom, people establish governments that have the authority to regulate behavior. The paradox is that too much government can be as much of a threat to freedom as too little government.

To achieve greatest freedom, a delicate balance between governmental authority and individual liberty must be struck (see Exhibit 1–7). Accordingly, individuals do not possess absolute freedom. As is commonly quipped, one person's freedom ends at the tips of the noses of other persons. While people do not possess absolute freedom, certain freedoms are protected in nearly all societies. In the United States, the Constitution establishes a zone of freedom over which government is prohibited from, or at least must have a very good reason for, regulating. The individual freedoms that comprise

Exhibit 1-7 MAXIMIZING SECURITY AND LIBERTY: THE TENSION BETWEEN FREEDOM AND THE NEED FOR GOVERNMENTAL PROTECTION

To reach the greatest individual freedom & personal security, unchecked individual freedom must be balanced with governmental authority to prevent & punish harmful behaviour.

civil liberties

■ Political liberties guaranteed by the Constitution and, in particular, by the Bill of Rights, especially the First Amendment.

this zone are known as individual rights, civil rights, or **civil liberties**. Said another way, civil rights are freedoms that are legally protected and enforceable.

The forefathers of the United States were sensitive to this relationship when they met in Philadelphia to draft the Constitution of the United States. Some characterize the relationship between a democratic republican form of government and its people as a contract. The people relinquish some freedoms in an effort to secure other freedoms. The preamble to the U.S. Constitution recognizes this principle. It states:

> "We, the People of the United States, in order to form a more perfect union, establish justice, insure domestic tranquility, provide for the common defense, promote the general welfare, and secure the blessings of liberty to ourselves and our posterity, do ordain and establish this Constitution for the United States of America."

The concept is also found in the Declaration of Independence, where Thomas Jefferson penned:

> ... that all Men are created equal, that they are endowed by their Creator with certain unalienable Rights, that among these are Life, Liberty, and the Pursuit of Happiness—That to secure these Rights, Governments are instituted among Men, deriving their just Powers from the Consent of the Governed."

So the contract was formed. The people are to receive the benefits of an organized, fair government. The government is to establish laws designed to protect the people from one another and from other nations. In exchange, the people agree to comply with the laws created by their government. Some would argue that the duty extends to require the people to participate in the activities of the government. You have probably heard people speak of a "duty" to vote. Clearly, this is the rationale for requiring individuals to sit as jurors.

Every government is different. Some governments permit little or no political participation by the people. Others permit more. In those nations where the people are active participants, the rights and duties of individuals can vary significantly. This is because values can vary significantly from culture to culture. Hence, what one society believes to be an important freedom and protects from government interference may not be so valued by other societies.

In nearly all nations, however, governmental involvement in the affairs of people is continually increasing. This is due in part to the fact that people are becoming less independent. That is, members of society now depend on one another to provide goods and services that were once commonly self-provided. In addition, the staggering increase in world population has caused people to have much more contact with each other than they did 100 years ago. The greater the population, contact between, and dependence of people on one another, the greater the number of conflicts that will arise requiring government intervention. As the population and dependence of people increase, so does the likelihood that one person's action may affect another. A person who lives alone in a forest far from other people can scream loudly in the middle of the night without bothering anyone. This person could dispose of trash in any manner desired. If that same person lived in the middle of a city, the scream could wake people, and the improper disposal of trash could cause the spread of disease as well as create an unpleasant environment. As the number of contacts between members of a society increases, so does the number of conflicts requiring government intervention. Even if the parties involved do not desire legal intervention to resolve their conflict, society will sometimes intervene through its government to prevent unacceptable behavior. For example, society has decided that duels are not an acceptable method of resolving disputes, even if two individuals wish to use this method. The government will try to prevent such behavior from occurring. If the duel is not discovered until after the fact, then the parties involved may be punished for participating.

As the need for government involvement in the private lives of citizens increases, it becomes more difficult to protect civil liberties. Many of these liberties are contained in the first 10 amendments to our Constitution, which are commonly known as the **Bill of Rights.** As the world becomes more populated and complex, the balance between permissible government involvement in the private lives of its citizens and impermissible encroachment upon those citizens' civil liberties becomes harder to maintain. As that line becomes thinner, the duty of the defense lawyer and the legal assistant to be zealous in preparation of their defenses increases.

As previously discussed, the attempt to control people's behavior is achieved through both civil law and criminal law. Generally, society reserves only those acts that are perceived as serious moral wrongs or extremely dangerous for sanction under criminal law. Those acts that are accidental or are not serious breaches of moral duty

Bill of Rights
■ The first 10 amendments (changes or additions) to the U.S. Constitution.

are usually not criminal, but may lead to civil liability. Beliefs about what acts should be considered under each category are very subjective and often change because a problem intensifies or because the public perceives an increased problem, even though the situation may not be any different than in years before.

For example, the 1980s saw an increased effort to stop people from driving while under the influence of alcohol. Many states enacted new laws increasing the penalty for violating their DUI statutes. In addition, a few states limited police discretion by requiring that violators be arrested. The practice once exercised by many police departments of taking drunk drivers home was stopped by legislative command. At one time, it can be argued that civil law was as much of a deterrent to driving under the influence as was criminal law. Fear of civil liability for causing property damage or personal liability was as great as fear of criminal liability, because of the inconsistent and often minor penalties that followed convictions for driving under the influence. However, as public concern over alcohol-related automobile accidents increased, the focus turned to criminal law to prevent such behavior. Increased penalties, consistent arrest policies, and mandatory alcohol treatment for those convicted are now common.

The extensive media coverage given to particular cases, such as the Larry Mahoney accident,[13] have increased the public awareness that one who drives while intoxicated risks arrest, conviction, and punishment, as well as civil liability for injuries to property and person. What this example teaches is that society determines what acts will be treated as criminal based on public perceptions of morality, the importance of deterrence, and the danger posed to the public by the acts in question. Do not forget that criminal acts are often the subject of civil suits. This is not always true, as noted earlier in this chapter, when the general purposes of civil law and criminal law were discussed.

THE PURPOSES OF PUNISHING CRIMINAL LAW VIOLATORS

You have already learned that the general goal of criminal law is to prevent behavior determined by society to be undesirable. The criminal justice system uses punishment as a prevention tool. Many theories support punishing criminal law violators. Although some people focus on one theory and use it as the basis for punishment, a more accurate approach, in this author's opinion, is to recognize that many theories have merit and that when a legislature establishes the range of punishment applicable to a particular crime, many theories were involved in motivating individual legislators. It is unlikely that every member of a legislature will be motivated by the same objective. It is also unlikely that an individual legislator will be motivated by one theory only. Rather, all of the following objectives influence legislative decision making to some degree.

Specific and General Deterrence

Specific deterrence seeks to **deter** individuals already convicted of crimes from committing crimes in the future. It is a negative reward theory. By punishing Mr. X for today's crime, we teach him that he will be disciplined for future criminal behavior. The arrest and conviction of an individual show that individual that society has the capability to detect crime and is willing to punish those who commit crimes.

General deterrence attempts to deter all members of society from engaging in criminal activity. In theory, when the public observes Mr. X being punished for his actions, the public is deterred from behaving similarly for fear of the same punishment. Of course, individuals will react differently to the knowledge of Mr. X's punishment. Individuals weigh the risk of being caught and the level of punishment against the benefit of committing the crime. All people do this at one time or another. Have you ever intentionally run a stoplight? Jaywalked? If so, you have made the decision to violate the law. Neither crime involves a severe penalty. That fact, in addition to the likelihood of not being discovered by law enforcement agents, probably affected your decision.

Presumably, if conviction of either crime was punished by incarceration (time in jail), then the deterrent effect would be greater. Would you be as likely to jaywalk if you knew that you could spend time in jail for such an act? Some people would; others would not. It is safe to assume, however, that as the punishment increases, so does compliance. However, one author observed that it is not as effective to increase the punishment as it is to increase the likelihood of being punished.[14] It is unknown how much either of these factors influences behavior, but it is generally accepted that they both do.

deter
- To discourage; to prevent from acting.

Incapacitation

Incapacitation, also referred to as restraint, is the third purpose of criminal punishment. Incapacitation does not seek to deter criminal conduct by influencing people's choices but prevents criminal conduct by restraining those who have committed crimes. Criminals who are restrained in jail or prison—or in the extreme, executed—are incapable of causing harm to the general public. This theory is often the rationale for long-term imprisonment of individuals who are believed to be beyond rehabilitation. It is also promoted by those who lack faith in rehabilitation and believe that all criminals should be removed from society to prevent the chance of repetition.

Crimes that are caused by mental disease or occur in a moment of passion are not affected by deterrence theories, because the individual does not have the opportunity to consider the punishment that will be inflicted for committing the crime before it is committed. Deterrence theories are effective only for individuals who are sufficiently intelligent to understand the consequences of their actions, are sane enough to understand the consequences of their actions, and are not laboring under such uncontrollable feelings that an understanding that they may be punished is lost.

Rehabilitation

Rehabilitation is another purpose of punishing criminals. The theory of rehabilitation is that if the criminal is subjected to educational and vocational programs, treatment and counseling, and other measures, it is possible to alter the individual's behavior to conform to societal norms. Another author noted:

> To the extent that crime is caused by elements of the offender's personality, educational defects, lack of work skills, and the like, we should be able to prevent him from committing more crimes by training, medical and psychiatric help, and guidance into law-abiding patterns of behavior. Strictly speaking, rehabilitation is not "punishment," but help to the offender. However, since this kind of help is frequently provided while the subject is in prison or at large on probation or parole under a sentence that carries some condemnation and some restriction of freedom, it is customary to list rehabilitation as one of the objects of a sentence in a criminal case.[15]

The concept of rehabilitation has come under considerable scrutiny in recent years, and the success of rehabilitative programs is questionable. However, the poor quality of prison rehabilitative programs may be the cause of the lack of success of these programs.

Retribution

Retribution, or societal vengeance, is the fifth purpose. Simply put, punishment through the criminal justice system is society's method of avenging a wrong. The idea that one who commits a wrong must be punished is an old one. The Old Testament speaks of an "eye for an eye." However, many people question the place of retribution in contemporary society. Is retribution consistent with American values? Jewish or Christian values? The question is actually moot, as there are few instances in which retribution stands alone as a reason for punishing someone who did not comply with the law. In most instances, society's desire for revenge can be satisfied while fulfilling one of the other purposes of punishment, such as incapacitation.

It has also been asserted that public retribution prevents private retribution.[16] That is, when the victim (or anyone who might avenge a victim) of a crime knows that the offender has been punished, the victim's need to seek revenge is lessened or removed. Therefore, punishing those who harm others has the effect of promoting social order by preventing undesirable conduct by victims of crimes. Retribution in such instances has a deterrent effect, as victims of crimes are less likely to seek revenge. This is a good example of how the various purposes discussed are interrelated.

Finally, consider a sociological note. Do not become so focused on criminal law as a method of social control that you forget the many other methods of control that exist.

> The criminal law is not, of course, the only weapon which society uses to prevent conduct which harms or threatens to harm these important interests of the public. Education, at home and at school, as to the types of conduct that society thinks good and bad, is an important weapon; religion, with its emphasis on distinguishing between good and evil conduct, is another. The human desire to acquire and keep the affection and respect of family, friends and associates no doubt has a great influence in deterring

most people from conduct that is socially unacceptable. The civil side of the law, which forces one to pay damages for the harmful results that one's undesirable conduct has caused to others, or which in inappropriate situations grants injunctions against bad conduct or orders the specific performance of good conduct, also plays a part in influencing behavior along desirable lines.[17]

Ethical Considerations

BASICS ON ETHICS IN CRIMINAL LAW

This feature, which appears in every chapter of this book, examines a particular ethical issue or dilemma that attorneys, judges, legal assistants, law enforcement officers, and parties confront in criminal cases.

In criminal cases, the various parties are governed by different sets of rules. Attorneys are regulated by state bar authorities. Most state bar authorities have adopted a modified version of the American Bar Association's (ABA) model rules. The ABA first issued a set of rules, the Canons of Professional Ethics, in 1908. In the 1960s, the ABA issued a new set of rules under the title Model Code of Professional Responsibility. Then, 20 years later, the Model Rules of Professional Conduct were issued. Today, it is the Model Rules that most states have adopted, typically with modifications. Accordingly, the Model Rules will be referenced in this book.

State bar authorities, not the ABA, enforce ethics rules. Typical sanctions for violations are reprimands, suspensions of the right to practice, restitution, and disbarment, which is the permanent removal from the practice of law. Additionally, judges possess the authority to discipline violations by attorneys (actually anyone appearing before the court) and contemptuous behavior with fines, temporary incarceration, and other penalties. Although not regulated by state or federal governmental authorities, paralegals are guided by the National Association of Legal Assistants and the National Federation of Paralegal Associations codes of professional conduct. More significantly, paralegals are indirectly regulated by state bars through their supervising attorneys, who are ultimately accountable for the research conducted by, and documents drafted by, their paralegals. Law enforcement officers are bound by state and federal laws and departmental rules.

Above all of these rules are the U.S. Constitution and the 50 state constitutions. Today, there is considerable constitutional case law that looks, smells, and tastes like ethics rules. Prosecuting attorneys, for example, are required to disclose evidence that tends to prove innocence to defendants. A violating prosecutor may be disciplined by a court, regardless of the bar's rules on the subject.

In each of the following chapters, a different dimension of ethics in criminal law will be explored more fully.

> **Web Links**
>
> **Courts and Prosecutors**
>
> What follows are a few of the excellent sites providing statistical data on United States courts and prosecutors:
>
> - http://www.albany.edu/sourcebook/
> - http://www.ncsconline.org (National Center for State Courts)
> - http://www.communitycourts.org (community courts page)

Key Terms

appellate courts	culpability	police power
Bill of Rights	damages	punitive damages
briefs	de novo	record
certiorari	deter	record on appeal
civil liberties	federalism	separation of powers
compensatory damages	inferior courts	statute
concurrent jurisdiction	intentional	strict liability
contract	interpret	terroristic
court of record	judicial review	tort
courts of general jurisdiction	jurisdiction	trial courts
courts of limited jurisdiction	negligence	

Review Questions

1. What is the primary duty of the executive branch of government in criminal law?
2. Define the term "court of record."
3. Define jurisdiction, and differentiate between a court of general jurisdiction and a court of limited jurisdiction.
4. What are the goals of criminal law? Civil law?
5. Who may file a civil suit? A criminal suit? How are these different?
6. What are compensatory damages? Punitive damages?
7. Should punitive damages be permitted in civil law? Explain your position.
8. Define culpability.

Problems & Critical Thinking Exercises

1. In 1973 the United States Supreme Court handed down the famous case *Roe v. Wade,* 410 U.S. 113 (1973), wherein the Court determined that the decision to have an abortion is a private decision that is protected from government intervention, in some circumstances, by the U.S. Constitution. Suppose that a state legislature passes legislation (a state statute) that attempts to reverse the *Roe* decision by prohibiting all abortions in that state. Which is controlling in that state, the statute or the decision of the United States Supreme Court? Explain your answer.
2. Same facts as in problem 1, except the state supreme court has determined that the state constitution protects the life of fetuses from abortion, except when the life of the mother is endangered. Which is controlling when a mother seeks to have an abortion and her life is not endangered to any greater amount than the average pregnancy—the state constitutional provision protecting fetuses or the decision of the United States Supreme Court? Explain your answer.
3. Assume that the United States Supreme Court has previously determined that regulation of traffic on county roads is a power reserved exclusively to the states. In reaction to this opinion, the United States Congress enacts a statute providing that the regulation of county roads will be within the jurisdiction of the United States Congress from that date forward. Your law office represents a client who is charged with violating the federal statute that prohibits driving on all roads while intoxicated. Do you have a defense? If so, explain.
4. In theory, people can increase their "freedom" by establishing a government and relinquishing freedoms (civil liberties) to that government. Explain why this paradox is true.
5. A bomb is exploded in a crowded shopping mall, killing 50 people and injuring hundreds of others. A written message is received at the local police station claiming that the attack was perpetrated by Foreigners for a New United States (FNUS), an established organization that has as its purpose the "destruction of the government of the United States and its citizens who support their government." Agents of the Federal Bureau of Investigation, working with local police, traced the message to Terry Ist, a leader of FNUS. Terry Ist was charged, convicted, and sentenced pursuant to the following federal statute:

Terrorism

i. Terrorist organization: The Attorney General, upon credible evidence that an organization has as a purpose to bring harm to the United States or its citizens, may declare such organization a terrorist organization by publishing notice of such declaration in the *Federal Register*.

ii. Any individual who is a member of a terrorist organization, as declared by the Attorney General in the previous section of this law, and who causes harm to person or property with the intent of (i) intimidating or coercing a civilian population; (ii) influencing the policy of a government by intimidation or coercion; or (iii) affecting the conduct of a government by mass destruction, assassination or kidnapping is guilty of terrorism, a felony.

iii. The government of the United States shall have exclusive jurisdiction to prosecute individuals for all crimes arising from acts of terrorism, as defined by this law herein.

After Terry Ist's conviction, the state where the bombing took place requested that Terry be turned over to it, where he was to be tried for murder and other offenses. The United States refused, citing section iii of the above law. Further, the United States Attorney filed a motion to have the case removed to federal court, along with an accompanying motion to dismiss the criminal action, asserting that section iii prohibits the state prosecution. Discuss the federalism issue, making the best case for both the state and federal governments. Conclude by explaining who should prevail and why.

To reach the greatest individual freedom & personal security, unchecked individual freedom must be balanced with governmental authority to prevent & punish harmful behaviour.

Endnotes

1. 18 U.S.C. §2331.
2. *Printz v. United States*, 521 U.S. 98 (1997)
3. *United States v. Morrison*, 529 U.S. 598 (2000)
4. *Jones v. United States*, 529 U.S. 848 (*2000*)
5. *Gonzales v. Raich*, 545 U.S. 1 (2005)
6. *United States v. Comstock*, 560 U.S. _____ (2010)
7. 28 U.S.C. § 41 *et seq.*
8. For more on the separation of powers and federalism, See Daniel E. Hall and John P. Feldmeier, *Constitutional Law: Governmental Power and Individual Freedoms,* 2nd ed. (Upper Saddle River, NJ: Prentice Hall Publishing, 2011), chapters 1–7. Chapter 1 contains a discussion of judicial review authority.
9. 517 U.S. 559 (1996).
10. 538 U.S. 408 (2003).
11. 554 U.S. 571 (2008).
12. 549 U.S. 346 (2007).
13. In May, 1988, Larry Mahoney, while driving under the influence of alcohol, struck a school bus, causing it to burst into flames. At the time he hit the bus, he was traveling in the wrong direction on an interstate highway. Twenty-four children and three adults died in the fire. On December 22, 1989, a Kentucky jury convicted Mr. Mahoney of second-degree manslaughter and other lesser offenses, and recommended that he be sentenced to 16 years in prison. Mahoney, who was characterized as a model prisoner, was granted early release from prison for good behavior in 1999, six years short of his sentence. "Drunken Driver Lives in Obscurity," *The Cincinnati Enquirer, May* 14, 2003.
14. *See* E. Puttkammer, *Administration of Criminal Law,* 16–17 (1953).
15. Schwartz and Goldstein, *Police Guidance Manuals* (Charlottesville: University of Virginia Press, 1968), Manual No. 3, at 21–32, reprinted in *Cases, Materials, and Problems on the Advocacy and Administration of Criminal Justice* 173 by Harold Norris (unpublished manuscript available in the Detroit College of Law library).
16. *See* Note, 78 *Colum. L. Rev.* 1249, 1247–59 (1978); LaFave and Scott, *Criminal Law* 26 (Hornbook Series, St. Paul: West, 1986).
17. LaFave and Scott at 23.

CHAPTER 2

INTRODUCTION TO CRIMINAL LAW

Chapter Outline

The Distinction Between Criminal Law and Criminal Procedure
Sources of Criminal Law
- *The Common Law*
- *Statutory Law*
- *Ordinances*
- *Administrative Law*
- *Court Rules*
- *The Model Penal Code*
- *Constitutional Law*

Ethical Considerations: Defending Individuals Charged with Horrendous Crimes

Chapter Objectives

After completing this chapter you should be able to:

- identify and describe the objectives of criminal law and begin thinking critically about these objectives.
- identify and describe the various sources of criminal law.
- brief a judicial opinion and you should have begun practicing your case analysis skills.
- outline and explain the fundamental history of the U.S. legal system.
- explain the tension between social control and freedom.

THE DISTINCTION BETWEEN CRIMINAL LAW AND CRIMINAL PROCEDURE

In all areas of legal study, a distinction is made between substance and procedure. Substantive law defines rights and obligations. Procedural law establishes the methods used to enforce legal rights and obligations. The substance of tort law defines what a tort is and what damages an injured party is entitled to recover from a lawsuit. Substantive contract law defines what a contract is, tells whether it must be in writing to be enforceable, who must sign it, what the penalty for breach is, and other such information. The field of civil procedure sets rules for how to bring the substance of the law before a court for resolution of a claim. To decide that a client has an injury that can be compensated under the law is a substantive decision. The question then becomes how injured clients get the compensation to which they are entitled. This is the procedural question. Procedural law tells you how to file a lawsuit, where to file, when to file, and how to prosecute the claim. Such is the case for criminal law and procedure.

Criminal law, as a field of law, defines what constitutes a crime. It establishes what conduct is prohibited and what punishment can be imposed for violating its mandates. Criminal law establishes what degree of intent is required for criminal liability. In addition, criminal law sets out the defenses to criminal charges that may be asserted. Alibi, insanity, and the like are defenses and fall under the umbrella of criminal law.

Criminal procedure puts substantive criminal law into action. It is concerned with the procedures used to bring criminals to justice, beginning with police investigation and continuing throughout the process of administering justice. When and under what conditions may a person be arrested? How and where must the criminal charge be filed? When can the police conduct a search? How does the accused assert a defense? How long can a person be held in custody by the police without charges being filed? How long after charges are filed does the accused have to wait before a trial is held? These are all examples of criminal procedure questions that As you will learn in later chapters, many of the rules of criminal procedure have their roots in both the U.S. and state Constitutions. Of course, statutory law is also important in this context. Do not worry if you cannot always distinguish between a procedural question and a substantive one. There is considerable overlap between the two concepts.

The first part of this text is devoted to criminal law and the latter part to criminal procedure. In the remainder of the book, the term "criminal law" is used often. In most cases, this refers to general criminal law, including both substantive criminal law and criminal procedure.

criminal law
■ The branch of the law that specifies what conduct constitutes crime and establishes appropriate punishments for such conduct.

criminal procedure
■ The rules of procedure by which criminal prosecutions are governed.

SOURCES OF CRIMINAL LAW

Criminal law is a body of many laws emanating from many sources. Today, most American criminal law is a product of legislative enactment. That has not always been so. Further, administrative regulations now make up a much larger percentage of criminal law than in the past. It is vital to successful legal research that that you understand the sources of criminal law. As you read this section, you will begin to see why an understanding of the functions of the three branches of government is important to an understanding of all criminal law.

The Common Law

The oldest form of criminal law in the United States is the **common law.** The common law developed in England and brought to the United States by the English colonists.

> The common law, as it exists in this country, is of English origin. Founded on ancient local rules and customs and in feudal times, it began to evolve in the King's courts and was eventually molded into the viable principles through which it continues to operate. The common law migrated to this continent with the first English colonists, who claimed the system as their birthright; it continued in full force in the 13 original colonies until the American Revolution, at which time it was adopted by each of the states as well as the national government of the new nation.[1]

But what exactly is this common law? Simply stated, the common law is judge-made law. It is law that has been developed by the hands of the judges of both England and the United States. To comprehend how the common law developed, an understanding of English legal history, particularly the concepts of precedence and **stare decisis,** is important. Beginning with William the Conqueror in 1066 (Norman Conquest), the English monarchy began using law to reinforce the authority of the monarchy, to increase fairness over the existing feudal systems, to promote economic stability and development, and to unify the kingdom. Prior to 1066, all law in England was local and varied. In the early years after the Norman Conquest, the king sent his judges to hear cases throughout the nation. These judges returned to London, where they discussed their decisions. This process, along with the creation of royal courts, led to the development of rules of court and legal doctrines that would be applied in all cases. One such doctrine, intended to make the law the judges were applying consistent and predictable, holds that when a court renders a legal decision, that decision is binding on itself and its inferior courts, whenever the same issue arises again in the future.

The decision of a court is known as a **precedent.** The principle that inferior courts will comply with that decision when the issue is raised in the future is known as "stare decisis et non quieta movera" (a Latin phrase meaning "stand by precedents and do not disturb settled points"). The Supreme Court of Indiana expressed its view of stare decisis:

> Under the doctrine of stare decisis, this Court adheres to a principle of law which has been firmly established. Important policy considerations militate in favor of continuity and predictability in the law. Therefore, we are reluctant to disturb longstanding precedent which involves salient issues. Precedent operates as a maxim for judicial restraint to prevent the unjustified reversal to a series of decisions merely because the composition of the court has changed.[2]

common law
■ The legal system that originated in England and is composed of case law and statutes that grow and change, influenced by ever-changing custom and tradition.

stare decisis
■ (Latin) The doctrine that judicial decisions stand as precedents for cases arising in the future.

precedent
■ Prior decisions of the same court, or a higher court, that a judge must follow in deciding a subsequent case presenting similar facts and the same legal problem, even though different parties are involved and many years have elapsed.

Most of the early decisions were based upon feudal law. The impact, however, of having royal courts with national authority recognize a feudal legal principle, and subsequently applying that principle throughout the kingdom, was that England, for the first time in its history, had a set of laws that were *common to all,* and hence is the explanation for the name of this type of law.

> The common law, as frequently defined, includes those principles, usages, and rules of action applicable to the government and security of persons and property which do not rest for their authority upon any express or positive statute or other written declaration, but upon statements of principles found in the decisions of courts. The common law is inseparably identified with the decisions of the courts and can be determined only from such decisions in former cases bearing upon the subject under inquiry. As distinguished from statutory or written law, it embraces the great body of unwritten law founded upon general custom, usage, or common consent, and based upon natural justice or reason. It may otherwise be defined as custom long acquiesced in or sanctioned by immemorial usage and judicial decision. . . .
>
> In a broader sense the common law is the system of rules and declarations of principles from which our judicial ideas and legal definitions are derived, and which are continually expanding. It is not a codification of exact or inflexible rules for human conduct, for the redress of injuries, or for protection against wrongs, but is rather the embodiment of broad and comprehensive unwritten principles, inspired by natural reason and an innate sense of justice, and adopted by common consent for the regulation and government of the affairs of men.[3]

As stated, the common law is fluid and dynamic, changing to meet societal values and expectations. As one court stated, "The common law of the land is based upon human experience in the unceasing effort of an enlightened people to ascertain what is right and just between men."[4]

While courts (and the monarch) were responsible for making law in the early years of the common law, the situation changed with the advent of Parliament in the thirteen and fourteenth centuries. While the early Parliament had very limited authority, it eventually evolved into the general lawmaking body of England, displacing courts in the lawmaking function. Today, legislatures in all common law nations are the primary lawmakers. In the United States, the Congress of the United States is the federal lawmaker and the legislatures of the states are each responsible for making state laws. However, for reasons detailed later, courts continue to play an important role in the development of the common law.

Historically what happened in criminal law is that courts defined crimes, as there was usually no legislative enactment that determined what acts should be criminal. As time passed, established "common-law crimes" developed. First the courts determined what acts should be criminal, and then the specifics of each crime developed; what exactly had to be proved to establish guilt, what defenses were available, and what punishment was appropriate for conviction. Although there is great similarity between the common laws of the many jurisdictions in the United States, differences exist because judicial decisions of one state are not binding on other states. However, courts may look outside their jurisdictions for opinions to guide them in their decisionmaking if no court in their jurisdiction has addressed the issue under consideration. Each state, as a separate and sovereign entity, has the power to decide whether to adopt the common law, in whole or in part, or to reject it.

The 13 original states all adopted the common law. Most did so through their state constitutions. Today, only Louisiana has not adopted the common law in some form. However, for reasons you will learn later, approximately half of the states no longer recognize common-law crimes.[5] Even in those states, though, the civil common law and portions of the criminal common law (i.e., defenses to criminal charges) continue in force. Most states have expressly adopted the common law either by statute or by constitutional authority. Generally, there is no federal common law; rather, federal courts, in certain civil cases, apply the common law of the states in which they sit. For example, a U.S. district court in New Jersey will apply New Jersey common law. Even though this may appear strange to you, it is common practice for federal courts to apply state law. Further discussion of this topic is beyond the scope of this text.

Finally, be aware that common law has been modified and even abolished in some jurisdictions. The modifications to, and nullifications of, common law have come about in many different manners. In some instances, courts have decided that the common law must be changed to meet contemporary conditions or to bring the law into conformity with state or federal constitutional principles. In extreme situations, parts of the common law have been totally abolished. Because legislatures are charged with the duty of making the laws, they have the final word on the status of the common law, unless there is a state constitutional provision stating otherwise. Some legislatures have expressly given their judiciaries the authority to modify the common law, often with limitations. State legislatures are free to modify, partially abolish, or wholly abolish the common law as long as their own state constitution or the U.S. Constitution is not violated by so doing.

The common law normally is inferior to legislation. This means that if a legislature acts in an area previously dealt with by common law, the new statute controls, absent a statement by the legislature to the contrary. For example, assume that under common law adultery was a crime in State Y. The legislature of State Y can change this by simply enacting a statute that provides that adultery is not criminal. The legislature may also amend the common law by continuing to recognize common-law adultery, but change the penalty for violation. If a state constitution, statute, or judicial decision has not abrogated the common law, presume that it continues in effect.

The Principle of Legality

The question of whether common-law crimes should continue to exist is debatable. Those who favor permitting common-law crimes like that it permits courts to "fill in the gaps" left by the legislatures when those bodies either fail to foresee all potential crimes or simply forget to include a crime that was foreseen. However, a separation-of-powers question is raised by this scenario: namely, should the judicial branch actively second-guess or clean house for the legislative branch? Such conduct does appear to be the exercise of legislative authority. However, few people want intentionally dangerous or disruptive behavior not to be criminalized, and it appears to be impossible for legislatures to foresee all possible acts that are dangerous and disruptive.

Those who oppose a common law of crimes point to the concept embodied in the phrase "nullum crimen sine lege," which translates roughly to "there is no crime if there is no statute." Similarly, "nulla poena sine lege" has come to mean that "there shall be no punishment if there is no statute." These concepts, when considered in concert, insist that the criminal law must be written, that the written law must exist at the time that the accused committed the act in question, and that criminal laws be more precise than civil laws.[6] This is the *principle of legality*.

The legality principle is founded on the belief that all people are entitled to know, prior to committing an act, that the act is criminal and that punishment could result from such behavior. This is commonly referred to as *notice*. The idea is sensible, as it appears to be a rule consistent with general notions of fairness and justice, not only in the United States but for peoples around the world. Does it appear fair to you to hold individuals criminally accountable for taking an act that they could not have known was prohibited? The legality principle remedies the notice problem by requiring that written law be the basis of criminal liability, not unwritten common law. Understand that the law imposes a duty on all people to be aware of written law; thus, all people are presumed to be aware of criminal prohibitions. The *Keeler* case discusses the legality principle. Today, the principle of legality is subsumed in the right to due process (a fair process) found in the Fifth and Fourteenth Amendments to the Constitution of the United States and in the constitutions of the various states.

---

sidebar

HOW TO BRIEF A CASE

You are about to read the first judicial decision found in this text. Decisions of courts are often written and are commonly referred to as *judicial opinions* or cases. These cases are published in law reporters so they may be used as precedent. Many cases appear in this text for your education. Your instructor may also require that you read other cases, often from your jurisdiction. The cases included in your book have been edited, citations have been omitted, and legal issues not relevant to the subject discussed have been excised. There is a common method that students of the law use to read and analyze, also known as briefing, cases. Please go to Appendix C now to learn more about how to brief a case.

sidebar (continued)

Most judicial opinions are written using a similar format. First, the name of the case appears with the name of the court, the cite (location where the case has been published), and the year. When the body of the case begins, the name of the judge, or judges, responsible for writing the opinion appears directly before the first paragraph. The opinion contains an introduction to the case, which normally includes the procedural history of the case. This is followed by a summary of the facts that led to the dispute, the court's analysis of the law that applies to the case, and the court's conclusions and orders, if any.

Most opinions used here are from appellate courts, where many judges sit at one time. After the case is over, the judges vote on an outcome. The majority vote wins, and the opinion of the majority is written by one of those judges. If other judges in the majority wish to add to the majority opinion, they may write one or more *concurring opinions*. Concurring opinions appear after majority opinions in the law reporters. When judges who were not in the majority feel strongly about their position, they may file dissenting opinions, which appear after the concurring opinions, if any. Only the majority opinion is law, although concurring and dissenting opinions are often informative.

During your legal education you may be instructed to brief a case. Even if your instructor does not require you to brief cases, you may want to, as many students understand a case better after they have completed a brief. Here are suggestions for reading and understanding cases:

1. Read the case. On your first reading, do not take notes; simply attempt to get a *feel* for the case. Then read the case again and use the following suggested method of briefing.
2. State the *relevant* facts. Often, cases read like little stories. You need to weed out the facts that have no bearing on the subject you are studying.
3. Identify the issues. *Issues* are the legal questions discussed by the court.
4. State the applicable rules, standards, or other law, as they apply to the issues you have identified.
5. Summarize the court's decision and analysis. Why and how did the court reach its conclusion? Note whether the court affirmed, reversed, or remanded the case.

For a more thorough discussion of briefing and to read a sample brief, see Appendix C.

KEELER V. SUPERIOR COURT
Supreme Court of California   2 Cal. 3d 619, 470 P.2d 617 (1970)

In this proceeding for writ of prohibition, we are called upon to decide whether an unborn viable fetus is a "human being" within the meaning of the California statute defining murder. We conclude that the legislature did not intend such a meaning, and that for us to construe the statute to the contrary and apply it to this petitioner would exceed our judicial power and deny petitioner due process of law.

The evidence received at the preliminary examination may be summarized as follows: Petitioner and Teresa Keeler obtained an interlocutory decree of divorce on September 27, 1968. They had been married for sixteen years. Unknown to the petitioner, Mrs. Keeler was then pregnant by one Ernest Vogt, whom she had met earlier that summer. She subsequently began living with Vogt in Stockton, but concealed the fact from petitioner. Petitioner was given custody of their two daughters, aged 12 and 13 years, and under the decree Mrs. Keeler had the right to take the girls on alternate weekends.

On February 23, 1969, Mrs. Keeler was driving on a narrow mountain road in Amador County after delivering the girls to their home. She met petitioner driving in the opposite direction; he blocked the road with his car, and she pulled over to the side. He walked to her vehicle and began speaking to her. He seemed calm, and she rolled down her window to hear him. He said, "I hear you're pregnant. If you are, you had better stay away from the girls and from here." She did not reply, and he opened the car door; as she later testified, "He assisted me out of the car . . . [I]t wasn't rough at this time." Petitioner then looked at her abdomen and became "extremely upset." He said, "You sure are. I'm going to stomp it out of you." He pushed her against the car, shoved his knee into her abdomen, and struck her in the face with several blows. She fainted, and when she regained consciousness, petitioner had departed.

Mrs. Keeler drove back to Stockton, and the police and medical assistance were summoned. She had suffered substantial facial injuries, as well as extensive bruising of the abdominal wall. A Caesarian section was performed, and the fetus was examined in utero. Its head was found to be severely fractured, and it was delivered stillborn. The pathologist gave as his opinion that the cause of death was skull fracture with consequent cerebral hemorrhaging, that death would be immediate, and that the injury could have been the result of force applied to the mother's abdomen. There was no air in the fetus' lungs, and the umbilical cord was intact. . . .

The evidence was in conflict as to the estimated age of the fetus; the expert testimony on the point, however, concluded "with reasonable medical certainty" that the fetus had developed to the stage of viability, i.e., that in the event of premature birth on the date in question, it would have had a 75 percent to 96 percent chance of survival.

An information was filed charging petitioner, in count I, with committing the crime of murder. . . .

Penal Code section 187 provides: "Murder is the unlawful killing of a human being, with malice aforethought." The dispositive question is whether the fetus which petitioner is accused of killing was, on February 23, 1969, a "human being" within the meaning of the statute. If it was not, petitioner cannot be charged with its "murder". . . .

* * *

We conclude that in declaring murder to be the unlawful and malicious killing of a "human being," the Legislature of 1850 intended that term to have the settled common law meaning of a person who had been born alive, and did not intend the act of feticide—as distinguished from abortion—to be an offense under the laws of California.

* * *

KEELER V. SUPERIOR COURT (continued)

The People urge, however that the sciences of obstetrics and pediatrics have greatly progressed since 1872, to the point where, with proper medical care, a normally developed fetus prematurely born ... is "viable" ... since an unborn but viable fetus is now fully capable of independent life. ... But we cannot join in the conclusion sought to be deduced: we cannot hold this petitioner to answer for murder by reason of his alleged act of killing an unborn—even though viable—fetus. To such a charge there are two insuperable obstacles, one "jurisdictional" and the other constitutional.

Penal Code section 6 declares in relevant part that "No act or omission" accomplished after the code has taken effect "is criminal or punishable, except as prescribed by this code...." This section embodies a fundamental principle of our tripartite form of government, i.e., that subject to the constitutional prohibition against cruel and unusual punishment, the power to define crimes and fix penalties is vested exclusively in the legislative branch. Stated differently, there are no common law crimes in California.... In order that a public offense be committed, some statute, ordinance or regulation prior in time to the commission of the act, must denounce it.

* * *

Applying these rules to the case at bar, we would undoubtedly act in excess of the judicial power if we were to adopt the People's proposed construction of section 187. As we have shown, the Legislature has defined the crime of murder in California to apply only to the unlawful and malicious killing of one who has been born alive. We recognize that the killing of an unborn but viable fetus may be deemed by some to be an offense of similar nature and gravity; but as Chief Justice Marshall warned long ago: "It would be dangerous, indeed, to carry the principle that a case which is within the reason or mischief of a statute, is within its provisions, so far as to punish a crime not enumerated in the statute, because it is of equal atrocity, or of kindred character, with those which are enumerated." ... Whether to thus extend liability for murder in California is a determination solely within the province of the Legislature. For a court to simply declare, by judicial fiat, that the time has now come to prosecute under section 187 one who kills an unborn but viable fetus would indeed be to rewrite the statute under the guise of construing it.... to make it "a judicial function"... "raises very serious questions concerning the principle of separation of powers."

The second obstacle to the proposed judicial enlargement of section 187 is the guarantee of due process of law. ...

The first essential of due process is fair warning of the act which is made punishable as a crime. "That the terms of a penal statute creating a new offense must be sufficiently explicit to inform those who are subject to it what conduct on their part will render them liable to its penalties, is a well-recognized requirement, consonant alike with ordinary notions of fair play and the settled rules of law."

Do not forget that *Keeler* is an opinion of the California Supreme Court; therefore, it is not the law of all of the United States. Similar decisions have been made in other states, however.

Also note that the court determined that the common law violates "ordinary notions of fair play" and that no warning or notice was given to Keeler that his act could be defined as murder. As the court noted, these requirements are embodied in

due process

■ The *due process* clauses of the Fifth and Fourteenth Amendments to the U.S. Constitution require that no persons be deprived of life, liberty, or property without having notice and a real chance to present their side in a legal dispute.

the **due process** clauses of the U.S. Constitution and the constitutions of the many states. There are two dimensions to due process, procedural and substantive. Procedural due process, in both civil and criminal law, requires that individuals be put on notice of impending government action, be given an opportunity to be heard and to present evidence, and in some cases, benefit from other rights, such as having counsel appointed and having the case heard by a jury. Substantive due process recognizes individual rights to act or not to act. For example, privacy is not explicitly protected in the Constitution of the United States. Regardless, the Supreme Court has found an implicit right to privacy in the due process clauses' protection of liberty. Through this implicit right, the Court has invalidated laws prohibiting interracial marriage, prohibiting the use of contraception by married persons, and prohibiting women from ending pregnancies in some circumstances.

Although common law crimes are suspect when viewed through a due process lens, the United States Supreme Court has determined that states may, under some circumstances, recognize common law crimes The court in *Keeler* based its decision on the California Constitution's Due Process Clause. You should remember that the California Supreme Court is the final word on California law, and *Keeler* teaches you that the California Constitution provides more protection than the U.S. Constitution in this regard. Still, the U.S. Constitution places limits on the use of the common law by the states to create crimes. This is done primarily through the Due Process Clause and the provision prohibiting ex post facto laws. You will learn more about the Due Process and Ex Post Facto Clauses later in this book when we examine defenses to criminal charges. If states, such as California in the *Keeler* case, want to increase a defendant's rights beyond what the U.S. Constitution protects, they may do so through their own statutes or constitutions.

Other Uses of the Common Law

Even in those jurisdictions that have abandoned use of the common law to create crimes, the common law continues to be important for many reasons.

First, many statutes mirror the common law in language. That is, legislatures often simply codify the common law's criminal prohibitions. Hence, when a question arises concerning whether a particular act of a defendant is intended to fall under the intent of a criminal prohibition, the case law handed down prior to codification of the common law may answer the question. The result is that the crime remains the same but the source of the prohibition has changed. It is also possible for a legislature to change only part of a common-law definition and leave the remainder the same. If so, prior case law may be helpful when considering the unaltered portion of the definition.

Second, many of the concepts developed at the common law are still recognized. For example, the distinction between felonies and misdemeanors continues today. Although jurisdictions vary in definition, a felony is a serious crime usually punishable by more than one year in prison. A misdemeanor is less serious and usually is punishable by one year or less in jail.

Third, legislatures occasionally enact a criminal prohibition without establishing the potential penalty for violation. In such cases, courts will often look to the penalties applied to similar common law crimes for guidance.

Fourth, in addition to defining crimes, the common law established many procedures that were used to adjudicate criminal cases. These procedures most often dealt with criminal defenses. What defenses could be raised, as well as how and when, were often answered by the common law. For example, the various tests to determine if a defendant was sane when an alleged crime was committed were developed under the common law. If a legislature has not specifically changed these procedural rules, they remain in effect, even if the power of courts to create common-law crimes has been abolished.

Statutory Law

As you have already learned, the legislative branch is responsible for the creation of law. You have also learned that legislatures possess the authority to modify, abolish, or adopt the common law, in whole or in part. During the nineteenth century, the codification of criminal law began.[7] This effectively displaced the role of the judiciary in defining crimes. Today, nearly all criminal law is found in criminal codes.

Although the power of the legislative branch to declare behavior criminal is significant, there are limits. The constitutions of the United States and of the many states contain limits on such state and federal authority. Most of these limits are found in the Bill of Rights. For example, the First Amendment to the federal Constitution prohibits government, with few exceptions, from punishing an individual for exercising choice of religion and for expressing opinions and thoughts. If a legislature enacts a law that violates a constitutional provision, it is the duty of the judicial branch to declare the law void. This is the power of judicial review, previously discussed in Chapter 1. For now, you need only understand that legislatures do not have unlimited authority to create criminal law.

Ordinances

The written laws of municipalities are termed **ordinances.** Ordinances are laws enacted by city, county, and other local governments. Ordinances can be administrative or civil in nature, e.g., zoning, building, construction, and related matters). Municipalities also be empowered by state law to make criminal laws. In some instances, criminal ordinances mirror state statutes but apply to those acts that occur within the jurisdiction of the city. For example, many cities have assault and battery ordinances, just as their states have assault and battery statutes. Traffic and parking violations may also be criminal, although some cities pursue these as civil violations, which permits enabling the state to pursue criminal charge for the same act.

Ordinances may not conflict with state or federal law. Any ordinance that is inconsistent with higher law may be invalidated by a court. States limit the power of cities to punish for ordinance violations, and most city court trials are to the bench, not to a jury.

ordinance

■ A local or city law, rule, or regulation.

Administrative Law

It is likely that during your life, you have likely had to deal with several administrative agencies. Agencies are governmental units, federal, state, and local, that administer the affairs of the government. Although often lumped together, the agencies are actually of two types: social welfare and regulatory. The two names reflect the purposes behind each type. Social welfare agencies put into effect government programs. For example, in Indiana, the State Department of Public Welfare administers the distribution of public money to those deemed needy. In contrast, state medical licensing boards are regulatory, because their duty is to oversee and regulate the practice of medicine in the various states. Regulatory and administrative agencies both receive their delegation of authority from the legislative branch.

Because legislatures do not possess the time or the expertise to write precise statutes, they often enact statutes that are very general, and in those statute grant one or more administrative agencies the authority to make more precise laws. Just as legislative enactments are known as statutes (or codes), administrative laws are known as **regulations** or rules. The extent to which a legislature may delegate its lawmaking authority, if at all, has been a continuing source of disagreement. Some scholars argue that legislatures may not grant such an important legislative function to agencies. Doing so is believed to be a violation of the principle of separation of powers, because agencies usually fall under the control of the executive branch, and the legislative branch is not permitted to delegate its powers to the executive branch, or vice versa.

In spite of these separation of powers problems, the United States Supreme Court has determined that agencies may create regulations that have the effect of law, including criminal prohibitions. The Court's opinion on how much authority may be delegated to administrative agencies has undergone a few changes over the years. In 1911, the United States Supreme Court handed down the opinion in the *Grimaud* case.

Grimaud is the law today. Agencies may be delegated penal rulemaking authority. However, the Supreme Court has said that although Congress may delegate to an agency the authority to make criminal laws, it may not delegate the responsibility of establishing penalties to an agency, with the possible exception of small fines. Congress must either set the precise penalty or set a range from which an agency can further determine the appropriate penalty.

An interesting question concerns how much guidance Congress must give an agency in its delegation. Because Congress is delegating its power to create law to an agency, it is expected to give the agency some guidance as to what it wants. This limits the discretion

regulation

■ Law created by governmental administrative agencies.

---

sidebar

FINDING ADMINISTRATIVE REGULATIONS

Federal administrative rules are found in the Code of Federal Regulations (C.F.R.). New rules that have not yet been added to the C.F.R. may be found in the *Federal Register*. Each state has its counterpart publications. For example, in Florida they are the Florida Administrative Code and the *Florida Administrative Weekly*, respectively.

of the agency and prevents it from becoming a substitute legislature.[8] Normally, Congress must provide an intelligible principle or sufficient standards to guide an agency.[9] It takes little congressional guidance to satisfy these tests. Due to the special nature of criminal law (i.e., the deprivation to liberty that may result from a criminal conviction), defendants have argued that Congress must be more specific, or give an agency less discretion, when delegating the authority to create penal rules, as opposed to non-penal rules. The Supreme Court refused to answer that question in *Touby v. United States*.

UNITED STATES V. GRIMAUD
United States Supreme Court 220 U.S. 506 (1911)

The defendants were indicted for grazing sheep on the Sierra Forest Reserve without having obtained the permission required by the regulations adopted by the Secretary of Agriculture. They demurred on the ground that the Forest Reserve Act of 1891 was unconstitutional, insofar as it delegated to the Secretary of Agriculture power to make rules and regulations and made a violation thereof a penal offense.

. . .

From the various acts relating to the establishment and management of forest reservations it appears that they were intended "to improve and protect the forest and to secure favorable conditions to water flows." . . . It was also declared that the Secretary "may make such rules and regulations and establish such service as will insure the objects of such reservation, namely, to regulate their occupancy and use to prevent the forests thereon from destruction; *and any violation of the provisions of this act or such rules and regulations shall be punished,*" as is provided in [the statute].

Under these acts, therefore, any use of the reservations for grazing or other lawful purpose was required to be subject to the rules and regulations established by the Secretary of Agriculture. To pasture sheep and cattle on the reservation, at will and without restraint, might interfere seriously with the accomplishment of the purposes for which they were established. But a limited and regulated use for pasturage might not be inconsistent with the object sought to be attained by the statute. The determination of such questions, however, was a matter of administrative detail. What might be harmless in one forest might be harmful to another. What might be injurious at one stage of timber growth, or at one season of the year, might not be so at another.

In the nature of things, it was impracticable for Congress to provide general regulations for these various and varying details of management. Each reservation had its peculiar and special features; and in authorizing the Secretary of Agriculture to meet these local conditions, Congress was merely conferring administrative functions upon an agent, and not delegating to him legislative power.

. . .

It must be admitted that it is difficult to define the line which separates the legislative power to make laws from the administrative authority to make regulations. This difficulty has often been recognized [as] referred to by Chief Justice Marshall . . . : "It will not be contended that Congress can delegate to the courts, or to any other tribunals, powers which are strictly and exclusively legislative. But Congress may certainly delegate to others, powers which the legislature may rightfully exercise itself." What

(continued)

UNITED STATES V. GRIMAUD (continued)

were these non-legislative powers which Congress could exercise but which also might be delegated to others was not determined, for he said: "The line has not been exactly drawn which separates those important subjects, which must be entirely regulated by the legislature itself, from those of less interest, in which a general provision may be made, and power given to those who are to act under such general provisions to fill up the details."

From the beginning of the Government, various acts have been passed conferring upon the executive officers power to make rules and regulations—not for the government of their departments but for administering the laws which did govern. None of these statutes could confer legislative power. But when Congress had legislated and indicated its will, it could give to those who were to act under such general provisions "power to fill up the details" by the establishment of administrative rules and regulations, the violation of which could be punished by fine or imprisonment fixed by Congress, or by penalties fixed by Congress or measured by the injury done.

• • •

It is true that there is no act of Congress which, in express terms, declares that it shall be unlawful to graze sheep on a forest reserve. But the statutes, from which we have quoted, declare that the privilege of using reserves for "all proper and lawful purposes" is subject to the proviso that the person shall comply "with the rules and regulations covering such forest reservation." The same act makes it an offense to violate those regulations.

• • •

The Secretary of Agriculture could not make rules and regulations for any and every purpose. As to those here involved, they all regulate matters clearly indicated and authorized by Congress.

TOUBY V. UNITED STATES
United States Supreme Court 500 U.S. 160 (1991)

Petitioners were convicted of manufacturing and conspiring to manufacture "Euphoria," a drug temporarily designated as a schedule I controlled substance pursuant to § 201(h) of the Controlled Substances Act. We consider whether § 201(h) unconstitutionally delegates legislative power to the Attorney General and whether the Attorney General's subdelegation to the Drug Enforcement Administration (DEA) was authorized by statute. . . .

[T]he Controlled Substances Act (Act) . . . establishes five categories or "schedules" of controlled substances, the manufacture, possession, and distribution of which the Act regulates or prohibits. Violations involving schedule I substances carry the most severe penalties, as these substances are believed to pose the most serious threat to public safety. Relevant here, § 201(a) of the Act authorizes the Attorney General to add or remove substances, or to move a substance from one schedule to another. . . .

When adding a substance to a schedule, the Attorney General must follow specified procedures. First, the Attorney General must request a scientific and medical evaluation from the Secretary of Health and Human Services (HHS), together with a recommendation as to whether the substances should be controlled. A substance cannot be scheduled if the Secretary recommends against it. . . . Second, the

TOUBY V. UNITED STATES (continued)

Attorney General must consider eight factors with respect to the substance, including its potential for abuse, scientific evidence of its pharmacological effect, its psychic or physiological dependence liability, and whether the substance is an immediate precursor of a substance already controlled.... Third, the Attorney General must comply with notice-and-hearing provisions of the Administrative Procedure Act... which permit comment by interested parties.... In addition, the Act permits any aggrieved person to challenge the scheduling of a substance by the Attorney General in a court of appeals....

It takes time to comply with these procedural requirements. From the time when law enforcement officials identify a dangerous new drug, it typically takes 6 to 12 months to add it to one of the schedules.... Drug traffickers were able to take advantage of this time gap by designing drugs that were similar in pharmacological effect to scheduled substances but differing slightly in chemical composition, so that existing schedules did not apply to them. These "designer drugs" were developed and widely marketed long before the Government was able to schedule them and initiate prosecutions....

To combat the "designer drug" problem, Congress in 1984 amended the Act to create an expedited procedure by which the Attorney General can schedule a substance on a temporary basis when doing so is "necessary to avoid an imminent hazard to the public safety."... Temporary scheduling under § 201(h) allows the Attorney General to bypass, for a limited time, several of the requirements for permanent scheduling. The Attorney General need consider only three of the eight factors required for permanent scheduling.... Rather than comply with the APA notice-and-hearing provisions, the Attorney General need provide only a 30-day notice of proposed scheduling in the Federal Register.... Notice also must be transmitted to the Secretary of HHS, but the Secretary's prior approval of a proposed scheduling is not required.... Finally... an order to schedule a substance temporarily "is not subject to judicial review."

Because it has fewer procedural requirements, temporary scheduling enables the government to respond more quickly to the threat posed by dangerous new drugs. A temporary scheduling order can be issued 30 days after a new drug is identified, and the order remains valid for one year. During this 1-year period, the Attorney General presumably will initiate the permanent scheduling process....

The Attorney General promulgated regulations delegating to the DEA his powers under the Act, including the power to schedule controlled substances on a temporary basis. Pursuant to that delegation, the DEA Administrator issued an order scheduling... "Euphoria" as a schedule I controlled substance....

While the temporary scheduling order was in effect, DEA agents, executing a valid search warrant, discovered a fully operational drug laboratory in Daniel and Lyrissa Touby's home. The Toubys were indicted for manufacturing and conspiring to manufacture Euphoria. They moved to dismiss the indictment on the grounds that § 201(h) unconstitutionally delegates legislative power to the Attorney General.... The United States District Court for the District of New Jersey denied the motion to dismiss ... and the Court of Appeals for the Third Circuit affirmed.... We granted certiorari... and now affirm.

The Constitution provides that "all legislative Powers herein granted shall be vested in a Congress of the United States." From this language the Court has derived the nondelegation doctrine: that Congress may not constitutionally delegate its legislative power to another Branch of government. "The nondelegation doctrine is rooted in the principle of separation of powers that underlies our tripartite system of Government."...

(continued)

> ## TOUBY V. UNITED STATES (continued)
>
> We have long recognized that nondelegation does not prevent Congress from seeking assistance, within proper limits, from its coordinate Branches. . . . Thus, Congress does not violate the Constitution merely because it legislates in broad terms, leaving a certain degree of discretion to executive or judicial actors. So long as Congress "lay[s] down by legislative act an intelligible principle to which the person or body authorized to [act] is directed to conform, such legislative action is not a forbidden delegation of legislative power." . . .
>
> Petitioners wisely concede that Congress has set forth in § 201(h) an "intelligible principle" to constrain the Attorney General's discretion to schedule controlled substances on a temporary basis. . . . Petitioners suggest, however, that something more than an "intelligible principle" is required when Congress authorizes another Branch to promulgate regulations that contemplate criminal sanctions. They contend that regulations of this sort pose a heightened risk to individual liberty and that Congress must therefore provide more specific guidance. Our cases are not entirely clear as to whether or not more specific guidance is in fact required. . . . We need not resolve the issue today. We conclude that § 201(h) passes muster even if greater congressional specificity is required in the criminal context.
>
> Although it features fewer procedural requirements than the permanent scheduling statute, § 201(h) meaningfully constrains the Attorney General's discretion to define criminal conduct. . . .
>
> It is clear that in § 201(h) and § 202(b), Congress has placed multiple restrictions on the Attorney General's discretion to define criminal conduct. These restrictions satisfy the constitutional requirements of the nondelegation doctrine.

So, an agency may be delegated the authority to declare acts criminal. Congress must provide at least an "intelligible principle," and possibly more, when making this type of delegation. Congress may not delegate the authority to set a penalty to an agency, although it may allow the agency to set the penalty for a violation from within statutory guidelines. An agency may not, however, establish more serious penalties, such an imprisonment, even if the sentences fall within statutory limits.

While agencies may not sentence individuals to imprisonment, legislatively endorsed, noncriminal deprivations of freedom may be ordered by agencies in rare circumstances, such as during quarantines, for psychiatric evaluations and treatment, and to detain illegal immigrants.

An interesting issue that has arisen in recent years is the extent to which private parties may be delegated governmental powers. For example, in some states, fines levied by homeowner and condominium associations are enforceable in courts. While this area of law is in development and much remains to be defined, a few general principles can be deduced. First, private parties may not, or have very limited authority to, punish individuals. Second, when private parties are acting on the behalf of a government, they are bound by the same rules that apply to the government.[10]

Court Rules

Just as administrative agencies need the authority to "fill in the gaps" of legislation because statutes are not specific enough to satisfy all of an agency's needs, so do courts.

The United States Congress and all of the state legislatures have enacted some form of statute establishing general rules of civil and criminal procedure. However, to fill in the gaps left by legislatures, courts adopt **court rules,** which also govern civil and criminal processes. Although court rules deal with procedural issues (such as service of process, limits on the length of briefs and memoranda, and timing of filing) and not substantive issues, they are important. Of course, court rules may not conflict with legislative mandates. If a rule does conflict with a statute, the statute is controlling. One exception to this rule may be when the statute is unconstitutional and the rule is a viable alternative, but discussion of this situation is best left to a course on constitutional law and judicial process.

Most court rules are drafted under the direction of the highest court of the state and become effective by either vote of the court or presentation to the state legislature for ratification. In the federal system, the rules are drafted by the Judicial Conference under the direction of the Supreme Court and then presented to Congress. If Congress fails to act to nullify the rules, they become law. Of course, Congress may amend the rules at will. Many jurisdictions also have local rules, that is, rules created by local courts for practice in those courts. The rules cannot conflict with either statutes or higher court rules. In the federal system, district courts adopt local rules. Being familiar with the rules of the courts in your jurisdiction is imperative. If you are not, you may miss important deadlines, file incomplete documents, or have your filings stricken.

rules of court
■ Rules promulgated by the court, governing procedure or practice before it.

The Model Penal Code

On occasion, the **Model Penal Code** will be referenced in this text. Actually entitled *Model Penal Code and Commentaries,* it was drafted by a group of scholars and practitioners expert in criminal law while working for the American Law Institute, a private organization. The intent of the drafters of the Code was to draft a consistent, thoughtful code that could be recommended to the states for adoption. The code itself is not law until adopted by a legislature.

According to one source, by 1985, 34 states had "enacted widespread criminal-law revision and codification based on its provisions; fifteen hundred courts had cited its provisions and referred to its commentary."[11] The Model Penal Code has been included in this text, in edited form, as Appendix B. You should refer to that as the Code is discussed in the following chapters.

Model Penal Code
■ A proposed criminal code prepared jointly by the Commission on Uniform State Laws and the American Law Institute.

Constitutional Law

Finally, constitutional law is included in this list of sources of criminal law, not because it defines what conduct is criminal, but because of its significant impact on criminal law generally. In particular, the U.S. Constitution, primarily through the Bill of Rights, is responsible for establishing many of the rules governing criminal procedure. This has been especially true in the past few decades. You will become more aware of why this is true as you learn more about criminal law and procedure. Pay close attention to the dates of the cases included in this text (see Exhibit 2–1); it is likely that many were handed down in your lifetime.

Exhibit 2–1 IMPORTANT DATES IN THE HISTORY OF THE CONSTITUTION OF THE UNITED STATES

May 25, 1787	Constitutional Convention opens in Philadelphia.
September 17, 1787	Constitutional Convention closes, delegates sign the Constitution, and it is sent to the states for ratification. This is recognized as Constitution (and Citizenship) Day by federal law.
December 6, 1787	Delaware is the first state to ratify the Constitution.
June 21, 1788	New Hampshire is the ninth state to ratify, and thereby provides the requisite number of ratifying states to adopt the Constitution for the entire United States.
May 29, 1790	Rhode Island is the thirteenth (last) state to ratify the Constitution.
December 15, 1791	Bill of Rights is ratified.
December 6, 1865	Thirteenth Amendment, abolishing slavery, is ratified.
July 28, 1868	Fourteenth Amendment, providing for due process, equal protection, and privileges and immunities, is ratified.
February 3, 1870	Fifteenth Amendment, prohibiting the vote from being withheld for race, color, or previous servitude, is ratified.
May 7, 1992	The Twenty-seventh Amendment, the last to date, was ratified. Addressing the raises for members of Congress, the amendment is the last to be ratified even though it was one of the original 12 amendments to be proposed.

Although it is common for courses in constitutional law to focus on the U.S. Constitution, do not forget that each state also has its own constitution with its own body of case law interpreting its meaning. Even though the dominant source for defending civil liberties has been the U.S. Constitution, it is possible that a shift to state constitutions will occur, as the current Supreme Court is expected to be more conservative on criminal issues, which means it is less likely to extend constitutional protections. Remember, the U.S. Constitution is the highest form of law, and the states may not decrease the individual protections secured by it. States, may, however, increase civil liberties through state law. Most state constitutions mirror the federal constitution, often verbatim. In spite of this, state courts are free to interpret their constitutional provisions as providing more protection than their federal counterparts, even if identical in text. See Exhibit 2–2 for a summary of the sources of criminal law.

Exhibit 2-2 SOURCES OF CRIMINAL LAW

Source	Comment
CONSTITUTIONS	The United States and every state have a constitution. The U.S. Constitution is the supreme law of the land. Amendment of the federal Constitution requires a 2/3 vote by both houses of the United States Congress and approval by 3/4 of the states or in the alternative, for 2/3 of the states to call for a constitutional convention and approval of 3/4 of the states of any suggested amendments. All existing amendments were enacted using the first method.
STATUTES	The written law created by legislatures, also known as codes. State statutes may not conflict with either their own constitution or the federal Constitution. State statutes also are invalid if they conflict with other federal law, and the federal government has concurrent jurisdiction with the states. Statutes of the United States are invalid if they conflict with the U.S. Constitution or if they attempt to regulate outside federal jurisdiction. Legislatures may change statutes at will.
COMMON LAW	Law that evolved, as courts, through judicial opinions, recognized customs, and practices. Legislatures may alter, amend, or abolish the common law at will. In criminal law, the common law is responsible for the creation of crimes and for establishing defenses to crimes.
REGULATIONS	Created by administrative agencies under a grant of authority from a legislative body. Regulations must be consistent with statutes and constitutions and may not exceed the legislative grant of power. The power to make rules and regulations is granted to "fill in the gaps" left by legislatures when drafting statutes.
ORDINANCES	Written law of local bodies, such as city councils. Must be consistent with all higher forms of law.
MODEL PENAL CODE	Written under the direction of the American Law Institute. It was drafted by experts in criminal law to be presented to the states for adoption. It is not law until a state has adopted it, in whole or in part. More than half of the states have adopted at least part of the Model Penal Code.
COURT RULES	Rules created by courts to manage their cases. Court rules are procedural and commonly establish deadlines, lengths of filings, etc. Court rules may not conflict with statutes or constitutions.

Ethical Considerations

DEFENDING INDIVIDUALS CHARGED WITH HORRENDOUS CRIMES

Defense attorneys are not held in the highest regard by all people, many of whom assume that a defense attorney's willingness to defend individuals charged with horrendous crimes is a reflection of the attorney's values. In actuality, this conclusion is correct, but there is a disconnect between the value that motivates an attorney to defend an individual charged with a horrendous crime and the value that many individuals apply in judging the attorney for the decision. Defense attorneys are often judged by individuals who apply personal values to them, while the attorneys must apply professional values.

The two model codes from which the states have enacted their rules that govern attorney ethics, the Model Rules of Professional Conduct and Model Code of Professional Responsibility, require attorneys to zealously represent their clients, regardless of the alleged crime. This requirement does not exist in a vacuum. The entire U.S. system of justice is built upon the idea that if you have two opposed parties, each with a loyal, zealous advocate, the truth will be unveiled to the fact finder. This *adversarial system* was developed in England and exists, in various forms, in all common-law nations.

The obligation of defense attorneys to zealously represent their clients and to maintain their clients' confidentiality is not without a price. Defense attorneys are the subject of public disdain and ridicule. In some circumstances, their professional and personal lives are injured when they are called upon to defend unpopular defendants. An example of this is the attorney featured in the case *People v. Belge*, which you will find in Chapter 3 of this book. In this case, two attorneys, Francis R. Belge and Frank H. Armani, represented a man accused of murder. During their conversations with the accused, he claimed to have committed three other murders. The attorneys confirmed two of the murders of young women by visiting the locations where his client had buried the bodies of his victims. After viewing the bodies, the attorneys discussed whether they should disclose the location of the bodies. They concluded that their duty to their client to maintain his confidence did not permit disclosure. They continuously denied knowing the location of the bodies throughout the case, even when asked by the families of the missing girls. When their client disclosed having told them, there was public outrage. Although accord was not universal, most ethics scholars agreed that the attorneys made the correct decision.

Ethical Considerations (continued)

But the decision came at a high price. Both men received death threats and began to carry guns. Belge was charged with the health crime of not reporting a dead body for burial (see Chapter 3), Belge's family life was injured, and his practice diminished. He ultimately moved to another state. Armani's experience was similar, but he remained in the region and his practice eventually recovered. Armani said of the decision they made:

> God only knows that this thing drove me crazy; it really bothered me. And if there was any way I could have, I would have told Mr. and Mrs. Hauck. But my hands were tied. And as a result, this thing has cost me dearly. My law practice failed. I spent nearly $40,000 defending Garrow. . . . I've lost about every friend I have. But there was nothing else I could do. Please believe that!

Unquestionably, if the attorneys had not visited the scene, they would have been correct in maintaining their client's confidence. However, the prosecutor who obtained the grand jury indictment against Belge alleged that the attorneys' presence at the crime scene changed matters. The court hearing the case, however, held that "Belge conducted himself as an officer of the Court with all the zeal at his command to protect the constitutional rights of his client. Both on the grounds of privileged communication and the interests of justice the Indictment is dismissed."

Source: Mark Gado, *Robert Garrow: The Predator*, Court TV, Crime Library, at *http://www.crimelibrary.com/serial_killers/predators/robert_garrow/1.html* (March 11, 2008).

Web Links

Findlaw

www.findlaw.com is an excellent site that contains state and federal statutory law, administrative law, and case law. In addition, FindLaw provides information on law schools, law firms, professional development, and legal news.

Key Terms

common law
court rules
criminal law
criminal procedure

due process
Model Penal Code
ordinance
precedent

regulations
stare decisis

Review Questions

1. What are civil liberties? Give two examples of civil liberties that are protected by the Constitution of the United States.
2. What is the common law? How do the concepts of stare decisis and precedent relate to the common law?
3. The common law is different in every state. Why?
4. What does the Latin phrase "nullum crimen sine lege" translate to? Explain the significance of that phrase.
5. Explain how the common law can violate the principle of legality.
6. State three uses the common law has in criminal law in those jurisdictions that do not permit common-law creation of crimes.
7. What is the source of most criminal law today? Where does that law come from?
8. What is an ordinance?
9. What is a regulation?
10. What is a court rule?
11. Place the following sources of law in order of authority, beginning with the highest form of law and ending with the lowest. Notice that both state and federal sources of law are included: U.S. Code, state constitutions, federal administrative regulations, ordinances, U.S. Constitution, state administrative regulations, state statutes.

Problems & Critical Thinking Exercises

1. List the various purposes for punishing criminal law violators. Using your answers from problem 2, determine if the goals of punishment can be achieved if prosecution is sought for the following acts (problems 3–5):
2. John, having always wanted a guitar, stole one from a fellow student's room while that student was out.
3. Jack suffers from a physical disease of the mind that causes him to have violent episodes. Jack has no way of knowing when the episodes will occur. However, the disease is controllable with medication. Despite this, Jack often does not take the medicine, as he finds the injections painful and inconvenient. One day, when he had not taken the medicine, Jack had an episode and struck Mike, causing him personal injury.
4. The same facts apply, as in problem 3, except there is no treatment or medication that can control Jack's behavior. He was diagnosed as having the disease years before striking Mike and has caused such an injury before during a similar violent episode.
5. Unknown to Kevin, he has epilepsy. One day while he was driving his automobile, he suffered his first seizure. The seizure caused him to lose control of his car and strike a pedestrian, inflicting a fatal injury.

Endnotes

1. 15A Am. Jur. 2d *Common Law* 6 (1976).
2. *Marsillett v. State*, 495 N.E.2d 699, 704 (Ind. 1986) (citations omitted).
3. 15A Am. Jur. 2d *Common Law* 1 (1976).

4. *Helms v. American Security Co.,* 22 N.E.2d 822 (Ind. 1986).
5. T. Gardner, *Criminal Law: Principles and Cases,* 4th ed. (Criminal Justice Series) (St. Paul: West, 1989).
6. P. Robinson, *Fundamentals of Criminal Law* (Boston: Little, Brown, 1988).
7. Today in the United Kingdom, where the common law originated, most law is created by Parliament (which dates to the 1300s), not by courts.
8. See *Schechter Poultry Corp. v. United States,* 2nd ed., 295 U.S. 495 (1935).
9. See D. Hall, *Administrative Law: Bureaucracy in a Democracy,* 5th ed., ch. 5 (Upper Saddle River, NJ: Prentice Hall, 2012).
10. For more on this subject, see D. Hall, *Administrative Law: Bureaucracy in a Democracy,* 5th ed., ch. 11 (Upper Saddle River, NJ: Prentice Hall, 2012).
11. J. Samaha, *Criminal Law,* 3rd ed. (St. Paul: West, 1990).

CHAPTER 3

INTRODUCTION AND PARTICIPANTS

Chapter Outline

Criminal Procedure Defined
A Common-Law, Adversarial, and Accusatorial System
The Due Process Model
The Participants
    Law Enforcement Officers
    Prosecutors
    Judges
    Defense Attorneys
    Victims
Liability of Governments and Their Officials

Chapter Objectives

After completing this chapter, you should be able to:

- explain the common-law, adversarial nature of the U.S. criminal justice systems.
- think critically about the due process and crime control models of criminal justice.
- describe the role and the ethics considerations of major players in the criminal justice system: law enforcement officers, defense attorneys, prosecutors, victims, and judges.
- describe the basic liability that government officials can incur when performing their duties.
- identify the material facts and legal issues in two-thirds of the cases you read and describe the court's analyses and conclusions in the cases.

CRIMINAL PROCEDURE DEFINED

The second section of this text addresses criminal procedure. *Criminal procedure*, as a field of law, describes the methods used in bringing an alleged criminal to justice. To state it another way, criminal procedure puts substantive criminal law into action.

Each state and the federal government has its own procedural rules. In some instances, the variation is significant. For the purpose of this text, most references will be to federal procedure. Many federal procedural rules can be found in the U.S. Code. A good number of procedures are judicially created (and approved by Congress) and are found in the Federal Rules of Criminal Procedure (Fed. R. Crim. P.). Finally, the constitutions of the national government and the states play a major role in defining procedures of criminal adjudications.

What follows is a discussion of the constitutional aspects of criminal procedure; the process, from investigation to appeal; searches and seizures; arrests; confessions and admissions; and the right to counsel.

A COMMON-LAW, ADVERSARIAL, AND ACCUSATORIAL SYSTEM

The colonists brought with them the common law of England. Today all states, except Louisiana, which is of the civil law family, are of the common law family.

In addition to being common law in nature, the legal system is **adversarial**. Adversarial adjudications resemble sporting events. There are two opposing parties and a neutral umpire. In criminal adjudications, these roles are played by the defendant, prosecutor, and judge. The judge in criminal adjudications is a passive participant, usually becoming involved only as needed by the parties or as required by law. Of course, the approach of judges varies; and some are more proactive than others. A pure adversarial system is not employed in the United States, and judges are expected to supervise the proceedings to assure fairness. The adversary system is built upon the theory that the truth is more likely to be discovered when there are two competing parties, each conducting its own investigation of the facts, asserting differing theories of fact and law, and each presenting its own case to the court.

Also, in the common law, judges are expected to remain impartial, neutral, and detached. This is believed to increase the fairness of the proceedings. In civil law jurisdictions, on the other hand, judges sometimes develop an opinion or theory, which may limit their consideration of alternatives and accordingly, limit the facts that are sought and the theories that are advanced. In the adversarial system, the parties are largely responsible for development of the case—that is, discovery of the evidence and, accordingly, the issues of law as well.

The adversarial system has its critics. Opponents contend that the truth is not found because the system encourages the opposing parties to present distorted, misleading, and sometimes untruthful accounts of the facts. The fact finder, who is not

---

adversary system

■ The system of law in the United States. The judge acts as the referee between opposite sides (between two individuals, between the state and an individual, etc.) rather than acting as the person who also makes the state's case or independently seeks out evidence.

part of the investigative process, is often left to choose between polarized versions of the same event. The adversarial system is also challenged as being unfair because it assumes two equally competent competing parties. However, because of differences in the abilities of counsel and the respective powers of the parties, this premise is questionable.

In addition to being adversarial, the criminal justice system is accusatorial. This means that the government, as the accuser, bears the burden of proving a defendant's guilt. If the government fails in its burden, then a defendant is entitled to a directed verdict or a judgement of acquittal. The accusatorial nature of the system extends beyond placing the burden of proof on the government at trial. The entire process is designed to minimize the risk of convicting an innocent person. The philosophy that it is better to free several guilty persons than to convict one innocent person is a major theme of the U.S. criminal justice system. Accordingly, the system is designed so that the accused enjoys several advantages, the most critical one being the presumption of innocence; the freedom from self-incrimination, the right to a jury trial, and the right to counsel are others.

The fact that a defendant enjoys a few advantages does not mean that the defendant has the advantage on whole. The government, state or federal, can commit substantial resources to a prosecution.

THE DUE PROCESS MODEL

Criminal justice systems are commonly characterized as falling on a continuum that is bracketed by the *crime control* and the *due process models*. The repression, detection, and efficient prosecution of crime is central to the crime control model. Failure to detect and successfully prosecute criminals is perceived as a failure of government. This failure leads to a loss of individual liberties because citizens live in constant fear of, and are actually subject to, criminal conduct. A secondary consequence is a loss of confidence in government by the public, thereby further hindering its ability to detect and prevent crime. Prosecution in such systems tends to be bureaucratic, that is, a form of "assembly-line" justice. Some civil law and socialist law nations tend toward the crime control model.

The due process model places a premium on the integrity of individual rights and the fairness of process, as well as factual guilt. Efficiency (speed, cost, identifying an punishing offenders) is secondary. The balance is different in crime control systems. Factual guilt and efficiency are emphasized. *Factual guilt* refers to whether a defendant has in fact committed a crime. *Legal guilt* is concerned not only with factual guilt, but also with whether the defendant's rights have been observed and respected by the government in the processes of investigation and prosecution. It is possible, under the due process model, to have sufficient evidence to prove a defendant factually guilty; but because of a civil rights violation, the defendant must be declared legally not guilty. The due process model has little tolerance for conviction of the innocent; the crime control model equally abhors crimes going unsolved and defendants unpunished. Investigation and adjudication of defendants is less efficient and more costly under the due process model than under the crime control model.

This is a simplification of the two models.[1] No system falls squarely into either of the two models, although most systems can be generally characterized as adhering to the principles of one more than the other. The United States follows the due process model. Individual rights and fair procedures are the hallmark of the U.S. system of criminal justice. All individuals are innocent until proven guilty. The process itself presumes innocence, and deprivations of liberties are sharply limited and regulated before guilt is found.

Exhibit 3–1   CRIME CONTROL AND DUE PROCESS MODELS COMPARED

	Model/Point on Continuum	
	Crime Control	**Due Process**
Philosophy	Discovering, apprehending, and punishing offenders, and deterring crime, is a priority. Civil liberties are protected, but not to the extent they jeopardize social control.	Discovering, apprehending, and punishing offenders is balanced against civil liberties. In some instances, civil liberties will prevail and crimes will go unpunished.
Process	Mechanistic; efficiency is a high priority. The criminal justice system is a machine through which the government processes its cases.	Cumbersome; efficiency is not a high priority. The criminal justice system is not so much a machine but a maze through which the government must navigate to secure a conviction.
Conviction Standard	Actual guilt of accused is required for conviction. Government's burdens of proof and production are less than in systems emphasizing due process.	Legal and factual guilt are required for conviction. Government has high burdens of production and proof.

Also, as the severity of the government's intrusions or deprivations increases, so must the evidence of guilt. For example, less evidence is required to establish probable cause to support a search of an automobile than to bind a defendant over to trial. This is because binding a defendant over to trial entails greater losses of liberty (possible pretrial detention and the cost and humiliation of being publicly tried) than does the search. You will learn many procedures that support the conclusion that the United States adheres to the due process model. Attempt to identify these characteristics as you read the following chapters. Chapters 4 through 7 examine the basic procedures and constitutional aspects of bringing criminals to justice. First, however, you must become familiar with the participants in this process.

THE PARTICIPANTS

Besides the accused and witnesses, there are six primary participants in criminal adjudications: law enforcement officers, prosecutors, judges, defense attorneys, victims, and jurors. What follows is a discussion of all these participants except jurors. Jurors are discussed later.

Law Enforcement Officers

The front line of law enforcement in the United States is what the public commonly refers to as the *police*. Law enforcement officers exist at the national, state, and local levels.

Federal law enforcement agencies include the Federal Bureau of Investigation, the Drug Enforcement Administration, Customs, the Coast Guard, U.S. Marshals, the Secret Service, and the Bureau of Alcohol, Tobacco, and Firearms, to name only a few.

Each state has a police department, and many have a counterpart to the FBI, such as the Kansas Bureau of Investigation (KBI). In addition, within each state, county sheriffs and municipal police departments enforce the laws of the state as well as the laws of their locality. There are more than 20,000 local law enforcement agencies in the United States. This includes 12,502 local police departments; 3,086 sheriffs' offices; 49 state police departments; and more than 700,000 sworn police officers and 300,000-plus civilian personnel. In addition, there were 105,000 federal officers who carry weapons and are authorized to make arrests in the 50 states and District of Columbia in 2004. Three-fourths of these officers work in the Department of Homeland Security. An additional 1,500 officers work in U.S. territories. Additional officers are stationed in foreign nations.[2]

Discretion

Law enforcement personnel are expected to keep the peace, investigate possible wrongdoing, enforce the laws, and further crime prevention. Although it is generally held that the police must enforce the laws, it is also recognized that not all the laws can be or should be enforced. Consequently, officers exercise much discretion when performing their daily duties. Deciding whether to conduct an investigation, whether to arrest an offender, or whether a search is necessary all usually fall within the individual officer's discretion. However, the conduct of police officers must comply with constitutional, statutory, and departmental policy standards.

Ethics

As is true of prosecutors and defense attorneys, the police officer's paramount ethical code is the Constitution. Police officers have a legal and ethical obligation to keep themselves within constitutional limits when performing their duties.

More specifically, the International Association of Chiefs of Police (IACP) has formulated a set of ethical principles intended to guide the law enforcement officer in the performance of his or her duties. The IACP has issued two ethics documents, the "Law Enforcement Code of Ethics" and the "Police Code of Conduct." The Code of Ethics is a general statement of ethical responsibility that may be used as an oath of office.

The Code of Ethics recognizes that police officers hold a special public trust and that they have an obligation not to violate that trust.

Although substantially the same, the Police Code of Conduct is more specific than the Code of Ethics. The Code of Conduct prohibits discriminatory treatment of individuals based upon status, sex, religion, political belief, or aspiration; the unnecessary use of force; the infliction of cruel, degrading, or inhuman treatment; violation of confidences, except when necessary in the performance of duties or as required by law; bribery; the acceptance of gifts; refusals to cooperate with other law enforcement officials; and other unreasonable and inappropriate behavior. The Code of Conduct further qualifies the necessary force requirement by stating that force should be used "only with the greatest restraint and only after discussion, negotiation and persuasion have been found to be inappropriate or ineffective."

Officers are expected to behave in a manner that inspires confidence and respect for law enforcement officials. Further, police officers are to attempt to obtain maximum public cooperation and to enforce all laws with courtesy, consideration, and dignity. Although the IACP has no enforcement authority, the codes do provide an excellent standard for adoption by law enforcement agencies, as well as by individual officers.

For the remainder of this book, references to police or law enforcement officers are to any one of the previously mentioned agencies.

Prosecutors

Prosecutors are also central to the administration of justice. *Prosecutors* are government attorneys responsible for prosecuting violators. This role includes preparing and filing documents; engaging in pretrial activity, such as discovery; and appearing in court. Prosecutors often also act as legal counsel to law enforcement officers, rendering advice on the law of searches, seizures, arrests, surveillance techniques, and similar matters. Prosecutors appear at grand jury hearings, where they present evidence and assist the jury in other ways. Finally, in some jurisdictions, prosecutors act in a supervisory capacity as the head of a law enforcement agency, such as the Attorney General of the United States, who is the head of the Department of Justice.

At the federal level, the highest law enforcement official and prosecutor is the attorney general, who undergoes the presidential nomination and senatorial confirmation process. The attorney general is a cabinet member who heads the Department of Justice.

Within each judicial district is one U.S. attorney, a subordinate of the attorney general, who also is selected through the nomination and confirmation process. U.S. attorneys, with the aid of several assistant U.S. attorneys (AUSAs), are responsible for most federal prosecutions. In rare cases, however, another attorney from the Department of Justice may travel to a district to handle a case. Federal law also provides for the appointment of an independent counsel (special prosecutor) when government officials are suspected of violating the law.

Similar to the federal government, each state has an attorney general. The states vary in the structure of their prosecutorial agencies, but most have locally elected prosecutors, who may be titled *prosecutor, district attorney*, or *state attorney*. The degree to which these individuals answer to the state attorney general differs greatly. Additionally, local forms of government have attorneys. In some localities, these attorneys prosecute ordinance violations.

Prosecutorial Discretion

Prosecutors enjoy considerable discretion in the performance of their duties. The decision whether to prosecute an individual is one aspect of prosecutorial **discretion.** This decision must be made by a prosecutor in most cases. In a small number of cases, however, the prosecutor may not be in a position to make this decision, such as when a traffic ticket acts as the charging instrument and the case proceeds directly to court without the prosecutor's involvement. However, most cases are initiated directly by a prosecutor, grand jury, or, as is usually the case, the police (through the arrest and complaint procedure). A case may not proceed under a complaint; rather, the prosecutor must file an information (or an indictment issued by a grand jury), which replaces the complaint. If a prosecutor refuses, or files a **nolle prosequi,** the case proceeds no further.

There are two general reasons that discretion must be exercised. First, the prosecutor's ethical obligation requires that he or she seek justice, not convictions. Prosecutors are not to maintain a prosecution simply because there is a probability of prevailing. Rather, the totality of the facts must be examined, and it must be determined that a prosecution will further justice. The justice obligation continues through the entire adjudicative process.

Economics is the second reason prosecutors cannot pursue every case. The resources of the prosecutor and law enforcement agencies are limited. Not every case can be prosecuted, because there are inadequate investigators, police officers, prosecutors, and other resources. Prosecutors must prioritize cases for prosecution. The decision whether to prosecute is influenced by many factors. The facts of the case; the accused's criminal, social, and economic history; the likelihood of success; the cost of prosecution, including the probable time investment; public opinion; the seriousness of the crime; the desires of the victims; police expectations and desires; political concerns; and whether the prosecution will further the administration of justice are all considered.

Although prosecutorial discretion is broad, it is not absolute. First, the authority to file a nolle prosequi, or dismissal, may be limited. The further along a case is in the process, the more involved the court becomes in the decision. Generally, the decision not to prosecute before the formal charge (information or indictment) is filed is left to the prosecutor without judicial intervention. However, a small number of states require judicial approval of nolle prosequi decisions.

Once the formal charge has been filed, judicial approval of dismissal is the rule rather than the exception. This is true in the federal system, which also requires leave of court to dismiss complaints.[3]

Second, decisions to prosecute that are motivated by improper criteria may violate equal protection. The Fourteenth Amendment prohibits each state from taking actions that "deny to any person within its jurisdiction the equal protection of the laws." Although the Fifth Amendment does not contain this language, the Supreme Court has interpreted the Fifth Amendment's Due Process Clause as requiring equal protection of the laws. A claim that it is unfair to prosecute a person because other known violators

discretion

■ The power to act within general guidelines, rules, or laws, but without either specific rules to follow or the need to completely explain or justify each decision or action.

nolle prosequi

■ (Latin) The ending of a criminal case because the prosecutor decides or agrees to stop prosecuting. When this happens, the case is "nolled," "nollied," or "nol. prossed."

are not prosecuted will not be successful, unless it can be shown that the accused has been singled out for an improper reason.

Generally, three elements must be shown to establish improper, discriminatory prosecution: first, that other people similarly situated were not prosecuted; second, that the prosecutor intentionally singled out the defendant; third, that the selection was based upon an arbitrary classification. As the Supreme Court stated in *Oyler v. Boles*,[4] for there to be an equal protection violation, it must be shown that "the selection was *deliberately* based upon an unjustified standard." What is an unjustified standard? Prosecutions based upon race, religion, and gender are examples. A prosecution intended to punish an individual for exercising a constitutional right is also improper. The Supreme Court discusses selective prosecution in *United States v. Armstrong* (1996).

To determine whether a classification is proper, equal protection analysis must be employed. Most decisions are tested under the rational relationship test. That is, if the decision to prosecute is rationally related to a legitimate governmental objective, it is valid. If a decision is based upon race or religion, or in retaliation for a person's exercise of a right, the decision is tested under the strict scrutiny test and is invalid unless it can be shown to further a compelling governmental interest. Finally, a few classifications, such as those based upon gender, are tested under a standard less demanding than strict scrutiny but more demanding than the rational relationship test. Such laws must bear a substantial relationship to a legitimate governmental interest. In reality, claims of selective enforcement are rarely successful.

Ethics

All attorneys are bound by ethical rules. Two sets of rules are used in the United States: the Model Code of Professional Responsibility and the Model Rules of Professional Conduct. The two are similar, and every state has adopted some form of these rules. Ethical violations may result in discipline by the bar, an offended court, or both. Common sanctions include private and public reprimands, suspension, and disbarment. Under court rules and rules of procedure, other sanctions, such as monetary penalties, may be assessed. Also, all courts possess the authority to punish for contempt.

Prosecutors have special ethical responsibilities. You have already learned that the mission of the prosecutor is to achieve justice. The Model Code of Professional Responsibility states that the "responsibility of a public prosecutor differs from that of the usual advocate; his duty is to seek justice, not merely to convict."[5]

Prosecutors have an ethical obligation to be sure that a prosecution is warranted and to seek dismissal immediately upon discovering that one is not. Prosecutors are not to trump up charges to increase their power during plea negotiations. Prosecutors are only to request a fair sentence from a court. Of course, prosecutors may not use perjured or falsified evidence to obtain a conviction. In addition, you will learn later in this text that prosecutors have a constitutional duty to disclose exculpatory evidence.[6] Evidence that mitigates the degree of an offense or reduces a sentence must also be disclosed.[7] Further, prosecutors are not to avoid pursuing evidence because it may damage the government's case or assist the defendant.[8] Through discovery rules, prosecutors have a duty to disclose other evidence prior to or during trial. In short, prosecutors have an obligation to deal with defendants fairly.

On the other side, prosecutors have an obligation to pursue a prosecution when the facts of the case demand it. At trial, unless a prosecutor becomes convinced that the accused is innocent, the prosecutor is to zealously pursue a conviction.

Judges

Judges are not executive branch officials, as are prosecutors and law enforcement officers. Judges are part of the judiciary, a separate and independent branch of government. Generally, the judiciary is responsible for the resolution of disputes and the administration of justice. In regard to criminal law, judges are responsible for issuing warrants, supervising pretrial activity, presiding over hearings and trial, deciding guilt or innocence in some cases, and passing sentence on those convicted.

Having a fair and impartial party make these determinations is an important feature of the U.S. criminal justice system, and is mandated by the Constitution in many instances, as you will learn in the following chapters. A judge has the obligation to remain unbiased, fair, and impartial in all cases before the bar.

Ethics

Like attorneys, judges are subject to a code of ethics. Most states have enacted the Code of Judicial Conduct. Judges are to be fair and impartial.[9] In criminal cases, judges must be sensitive to defendants' rights and be careful not to imply to a jury that a defendant is guilty.

Defense Attorneys

Because of the complexity of the legal system and the advantage of having an advocate, competent legal counsel has become an important feature of the American system of criminal justice. The Sixth Amendment to the Constitution provides that all persons have a right to be represented by counsel in criminal cases. Today, indigent defendants have a right to counsel in all cases that may result in incarceration. Counsel for indigent defendants may be appointed from the private bar or, as is the case in most jurisdictions, a public defender will be assigned. Public defenders are provided to defendants at no cost. Regarding professional responsibility, defense counsel—whether a paid private defender or a public defender—owes his or her client the same loyalty and zeal in representation.

Ethics

Defense attorneys have high, and sometimes morally challenging, ethical responsibilities. Unlike the prosecutor, whose duty is to see that justice is achieved, the defense attorney must zealously represent the accused, within the bounds of the law,[10] regardless of innocence or guilt.

This obligation is the cause of some public disrespect for the legal profession. Attorneys are perceived as hired guns, not as advocates of civil liberties. Defense lawyers are frequently asked how they can defend people they know are guilty. There are two responses to this inquiry. First, defense attorneys often do not know whether their clients are in fact guilty, as this question is rarely asked. Second, defense attorneys are not defending the actions that the defendant is accused of committing; rather, defense attorneys are defending the rights of the accused, specifically, the right to have the government prove its case beyond a reasonable doubt using lawfully obtained evidence. In defending the rights of one person against governmental oppression, the rights of all the people are defended.

This approach, which is a vital part of the U.S. criminal justice system, is often misunderstood by the public. The defense attorney who fulfills this constitutional and ethical mission is often the source of public animosity and ridicule.

Communications between attorneys and clients are confidential and privileged. Attorneys are generally prohibited from disclosing those communications.[11] In the *Belge* case, an attorney was indicted for not revealing a client's privileged communication and was the subject of considerable public disdain. The indictment was dismissed in the interests of justice, namely, preservation of the attorney-client privilege. However, the court could do nothing to restore the attorney's good reputation and standing in his community.

Belge turned on the fact that the crimes had already occurred and the defendant posed no threat. An attorney is allowed, but not required, to report a client's intention to commit a crime.[12] Therefore, if a client informs his counsel that he intends to kill a witness if he is released on bond, the attorney may disclose this information without breaching any ethical obligations.

Attorneys are generally obligated to represent criminal defendants when appointed by a court or upon request by a bar association. However, an attorney may be excused for compelling reasons. In no event is belief in a defendant's guilt or disgust with the alleged acts compelling.[14]

An interesting ethical dilemma is presented when a defense attorney knows (or has a strong belief) that either the client or one of the defense witnesses has given or intends to give false testimony. On the one hand, the attorney is an officer of the court and thus prohibited from defrauding the court. On the other hand, the defense attorney has an obligation to the client. There is a split in the jurisdictions concerning how this situation is to be handled. There are three possibilities. First, the most preferable, the defense attorney dissuades the client from committing perjury. Second, the attorney moves to withdraw from the case, keeping the reason secret. Third, the attorney discloses the client's intention to commit perjury to the court. The law in each jurisdiction must be examined to determine which of these options is permitted or preferred.

Defense attorneys are sometimes asked to represent co defendants. This can create a conflict of interest for a defense attorney if the defendants have conflicting or antagonistic defenses. Because of the inherent dangers of representing co defendants, many defense attorneys refuse joint representation. It is a violation of a defendant's Sixth Amendment right to the assistance of effective counsel to have a lawyer with divided loyalties.

Finally, trial counsel for criminal defendants have an obligation to continue on appeal unless new counsel is retained or the court has authorized withdrawal. This is different from civil cases, where there is no general obligation to continue after trial.

Legal Assistants

Legal assistants are employed by both prosecutors and defense attorneys, with the latter being more common.[15] In the defense context, legal assistants may be asked to perform several tasks, including conducting initial interviews, conducting legal research, preparing drafts of motions and other documents, maintaining and organizing files, acting as a contact with incarcerated clients, assisting in preparing the defendant and other witnesses for trial, and preparing the defendant for the presentence investigation interview. Some paralegals are called upon to conduct investigations.

As employees of attorneys, legal assistants must also follow ethical guidelines and responsibilities. Although no state has yet established mandatory certification of legal assistants, and therefore there is no enforceable set of ethics rules, the National Federation of Paralegal Organizations and the National Association of Legal Assistants (NALA) have promulgated Codes of Ethics.

The NALA Code states that, first, legal assistants may not engage in the practice of law.[16] This includes rendering legal advice, establishing an attorney-client relationship, setting fees, and appearing in court on behalf of a client. Although some administrative agencies permit legal assistants to represent clients at hearings, this is never so in criminal law. The unauthorized practice of law is both criminal and unethical. Further, legal assistants are to act prudently in determining the extent to which a client may be assisted without the presence of a lawyer.[17] Finally, it is imperative that the attorney directly supervise the legal assistant's work in criminal law.[18]

Second, all employees of an attorney are bound by the confidentiality rule.[19] All communications made by a client to a legal assistant fall within the scope of the attorney-client privilege and may not be disclosed by the legal assistant.

Third, legal assistants must be careful not to suborn perjury when preparing the client and witnesses for trial. Instructing a witness in effective techniques, including dress and personal appearance, and methods of responding to inquiries (e.g., answer directly, honestly, and as succinctly as possible; look at the jury during your response) is proper. Suggesting, urging, encouraging, or directing a witness to lie or mislead a court is suborning perjury.

Fourth, legal assistants are bound through their attorney-supervisors by the American Bar Association's Model Rules of Professional Conduct and Model Code of Professional Responsibility.[20]

Victims

Recall that the legal victim of crimes is the government. That is why criminal prosecutions are brought in the name of the government. However, most crimes have another victim, the victim-in-fact. This is the person assaulted, battered, raped, or robbed. Victims affect criminal adjudications in a number of ways.

First, law enforcement officers may decline to make an arrest or conduct an investigation if the victim is disinterested in having the matter pursued. Second, the prosecutor may file a nolle prosequi, if there has been an arrest, or otherwise refuse to proceed with a prosecution if that is the victim's desire. Third, if the matter proceeds to trial, the victim may be required to testify at both pretrial hearings and trial. A victim may choose to attend even if his or her testimony is not required. Fourth, the victim may participate in the sentencing portion of the trial. As you will learn, statements concerning how a victim and a victim's family have been affected may be considered by judge and jury when passing sentence. Restitution is also made a condition of some sentences.

Victims' rights have received considerable attention since the mid-1980s. Victims' rights organizations have strenuously—and successfully—lobbied to introduce both state constitutional amendments and legislation concerning victims' rights. For example, the Arizona Constitution was amended to include a "Victims' Bill of Rights." Through that amendment and its enabling legislation, crime victims are allowed to participate in the initial appearance, be heard on conditions of release, be present at all court proceedings, confer with the prosecutor concerning disposition of the case, refuse a defense interview or other discovery request, provide an impact statement for sentencing, receive restitution and other damages, receive notice of probation modifications of the perpetrator, and receive notice of parole or death of the perpetrator.[21]

Rape shield legislation is another form of victims' rights laws. Rape shield laws exclude from trial evidence of a rape victim's sexual history (except evidence of sexual history with the accused) and reputation in the community. These laws were enacted to protect the rape victim from embarrassing, harassing, and intimidating inquiries.

In most jurisdictions, victims' rights are a matter of statutory, not constitutional, law. Change came quickly in this area. In 1982, only 4 states had victims' bills of rights. That number increased to 44 by 1987. In 1982, only 8 states allowed the use of **victim impact statements** at sentencing. By 2013, the number of states permitting victim impact evidence to be considered by sentencing judges and juries increased to 50 and 32 states now provide for victims rights in their constitutions.[22]

In addition to laws providing for victim participation in court proceedings, laws have been enacted for the protection of both victims and witnesses. These laws provide for the relocation of a witness or victim whose cooperation with an investigation or prosecution endangers his or her life. The federal law is well known. It provides for relocation of the victim or witness and his or her immediate family at taxpayer expense. Further, the United States provides the family with a new identity.[23]

Victims are likely to have civil remedies against perpetrators under traditional civil law theories. Intentional tort actions for assault, battery, invasion of privacy, and conversion are examples.

Finally, *victim assistance organizations* are available in many jurisdictions. Some are independent, not-for-profit corporations, and others are governmental entities. These organizations provide information, counseling, and other assistance to victims. Also, most states have enacted *victim compensation programs*. In many instances restitution proves inadequate, such as when the perpetrator is indigent. In these instances, a victim can request compensation from a state victim compensation fund. These programs reimburse victims for medical expenses and, sometimes, loss of income. Generally, they do not compensate victims for property losses.

victim impact statement

■ At the time of sentencing, a statement made to the court concerning the effect the crime has had on the victim or on the victim's family.

LIABILITY OF GOVERNMENTS AND THEIR OFFICIALS

Government officials, including law enforcement officers, prosecutors, and judges, are not above the law. Violation of an individual's rights by an official, even if during the performance of official duties, may lead to civil and criminal liability.[24] It is not in society's best interest, however, to create an environment where officials are threatened with civil or criminal liability for every incorrect decision and action, especially when they act in good faith and after thoughtful consideration of alternatives and repercussions. In such a world, civil authorities would be afraid to act and government would be paralyzed. Therefore, the laws governing liability of government officials are designed to provide remedies only for acts that are outrageous, malicious, shocking, or in clear violation of established rights.

States have laws that may provide remedies to the victims of improper governmental conduct. A police officer who commits an unjustified assault, battery, or false imprisonment may be liable under traditional tort and criminal law theories. These and other actions may lead to civil and criminal liability under state civil rights laws. In addition, violations of federally secured rights by state or federal officers can result in both civil and criminal prosecutions under federal civil rights statutes.[25] It was under these laws that several Los Angeles police officers were prosecuted for violating the civil rights of Rodney King in 1993. Similarly, a prosecutor who violates a person's civil rights may be liable under federal law,[26] or a similar state law, or under a state tort theory. In fewer instances, judges may also be liable for their actions.

The civil liability of officials is limited by immunity doctrines. Immunities developed at common law, and the United States Supreme Court, has determined that Congress did not intend to abolish these immunities when it enacted the civil rights acts.[27] Therefore, governmental officials may assert immunity as a defense if sued under the federal civil rights statutes.

There is a judicial immunity. Any action that is judicial in nature is shielded by *absolute immunity*. Because it is absolute, a government official is free from both suit and liability when performing judicial functions. Issuing orders (including warrants) and presiding over hearings are examples of judicial acts.

Most judicial acts are performed by judges, but not all. Prosecutors perform quasi-judicial acts and are shielded with absolute immunity for the performance of these acts. Appearing in court (including ex parte warrant application hearings) and complying with court orders are considered quasi-judicial acts. The Supreme Court has held, in *Van de Kamp v. Goldstein*, 555 U.S.—(2009) that this immunity extends to the supervisory and training functions of prosecutors when the functions in question are intimately associated with the judicial phase of a case. So, failure to supervise or properly train junior prosecutors in trial rules is immunized conduct. Other, more administrative conduct, such as recruitment, hiring, and awarding contracts is not shielded. Similar to prosecutors, police officers are shielded with absolute immunity when enforcing court orders (including warrants) and when testifying in court but not when performing non judicial tasks.

In other situations, another form of immunity may apply. A person entitled to *qualified immunity* is free from liability but not necessarily free from suit. That means that the process of establishing nonliability may involve a greater commitment of time, energy, and money by a defendant. Under absolute immunity, issues of malice, intent, or the nature of the right alleged to be violated are immaterial, because the defendant is immune regardless. In contrast, whether an official acted with malice or whether the alleged right violated was clearly established at law are material in the qualified immunity case. Under some laws, an official is liable only if malice is shown, or, as required by federal law, a plaintiff can prove that a clearly established right was violated.

So, under federal law, although prosecutors are absolutely immune from civil liability for quasi-judicial acts, such as appearing in court and filing charges, they enjoy only a qualified immunity when performing other acts, such as rendering legal advice to law enforcement officers.[28] Similarly, judges are protected by qualified immunity when performing nonjudicial but work-related functions, such as making personnel decisions.[29] Police officers are shielded by qualified immunity when conducting investigations, making warrantless searches or seizures, and engaging in administrative and personnel matters.

Finally, the government itself may be sued in some circumstances. A serious obstacle, which must be overcome to establish governmental liability, is **sovereign immunity**. The doctrine of sovereign immunity holds that the government is immune from lawsuits. Therefore, governments must consent to be sued. This is true of both state and federal governments. Most states have abolished sovereign immunity to some degree, some by statute, and a few by judicial decision.

The federal government has consented to be sued under several laws. Through the Federal Tort Claims Act (FTCA),[30] the United States has waived immunity from suit for a number of torts. In 1974, the statute was amended to permit suits based upon assault, battery, false imprisonment, false arrest, abuse of process, or malicious prosecution committed by federal law enforcement officers.

States may not be sued directly under federal civil rights statutes, nor may the federal government. However, local forms of government may be sued under federal civil rights laws if the acts alleged to have violated the plaintiff's civil rights were committed pursuant to an ordinance, regulation, policy, or decision of the locality.[31]

---

sovereign immunity

■ The government's freedom from being sued. In many cases, the U.S. government has waived immunity by a statute such as the Federal Tort Claims Act; states have similar laws.

Web Links

International Criminal Justice

The United Nations collects data on crime and criminal justice systems around the World. See, for example, the website for the United Nations Interregional Crime and Justice Research Institute and a survey of crime trends around the World http://www.uncjin.org/Statistics/WCTS/wcts.html

Key Terms

adversarial
discretion

nolle prosequi
sovereign immunity

victim impact statements

Review Questions

1. What is the constitutional mission of a prosecutor?
2. What is the policy behind requiring defense attorneys to zealously represent guilty persons?
3. What is the attorney-client privilege?
4. Legal assistants and other nonlawyers are prohibited from practicing law. What acts constitute the practice of law?
5. Are legal assistants who are employed in law offices obligated to maintain client confidences?
6. What are victims' bills of rights? Name three rights typically included in such a law.
7. According to the Police Code of Conduct promulgated by the International Association of Chiefs of Police, when may force be used?
8. What do "U.S.C." and "Fed. R. Crim. P." represent?

Problems & Critical Thinking Exercises

1. Create a set of facts under which co defendants could not be represented by the same attorney. Explain why separate counsel is necessary under your scenario.
2. Do you believe that a defense attorney should be required to zealously represent a client who has admitted guilt to the lawyer? What if the result is the release of a violent criminal (i.e., acquittal or dismissal of charges)? Can you suggest an alternative method?
3. Do you believe that police officers should arrest every violator they encounter, discover, or are made aware of? Support your answer. What factors should an officer consider when deciding whether to arrest or otherwise pursue a prosecution?
4. In some nations, prosecutors are required to file a criminal charge if sufficient evidence exists. What are the advantages of such a system? What are the disadvantages of such a system? Should

this form of compulsory prosecution replace the U.S. model of prosecutorial discretion? Explain your answer.

5. In some nations, individual victims are permitted to file a criminal charge against the person(s) who committed the alleged act(s). In these nations, the victim may prosecute the case or a public prosecutor may prosecute on the victim's behalf. Should such a method be employed in the United States? Explain your answer.

Endnotes

1. For more information concerning the due process and crime control models, *see* N. Gary Holten & Lawson Lamar, *The Criminal Courts* ch. 1 (City: McGraw-Hill, 1991).
2. Bureau of Justice Statistics, Bulletin: *Federal Law Enforcement Officers*, 2004 (2006).
3. Fed. R. Crim. P. 48.
4. 368 U.S. 448 (1962).
5. Ethical Consideration (EC) 7-13.
6. *Id. See also Brady v. Maryland*, 373 U.S. 83 (1963).
7. Model Code of Professional Responsibility, Disciplinary Rule (DR) 7-103.
8. EC 7-13.
9. Code of Judicial Conduct, Canon 3.
10. EC 7-1; DR 7-101.
11. DR 4-101.
12. Model Code of Professional Responsibility, DR 4-101(c)(3); Model Rules of Professional Conduct 1.6(b)(1).
13. The decision was affirmed on appeal. *See* 376 N.Y.S.2d 771 (1975) and 390 N.Y.S.2d 867 (1976).
14. EC 2-29.
15. Approximately 13 percent of all paralegals in the United States work in criminal law. *See* Angela Schneeman, *Paralegals in American Law* (Lawyers Cooperative) City: Delmar Publishers 1994).
16. NALA Code of Ethics, Canons 1, 3, 4, and 6.
17. *Id.*, Canon 5.
18. *Id.*, Canon 2.
19. *Id.*, Canon 7.
20. *Id.*, Canon 12.
21. Christopher Johns, "Criminal Justice in America—Part One, The Costs of Victims' Rights," 29 *Arizona Attorney* 27 (Oct. 1992).

22. See National Center for Victims of Crime website, policy pages at victimsofcrime.org.
23. Victim and Witness Protection Act, 18 U.S.C. § 224.
24. For a more thorough discussion of governmental liability, including the liability of government officials, *see* Daniel E. Hall, *Administrative Law: Bureaucracy in Democracy*, 4th ed. (Upper Saddle River, NJ: Pearson Prentice Hall, 2009).
25. *See* 42 U.S.C. § 1983; 18 U.S.C. § 241 *et seq.*
26. *See* 42 U.S.C. § 1983.
27. *See Burns v. Reed*, 111 S. Ct. 1934 (1991); *Pierson v. Ray*, 386 U.S. 547 (1967).
28. *See* Daniel Hall, *Administrative Law: Bureaucracy in Democracy*, 4th ed., ch. 11 (Upper Saddle River, NJ: Pearson Prentice Hall, 2009), for a discussion of prosecutorial immunity.
29. *Id.*
30. 28 U.S.C. §§ 1291, 1346, 1402, 1504, 2110, 2401–2402, 2411–2412, -2671–2678, and 2680.
31. *Monell v. Department of Social Services*, 436 U.S. 658 (1978). *Also see* Hall, *Administrative Law*, ch. 11, *supra*, fn. 28.

CHAPTER 4
CONSTITUTIONAL ASPECTS OF CRIMINAL PROCEDURE

Chapter Outline

Introduction
Incorporation
Expansion of Rights
Exclusionary Rule
Fruit of the Poisonous Tree
 Exceptions
Standing
State Constitutions and the
 "New Federalism"

Chapter Objectives

After completing this chapter, you should be able to:

- identify and describe the major provisions in the Constitution of the United States and its amendments that apply in the criminal context.
- explain why the U.S. Constitution's prominence in criminal justice has increased in recent decades.
- define, identify the landmark cases, and explain the underlying theory and rationale of the exclusionary rule, fruit of the poisonous tree, and related doctrines.
- describe the authority of the states to increase individual liberties through their constitutions and describe the relationship of federal and state constitutional and statutory law in this context.
- identify the material facts and legal issues in two-thirds of the cases you read, describe the courts' analyses and conclusions in the cases, and demonstrate the ability to synthesize and think critically about the law of the subject.

INTRODUCTION

Criminal justice is a policy subject that belongs largely to the states. Nearly 95 percent of all criminal prosecutions occur in state courts. Not only do the states conduct most criminal prosecutions, but each state is free, with few limitations, to design its criminal justice system in any manner it chooses. This was especially true in the early years of the United States. For the most part, the national government did not involve itself in state criminal law for 150 years.

This situation began to change in the 1950s, with significant changes occuring in the 1960s. Today the United States plays a major role in defining the rights of criminal defendants in state prosecutions, as well as federal. The source of federal involvement is the U.S. Constitution, and two developments account for its increased role in state criminal law. First, the reach of the Constitution has been extended to the states through what is known as *incorporation*. Second, the rights found in the Bill of Rights have significantly expanded.

INCORPORATION

Prior to the adoption of the Fourteenth Amendment, the Bill of Rights guarantees were interpreted by the Supreme Court as restricting the authority of the federal government only. The history of the amendments on the subject was so clear that Chief Justice Marshall opined that the question was one of great importance but could be decided without difficulty in the 1833 decision *Barron ex rel. Tiernan* v. *Mayor of Baltimore*, 7 Pet. 243 (1833). Accordingly, fundamental rights in the U.S. Constitution, such as the right to counsel and the right to be free from unreasonable searches and seizures, were guaranteed to a defendant only when prosecuted in federal court. If a state did not have a constitutional or statutory provision granting the right, the defendant was not entitled to its protection when prosecuted in state court.

In 1868 the Fourteenth Amendment to the U.S. Constitution was adopted. One objective of the Fourteenth Amendment is to protect certain civil liberties from state action. Section One of that amendment reads:

> All persons born or naturalized in the United States, and subject to the jurisdiction thereof, are citizens of the United States and of the State wherein they reside. No State shall make or enforce any law which shall abridge the privileges or immunities of citizens of the United States; nor shall any State deprive any person of life, liberty, or property, without due process of law; nor deny to any person within its jurisdiction the equal protection of the laws.

The language of the Fourteenth Amendment is similar to that found in the Fifth Amendment, insofar as they both contain a Due Process Clause. It is through the Due Process Clause and the Equal Protection Clause that the powers of the states are limited. However, what is meant by *due process* has been the subject of great debate among jurists and Supreme Court justices.

Note that the language of the Fourteenth Amendment does not include any of the specific guarantees found in the Bill of Rights, except that it requires the states to afford due process whenever depriving a person of life, liberty, or property. Thus, one of the most important issues raised in the context of the Fourteenth Amendment is whether it includes the rights found in the Bill of Rights, such as the rights to counsel, to freedom of the press, to freedom of speech, to be free from self-incrimination, to be free of unreasonable searches and seizures, and to be free from cruel and unusual punishments. That is, does the requirement that states treat citizens with fairness (due process) mean that states must provide juries in criminal trials, be reasonable when searching persons and homes, etc.? Today, the idea that the Fourteenth Amendment is a vehicle for the application of the Bill of Rights against the states is known as incorporation. Eleven years after the adoption of the Fourteenth Amendment the Supreme Court answered the incorporation question in the negative.[1] But the Court slowly changed its position. The first right to be incorporated was the Fifth Amendment's Takings Clause, in 1897.[2] The first application of incorporation in a criminal case occurred in 1925.[3] In the years that followed, several theories concerning which rights applied to the states developed.

At one extreme is the *independent content approach*. Under this theory, the Fourteenth Amendment's Due Process Clause does not include any right found in the Bill of Rights; that is, due process does not overlap with the Bill of Rights. Rather, due process has an independent content, and none of the rights secured in the Bill of Rights apply against the states. The Supreme Court has never adopted this position.

At the other extreme is *total incorporation*. Proponents of total incorporation, who included Supreme Court Associate Justice Black, argue that the entire Bill of Rights is incorporated by the Fourteenth Amendment and that all the rights contained therein may be asserted by defendants in both state and federal courts. The incorporation occurs automatically, as the proponents of this position believe that the drafters of the Fourteenth Amendment intended to incorporate the entire Bill of Rights. Under this approach, however, the Due Process Clause was limited to recognizing rights contained in the Bill of Rights. Another group of jurists have been labeled *total incorporation plus,* because they contend that the Due Process Clause not only incorporates the Bill of Rights but also secures additional independent rights. Neither of these positions has been adopted by the Supreme Court.

Another position, which was held by the Supreme Court until the 1960s, is known as *fundamental fairness*. Those rights that are "fundamental" and "essential to an ordered liberty" are incorporated through this approach. The fundamental fairness doctrine held that no relationship existed between the Bill of Rights and those deemed fundamental, although the rights recognized under the fundamental fairness doctrine may parallel rights recognized by the Bill of Rights.

The Supreme Court rejected the fundamental fairness doctrine in the 1960s and replaced it with the *selective incorporation doctrine*. Similar to the fundamental fairness doctrine, a right is incorporated under this doctrine if it is both fundamental and essential to the concept of ordered liberty. Like the fundamental fairness approach, independent rights are also recognized under selective incorporation analysis.

However, the two approaches differ in two major respects. First, under the fundamental fairness approach, cases were analyzed case by case. That is, it was possible to have essentially the same facts with different outcomes under the fundamental fairness

Exhibit 4–1 INCORPORATION PROCESS

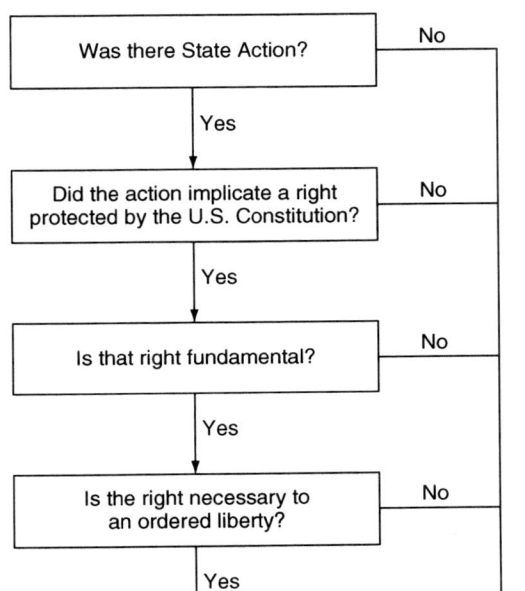

doctrine. Critics charged that the approach was too subjective. Under the selective incorporation method, blanket rules are established to act as precedent for all similar cases in the future. In addition, the entire body of precedent interpreting a federal amendment becomes applicable to the states as a result of an amendment's incorporation. Exhibit 4–1 shows the incorporation process.

Second, selective incorporation gives special attention to the rights contained in the Bill of Rights. A right secured by the Bill of Rights is more likely to be protected by the Fourteenth Amendment's Due Process Clause than are other rights. Selective incorporation continues to be the approach of the Supreme Court today.

Nearly the entire Bill of Rights has been incorporated under the selective incorporation doctrine. The right to grand jury indictment has not been incorporated,[4] nor has the right to a jury trial in civil cases, nor the Eighth Amendment's right to be free from excessive bail or fines. The right to bear arms was incorporated in 2010, the most

Exhibit 4–2 THE BILL OF RIGHTS AND INCORPORATION

Right	Status
First Amendment speech	Incorporated in *Gitlow v. New York*, 268 *U.S.* 652 (1925)
First Amendment—religion	Incorporated in *Everson v. Board of Education*, 330 *U.S.* 1 (1947) and *Cantwell v. Connecticut*, 310 *U.S.* 296 (1940)
First Amendment press	Incorporated in *Near v. Minnesota*, 283 *U.S.* 697 (1931)
First Amendment assembly	Incorporated in *DeJonge v. Oregon*, 299 *U.S.* 353 (1937)
First Amendment grievances	Incorporated in *Edwards v. South Carolina*, 372 *U.S.* 229 (1963)
Second Amendment—arms	Incorporated in *McDonald v. Chicago*, 561 *U.S.* 3025 *(2010)*
Third Amendment	Not incorporated (lower courts have held that it is incorporated)
Fourth Amendment	Incorporated. Different requirements incorporated through several cases, including *Mapp v. Ohio*, 367 *U.S.* 643 (1961)
Fifth Amendment—grand jury	Not incorporated
Fifth Amendment—self incrimination	Incorporated in *Malloy v. Hogan*, 378 *U.S.* 1 (1964)
Fifth Amendment—double jeopardy	Incorporated in *Benton v. Maryland*, 395 *U.S.* 784 (1969)
Fifth Amendment takings	Incorporated in *Chicago, Burlington & Quincy Railroad Co. v. City of Chicago*, 166 U.S. 226 (1897)
Fifth Amendment—due process	Fourteenth Amendment contains due process clause
Sixth Amendment—counsel	Incorporated in *Gideon v. Wainwright*, 372 *U.S.* 335 (1963)
Sixth Amendment—public trial	Incorporated in *In re Oliver*, 333 *U.S.* 257 (1948)
Sixth Amendment—jury trial	Incorporated in several cases upholding right to impartial jury, number of jurors, etc.
Sixth Amendment—speedy trial	Incorporated in *Klopfer v. North Carolina*, 386 *U.S.* 213 (1967)
Sixth Amendment—confront accusers	Incorporated in *Pointer v. Texas*, 380 *U.S.* 400 (1965)
Sixth Amendment—compulsory process	Incorporated
Sixth Amendment—notice of charge	Incorporated
Seventh Amendment	Not incorporated
Eighth Amendment—cruel punishments	Incorporated in *Robinson v. California*, 370 *U.S.* 660 (1962)
Eighth Amendment—excessive bail/fines	Not incorporated (dicta in Supreme Court opinions indicate that it will be if the Court hears the issue)
Ninth Amendment	Has never been used by Supreme Court to establish a right, although it has been cited as support for incorporated rights
Tenth Amendment	Not applicable

recent right to be recognized as fundamental. Exhibit 4–2 contains a chart of rights that have been incorporated.[5] Once incorporated, a right applies against the states to the extent and in the same manner as it does against the United States. Also, several independent due process rights have been declared. You will learn many of these in the following chapters.

EXPANSION OF RIGHTS

Another major development in the area of constitutional criminal procedure has been the expansion of many rights. The language of the Constitution is concise. It refers to "unreasonable searches and seizures," "due process," "equal protection," "speedy and public trial," and so on. No further definition or explanation of the meaning of these provisions is provided. The process of determining the meaning of such phrases is known as *constitutional interpretation*. It is possible to make each right ineffective by reading it narrowly. The opposite is also true.

During the 1960s, many rights found in the Bill of Rights were expanded by court decisions. *Expansion* refers to extending a right beyond its narrowest reading. The effect of expansive interpretation is to increase defendants' rights. An example of an expansive interpretation is the *Miranda v. Arizona* decision, 384 U.S. 436 (1966). Although the language of the Fifth Amendment does not explicitly state that a defendant must be advised of the right to remain silent, to have the assistance of counsel, and so forth, the Court now requires that such admonishments be given because of an expanded interpretation of the Fifth Amendment.

Another example of expanded individual rights is the right to privacy. No explicit constitutional language provides for a right to privacy. However, the Supreme Court has found a right to privacy to be implicit in the Constitution. The Court has held that the right to privacy protects a woman's right to abortion, in some circumstances,[6] and a couple's right to use contraceptives,[7] among many other rights. Many more expansions will be discussed later.

EXCLUSIONARY RULE

Another important constitutional development was the creation of the **exclusionary rule**. The rule is simple: Evidence that is obtained by an unconstitutional search or seizure is inadmissible at trial.

The rule was first announced by the Supreme Court in 1914.[8] However, at that time the rule had not been incorporated, and therefore the exclusionary rule did not apply to state court proceedings. This changed in 1961 when the Supreme Court declared that evidence obtained in violation of the Constitution could not be used in state or federal criminal proceedings. The case was *Mapp v. Ohio*.

exclusionary rule

■ "The exclusionary rule" often means the rule that illegally gathered evidence may not be used in a criminal trial. The rule has several exceptions, such as when the evidence is used to impeach a defendant's testimony and when the evidence was gathered in a good-faith belief that the process was legal.

The exclusionary rule has been the subject of intense debate. There is no explicit textual language establishing the rule in the Constitution. For that reason, critics contend that the Supreme Court exceeded its authority by creating it; that it is the responsibility of the legislative branch to make such laws.

On the other side is the argument that without the exclusionary rule, the Bill of Rights is ineffective. Why have constitutional standards if there is no method to enforce them? For example, why require that the officers in the *Mapp* case have a search warrant, yet permit them to conduct a warrantless search and use the evidence obtained against the defendant? These questions go to the purpose of the exclusionary rule: it discourages law enforcement personnel from engaging in unconstitutional conduct.

The Court has been criticized for creating such a rigid, single-remedy approach to police misconduct. In fact, most nations, including those in the Western world who share a legal heritage with the United States, do not employ the rule. Instead, they attempt to deter police misconduct in ways that have lesser social expense (e.g., releasing a dangerous individual back into the public as can occur following the suppression of key evidence in the United States). Administrative discipline, civil liability, and personal criminal liability for offending officers are examples of alternatives. Indeed, the Court has begun to soften the exclusionary rule, as evinced in the *Hudson* case.

When it applies, the exclusionary rule prevents the admission into evidence of any item, confession, or other thing that was obtained by law enforcement officers in an unconstitutional manner.

The evidence must be obtained by the police in an unlawful manner. However, if a private citizen working on his or her own obtains evidence illegally and then turns it over to the police, it may be admitted.[9] People hired or authorized to assist the police are considered agents of the government, and therefore the exclusionary rule applies to their actions.

The exclusionary rule does not apply to pretrial matters. A defendant may not challenge a grand jury indictment because the grand jury considered illegally obtained evidence. The defendant's remedy is at trial. In most cases, but not all, evidence obtained illegally may be used at sentencing.

Another important exception to the exclusionary rule allows the government to use illegally seized evidence to rebut statements made by a defendant.[10] The government may not use the evidence if the defendant does not "open the door." That is, the government may use the evidence if the defense refers to it in its case.

Most exclusionary rule issues are resolved prior to trial by way of a motion to suppress, or exclude, evidence. In some instances the motion may be made at the moment the prosecutor attempts to introduce such evidence at trial. This is known as a *contemporaneous objection*.

FRUIT OF THE POISONOUS TREE

The exclusionary rule applies to *primary evidence,* that is, evidence that is the direct result of an illegal search or seizure. It is possible that such primary evidence may lead the police to other evidence. For example, suppose a special agent of the Federal Bureau of Investigation searches a home in violation of the Fourth Amendment.

The agent discovers on the homeowner's computer a plan to rob a federally insured bank. The plan includes a list of supplies that are needed and where they are hidden. Two of the items, a gun and a mask, are buried under a tree in a public park. The agent leaves the home, drives to the park, and digs up the items. Because the items were in a public space, the agent didn't need to obtain a warrant to search for them. But because they were found as a consequence of the illegal search, both the primary evidence (the plan) and the secondary or derivative evidence (the gun and mask) are inadmissible at trial. Such secondary evidence is known as **fruit of the poisonous tree**. Generally, evidence that is "tainted" by the prior illegal conduct is inadmissible. The rule does not make all evidence later obtained by law enforcement inadmissible. In some instances, evidence may be admissible because the connection between the illegally seized evidence and the subsequently obtained evidence is marginal, or as the Supreme Court has stated it, "the causal connection . . . may have become so attenuated as to dissipate the taint."[11]

fruit of the poisonous tree doctrine

■ The rule that evidence gathered as a *result* of evidence gained in an illegal search or questioning cannot be used against the person searched or questioned even if the later evidence was gathered lawfully.

Exceptions

Several exceptions to the exclusionary rule (and fruit of the poisonous tree) exist. First, such evidence is admissible at court hearings where determinations of guilt are not made, such as grand jury proceedings, pretrial hearings, and sentencing, for example. Also, if a defendant opens the door by referring to such evidence, a prosecutor may refer to it as well in rebuttal or to impeach the testimony of a defendant. This was the case in *Kansas v. Ventris* (2009),[12] where a confession was obtained illegally by a government informant. While such evidence could not be admitted at trial to prove guilt, the Supreme Court held that it could be used to impeach the defendant's testimony that he didn't commit the crime. The Court found the deterrent effect on police by excluding the evidence at trial to prove guilt was adequate and that the exclusion didn't need to extend to rebutting the defendant's testimony. In the Court's words, "[O]nce the defendant testifies inconsistently, denying the prosecution 'the traditional truth-testing devices of the adversary process,' is a high price to pay for vindicating the right to counsel at the prior stage. On the other hand, preventing impeachment use of statements taken in violation of *Massiah* would add little appreciable deterrence for officers, who have an incentive to comply with the Constitution, since statements lawfully obtained can be used for all purposes, not simply impeachment."

Another situation in which illegally obtained evidence may be admitted is when an independent source exists. An **independent source** must be an alternative, unconnected, and legal pathway to the same evidence. Consider the preceding bank robbery example. If a co-conspirator in the robbery also told the police where the money is, it is admissible regardless of the illegal confession, so long as the co-conspirator's admission was lawfully obtained.

Evidence that would be inevitably discovered by law enforcement may be admitted. This doctrine is similar to the independent source doctrine. However, police must actually obtain evidence from an untainted, lawful source to invoke the independent

independent source

■ The general rule that if new evidence can be traced to a source completely apart from the illegally gathered evidence that first led to the new evidence, it may be used by the government in a criminal trial.

inevitable discovery rule

The principle that even if criminal evidence is gathered by unconstitutional methods, the evidence may be admissible if it definitely would have come to light anyway.

source doctrine. The **inevitable discovery doctrine** holds that evidence that is the fruit of an illegal search, seizure, or arrest may be admitted if it is probable that the evidence would have been obtained lawfully at a later date.

Another limitation of the fruits doctrine is the admissibility of secondary or derivative evidence in cases where suspects have not been given *Miranda* warnings but have made voluntary statements leading to the seizure of secondary or derivative evidence. You will learn more about *Miranda* and this exception later.

Because the Constitution's individual rights only limit governmental authority, evidence that is obtained illegally by private individuals and turned over to law enforcement may be admitted. Of course, the individual who illegally obtained the evidence may be prosecuted for the underlying offense, e.g. trespass or theft. If the private individual was asked or encouraged to find the evidence by the government, the evidence will be excluded under agency doctrine (although not an employee, the individual was acting as an agent of the government).

STANDING

standing

■ A person's right to bring (start) or join a lawsuit or to raise a particular issue because he or she is directly affected by the issues raised.

A defendant must have **standing** before he or she may successfully have evidence suppressed. There are two aspects to standing. First, the person challenging the evidence must have an adversarial interest in the proceeding. Basically, only defendants in criminal cases may challenge evidence as seized in violation of the Fourth Amendment. A defendant's mother may not intervene in the criminal case and attempt to have evidence suppressed because her Fourth Amendment rights were violated by an illegal search and seizure—even if the claim is true. A mother lacks standing to make the claim.

The second aspect concerns the defendant's interest in the area searched or thing seized. A defendant must have a reasonable expectation of privacy to a place or thing before he or she can have it excluded at trial. To say it another way, the defendant's constitutional rights must have been violated before evidence will be suppressed. Therefore, the defendant may not assert his mother's right to be free from illegal searches and seizures.

Note that in *Simmons v. United States,* [13](1968), the Supreme Court held that a defendant may testify at a suppression hearing without waiving the right not to testify at trial and that any testimony given at a suppression hearing by a defendant may not be used against him or her at trial.

Simmons eliminated the quandary many defendants had: Should they give incriminating evidence during a suppression hearing in hopes of having the evidence excluded? Of course, if the suppression claim was unsuccessful, then a defendant faced the incriminating testimony at trial. This put many defendants in a position of having to choose one right or another: the right to be free from self-incrimination versus the right to have illegally seized evidence excluded from trial. The Supreme Court held that defendants should be free from such dilemmas.

During the 1960s and early 1970s, many jurists predicted that the Supreme Court would become so involved with criminal procedure that it would, in effect, write its own "constitutional criminal procedure code." This prediction has not proven to be true; however, many areas of criminal procedure are greatly influenced by Supreme Court decisions. It is common to refer to the expansion of individual rights and the extension of those rights to the states as the *constitutionalization* of criminal procedure.

In recent years, though, there appears to be a trend away from expansive interpretation. This is largely because the composition of the Supreme Court is more conservative than it was during the 1960s. Some believe that the trend of increasing individual rights was hindering law enforcement and welcome regression. Those who believe strongly in the rights of the individual point out that the Framers intended to create an inefficient government, in favor of protecting liberties, and proclaim that it is better to free several guilty persons than to imprison one innocent person.

STATE CONSTITUTIONS AND THE "NEW FEDERALISM"

Each state has its own constitution. State constitutions typically differ from the U.S. Constitution in several ways. Most are longer than the U.S. Constitution. This is often a consequence of greater elaboration of governmental structures, often including how local forms of government are to be created and organized. Short of demanding a republican form of government, the federal Constitution is silent about the internal organization of state governments. State constitutions also typically provide more details about the organization of state government than the U.S. Constitution does about the federal government. It is also common for state constitutions to have more amendments than the federal Constitution. This is because amendment is easier in most states. In many, amendment can occur through public referendum. This leads to another difference between state and federal constitutions. Because state constitutions are easier to amend, they are more likely to address specific issues, and they are more likely to be internally inconsistent than is the federal Constitution.

One area where the two are very similar is in their respective bills of rights. Most states' bills of rights are identical, or nearly identical, in language to the national Constitution's Bill of Rights. There are exceptions, however. For example, several states protect privacy explicitly, while the federal Constitution does not. The Supreme Court has held, however, that there is an implicit right to privacy in several of the provisions of the U.S. Constitution, most notably, the Fourth Amendment and the due process clauses of the Fifth and Fourteenth Amendments. States that explicitly protect privacy include Alaska, Arizona, California, Hawaii, Illinois, Louisiana, Montana, and Washington, D.C., while the federal Constitution does not and only recently was the right held to be implicit in several provisions found in the Bill of Rights. California's right, found in Art. I, § 1, reads:

> All people are by nature free and independent and have inalienable rights. Among these are enjoying and defending life and liberty, acquiring, possessing, and protecting property, and pursuing and obtaining safety, happiness, and privacy.

Montana's Constitution, at Art. II, § 10, provides that

> The right of individual privacy is essential to the well-being of a free society and shall not be infringed without the showing of a compelling state interest.

Until recently, state constitutions have not played an important role in defining civil liberties. This is because both state and federal courts have looked almost exclusively to the national Constitution to answer questions concerning civil liberties, particularly in criminal cases. It is also due to the tendency of state courts to interpret state constitutional rights as identical to those secured by the national Constitution.

Increasingly, this is not the case. During the past two decades, commentators, judges, and attorneys have exhibited a renewed interest in state constitutional law. Concerned that the Supreme Court of the United States was backing away from the protections recognized by the Court in the 1960s, former Justice William Brennan of the United States Supreme Court urged states and their courts to turn to their own constitutions to protect liberties.[14]

The resurgence in state constitutional law is known as "New Federalism." State constitutions can be an independent source of civil liberties. Of course, a state constitution cannot be used to limit or encroach on a federally secured right, but it can be used to extend the scope of a right. This trend was buttressed by the Rehnquist and early Roberts Court decisions favoring dual sovereignty, for example, limited federal authority and more expansive state authority.

In several instances, state courts have determined that their state constitutions protect criminal defendants to a greater extent than does the national Constitution. The Supreme Court of Pennsylvania strongly asserted that its state's constitution has its own meaning separate and independent from the federal Constitution. In a 1991 case, that Court stated:

> [T]he decisions of the [U.S. Supreme] Court are not, and should not be, dispositive of questions regarding rights guaranteed by counter-part provisions of State Law. Accordingly, such decisions are not mechanically applicable to state law issues, and state court judges and members of the bar seriously err if they so treat them. Rather, state court judges, and also practitioners, do well to scrutinize constitutional decisions by federal courts, for only if they are found to be logically persuasive and well-reasoned, paying due regard to precedent and the policies underlying specific constitutional guarantees, may they properly claim persuasive weight as guide posts when interpreting counter-part state guarantees.[15]

The California courts have taken a similar approach. Even if a provision's interpretation parallels national law, the courts favor citing state law over federal law.

Whether a state court depends on state or federal law in defining a right determines what court has the final word on the subject. If a right is founded upon federal law, the Supreme Court of the United States is the final arbiter. If a right is founded upon state law, the highest court of the state is the final arbiter, again assuming that no federal right is encroached upon by the state decision. This problem normally arises when one person's exercise of a right affects another person's rights. For example, if a state court were to find that a fetus has a right to life in every instance, the decision would be void as violative of the federally secured right to privacy held by the mothers to elect abortions in some circumstances.

If a state court relies upon federal law when defining a right, the possibility of reversal by a federal court, usually the Supreme Court, exists. This is what occurred in California concerning the use of peyote, a drug made from cactus, by Native Americans. The Supreme Court of California decided in 1965 that the use of peyote by Native Americans during religious ceremonies was protected by the U.S. Constitution's First Amendment free exercise of religion clause.[16] That decision was not disturbed until 1990, when the Supreme Court of the United States decided that the regulation of peyote as a drug was a reasonable burden upon the First Amendment[17] and therefore overruled the 1965 California decision. Although the defendant asserted both the federal and state free exercise guarantees, the California Supreme Court relied entirely upon federal law in making its decision.

Although there has been an increase in the number of state courts that have turned to their own constitutions to protect liberties since Justice Brennan issued his famous challenge, the response hasn't been as significant as many civil libertarians had hoped. But examples of state rights expanding beyond their federal counterparts exist and even when state courts rely on federal law, it is more common today than before to cite state law as well, thereby providing an alternative basis upon which a reviewing court can affirm a decision protecting a liberty.

The *Leon* case, issued by the Supreme Court of the United States, recognized a good-faith exception to the exclusionary rule; the *Edmunds* decision, by the Supreme Court of Pennsylvania, expressly rejects the good-faith exception in state prosecutions.

As another example, several states have not followed the Supreme Court's lead in allowing statements made in violation of *Miranda* to be used by the prosecution in impeachment of a defendant.[18] These are but a few of the many instances in which a right has received greater protection under state law than under federal law.[19]

As mentioned earlier, state laws may not reduce federally secured rights. Similarly, state laws may not enlarge federally secured rights. They may, through state law, enlarge rights also protected by federal law. In the following case, decided in 2008, the distinction that was just drawn was at issue.

> **Web Links**
>
> **Metasearching the World Wide Web**
>
> Savvy Search at *http://www.search.com/* is a multiengine search tool. Savvy Search claims that your search terms are run through 12 search engines at one time, thus increasing total hits between 200% and 800% and relevant hits by 60%. This should enhance searches in any subject, including law and justice.

Key Terms

exclusionary rule
fruit of the poisonous tree
independent source
inevitable discovery doctrine
standing

Review Questions

1. What is selective incorporation? Total incorporation? Which reflects current law?
2. Name three rights that have been incorporated and one that has not.
3. What is the exclusionary rule?
4. Give an example of when evidence would be fruit of the poisonous tree.
5. Name three exceptions to the fruit of the poisonous tree doctrine.
6. What is the "New Federalism" in the context of constitutional law?

Problems & Critical Thinking Exercises

1. The Constitution of the United States significantly affects all criminal law. Why is that so when more than 95 percent of all prosecutions occur in state courts?
2. Do you believe that evidence that has been obtained by law enforcement in an unconstitutional manner should be inadmissible at trial? Explain your position.
3. England does not employ the exclusionary rule. Rather, police officers are subject to civil liability for illegal searches. Is this a satisfactory remedy that should be employed in the United States? Can you think of alternative remedies?

Endnotes

1. *United States v. Cruikshank,* 92 U.S.w42 (1876).
2. *Chicago, Burlington & Quincy Railroad Co. v. City of Chicago,* 166 U.S. 226 (1897).
3. *Gitlow v. New York,* 268 U.S. 652 (1925).
4. *Hurtado v. California,* 110 U.S. 516 (1884).
5. *McDonald v. Chicago,* 561 U.S. __ (2010).
6. *Roe v. Wade,* 410 U.S. 113 (1973).
7. *Griswold v. Connecticut,* 381 U.S. 479 (1965).
8. The rule, as it applied in federal courts, was announced in *Weeks v. United States,* 232 U.S. 383 (1914). However, it appears that the rule was applied in at least one case prior to that date. See LaFave & Israel, Criminal Procedure 78 (Hornbook Series) (St. Paul: West, 1985).
9. *Burdeau v. McDowell,* 256 U.S. 465 (1921).
10. *Walder v. United States,* 347 U.S. 62 (1954); *United States v. Havens,* 446 U.S. 620 (1980).
11. *Nardone v. United States,* 308 U.S. 338 (1939).
12. 556 U.S. 586 (2009).
13. 390 U.S. 377.
14. William J. Brennan, Jr., *State Constitutions and the Protection of Individual Rights,* 90 Harv. L. Rev. 489 (1977).
15. *Commonwealth v. Ludwig,* 527 Pa. 472, 478 (1991).
16. *People v. Woody,* 61 Cal. 2d 716, 394 P.2d 813 (1965).
17. *Department of Human Resources v. Smith,* 494 U.S. 872 (1990).
18. See *People v. Disbrow,* 16 Cal. 3d 101, 545 P.2d 272 (1976) (California law); *State v. Santiago,* 53 Haw. 254, 492 P.2d 657 (1971) (Hawaii law); *Commonwealth v. Triplett,* 462 Pa. 244, 341 A.2d 62 (1975) (Pennsylvania law).
19. See Joseph Cook, *Constitutional Rights of the Accused,* 2d ed., § 1:8, n.16 (Lawyers Cooperative, 1989) for a more thorough list.

CHAPTER 5

THE PRETRIAL PROCESS

Chapter Outline

Introduction
Discovery and Investigation of Criminal Activity
Arrest
The Complaint
Initial Appearance
Pretrial Release and Detention
    Types of Release
    Eighth Amendment
    Detention
Preliminary Hearing
The Formal Charge
    Indictment and Grand Jury
    Information
Arraignment
Pretrial Activity
    Discovery
    Motion Practice
    Pretrial Conference
Extradition and Detainers
Removal

Chapter Objectives

After completing this chapter, you should be able to:

- outline the process of a criminal case from discovery of the criminal act to preparation for trial.
- describe the two formal criminal charges that are filed against defendants in the United States.
- discuss the history, purpose, and procedures of grand juries, and contrast that with contemporary grand juries.
- describe and apply to fact scenarios the law of pretrial release of defendants.
- identify the material facts and legal issues in nearly all of the cases you read, describe the courts' analyses and conclusions in the cases, and demonstrate the ability to synthesize and think critically about the law of the subject.

INTRODUCTION

What follows is an outline of the basic process a case goes through, from before arrest to after trial. As previously mentioned, each state and the federal government have different processes. The federal process is used for illustration. Exhibit 5–1 provides a visual summary of the process. You may find it helpful to refer to it as you learn the different stages of the process.

DISCOVERY AND INVESTIGATION OF CRIMINAL ACTIVITY

The process begins when law enforcement officials learn of a crime that has been committed (or is to be committed). Police learn of criminal activity in two ways: They may discover it themselves, or a citizen may report such activity.

Once police are aware of criminal activity, the pre-arrest investigation begins. There are two objectives to this stage. First, police must determine whether a crime

Exhibit 5–1 VISUAL SUMMARY OF THE BASIC CRIMINAL PROCESS

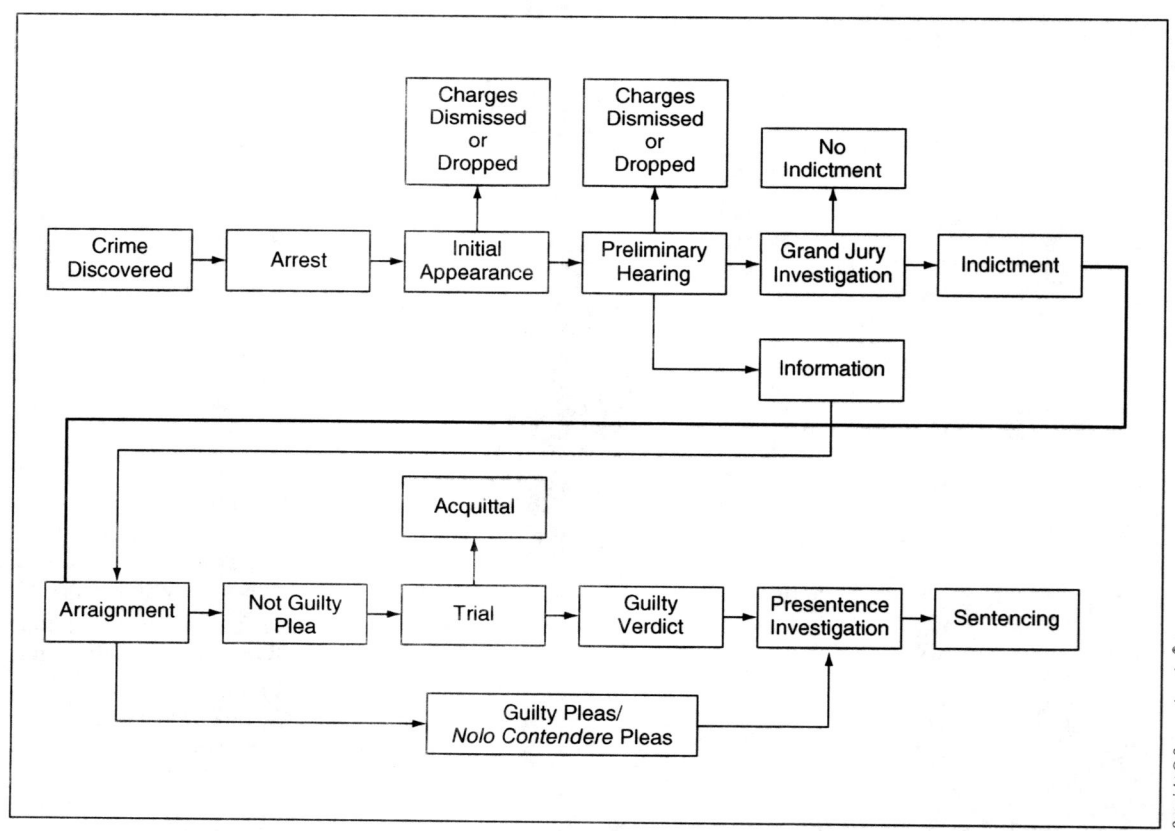

has been committed. Second, if a crime has been committed, police attempt to gather sufficient evidence to charge and convict the person believed to have committed the crime.

ARREST

Once adequate evidence exists, an **arrest** is made in most cases. However, in some misdemeanor cases a defendant is asked to come to the police station, and an arrest is not made unless the defendant refuses. The arrest may be made without an arrest warrant in some situations. In others, an ex parte hearing may be held to determine if probable cause exists to believe that the person under investigation committed the crime. If so, the judge may issue an arrest warrant.

At the time of arrest, police ordinarily search the defendant. Once at the police station, the defendant is "booked." *Booking* consists of obtaining biographical information about the defendant (name, address, etc.), fingerprinting the defendant, and taking the defendant's photograph, commonly known as a "mug shot." The defendant is usually permitted to make a telephone call at this stage.

The defendant is then searched (sometimes deloused and showered) and held in jail until further arrangements are made. For minor offenses, the defendant may be able to post bail prior to appearing before a judge. In such cases, defendants are out of jail within hours. All others have to wait for a judge to set a bail amount at an initial appearance. During and after this stage, law enforcement investigation and gathering of evidence may continue.

arrest

■ The official taking of a person to answer criminal charges. This involves at least temporarily depriving the person of liberty and may involve the use of force. An arrest is usually made by a police officer with a warrant or for a crime committed in the officer's presence.

THE COMPLAINT

At this stage, a police officer, or in some instances a prosecutor, files a **complaint,** which acts as the charging instrument. Fed. R. Crim. P. 3 states: "The complaint is a written statement of the essential facts constituting an offense charged. It shall be made upon oath before a magistrate." The complaint need not be written upon personal knowledge. That is, an officer may use hearsay and circumstantial evidence in a complaint. Affidavits from those who have personal knowledge, such as witnesses and victims, are often attached to the complaint.

When a warrant is sought to arrest a defendant, the complaint is often produced in support of the request for a warrant. This occurs at the ex parte hearing mentioned earlier. Federal law requires that a warrant be issued if probable cause is established by the complaint and its accompanying affidavits. Upon the request of the government, a summons (an order to appear) may be issued rather than an arrest warrant.[1]

If the defendant was arrested without a warrant, the complaint serves as the charging document at the initial appearance or preliminary hearing.

For traffic violations and some lesser misdemeanors, the complaint acts as both a summons to appear in court and the charging document. In such cases the defendant appears in court on only one occasion, and the ticket is used in place of an information or indictment. See Exhibits 5–2 and 5–3.

complaint

■ A *criminal complaint* is a formal document that charges a person with a crime.

Exhibit 5–2   CRIMINAL COMPLAINT

AO 91 (Rev. 5/85) Criminal Complaint

United States District Court

_____ DISTRICT OF _____

UNITED STATES OF AMERICA

V.

CRIMINAL COMPLAINT

CASE NUMBER:

(Name and Address of Defendant)

I, the undersigned complainant being duly sworn state the following is true and correct to the best of my knowledge and belief. On or about _____ in _____ county, in the _____ District of _____ defendant(s) did,
(Track Statutory Language of Offense)

in violation of Title _____ United States Code, Section(s) _____. I further state that I am a(n) _____ and that this complaint is based on the following facts:

Continued on the attached sheet and made a part hereof: ☐ Yes   ☐ No

_____
Signature of Complainant

Sworn to before me and subscribed in my presence,

_____ at _____
Date   City and State

_____   _____
Name & Title of Judicial Officer   Signature of Judicial Officer

Source: http://www.uscourts.gov/uscourts/FormsAndFees/Forms/AO091.pdf

Exhibit 5–3   SUMMONS IN A CRIMINAL CASE

AO 83 (Rev. 5/85) Summons in a Criminal Case

United States District Court

_____ DISTRICT OF _____

UNITED STATES OF AMERICA

SUMMONS IN A CRIMINAL CASE

CASE NUMBER:

(Name and Address of Defendant)

YOU ARE HEREBY SUMMONED to appear before the United States District Court at the place, date and time set forth below.

Place	Room
	Date and Time
Before:	

To answer a(n)
☐ Indictment   ☐ Information   ☐ Complaint   ☐ Violation Notice
☐ Probation Violation Petition

Charging you with a violation of Title _____ United States Code, Section _____.

Brief description of offense:

_____   _____
Signature of Issuing Officer   Date

_____
Name and Title of Issuing Officer

(continued)

Exhibit 5–3   *(continued)*

AO 83 (Rev. 5/85) Summons in a Criminal Case

RETURN OF SERVICE

Service was made by me on:[1]   Date

Check one box below to indicate appropriate method of service

☐ Served personally upon the defendant at: _____

_____

☐ Left summons at the defendant's dwelling house or usual place of abode with a person of suitable age and discretion then residing therein and mailed a copy of the summons to the defendant's last known address. Name of person with whom the summons was left:
_____

_____

☐ Returned unexecuted: _____

_____

_____

_____

I declare under penalty of perjury under the laws of the United States of America that the foregoing information contained in the Return of Service is true and correct.

Returned on _____   _____
                    Date   Name of United States Marshal

                                                                      _____
                                                                      (by) Deputy United States Marshal

1) As to who may serve a summons see Rule 4 of the Federal Rules of Criminal Procedure

Source: http://www.nvd.uscourts.gov/Files/AO_083_0109.pdf

INITIAL APPEARANCE

After arrest, the defendant is taken "without unnecessary delay" before the nearest available federal magistrate.[2] In most cases this means that a defendant will be brought before the judge within 24 hours. However, if a defendant is arrested on a weekend, it may be the following Monday before the defendant has the initial appearance, unless a weekend session of court is held.

The first appearance is brief. If the arrest was executed under an arrest warrant, it is the duty of the presiding judge to make sure that the person arrested is the person named in the warrant. The defendant is also informed of various rights, such as the rights to remain silent and to have the assistance of counsel. If the defendant is indigent, the court will appoint counsel. The right to counsel is discussed more fully later. If the arrest was warrantless, an initial probable cause determination must occur.

In 1991, the United States Supreme Court examined the need for prompt probable cause determinations in warrantless arrest situations. In *County of Riverside v. McLaughlin*,[3] the Court held that persons arrested without a warrant must have a probable cause determination within 48 hours after arrest or quicker if reasonable. A defendant who asserts unreasonable delay, but was held less than 48 hours before a probable cause hearing was conducted, bears the burden of proving that the delay was unreasonable under the Fourth Amendment. If a defendant is held longer than 48 hours without a probable cause hearing, the burden of showing a bona fide emergency or other extraordinary circumstance falls on the government.

Time to gather additional evidence, ill will, or the fact that the defendant was arrested on a weekend are not sufficient to delay the probable cause determination longer than 48 hours.

Finally, a preliminary hearing date is set, and if the defendant is in jail, the court determines whether he or she should be released prior to trial.

PRETRIAL RELEASE AND DETENTION

In many cases, defendants are released prior to trial. A court may order many types of release, but the predominantly used methods are cash bail, surety bond, property bond, and personal recognizance.

Types of Release

The most obvious method of gaining release is to post **bail**. A defendant who has the resources may simply pay into the court the amount of the bail.

Whenever a third party, usually a professional bondsman, agrees to pay the bond for a defendant, a surety bond is created. The common practice is for the defendant to pay the surety 10 percent or more of the bond amount in exchange for the bondsman making the defendant's bail. The 10 percent is not refunded to the defendant after the case is concluded.

bail
■ The money or property given as security for a defendant's appearance in court. The money, often in the form of a bail bond, may be lost if the defendant released does not appear in court.

Some sureties require security (collateral) before a bond will be issued. Defendants may pledge cars, houses, or other property to obtain release. This is a property bond.

For many misdemeanors and a few felonies, a defendant may be released on personal recognizance. To gain such a release, a defendant need only promise to appear.

Regardless of the type of release, courts frequently impose conditions upon the defendant. Defendants who are arrested or caught intimidating witnesses or interfering with the judicial process may be jailed until trial.

Eighth Amendment

The Eighth Amendment proscribes the imposition of "excessive bail." This provision may be applicable to the states through the Fourteenth Amendment. The purpose of imposing money bail is to assure the defendant's appearance at trial, not to inflict punishment. Bail set higher than necessary to accomplish this purpose is deemed excessive.[4] In practice, courts have significant discretion in setting bail and are rarely reversed.

The Supreme Court has held that the mere fact that a defendant cannot pay the amount set by a court does not make it excessive. Additionally, the Court has stated that not all defendants have a right to bail. Defendants who are a danger to the community or unlikely to appear for trial may be held without bail.

The exact meaning of the Eighth Amendment has not been spelled out by the Supreme Court. Whether pretrial detention laws, especially those that create a presumption of detention, are constitutional remains to be seen.

Detention

The federal government (and presumably most states, if not all) provides for detention of some defendants prior to trial.

Pretrial detention may not be used to punish a person. To do so violates a person's due process right to be free from punishment without a fair trial. However, a defendant may be detained if there is reason to believe that he or she will not appear for trial or if he or she poses a threat to others.

In the federal system, the defendant is entitled to an adversary hearing concerning pretrial detention, and the government must prove by clear and convincing evidence that the defendant is either dangerous or unlikely to appear for trial.[5] The adversary hearing must be held at the initial appearance; or upon the motion of the defendant or the government, it may be continued.

Although the general rule is that the government bears the burden of proving that a defendant must be detained, there are exceptions. There are two classes of presumptions in the federal statute. One presumes that certain defendants will not appear for trial, and another presumes that certain defendants are a danger to the community. For example, defendants charged with crimes of violence who have a prior conviction for a crime of violence, which was committed while the defendant was released pending trial, are presumed to be dangerous to the community. It is also presumed that defendants charged with drug crimes that carry 10 years or more imprisonment will flee. These presumptions also apply to many other defendants.[6] The presumption is rebuttable, and the defendant has the burden of disproving it. Some question the constitutionality of such presumptions, and it remains to be seen whether such statutes will be reversed or upheld.

Many states have statutes that require detention of persons charged with crimes punishable by life imprisonment or death, provided that the proof of guilt is great.

PRELIMINARY HEARING

The defendant's second appearance before a judge is the **preliminary hearing.** How this stage is handled by the states varies significantly. At the preliminary hearing, the court determines if probable cause exists to believe the accused committed the crime. If probable cause is found, the defendant is "bound over" to the next stage of the process. The next stage is either trial or review by grand jury. If probable cause is not established, the defendant is released.

If indictment by grand jury is required, the case is bound over to the grand jury. The grand jury is not bound by the judge's decision that probable cause exists; it makes an independent decision whether to charge the defendant. If grand jury review is not required, the defendant is bound over for trial.

The purpose of the preliminary hearing is to have an impartial third party review the facts to be sure that probable cause exists. There is no constitutional requirement for a preliminary hearing.[7] However, many states do provide for preliminary hearings.

It is common to permit prosecutors to bypass the preliminary hearing either by submitting the case to a grand jury or by directly filing an information. Defendants often waive the preliminary hearing. In some states, prosecutors may demand a preliminary hearing over the objection of the defendant.

The preliminary hearing can be quite lengthy compared to a defendant's initial appearance. The hearing is adversarial. Witnesses are called, and the attorneys are allowed to make arguments. Rules of evidence are applied in modified form, so hearsay and illegally obtained evidence are often considered. Defendants have a right to counsel and may also be allowed to cross-examine the prosecution witnesses and to present defense witnesses. The right to counsel is a matter of federal constitutional law. The other two rights are granted by state laws. The preliminary hearing can be an important asset to both prosecution and defense, as it can serve as a source of discovery.

The preliminary hearing is different from the initial probable cause determination required by *County of Riverside v. McLaughlin*. The initial determination is constitutionally required, whereas the preliminary hearing is not. Further, although the same terminology is used (i.e., probable cause), less evidence is needed to satisfy the government's obligation at the initial determination than at the preliminary hearing. Probable cause at the initial hearing equates with the probable cause required to obtain a warrant, which is generally recognized as requiring less proof than does probable cause at the later preliminary hearing. Also in contrast is the fact that the probable cause hearing required by *County of Riverside* will likely be one-sided. That is, only the government will present evidence. Some states, however—such as California—permit defendants to present evidence at preliminary hearings.

preliminary hearing
■ The first court proceeding on a criminal charge, in federal courts and many state courts, by a magistrate or a judge to decide whether there is enough evidence for the government to continue with the case and to require the defendant to post bail or be held for trial.

Fed. R. Crim. P. 5 requires that the date for "preliminary examination" be scheduled at the defendant's initial appearance. It shall be held within 10 days of the initial appearance if the defendant is in custody and within 20 days if the defendant has been released.

In federal courts and in many states, probable cause may be founded upon hearsay evidence.[8] Motions to suppress illegally seized evidence are made after the preliminary hearing, so such evidence may be considered at the preliminary examination stage. If a grand jury has issued an indictment, the preliminary hearing may be dispensed within the federal system.[9] Many states have a similar rule.

THE FORMAL CHARGE

information
■ A formal accusation of a crime made by a proper public official such as a prosecuting attorney.

indictment
■ A sworn, written accusation of a crime, made against a person by a prosecutor to a *grand jury*.

grand jury
■ Persons who receive complaints and accusations of crime, hear preliminary evidence on the complaining side, and make formal accusations or indictments.

There are two formal charges: the **information** and the **indictment.** Informations are charges filed by prosecutors. Indictments are charges issued by grand juries. Once filed, an information or indictment replaces the complaint and becomes the formal charging instrument.

Indictment and Grand Jury

Purpose of the Grand Jury

In early American history, **grand juries** were used to guard against unfair and arbitrary government prosecutions and to preserve the reputation of persons investigated but not indicted. The Framers of the U.S. Constitution believed grand jury review so important that they stated in the Fifth Amendment: "[N]o person shall be held to answer for a capital, or otherwise infamous, crime, unless on a presentment or indictment of a Grand Jury."

Grand juries consist of 12 to 23 persons who are usually selected in the same method as petit juries (juries that determine guilt or innocence). Grand juries sit for longer periods of time and are called to hear cases as needed.

The primary objective of grand jury review is the same as that of the preliminary hearing: to determine whether there is probable cause to believe that a target of the investigation committed the alleged crime. The grand jury, therefore, was intended to protect individuals from unwarranted prosecutions. Because the grand jury proceedings are closed, individuals investigated but not charged are not subjected to the public humiliation and damage to reputation that often results from a more public investigation. The secondary objective of the grand jury has become its primary purpose, as defined by prosecutors: to facilitate investigation. See Exhibit 5–4.

Procedures of the Grand Jury

First, grand juries are closed. The public, including the defendant, is not entitled to attend. Second, the prosecutor runs the show before the grand jury, and the defendant has no right to present evidence or to make a statement. Third, the actions of grand juries are secret. Those who attend are not permitted to disclose what transpires. Defendants have no right to know what evidence is presented to a grand jury, unless it is exculpatory (tends to prove the defendant's innocence). Fourth, those who testify before the grand jury are not entitled to have counsel in the jury room.[10] In most states witnesses are permitted to

Exhibit 5–4 SUBPOENA TO TESTIFY BEFORE GRAND JURY

AO 106 (Rev. 5/85) Subpoena to Testify Before Grand Jury

United States District Court

_____ DISTRICT OF _____

To

**SUBPOENA TO TESTIFY
BEFORE GRAND JURY**

SUBPOENA FOR:
☐ PERSON   ☐ DOCUMENT(S) OR OBJECT(S)

YOU ARE HEREBY COMMANDED to appear and testify before the Grand Jury of the United States District Court at the place, date, and time specified below.

PLACE	COURTROOM
	DATE AND TIME

YOU ARE ALSO COMMANDED to bring with you the following document(s) or object(s):[1]

☐ *Please see additional information on reverse*

This subpoena shall remain in effect until you are granted leave to depart by the court or by an officer acting on behalf of the court.

CLERK	DATE
(BY) DEPUTY CLERK	

This subpoena is issued on application of the United States of America	NAME, ADDRESS AND PHONE NUMBER OF ASSISTANT U.S. ATTORNEY

[1] If not applicable, enter "none"

(continued)

Exhibit 5–4 *(continued)*

AO 110 (Rev. 5/85) Subpoena to Testify Before Grand Jury

RETURN OF SERVICE[1]

RECEIVED BY SERVER	DATE	PLACE
SERVED	DATE	PLACE

SERVED ON (NAME)		

SERVED BY	TITLE	

STATEMENT OF SERVICE FEES

TRAVEL	SERVICES	TOTAL

DECLARATION OF SERVER[2]

I declare under penalty of perjury under the laws of the United States of America that the foregoing information contained in the Return of Service and Statement of Service Fees is true and correct.

Executed on _____   _____
              Date   *Signature of Server*

                              _____
                                      Address of Server

ADDITIONAL INFORMATION

(1) As to who may serve a subpoena and the manner of its service see Rule 17(d), Federal Rules of Criminal Procedure, or Rule 45(c), Federal Rules of Civil Procedure.

(2) "Fees and mileage need not be tendered to the witness upon service of a subpoena issued on behalf of the United States or an officer or agency thereof (Rule 45(c), Federal Rules of Civil Procedure Rule 17(d), Federal Rules of Criminal Procedure) or on behalf of certain indigent parties and criminal defendants who are unable to pay such costs (28 USC 1825, Rule 17(b) Federal Rules of Criminal Procedure)."

Source: http://www.uscourts.gov/uscourts/FormsAndFees/Forms/AO110.pdf

leave the proceeding to confer with counsel waiting directly outside. Because statements made to a grand jury can be used later, the Fifth Amendment right to be free from self-incrimination is available to witnesses. Grand juries can overcome Fifth Amendment claims (refusals to testify) by granting witnesses immunity from prosecution. Also, witnesses may not refuse to testify because the inquiry is the result of illegally seized evidence. To permit refusal or exclusion would not further the objective of the exclusionary rule (to deter police misconduct) and would substantially interfere with the grand jury process.[11]

Grand juries possess the power to order people to appear, to subpoena documents, to hold people in contempt, and to grant immunity in order to procure testimony.

As a general proposition, prosecutors control grand juries. For the most part, grand juries convene only when called by the prosecutor. The prosecutor decides what witnesses need to be called and who should be given immunity. Nearly all people targeted (the person the prosecutor believes guilty) by prosecutors are indicted. Many criticize the grand jury system for this reason: The government has too much control over the grand juries. The argument is reasonable when one considers the historical purpose of grand jury review.

The proponents of abolishing the grand jury system argue that grand juries have not only lost their independence, but they also now act to the benefit of prosecutors by allowing discovery of information that may otherwise have been unavailable.

The Indictment

After a grand jury has completed its investigation, a vote on whether to charge is taken. In the federal system, grand juries consist of 16 to 23 people. At least 12 must vote for indictment.[12] In many cases indictments are sealed until the indicted defendant is arrested.

The Constitution requires that all federal prosecutions for capital and infamous crimes be by indictment. However, if a defendant waives the right to grand jury review, he or she may be charged by information. The waiver of indictment form used in federal court is shown in Exhibit 5–5. Crimes punishable by 1 year or longer in prison are "infamous."[13] A defendant may not waive indictment in federal capital cases. It is always proper to charge corporations by information, as imprisonment is not possible.

The United States Supreme Court has ruled that grand jury review is not a fundamental right; therefore, the Fifth Amendment requirement for indictment is not applicable against the states. However, many states have grand juries and require that serious charges be brought by indictment.

Indictments must be written and state in "plain and concise" terms the essential facts constituting the offense charged.[14] Indictments are liberally read, and technical errors do not make them invalid. However, an indictment must contain all the essential elements of the crime charged. If an indictment charges more than one crime, each crime must be made a separate count.[15] Jurisdiction must be noted, and the law upon which the charge is made must be cited. It was upon this indictment that Ted Bundy was prosecuted, convicted, and executed.

If a defendant believes that an indictment is fatally deficient, it may be attacked by a **motion** to **quash.** Indictments are not quashed because of technical errors. An example of a valid reason to quash is failure to allege an essential element of the crime

motion
■ A request that a judge make a ruling or take some other action.

quash
■ Overthrow; annul; completely do away with. *Quash* usually refers to a court stopping a subpoena, an order, or an indictment.

Exhibit 5–5 WAIVER OF INDICTMENT

AO 455 (Rev.5/85) Waiver of Indictment

United States District Court

_____ DISTRICT OF _____

UNITED STATES OF AMERICA
   V.

WAIVER OF INDICTMENT

CASE NUMBER:

I, _____, the above named defendant, who is accused of being advised of

the nature of the charge(s), the proposed information, and of my rights, hereby waive in open court on _____ prosecution by indictment and consent that the proceeding may be by information rather than by indictment.
Date

_____
Defendant

_____
Counsel for Defendant

Before _____
    Judicial Officer

Source: http://www.uscourts.gov/uscourts/FormsAndFees/Forms/AO455.pdf

charged. It is not violative of the Fifth Amendment's Double Jeopardy Clause for a grand jury to issue a second indictment after the first has been quashed or dismissed.

In some jurisdictions, a prosecutor may refuse to prosecute, even though an indictment has been issued. In that situation, the prosecutor must assist the jury in preparing the document and must usually explain why a prosecution will not be maintained. In other instances, the prosecutor *must* pursue the case. The former situation represents federal law; that is, the decision on whether to prosecute falls within the purview of the federal prosecutor, who may properly refuse to sign an indictment and prosecute the case.[16]

Information

The second formal method of charging someone with a crime is by information. Informations are filed by prosecutors without grand jury review. The current trend is away from indictments and toward charging by information.

If a defendant has been initially charged by complaint, the prosecutor must independently review the evidence and determine whether a prosecution is warranted. If not, a prosecutor may file a nolle prosequi. If so, the information is filed.

Informations serve the same function as indictments. Under the federal rules, informations must take the same form as indictments. They must be plain, concise, and in writing. All essential elements, as well as the statute relied upon by the government, must be included.[17] (See the sample criminal information in Chapter 9.) As is true of indictments, informations must be filed with the appropriate court.

Defendants may seek to have defective informations quashed or dismissed. The rules regarding defectiveness are the same for informations as for indictments. Technical errors are not fatal.

ARRAIGNMENT

After the formal charge has been filed, the defendant is brought to the trial court for **arraignment.** This is the hearing at which the defendant is read the formal charge and is asked to enter a **plea.**

Defendants may plead guilty, not guilty, or nolo contendere. By pleading guilty a defendant admits all the charges contained in the charging document, unless a plea agreement has been reached with the government. A **plea agreement,** also known as a *plea bargain,* is the product of negotiations between the prosecutor and the defendant. It is common for the prosecution to dismiss one or more charges of a multi-count charge or to reduce a charge in exchange for a defendant's plea of guilty. Judges are not permitted to participate in plea negotiations and a judge's involvement, including urging a defendant to plead guilty, can be cause for a reversal of a conviction.[18]

Plea bargaining is an important aspect of criminal procedure. More than 90 percent of all felony cases are disposed of by pleas of guilty. Most guilty pleas are the result of plea bargaining.

arraignment
■ The hearing at which a defendant is brought before a judge to hear the charges and to enter a plea (guilty, not guilty, etc.).

plea
■ The *defendant's* formal answer to a criminal charge. The defendant says: "guilty," "not guilty," or "nolo contendere" (no contest).

plea bargain (plea agreement)
■ Negotiations between a prosecutor and a criminal defendant's lawyer, in the attempt to resolve a criminal case without trial.

By pleading guilty, defendants waive a host of rights. The right to a jury trial and to be proven guilty beyond a reasonable doubt are two of the rights waived by a guilty plea. Due to the significance of such waivers, courts must be sure that guilty pleas are given knowingly and voluntarily. To be knowing, a defendant must understand his or her rights and that he or she is waiving them by making the plea. The plea must be free of coercion or duress to be voluntary. Of course, the inducement of a plea bargain is not coercion.

The court must also find that a factual basis exists before a plea of guilty can be accepted. This means there must be sufficient facts in the record to support the conclusion that the defendant committed the crime. A defendant has no right to plead guilty to a crime he or she did not commit. The factual basis may be established by the testimony of the investigating officer or by the defendant recounting what transpired. Once the plea is taken, the court will either impose sentence or set a future date for sentencing.

If a defendant enters a not-guilty plea, the court will set a trial date. In some instances, courts will set a pretrial schedule, which will include a pretrial conference date and a deadline for filing pretrial motions.

Finally, a plea of nolo contendere may be entered. *Nolo contendere* is a Latin phrase that translates to "I do not contest it." The defendant who pleads nolo contendere neither admits nor denies the charges and has no intention of defending himself or herself.

Nolo contendere is treated as a plea of guilty. That is, the government must establish that a factual basis exists to believe the defendant committed the offense, and the court accepting the plea must be sure that the plea is made voluntarily and knowingly. In most jurisdictions a defendant may plead nolo contendere only with the court's approval. This is true in the courts of the United States.[19]

The advantage of a no-contest plea over a guilty plea is that the no-contest plea cannot be used in a later civil proceeding against the defendant, whereas a guilty plea may be used. If the case is not disposed of by a plea of guilty or nolo contendere, the parties begin preparing for trial.

PRETRIAL ACTIVITY

Discovery

discovery

■ The formal and informal exchange of information between the prosecution and the defense.

Discovery refers to a process of exchanging information between the prosecution and defense. Discovery is not as broad in criminal cases as in civil.

The amount of discovery that should be allowed is heavily debated. Those favoring broad discovery contend that limited discovery leads to "trial by ambush," which is not in the best interests of justice. The purpose of a trial is to discover the truth and achieve justice, not to award the better game player. Proponents of this position claim that unexpected evidence at trial is inefficient, costly, and unfair. It is inefficient because trials often have to be delayed to give one party time to prepare a response to the unexpected evidence. Such tactics lead to time problems for the parties as well as the trial court. They may also be unfair. Evidence that was once available may not be so at trial. If the party surprised at trial had known about the unexpected evidence, other contrary evidence could have been secured and a proper defense or response could have been prepared.

Finally, it appears unfair to subject defendants to the possibility of surprise when the government is insulated from certain surprises. For example, affirmative defenses must be specially pled. Intent to rely on alibi and insanity defenses must be provided to the government in most jurisdictions, often with strict enforcement of time requirements. The purpose of these rules is to prevent surprises to the government at trial. Those who support expanded discovery feel that it is unfair to place such requirements upon defendants, but not upon the government.

Those opposed contend that expansive discovery increases the likelihood that defendants will manipulate the system. In particular, defendants might intimidate government witnesses. Additionally, opponents contend that it is easier for a defendant to skillfully plan his or her testimony, even if false, if a defendant knows the government's entire case. For example, if a defendant originally planned to assert an alibi but finds out through discovery that the government has a witness placing him at the location of the crime, he has been provided an opportunity to change his defense. Today, discovery in criminal proceedings is quite limited in many jurisdictions, including federal courts. A few states have enlarged what information may be obtained prior to trial.

What follows is an examination of the federal rules, as well as constitutional requirements for discovery.

Bill of Particulars

One method that defendants have to obtain information about the government's case is through a **bill of particulars.** The purpose of bills of particulars is to make general indictments and informations more specific. Fed. R. Crim. P. 7(f) allows district courts to order prosecutors to file a bill of particulars.

Bills of particulars are not true discovery devices. If the charging instrument is sufficiently clear and detailed, the court will not grant a defense motion for particularization of the charge. A bill of particulars is intended to provide a defendant with details about the charges that are necessary for the preparation of a defense and to avoid prejudicial surprise at trial.[20] The test is not whether the indictment is sufficiently drawn; the question is whether the information is necessary to avoid prejudice to the defendant.

bill of particulars
■ A detailed, formal, written statement of charges or claims by a plaintiff or the prosecutor (given upon the defendant's formal request to the court for more detailed information).

Statements of the Defendant

Fed. R. Crim. P. 16(a) (1) (A) states that upon request the government must allow the defendant to inspect, copy, or photograph all prior relevant written and recorded statements made by the defendant. This includes testimony that defendants give before grand juries—an exception to the rule of secrecy of grand jury proceedings.

Prosecutors are required to allow inspection of all statements made by the defendant that are in the possession of the prosecution or that may be discovered through due diligence. Hence, if a defendant makes a statement to an arresting officer and the statement is recorded or reduced to writing, the prosecutor must allow defense inspection even though the statement may be in the possession of the officer and not the prosecutor.

In addition to recorded statements and writings, the government is required to inform the defendant of "the substance of any oral statement that the government intends to offer in evidence." This means that statements made by a defendant that are summarized by the police (or other government agent), but not verbatim or signed by the defendant, are also discoverable. However, such evidence is discoverable only if the prosecution intends to use it at trial. This is not true of written and recorded statements of a defendant.

Criminal Record of the Defendant

Fed. R. Crim. P. 16 also requires prosecutors to furnish a copy of the defendant's criminal record to the defendant. This includes not only the records known to the prosecutor but also those that can be discovered through due diligence.

Documents and Tangible Objects

Under Rule 16, defendants are also entitled to inspect and copy photographs, books, tangible objects, papers, buildings, and places that are in the possession of the government if:

1. The item is material to preparation of the defendant's defense, or
2. The item is going to be used by the government at trial, or
3. The item was obtained from, or belongs to, the defendant.

The situations in which this rule might apply are countless. For example, if the police take pictures of the scene of a crime, this provision allows the defendant to view and copy those pictures prior to trial. Or, if the police seize a building that was used to manufacture drugs, the defendant can invoke this rule to gain access to the premises.

This section of Rule 16 has a reciprocal provision. That is, defendants must allow the government to inspect and copy defense items. However, the rule is not as broad for government discovery. Defendants only have to permit inspection and copying of those items intended to be used at trial.

Scientific Reports and Tests

All scientific reports and tests in the possession of the government (or that can be discovered through due diligence) must be turned over to the defendant, if requested.

This provision includes reports and conclusions of mental examinations of the defendant, autopsy reports, drug tests, fingerprint analysis, blood tests, DNA (genetic) tests, ballistic tests, and other related tests and examinations.

The defendant must accord the government reciprocity, if requested. For example, if a defendant undergoes an independent mental examination, the government is entitled to review the report of the evaluator prior to trial.

Statements of Witnesses/Jencks Act

Many jurisdictions require that the prosecution, and in some the defense, provide a list of intended trial witnesses. It is common to require additional information about expert witnesses, such as background and reports they have prepared.

In the federal system, defendants are not entitled to inspect or copy statements of prosecution witnesses prior to trial. However, a federal statute, commonly known as the Jencks Act,[21] permits a defendant to review a prior written or recorded statement after the witness has testified for the government. Reviewing such statements may prove important to show that a witness is inconsistent, biased, or has a bad memory.

This procedure often causes trial delay, as defendants usually request time between direct examination and cross-examination to review such statements. For this reason, some federal prosecutors provide such information prior to trial. The Jencks Act is a matter of federal statutory law and does not apply in state criminal prosecutions.

Depositions

A **deposition** is oral testimony given under oath, not in a court. In civil procedure, depositions are freely conducted. Upon notice to a party or subpoena to a witness, an attorney can call a person to testify prior to trial. This is not so in criminal practice.

Fed. R. Crim. P. 15 allows depositions only when "exceptional circumstances" exist. Expected absence of a witness at trial is an example of an exceptional circumstance. If such a circumstance is shown, the deposition may be ordered by the trial court, and the deposition may be used at trial. Of course, both the defendant and government have the opportunity to question the witness at the deposition.

deposition

■ The process of taking a witness's sworn out-of-court testimony. The questioning is usually done by a lawyer, and the lawyer from the other side is given a chance to attend and participate.

Brady Doctrine

Although most discovery occurs under the authority of statutes and court rules, the Constitution also requires disclosure of information by the government in some situations. In *Brady v. Maryland*, the Supreme Court announced what is now referred to as the Brady doctrine.

Obviously, *Brady* applies to both state and federal prosecutions. Note that only exculpatory evidence must be provided. Evidence that tends to prove a defendant's innocence is exculpatory. *Brady* does not stand for the proposition that prosecutors must reveal incriminating evidence to defendants. Failure to disclose to a defendant will result in reversal of a conviction if there is a reasonable probability that the likelihood of a different result is great enough to undermine confidence in the outcome of the trial.[22]

In most situations, disclosure at trial will satisfy *Brady*. However, if disclosure at trial would prejudice a defendant, pretrial disclosure may be constitutionally required. As is sometimes the case with Jencks Act materials, prosecutors may provide such information prior to trial as a courtesy.

In a case related to *Brady*, the Supreme Court found that it is violative of due process for prosecutors to use perjured testimony or to deceive juries. This is true even if the perjury was unsolicited by the prosecuting attorney. As such, a prosecutor has a duty to correct any testimony of a witness that he or she knows is false.[23]

Although *Brady* and related cases are law in both state and federal prosecutions, the other discovery rules differ. Be sure to check local law to determine what your client has a right to discover.

Freedom of Information Laws

The federal government and most, if not all, states have statutes requiring the public disclosure of files, documents, and other information in the possession of the government.[24] The federal statute is known as the Freedom of Information Act (FOIA).[25]

There are nine exemptions to the federal FOIA. If a request for information falls into one of the nine exemptions, the government may withhold disclosure. Otherwise, disclosure is mandated.

One of the exemptions provides that law enforcement records may be withheld if disclosure will:

1. Interfere with enforcement proceedings.
2. Deprive a person of a fair trial or an impartial adjudication.
3. Constitute an unwarranted invasion of personal privacy.
4. Disclose the identity of a confidential source.
5. Disclose investigative techniques and procedures.
6. Endanger the life or physical safety of law enforcement personnel.

The FOIA is not a discovery device. It is a statute of general applicability, and any person may request inspection or production of documents under its authority. The purpose of the FOIA, which is unrelated to litigation, is the promotion of democracy by having an informed citizenry; it keeps the governors accountable to the governed.

Even though the FOIA was not specifically intended to be used for discovery in litigation, it does not foreclose that use. However, although the FOIA may be used to obtain information, it is not intended to displace or supplement the recognized forms of discovery.[26] Nor shall the process of obtaining information through the FOIA be cause for delaying a criminal proceeding. Therefore, requests for information under the FOIA are separate from a defendant's discovery requests in a criminal case.[27]

Hence, defendants may seek information under the FOIA, but such requests are not part of the criminal discovery process, and criminal proceedings will not be delayed to wait for such requests to be answered or disputes over disclosure to be adjudicated.

The same principles apply to other disclosure laws. For example, the federal Privacy Act[28] provides that individuals have a right to discover the contents of files containing information about them. Again, requests for information under this law are aside from, not in addition to, criminal discovery rules.

Reciprocal Discovery

The Fifth Amendment's freedom from self-incrimination clause, as well as due process, greatly limits what can be expected of defendants in discovery. Requiring defendants to give notice of affirmative defenses, such as alibi and insanity, is common and constitutional. Many jurisdictions also expect defendants to provide witness lists, pretrial statements of the witnesses, and to detail expert testimony and reports that will be offered at trial.

Motion Practice

In both civil and criminal practice, a motion is a request made to a court for it to do something. In most cases a party that files a motion is seeking an order from the court. Generally, when a person desires something from a court, a formal motion must be filed and copies sent to opposing counsel. On occasion, oral motions are made. This is most common during trials and hearings. Some of the most common motions are discussed here.

Motion to Dismiss/Quash

If a defendant believes that the indictment or information is fatally flawed, the appropriate remedy is a motion to dismiss. In some jurisdictions, this would be called a motion to quash. Examples of fatal flaws in the charging instrument are as follows: the court lacks jurisdiction; the facts alleged do not amount to a crime; an essential element is not charged; or the defendant has a legal defense, such as double jeopardy.

If the form of the charging instrument is attacked, courts often permit prosecutors to amend the charge rather than dismissing it entirely. Dismissal of an indictment or information does not mean that the defendant cannot be recharged. A person is not in "jeopardy" under the Fifth Amendment until later in the proceeding.

Motion to Suppress

You have already learned that evidence obtained in an unconstitutional manner may not be used at trial. Objection at trial to the admission of such evidence is one method of excluding such evidence. Another is by way of a motion to suppress prior to trial.

A separate hearing is conducted prior to trial to determine whether the motion to suppress should be granted. Defendants may testify at suppression hearings, and their testimony may not be used against them at trial.[29] To allow a defendant's testimony from a suppression hearing to be used at trial would place the defendant in a position of choosing between the right to suppress evidence and the right to be free from self-incrimination. The best alternative is to allow the defendant to testify and to prohibit that testimony from being used later.

Who has the burden of proof in suppression hearings varies by jurisdiction and on what the defendant wishes to be suppressed. For example, most jurisdictions place the burden of proving that a search pursuant to a warrant was unconstitutional on the defendant. The opposite is true if there was no warrant; the government bears the burden of proving the propriety of the search. Most jurisdictions also place the burden of proving that a confession was voluntary upon the prosecution.

Motion for Change of Venue

Venue means "place for trial." In state criminal proceedings, venue usually lies in the county where the crime occurred. In federal proceedings, venue lies in the district where the crime occurred. Many federal crimes are interstate in character, and the charges may be filed in any district where the crime took place.

Fed. R. Crim. P. 21 permits transfer of a case from one district to another if "the defendant cannot obtain a fair and impartial trial" at the location where the case is pending. In addition, a district judge may transfer a case if it is most convenient for the defendant and witnesses.

Pretrial publicity of criminal matters may be cause to transfer a case (change venue in state proceedings). If a defendant receives considerable negative media coverage, it may be necessary to try the defendant in another location. Several factors are taken into consideration when a defendant moves for a change of venue due to excessive negative publicity, including the total amount of coverage, whether media attention had increased or waned since the case first became public, the length of time between first coverage and trial, the extent to which the coverage itself directly accused or implied guilt, and the nature of the facts that had been brought to light.

The early 2000s witnessed some of the largest and most costly financial scandals in U.S. history. Millions of people lost money and the economies of many nations suffered as a result of corruption in the accounting, banking, investment, energy, and other industries. Enron, one of the United States' largest corporations, found itself bankrupt in 2001. Jeffrey Skillings, its president and CEO, was charged and convicted, among others, as having lied to shareholders and others about the financial status of the company pre-bankruptcy. The case generated considerable attention around the world. Believing he could not be given a fair trial in Houston, Texas, the site of Enron's headquarters and where the charges were filed, he sought a change of venue. The trial court denied his motion. Eventually, the Supreme Court heard his case.

Because of the First Amendment free press issue, judges are generally prohibited from excluding the press or public from hearings.[30] In some instances judges may order the attorneys involved in a case not to provide information to anyone not involved in the proceeding.

Motion for Severance

Fed. R. Crim. P. 8 permits two or more defendants to be charged in the same information or indictment if they were involved in the same crime. That rule also permits joinder of two offenses by the same person in one charging instrument, provided they are similar in character or arise out of the same set of facts.

In some situations, severance of the two defendants may be necessary to assure fair trials. For example, if two defendants have antagonistic defenses, severance must be granted. Defenses are *antagonistic* if the jury must disbelieve one by believing the other. For example, if Defendant A denies being at the scene of a crime, and Defendant B claims that they were both there, but also claims that A forced him to commit the crime, their defenses are antagonistic.

If a defendant is charged with two or more offenses, it may be necessary to sever them to have a fair trial. For example, if a defendant plans to testify concerning one charge and not the other, severance is necessary.

Motion in Limine

Prior to trial, both the defendant and the prosecution may file motions in limine. This is a request that the court order the other party not to mention or attempt to question a witness about some matter. A motion in limine is similar to a motion to suppress, except that it encompasses more than admission of illegally seized evidence.

For example, if one anticipates that the opposing counsel will attempt to question a witness about evidence that is inadmissible under the rules of evidence (e.g., hearsay), a motion in limine may be filed to avoid having to object at trial. This is important, as often a witness may blurt out the answer before an attorney has had an opportunity to object. In addition, knowing whether the judge will permit the admission of evidence prior to trial helps an attorney to plan the case.

Other Motions

A variety of other motions may be filed. If the prosecution fears that revealing information required under a discovery rule will endanger the case or a person's life, a motion for a protective order may be filed. In such cases the trial court reviews the evidence in camera and decides if it is necessary to keep it from the defendant. If so, the judge will enter a protective order so stating.

Motions for continuance of hearings and trial dates are common. In criminal cases, courts must be careful not to violate speedy trial requirements.

If two defendants have been charged jointly, one or both may file a motion for severance of trial. If defense counsel believes that the defendant is not competent to stand trial, a motion for mental examination may be filed.

Pretrial Conference

Sometime prior to trial, the court will hold a pretrial conference. This may be weeks or only days before trial.

At this conference the court will address any remaining motions and discuss any problems the parties have. In addition, the judge will explain his or her method of trying a case, such as how the jury will be selected. The next stage is trial.

EXTRADITION AND DETAINERS

If wanted persons are located outside the jurisdiction where they are, or will be, charged, **extradition** is one method of securing their presence in the charging jurisdiction. *Extradition* is the surrender of a person from one jurisdiction to another where the person has been charged or convicted of a crime.

Extradition usually occurs under the provisions of a treaty. Extradition includes transfers between states, as well as between nations. Extradition, especially international, is as much a political decision as a legal one.

Pursuant to the Uniform Interstate Criminal Extradition Act, which has been adopted by 47 states,[31] the request for extradition is made between governors. If a governor determines that the person sought should be delivered, an arrest warrant is issued by that governor.

Once seized, the arrestee is brought before a judge and may file a petition for writ of habeas corpus. During the proceedings, release on bail is permitted, unless the crime charged is one punishable by death or life imprisonment in the state where the crime was committed. If the person sought is under charge in the sending state, the governor may order his or her surrender immediately or may wait until the prosecution and punishment are completed in the first state.

extradition

■ One country (or state) giving up a person to a second country (or state) when the second requests the person for a trial on a criminal charge or for punishment after a trial.

Generally, the guilt or innocence of the accused may not be considered by the governor or courts during the proceedings; that issue is left to the requesting jurisdiction. It is the obligation of the governor and courts of the sending state to be sure that the correct person is seized and that proper procedures are followed.

Defendants may waive extradition. This waiver must be made in court, and defendants must be informed of their rights, including habeas corpus, for waivers to be valid.

The law permits arrests by police officers from outside a state in hot-pursuit situations. If an arrest is made in hot pursuit, the officer is to bring the accused before a local court, which is to order the defendant held, or released on bail, until an extradition warrant is issued by the governor.

The Supreme Court has held that the exclusionary rule does not exclude persons who have been illegally seized from trial. In *Frisbie v. Collins*, 342 U.S. 519 (1952), the fact that Michigan police officers kidnapped a defendant from Illinois and returned him to Michigan, disregarding extradition laws, did not affect the court's jurisdiction to try the defendant. The same result was reached in a case in which international extradition laws were not followed.[32] Today, if the government's conduct in seizing a defendant were outrageous or shocking, there is a possibility that a court would bar prosecution.[33]

You may recall from discussion of double jeopardy earlier in this text that the Fifth Amendment's Double Jeopardy Clause does not prevent two sovereigns from charging an individual for the same crime or two crimes arising from the same facts. Accordingly, one state may grant immunity to an individual and then extradite that individual to another state to be tried for the immunized crime.

A **detainer** is a request (or order) for the continued custody of a prisoner. For example, suppose federal charges are pending against a Utah prisoner. The United States would issue a detainer requesting that Utah hold the prisoner after his or her sentence is completed, so that the United States may take custody. This situation does not raise jurisdictional issues, as federal authorities have nationwide jurisdiction. As to interstate detention, the detainer is used in conjunction with extradition.

Pursuant to the Interstate Agreement on Detainers, a state may request the temporary custody of a prisoner of another state in order to try the person. Once the trial is completed, the prisoner is returned, regardless of the outcome. If the prisoner is convicted, a detainer is issued and he or she is again returned after the sentence is completed in the sending state.

The Agreement also provides that prisoners are to be notified of any detainers against them. Further, if a state issues a detainer for a prisoner, that prisoner may request to be temporarily transferred to that state for final disposition of that case. A request for final disposition by a prisoner is deemed a waiver of extradition to and from the sending state. Also, it is deemed a waiver of extradition to the receiving state to serve any resulting sentence after the sentence in the sending state is completed.

It is a common practice for jail and prison officials to conduct warrant checks before releasing or transferring prisoners. The importance of this practice was highlighted by the tragic events leading to the death of 6-year-old Jake Robel. On February 20, 2000, a local jail in Missouri released Kim Davis. Within hours of his

detainer

■ A warrant or court order to keep a person in custody when that person might otherwise be released. This is often used to make sure a person will serve a sentence or attend a trial in one state at the end of a prison term in another state or in a federal prison.

release, Davis carjacked an automobile owned by Christy Robel. Christy's son, Jake Robel, was in the automobile at the time Kim Davis stole the car. Ms. Robel attempted to remove her son from the car, but he became entangled in the seatbelt and her pleas to Kim Davis to stop were ignored. She was dragged for a short distance before she lost her grip of the car. Tangled in the seatbelt and hanging out of the car, Jake Robel was dragged five miles by Kim Davis while driving at speeds reaching 80 miles per hour. Jake was dead by the time Kim Davis was forced to stop the vehicle. It was discovered that there was an outstanding warrant for the arrest of Kim Davis when he was released and that a warrants check had not been conducted by jail officials. Kim Davis was subsequently convicted of second-degree murder and sentenced to life imprisonment. In response to the records check oversight, Missouri enacted "Jake's Law," a statute requiring records checks of individuals scheduled for release from jails and prison in Missouri.

REMOVAL

Congress has provided that, in certain circumstances, criminal cases may be removed from state courts to federal courts. Removal is premised upon the principle that certain cases are more properly adjudicated in a federal, rather than state, court. The purpose of removal is to preserve the sovereignty of the federal government by assuring a fair trial to particular criminal defendants. Otherwise, the states could interfere with the functioning of the federal government by harassing federal officials through criminal proceedings.

28 U.S.C. § 1442 provides that a federal official sued in state court, whether the action is civil or criminal, may remove the case to the federal district court where the action is pending, if the suit concerns the performance of his or her official duties. Similarly, 28 U.S.C. § 1442(a) provides for removal of cases, civil or criminal, filed against members of the U.S. armed forces for actions taken in the course of their duties. 28 U.S.C. § 1443 provides for removal of certain civil rights cases.

Removal of criminal cases is the same as for civil: The defendant must file a notice of, and petition for, removal.[34] Improperly removed actions are remanded to the state court from which they came.[35]

Web Links

Directory of Attorneys

For a listing of attorneys, try one of these two sites: Martindale-Hubbell at http://www.martindale.com/ or http://lawyers.findlaw.com

Key Terms

arraignment
arrest
bail
bill of particulars
complaint
deposition
detainer
discovery
extradition
grand juries
indictment
information
motion
plea
plea bargain (plea agreement)
preliminary hearing
quash

Review Questions

1. For what two reasons may a defendant be detained prior to trial?
2. What is the difference between an indictment and an information?
3. What are the purposes of indictments and informations?
4. If a defendant needs more information than appears in the indictment to prepare a defense, what should be done?
5. What advantage does a plea of nolo contendere have over a guilty plea?
6. Kevin has been charged with murder. He believes a weapon that the prosecutor plans on using at trial was unconstitutionally seized from his home. How can he raise this issue prior to trial?
7. Place the following in the proper order of occurrence: preliminary hearing; formal charge; initial appearance; arraignment; trial; and complaint.
8. What is the Brady doctrine?
9. When is removal from state to federal court allowed?
10. What is extradition?

Problems & Critical Thinking Exercises

1. What is the historical purpose of the grand jury? Many feel that grand juries should be abolished. Why?
2. Discovery in civil cases is very broad. Fed. R. Civ. P. 26 permits discovery of anything "reasonably calculated to lead to the discovery of admissible evidence." Should discovery in criminal cases be broader? Explain your position.
3. Do you believe that indictment by grand jury should be incorporated? Explain your position.

Endnotes

1. Fed. R. Crim. P. 4.
2. Fed. R. Crim. P. 5.
3. 500 U.S. 44 (1991).
4. *Stack v. Boyle*, 342 U.S. 1 (1951).

5. 18 U.S.C. § 3142(f).
6. 18 U.S.C. § 3142(e), (f).
7. *Gerstein v. Pugh,* 420 U.S. 103 (1975).
8. Fed. R. Crim. P. 5.1; 18 U.S.C. § 3060.
9. 18 U.S.C. § 3060(e).
10. *United States v. Mandujano,* 425 U.S. 564 (1976).
11. *United States v. Calandra,* 414 U.S. 338 (1974).
12. Fed. R. Crim. P. 6.
13. *Ex parte Wilson,* 114 U.S. 417 (1884). *See also* Fed. R. Crim. P. 7.
14. Fed. R. Crim. P. 7(c).
15. Fed. R. Crim. P. 8(a).
16. *See United States v. Cox,* 342 F.2d 167 (5th Cir.), *cert. denied,* 381 U.S. 935 (1965).
17. Fed. R. Crim. P. 7(c).
18. See *United States v. Davila,* U.S. (2013)
19. Fed. R. Crim. P. 11.
20. *United States v. Diecidue,* 603 F.2d 535 (5th Cir.), *cert. denied,* 445 U.S. 946 (1979).
21. 18 U.S.C. § 3500.
22. *Smith v. Cain,* 564 U.S.(2012).
23. *Mooney v. Holohan,* 294 U.S. 103 (1935).
24. See Daniel Hall, *Administrative Law: Bureaucracy in a Democracy,* 4th ed., ch. 10 (Upper Saddle River, NJ: Pearson: Prentice Hall, 2009), for a more thorough discussion of the Freedom of Information Act.
25. 5 U.S.C. § 552.
26. *John Doe Corp. v. John Doe Agency,* 493 U.S. 146 (1989).
27. *North v. Walsh,* 881 F.2d 1088 (D.C. Cir. 1989).
28. 5 U.S.C. § 552(a).
29. *Simmons v. United States,* 390 U.S. 377 (1968).
30. *Richmond Newspapers, Inc. v. Virginia,* 448 U.S. 555 (1980).
31. Rhonda Wasserman, "The Subpoena Power: *Pennoyer's* Last Vestige," 74 *Minn. L. Rev.* 37 (1989).
32. *Ker v. Illinois,* 119 U.S. 436 (1886).
33. *See United States v. Toscanino,* 500 F.2d 267 (2d Cir. 1974).
34. 28 U.S.C. § 1446.
35. 28 U.S.C. § 1447.

CHAPTER 6
TRIAL

Chapter Outline

Trial Rights of Defendants
    The Right to a Jury Trial
    The Right to a Public Trial
    The Right to Confrontation and Cross-Examination
    The Presumption of Innocence/ Burden of Proof
    The Right to Speedy Trial
    The Right to Counsel

Trial Procedure
    Voir Dire
    Preliminary Instructions
    Opening Statements
    The Prosecution's Case in Chief
    The Defense Case
    Rebuttal
    Closing Arguments
    Final Instructions
    Jury Deliberations and Verdict
    JNOV/New Trial

Chapter Objectives

After completing this chapter, you should be able to:

- identify and explain, in sequence, the various steps and procedures of trial.
- list, describe, and identify the landmark cases discussed in the book for the constitutional rights possessed by defendants at trial, such as the right to a public, speedy, jury trial, counsel, to remain silent, to cross-examine witnesses, and to confront accusers.
- identify the material facts and legal issues in nearly all of the cases you read, describe the courts' analyses and conclusions in the cases, and demonstrate the ability to synthesize and think critically about the law of the subject.

TRIAL RIGHTS OF DEFENDANTS

The Right to a Jury Trial

A trial is a method of determining guilt or innocence. In medieval England, trials by ordeal, combat, and compurgation were used.

To demonstrate how trials have changed, consider trial by ordeal. Trial by ordeal was considered trial by God; that is, God determined the person's guilt or innocence. There were two ordeals: by water and fire. Two water ordeals were used. In the first the accused was thrown into a body of water. If he sank he was adjudged innocent, and if he floated he was guilty. In the second water ordeal, the accused's arm was submerged in boiling water. The defendant had to survive this unhurt to be proven innocent. The fire ordeal was similar, the accused having to walk over fire or grasp hot irons.

Trial as we know it today finds its roots in the Magna Carta (1215), which guaranteed free men trial by their peers. Unlike juries today, those juries comprised people who knew the facts of the case. The concept of trial by a jury of one's peers was of great importance to the colonists of the United States and made its way into the Constitution of the United States.

The Sixth Amendment to the U.S. Constitution reads, in part, "[i]n all criminal prosecutions, the accused shall enjoy the right to a speedy and public trial, by an impartial jury of the State and district wherein the crime shall have been committed." The Sixth Amendment is fully applicable against the states via the Fourteenth Amendment. See exhibit 6-1 for an illustration of the trial rights found in the Sixth Amendment.

The Sixth Amendment has been interpreted to mean that defendants have a right to a jury trial for all offenses that may be punished with more than six months' imprisonment. Most crimes that have as their maximum punishment less than six months are "petty offenses," and there is no right to trial by jury.[1]

Note that the term "most" is used. Some argue that when fines become large enough, one is entitled to a jury trial, regardless of the amount of time one could be sentenced to spend in jail. In addition, it is argued that crimes that are moral in nature and subject the defendant to ridicule and embarrassment justify trial by jury, even when the punishment is less than six months' imprisonment. The same question is raised concerning crimes that were indictable at common law. The Supreme Court has not answered these questions, and the lower courts that have addressed these issues are split.

The maximum penalty allowed determines if a crime is petty, not the actual sentence. For example, if a crime is punishable by from three months to one year in jail, the defendant is entitled to a jury, even if the trial judge routinely sentences those convicted to three months for the offense. Some crimes do not have a legislatively established punishment, such as contempt. In such cases the issue is whether the defendant is sentenced to more than six months in jail. If so, the defendant is entitled to a jury.

Although the right to a jury trial for nonpetty offenses nearly always attaches, there are a few exceptions. There is no right to a jury in military trials. In addition, those appearing in juvenile court (delinquency proceedings) are not entitled to a jury trial.[2] Of course, juveniles who are tried as adults are entitled to the same rights as adults, including the right to have a jury trial.

Juries sit as fact finders. A defendant may be entitled to have a jury decide guilt or innocence, and as you learn in the next chapter, there is also a right to have juries decide the facts that are essential to passing sentence. Some jurisdictions have juries actually impose sentence, or make a sentence recommendation to the trial court; however, this is not usually the practice and there is no federal constitutional reason for it.

The Supreme Court has held that there is no constitutional requirement for 12 jurors.[3] Nor does the Constitution require juror unanimity. There is a limit to how small a jury may be and how few jurors must concur in a verdict. In one case, the Supreme Court found a law unconstitutional that required trial by six jurors and permitted conviction with a vote of five to one.[4]

It is common for six-person juries to be used for misdemeanors. However, a unanimous verdict is constitutionally required for conviction. If a 12-member jury is used, it is constitutional to permit conviction upon a concurrence of 9 or more jurors.

A defendant cannot be penalized for choosing to proceed to trial rather than pleading guilty. In *United States v. Jackson*, 390 U.S. 570 (1968), the Supreme Court found that a statute making the death penalty available for those who were tried and not for those who pled guilty was violative of the Sixth Amendment. An interesting question that has received considerable attention from the Supreme Court in recent years is exactly what facts must be found by a jury. As you will learn in the next chapter, the responsibility of juries extends beyond the guilt decision. They must also find all facts that are essential to the sentencing decision.

The Right to a Public Trial

The Sixth Amendment also guarantees the right to a public trial. This guarantee applies throughout the trial, from openings to return of the verdict; it also applies to many pretrial hearings, such as suppression hearings. The presence of the public is intended to keep prosecutions "honest." As the Supreme Court stated in *Estes v. Texas*, 381 U.S. 532 (1965): "History has proven that secret tribunals were effective instruments of oppression."

The right to a public hearing does not mean that everyone who wishes to attend has to be permitted in. The trial judge is responsible for maintaining order in the courtroom and may require the doors to be shut once all seats have been filled. Also, a disruptive citizen may be removed.

The defendant's right to a public trial is not absolute. Trial judges, acting with extreme caution, may order that a hearing be conducted in private. Facts that support excluding the public are rare. An example of when exclusion of the public may be justified is when an undercover law enforcement agent testifies, and public exposure would put the officer's life in jeopardy.

If a court closes a hearing (or trial) without justification, the defendant is entitled to a new hearing, regardless of whether the defendant was actually harmed. The 1998 First Circuit Court of Appeals case, *United States v. DeLuca*, addressed both the presumption of innocence and the right to a public trial in what are rather unusual circumstances.

Generally members of the press have no greater right to attend a hearing than do other members of the public. However, many judges provide special seating for reporters.

The Right to Confrontation and Cross-Examination

The Sixth Amendment also contains a right to confront one's accusers. This means that a defendant has the right to cross-examine the witnesses of the prosecution. Each state drafts its own rules of evidence; however, it may not enact a rule of evidence that conflicts with a defendant's right to confrontation.

For example, a state procedure permitting government witnesses to refuse to identify themselves was found violative of the Sixth Amendment.[5] The Supreme Court reasoned that the procedure was invalid because it did not permit the defendant to conduct his or her own investigation into the credibility of government witnesses.

Statutes allowing victims to testify remotely, such as by closed-circuit television, also raise confrontation issues. However, the Supreme Court has stated that the Confrontation Clause does not per se prohibit child witnesses in child abuse cases from testifying outside the defendant's physical presence by one-way closed-circuit television. Before such a procedure is used, however, the court must examine the facts of the case and determine that remote testimony is necessary.[6] Failure to make such a finding (e.g., the child fears the defendant) can lead to reversal.[7]

The Confrontation Clause does not give defendants carte blanche to probe any area on cross-examination. If a state can show a compelling reason, it may prohibit cross-examination of a subject. For example, rape shield laws prohibit defendants from inquiring into a rape victim's sexual background in most cases. Courts have affirmed such laws, finding that the protection of the rape victims from unwarranted personal attacks is a legitimate reason to limit defense cross-examination.

The Confrontation Clause also restricts the government's use of hearsay evidence. *Hearsay* is a statement made by a person out of court that is intended to *prove the matter asserted*. To prove the matter asserted means, in plain language, that the out of court statement must prove, or support, the matter fact that the attorney is trying to make. For example, in a trial of Samuel for murder, it is hearsay for him to testify that a third person, Ambrose, told him that he observed Samuel commit the murder because the purpose of the testimony is to prove the matter asserted, e.g. Samuel committed the murder. The prosecutor in this instance must find and call Ambrose to testify.

There are exceptions to the hearsay rule, and hearsay is commonly admitted in civil trials. However, the Confrontation Clause limits the admissibility of hearsay in criminal trials. To be admissible, it must be shown that the (1) witness is unavailable at trial and (2) the defendant had a prior opportunity to examine the witness. This standard was announced by the Court in *Crawford v. Washington,* a case where a wife's statement to police that incriminated her husband had committed a crime was determined to be inadmissible because she was unavailable at trial to the prosecutor because of the marital privilege. The Court limited its Confrontation Clause protection to hearsay—evidence that is introduced to prove the matter asserted. Since the matter at hand in *Crawford* was intended to prove the guilt of the husband, the wife's incriminating statements to the police were excluded. As you will learn in a moment, the exception for non-testimonial statements will prove significant in a later case.[8]

The Confrontation Clause implicitly includes a right of a defendant to be at the trial. This right includes the entire trial, from selection of the jury to return of the verdict. It also includes many pretrial matters, such as suppression hearings. Of course, defendants have a right to be present at both sentencing and probation revocation hearings. Although the right to be present during one's trial is fundamental, it may be lost by disruptive behavior.

There is a long and widely accepted exception to evidence and Confrontation Clause rules that permits purely scientific evidence to be admitted through a report. Unless a defendant had evidence to challenge the validity of such a test, courts in most states and in the federal system admit scientific reports without requiring the scientist or lab attendant to testify. The Supreme Court appeared to have altered this long-standing practice in two cases, *Melendez-Diaz* and *Bullcoming*.

Note that a strongly worded dissent by four justices criticized the majority for setting aside over two hundred years of evidentiary law that permitted the admission of scientific testing through authenticated reports, citing the concern that the requirement of having analysts testify in all cases where scientific reports are introduced will be burdensome, expensive, and often difficult to implement.

In spite of the strongly worded dissent, the Court reaffirmed *Melendez-Dias* in the 2011 case *Bullcoming v. New Mexico*, where the use of a surrogate lab technician who testified on behalf of the technician who conducted a blood alcohol test was invalidated by the Court as contrary to the Confrontation Clause. The Court found that the analyst who conducted the test had to testify at trial or be available pretrial to testify and be subjected to cross-examination by the defendant.[9]

What appeared to be clear and settled law was dealt a confusing blow in 2012. In a 5-4 decision with no one rationale commanding a majority of justices, the Court decided in *Williams v. Illinois*[10] that the testimony of a forensic DNA expert who testified that the DNA of semen taken from a vaginal swab of a rape victim and analyzed at a private lab, Cellmark, which matched the defendant, was admissible. This expert did not conduct the testing and most likely had never been in the Cellmark lab.

Because the justices were divided, it is difficult to identify exactly how they distinguished the case from *Crawford, Melendez-Diaz,* and *Bullcomings*. But a few ideas can be extracted from the opinions. First, the testing occurred before the defendant had been identified as a suspect. The DNA profile had been built in order to identify an unknown rapist. Accordingly, the profile was not aimed at the defendant. Accordingly, the important purpose of enabling defendants to cross-examine witnesses "against them" would not have been satisfied by prohibiting the expert's testimony.

Second, the expert's statements were not hearsay. She didn't testify to prove the matter asserted—that is, she didn't testify as to the testing or the contents of the testing report. The Court summarized the expert's testimony as such:

> In order to assess petitioner's Confrontation Clause argument, it is helpful to inventory exactly what Lambatos said on the stand about Cellmark. She testified to the truth of the following matters: Cellmark was an accredited lab; the ISP occasionally sent forensic samples to Cellmark for DNA testing; according to shipping manifests admitted into evidence, the ISP lab sent vaginal swabs taken from the victim to Cellmark and

later received those swabs back from Cellmark; and, finally, the Cellmark DNA profile matched a profile produced by the ISP lab from a sample of petitioner's blood. Lambatos had personal knowledge of all of these matters, and therefore none of this testimony infringed petitioner's confrontation right.

Third, the case was tried before a judge. The law assumes that judges have a better understanding of the law and are better at categorizing evidence and not considering it for purposes beyond what is permitted than jurors. In this case the expert's testimony was not admitted to prove that the quality of the testing and the judge is presumed to have not considered it for such purposes. Whether the decision would have been different if the case had been tried before a jury is unclear. But it easy to imagine that many jurors would interpret the testimony as proving the guilt of the defendant. The full impact of this decision will be revealed in the years to come.

The Presumption of Innocence/Burden of Proof

One of the most basic rights underlying the right to a fair trial is the presumption of innocence. All those accused must be proven guilty by the government. Criminal defendants have no duty to defend themselves and may remain silent throughout the trial. In fact, the government is prohibited from calling defendants to testify, and defendants cannot be made to decide whether they will testify at the start of the trial.[11] The fact that a defendant chooses not to testify may not be mentioned by the prosecutor to the jury. Defendants may testify in their own behalf. If so, they are subject to full cross-examination by the prosecutor. The Fifth Amendment right to be free from self-incrimination is discussed more fully in Chapter 14.

The standard imposed upon the government in criminal cases is to prove guilt **beyond a reasonable doubt.** A doubt that would cause a reasonable or prudent person to question the guilt of the accused is a reasonable doubt. Although not precisely quantified, beyond a reasonable doubt is greater than the civil preponderance (51 percent likely) and less than absolute (100 percent confidence of guilt). See the standards of proof graphic in Chapter 12 to refresh your understanding of the different standards that are employed in criminal law. The prosecution must prove every element of the charged crime beyond a reasonable doubt. The reasonable doubt standard is an important feature of the accusatorial system of the United States and is required by due process.[12] A juror must vote for acquittal if he or she harbors a reasonable doubt.

To further the presumption of innocence, judges must be careful not to behave in a manner that implies to a jury that a defendant is guilty.

The court and government must be careful not to create a physical setting that implies guilt. The Supreme Court has stated that the presence of a defendant at a jury trial in prison clothing is prejudicial.[13] In the *Young* case, a federal appellate court reviewed the use of "prisoner docks" for a Sixth Amendment violation. Similarly, a criminal defendant also has a right to be free from appearing before the jury in handcuffs or shackles.

beyond a reasonable doubt

■ The level of proof required to convict a person of a crime. Precise definitions vary, but moral certainty and firm belief are both used. Beyond a reasonable doubt is not absolute certainty. This is the highest level of proof required in any type of trial.

The government's needs are balanced against the defendant's, however. In *Holbrook v. Flynn*, 475 U.S. 560 (1986), the Court stated that not all practices that single out the defendant are excessively prejudicial. The Court held that some prejudice may exist. The question is whether there is unacceptable prejudice that is not justified by governmental necessity. Using this standard, the Court allowed a conviction to stand where the defendant objected to the presence of four police officers in the first row of the spectator gallery, directly behind the defendant, during trial.

Trial judges also have a responsibility to monitor private conduct in the courtroom to ensure unacceptable unfairness to the defendant does not happen. For example, spectators are not permitted to express opinions about the case to jurors. Whether more subtle behaviors, such as wearing a button with a photo of the victim, are unacceptably prejudicial remains to be seen.[14]

This right to be free of restraint is not absolute. Judges have the authority to take whatever measures are necessary to assure safety in the courtroom and to advance the administration of justice. Accordingly, a defendant who is disorderly may be expelled from the trial. However, before exclusion is ordered the court should consider other alternatives. Defendants who are threatening may be restrained, and those who verbally interfere with the proceeding may be gagged.[15]

The Right to Speedy Trial

All criminal defendants have a right to a speedy trial. It is the Sixth Amendment, as extended by the Fourteenth Amendment to the states, that guarantees speedy trial. This right has a history dating back to at least the Magna Carta.

To date, the United States Supreme Court has not set a specific number of days within which trial must be conducted. Rather, the Court said in *Barker v. Wingo* that four factors

Exhibit 6–1 SIXTH AMENDMENT TRIAL RIGHTS

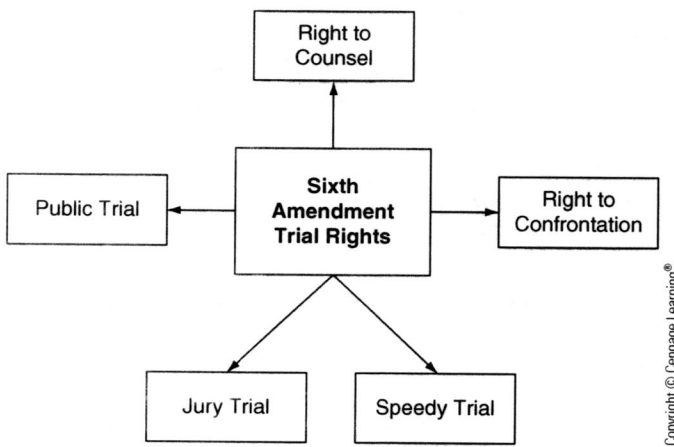

must be considered when determining if a defendant has enjoyed a speedy trial. First, the length of the delay; second, the reason for the delay; third, whether the defendant has asserted the right to a speedy trial; fourth, how seriously the defendant was prejudiced.[16]

Time for speedy trial begins once the defendant is arrested or formally charged.[17] If a defendant is charged by sealed indictment, speedy trial does not start until the indictment has been opened.

Dismissal with prejudice is the remedy for violation of speedy trial. That is, the charge is dismissed and may not be refiled by the prosecutor.

All the states and the national government have enacted speedy trial acts. The Speedy Trial Act of 1974[18] is the federal statute. That act requires that individuals be formally charged within 30 days from the date of arrest and tried within 70 days of the filing date of the information or indictment, or of the date the defendant had the initial appearance before the court that will try the case, whichever is later.

To avoid prejudice by having a trial before a defendant has had an opportunity to prepare a defense, the statute provides that trial shall not occur for 30 days, unless the defendant consents to an earlier date.

The statute specifies certain delays that are excluded from computing time for purpose of speedy trial. A few of the periods excluded by the Speedy Trial Act of 1974 are when the defendant is a fugitive; when trial is delayed because an issue is on appeal; when delays are caused by motions of the parties; and when delays result from mental examinations of the defendant.

The Speedy Trial Act of 1974 gives the trial court the discretion to decide whether violation of its provisions justifies a dismissal with or without prejudice. Factors that must be considered are the seriousness of the offense, the reason for delay, other facts of the case, and the impact of reprosecution on the administration of justice.[19]

Because the United States Supreme Court has not established specific time requirements for speedy trial, each state has its own time requirements. Of course, states must comply with the requirements of *Barker v. Wingo*. Most states have speedy trial provisions in their constitutions, which are similar, if not identical, to the Sixth Amendment. Other states set their speedy trial requirements out in statute or court rules. Time requirements differ, but trial within six months is common.

The Right to Counsel

The Sixth Amendment to the U.S. Constitution provides that "in all criminal prosecutions, the accused shall enjoy the right . . . to have the Assistance of Counsel for his defense." The right to counsel is one of the most fundamental rights guaranteed to criminal defendants and is fully applicable to the states.

The right to the assistance of counsel is found not only in the Sixth Amendment but also in the Fifth and Fourteenth Amendments. These alternative sources are discussed later in the particular contexts within which they apply.

Indigency

It has always been clear that criminal defendants are entitled to retain the attorney of their choice. It was not until 1923 that the United States Supreme Court recognized a constitutional right to appointed counsel for indigent defendants in *Powell v. Alabama*, 287 U.S. 45 (1923).

In the *Powell* case (commonly known as the Scottsboro case), nine young black males were charged with the rape of two white girls. Within one week of arrest, the defendants were tried. Eight of the "Scottsboro boys" were convicted and sentenced to death. The defendants appealed, claiming that they should have been provided counsel. The Supreme Court agreed.

However, the right to appointed counsel in *Powell* was not founded upon the Sixth Amendment, but upon the Fourteenth. The Court reasoned that the absence of counsel deprived the defendants of a fair trial, and, accordingly, violated the defendants' due process rights. This decision was narrow: It applied only to capital cases where the defendant was incapable of preparing an adequate defense and did not have the resources to hire an attorney.

The due process right to counsel was subsequently extended to all situations in which a defendant would not have a fair trial in the absence of defense counsel. Whether counsel was required depended on each particular case's "totality of facts." If denial of counsel was "shocking to the universal sense of justice," then the defendant's right to a fair trial, as guaranteed by the Fourteenth Amendment, was violated.[20] The Court refused to extend the right to counsel to all state criminal proceedings. Cases that involve complex legal issues or a defendant of low intelligence are the types of situation that required the appointment of counsel under the *Betts* due process standard.

In 1938 the Court decided *Johnson v. Zerbst*, 304 U.S. 458 (1938), which held that the Sixth Amendment guarantees a right to counsel. The Sixth Amendment right to counsel was found to be broader than the right to counsel announced in *Powell*, as it applied to all criminal prosecutions. However, *Zerbst* did not apply to state proceedings. Eventually, the Sixth Amendment right to counsel was extended to all state felony proceedings, in *Gideon v. Wainwright*.

Subsequently, the right to counsel was again extended to encompass all criminal cases punished with a jail term. Whether the crime is labeled a misdemeanor or felony is not dispositive of the right-to-counsel issue.[21] In the 2002 case, *Alabama v. Shelton*, the Supreme Court extended the right again. In *Shelton*, the right to counsel was found for a convictee who was sentenced to imprisonment, even though the entire sentence was suspended to probation.

In some cases, it may be to the prosecution's advantage for a defendant to have counsel, even though a sentence of imprisonment is not available for a first conviction, but is available for subsequent convictions. This is because a sentence may not be enhanced to include jail time based on a prior conviction where the defendant possessed a right to, but was denied, counsel.[22] For example, the penalty for first-offense drunk driving is not punished by a term in jail; however, subsequent violations are. If Jack is arrested and convicted without counsel for his first offense, he may not be sentenced to jail time for his second drunk driving conviction, because he did not have counsel during his first trial.

To qualify for appointed counsel, a defendant does not have to be financially destitute. It need only be shown that the defendant's financial situation will prevent him or her from being able to retain an attorney. An indigent defendant does not have a right to choose the appointed attorney; this decision falls within the discretion of the trial court. See Exhibit 6–2 for a summary of when the right to counsel attaches.

Exhibit 6–2 THE RIGHT TO COUNSEL

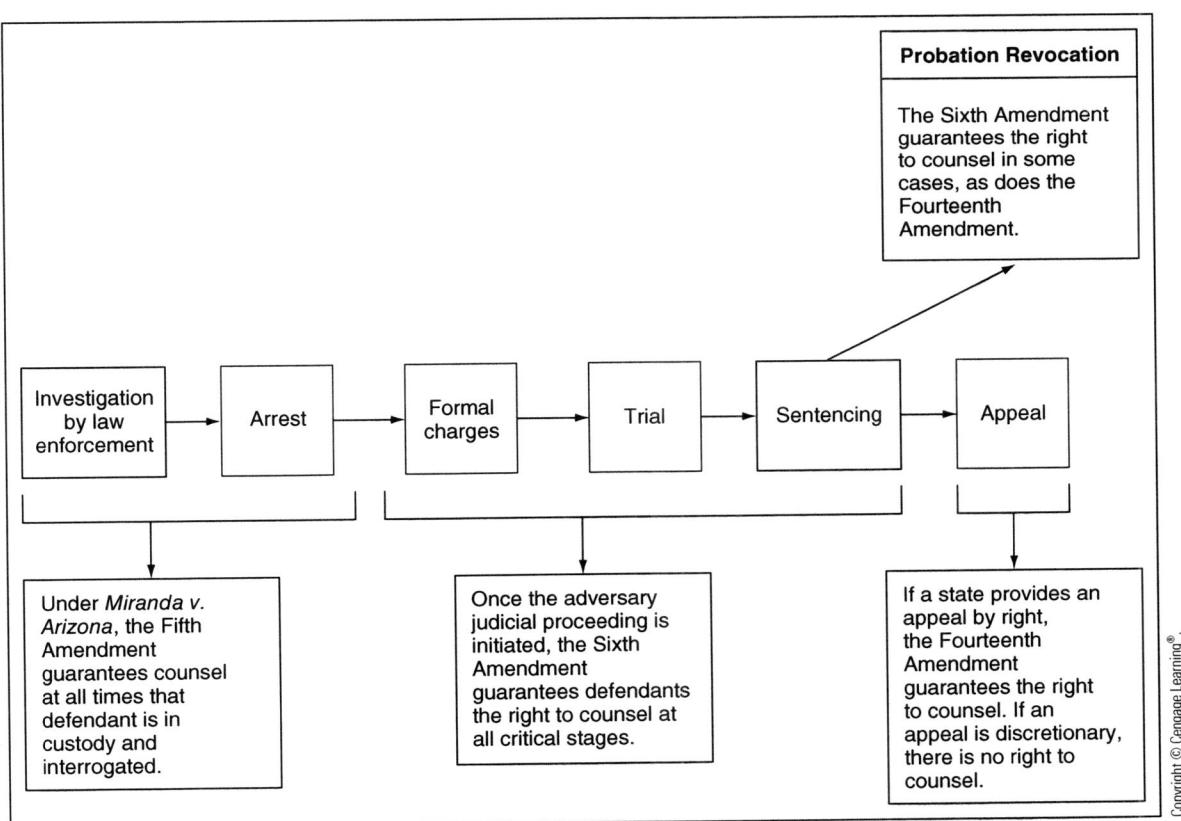

Effective Assistance of Counsel

Defendants are entitled not only to have an attorney but also to receive the "effective assistance of counsel." On appeal, defendants may challenge their convictions by claiming that at a lower level (trial or appellate) they did not have effective counsel.

To succeed with such a claim, two facts must be shown. First, the representation must be extremely inadequate. Second, the defendant must show that he or she was actually harmed by the lack of adequate counsel. So, if an appellate court determines that a defendant would have been convicted with the best of attorneys, the defendant's claim of inadequate counsel fails.

A Sixth Amendment claim of ineffective assistance of counsel can take many forms. Incompetence of counsel is often claimed, but rarely successful. Attorneys are expected to make the legal and tactical decisions of the defense. The fact that defense counsel rendered incorrect legal advice is not determinative. The issue is whether the defendant's representation was shockingly substandard.

A defendant has a right to the "undivided loyalty" of defense counsel. Hence, it is common to have ineffective assistance of counsel claims where one attorney is representing codefendants. In *Cuyler v. Sullivan*, 446 U.S. 335 (1980), it was held that an ineffective assistance of counsel claim based upon an alleged conflict of interest will succeed only if the defendant can show that the conflict "adversely affected" his or her rights.

Also, the accused has a right to confer with counsel to prepare a defense. If a court denies a defendant access to his or her counsel, a Sixth Amendment claim may be made.

Governmental eavesdropping on a defendant's conversation with his or her counsel is also improper and violative of the Sixth Amendment.

The Right to Self-Representation

In *Faretta v. California*, 422 U.S. 806 (1975), the right to self-representation was established. The Supreme Court recognized that the assistance of trained legal counsel is essential to preparing and presenting a defense. However, in balance, the Court found that a defendant's right of choice has greater importance. Therefore, defendants may choose to act as their own counsel (pro se), even though the decision increases the probability of a conviction.

The record must clearly show that a defendant who has chosen to proceed pro se has done so voluntarily and knowingly. The defendant "must be made aware of the dangers and disadvantages of self-representation." Whether the defendant possesses any legal training or education is not relevant.

Trial judges are permitted to appoint "standby counsel" for trial. This attorney attends the trial and is available to counsel the defendant or take over the defense, if necessary. The Court later approved the practice of appointing standby counsel over the objection of the defendant. This is routinely done in felony cases in which the defendant has opted to proceed pro se.

The right to self-representation is not absolute. A defendant who engages in disruptive behavior during the proceeding may be relieved of pro se status. Standby counsel, if appointed, may be ordered to complete the trial.

The Scope of the Right

Through *Gideon*, the right to counsel in criminal prosecutions was extended to the states. *Argersinger* made it clear that counsel must be provided in all cases in which the defendant is sentenced to actual imprisonment. But when does the right begin?

The United States Supreme Court has stated that the Sixth Amendment right to counsel applies to all critical stages of a criminal prosecution. This definition requires that a "prosecution" be initiated before the right to counsel, under the Sixth Amendment, attaches. Accordingly, the Sixth Amendment does not apply to juvenile proceedings, nor to administrative hearings such as parole determination and revocation.

The right starts whenever the "adversary judicial proceeding" is initiated. Police contacts prior to the initiation of an adversary judicial proceeding are not covered by the Sixth Amendment.

In determining what constitutes a critical stage, courts focus on "whether substantial rights of the defendant may be affected." The greater the contact between the prosecutor and the defendant, the more likely the event is at a critical stage.

The first critical stage is normally the initial appearance or the arraignment. Courts have also determined that a defendant may be entitled to counsel at a police lineup, sentencing, preliminary hearing, and during a probation revocation hearing. Once charges are filed, all interrogations of the defendant by the government are critical stages.

The Sixth Amendment is not the only constitutional provision assuring counsel. The Fifth Amendment's right to be free from self-incrimination also guarantees counsel in some instances, as does the Fourteenth Amendment's Equal Protection and Due Process Clauses.

TRIAL PROCEDURE

Voir Dire

The first stage of trial is the **voir dire.** This is a French phrase that translates "look speak" (to speak the truth). Voir dire is also known as *jury selection.*

The process of selecting a jury differs among the jurisdictions. In all jurisdictions, prospective jurors are asked questions bearing upon their individual ability to serve fairly and impartially. Each state differs in how this information is obtained. In many, the judge is responsible for asking most of the questions. In others, the judge makes only a few brief inquiries, and the lawyers do most of the questioning.

There are two ways of eliminating a juror. First, if one of the attorneys believes that a juror could not be fair and impartial, the juror can be **challenged for cause.** If the judge agrees, the juror is released. An unlimited number of jurors may be eliminated for cause.

In addition to challenges for cause, a juror may be eliminated by a party using a **peremptory challenge.** Each party is given a specific number of peremptory challenges at the start of the trial and may strike jurors until that number is exhausted. A party is free to eliminate, without stating a reason, any potential juror. However, a juror may not be eliminated because of race.[23]

In the federal system, both defendant and prosecutor have 20 peremptory strikes in death cases and 3 in misdemeanors; in noncapital felony cases the defendant gets 10 and the government 6.[24] States have similar rules. The authority of the parties to use peremptory challenges is nearly absolute. Two limitations exist, though—the use of a challenge to eliminate a prospective juror for race and sex. Such criteria violate the Fifth and Fourteenth Amendments' equal protection guarantees.[25] Other than these

voir dire examination
▪ (French) "To see, to say"; "to state the truth." The preliminary in-court questioning of a prospective witness (or juror) to determine competency to testify (or suitability to decide a case). [pronounce: vwahr deer]

challenge for cause
▪ A formal objection to the qualifications of a prospective juror or jurors.

peremptory challenge
▪ The automatic elimination of a potential juror by one side before trial without needing to state the reason for the elimination.

limitations, parties often go to great lengths to try to understand the psychological profile of venireman. When resources permit, experts are retained who make recommendations about whether venireman should be retained or struck using models that predict how a prospective juror will react to the facts of the case.

In addition to challenging individual jurors, entire jury panels may be challenged. For example, a defendant may challenge the method used to select prospective jurors if the method does not select individuals who represent a fair cross section of the community. In many instances, these challenges concern race or ethnicity.

Preliminary Instructions

The next stage in the trial proceeding is for the judge to give preliminary instructions to the jury. The trial judge explains to the jury what its obligation is and gives a brief introduction to the law and facts of the case. The judge may read the formal charge verbatim to the jury or may summarize its contents.

The presumption of innocence is explained, and the judge admonishes the jury not to discuss the case prior to deliberating. Jurors are told not to read newspaper articles or watch television reports concerning the trial. In rare cases, it may be necessary to keep the jurors' identities secret and to conduct the voir dire in private. Threat to the safety of the jurors is an example of such an instance. This method is to be used cautiously, as it encroaches upon First Amendment rights of media and of the defendant to a public trial. Moreover, when using this method, the trial judge should be careful not to prejudice the jury. If the reason for secrecy is a perceived threat, the judge should instruct the jury as to another reason, such as concern over pretrial publicity.[26]

Opening Statements

After the judge has given the preliminary instructions, the parties address the jury. These statements are commonly known as *opening statements*. The purpose of opening statements is to acquaint the jury with the basic facts of the case. Opening statement is not the time for counsel to argue the law; only the facts expected to be presented should be mentioned.

In some cases the defense attorney may be permitted to wait until after the prosecution has put on its case before giving an opening. Because the purpose of opening statements is to present the facts surrounding the charge to the jury, opening statements are often waived in bench trials.

The Prosecution's Case in Chief

The United States employs an adversarial system of adjudication. In adversarial systems, the parties take the lead, not the court, in the development of the facts and theories of the case. At trial the parties are responsible for introducing the evidence, calling and examining the witnesses, and presenting theories to juries. Judges occasionally ask questions of witnesses and even less often, call witnesses. Historically jurors have been expected to sit silently during trials. They do not call or questions witnesses. In recent years there has been a small movement in the direction of jury participation. Arizona, Florida, and a few other states, for example, now permit jurors to ask questions of witnesses. State rules vary in how this happens. It is common, for example, to require questions to be submitted to the Court for review. In some jurisdictions the parties are permitted to review and object to questions. It is common for the judge to ask the questions that are approved.

Because the government has brought the charges, it puts its case on first. This consists of calling witnesses to testify and producing exhibits.

All jurisdictions have rules of evidence that govern procedure and the admissibility of evidence. The Federal Rules of Evidence are used in the federal courts, and many states have modeled their rules after the federal ones.

Many evidentiary questions can be resolved prior to trial through a motion **in limine.** Those arising during trial are handled through **objections.** Any time an attorney believes that a question, statement, or action of the opposing lawyer is improper, he or she may object. The court will then rule on the objection, and the trial will continue. In some instances the attorneys will want to argue the objection outside the hearing of the jury. In such cases a **sidebar** may be held, or the judge may order that the jury be removed until the matter is resolved.

The Confrontation Clause assures the defendant the right to cross-examine the prosecution's witnesses. Normally, cross-examination is limited to matters raised during the prosecution's direct examination. The defense also has the right to review an exhibit before it is shown to the jury.

The Supreme Court has held that prosecutors may not call defendants to testify. While a defendant may assert the privilege and refuse to testify once called, the Court has found that to demand this of a defendant creates an appearance of guilt. Furthermore, prosecutors may not refer to a defendant's failure to testify in closing arguments. Of course, a prosecutor may cross-examine a defendant who chooses to testify. However, in the 2013 case *Salinas v. Texas,*[27] the Supreme Court held that a defendant's silence in response to a question during a voluntary interview by police may be mentioned by a prosecutor as evidence of guilt to a jury.

Directed Verdict and Judgement of Acquittal

After the government has rested (finished its case), the defendant may move for a directed verdict or, as it is also known, a judgement of acquittal. Upon such motion the trial judge reviews the evidence presented by the government. If the evidence to support a conviction is insufficient, the judge will enter a directed verdict favoring the defendant. A directed verdict may never be entered favoring the government.

The prosecution's evidence is insufficient if reasonable persons could not conclude that the defendant is guilty. If the trial court grants a motion for directed verdict, the jury never deliberates and is discharged. Directed verdicts are rarely granted, as most judges prefer to have the jury return a verdict.

The Defense Case

If the motion for directed verdict is denied, the defense may put on its case. The defendant is not required to put on a defense, and juries are instructed not to infer guilt by the absence of a defense.

in limine
■ (Latin) "At the beginning"; preliminary. A motion in limine is a (usually pretrial) request that prejudicial information be excluded as trial evidence.

objections
■ A claim that an action by your adversary in a lawsuit (such as the use of a particular piece of evidence) is improper, unfair, or illegal, and you are asking the judge for a ruling on the point.

sidebar
■ An in-court discussion among lawyers and the judge that is out of the hearing of witnesses and the jury. Sidebar conferences are usually *on* the record.

If a defendant chooses to present a defense, the rules are the same as for the prosecution. The defendant may call witnesses and introduce exhibits, as limited by the rules of evidence. Defense witnesses are subject to cross-examination by the prosecutor. Defendants do not have to testify but may choose to do so. If a defendant does testify, he or she is subject to cross-examination by the prosecutor.

Rebuttal

After the defense has concluded, the prosecution may call rebuttal witnesses in an effort to disprove the evidence of the defense. No new issues may be raised during rebuttal. The defense is then permitted to rebut the prosecution's rebuttal evidence.

Closing Arguments

After the evidentiary stage of the trial has concluded, the parties present their closing arguments. The length of closing arguments is left to the discretion of the trial judge.

Attorneys may argue both the facts and the law during closing arguments. However, an attorney may not argue law different from what the judge will express to the jury as controlling in the case. Closing arguments give the parties an opportunity to summarize the evidence and explain their positions to the jury.

Attorneys must not make incorrect factual or legal statements to the jury. Objections to such statements may be made. If an objection is sustained, the jury will be instructed by the judge to disregard the statement. Prosecutors must be especially careful not to make inflammatory remarks about the defendant or defense counsel. Such remarks, if extreme, can lead to mistrial.

Final Instructions

After closing arguments are completed, the judge will instruct the jury. Through these instructions the judge explains the law to the jury. The information contained in the judge's instructions includes the prosecutorial burden, the standard of proof, the elements of the charged crime, how to weigh and value evidence, and rules for reaching a verdict.

Jury Deliberations and Verdict

After receiving its instructions, the jury goes into deliberations. Jury deliberations are secret in all cases.

Generally, no person has contact with the jury when it is deliberating. If the jury has a question for the judge, it is escorted into the courtroom where all the parties may hear the question. Some judges, but not all, permit juries to take the exhibits and instructions with them into the jury room.

As mentioned earlier, juror unanimity is not required when twelve jurors are empanelled. As few as nine jurors may support a guilty verdict. This is not true, however, in capital cases where a unanimous vote is required. Unanimity is also required if only six jurors sit in judgement.

On occasion, a jury may communicate to the judge that a verdict cannot be reached. Some courts will then give the jury an "*Allen* charge," an instruction encouraging jurors in the minority to reexamine their position. The charge gets its name from *Allen v. United States*, 164 U.S. 492 (1896), wherein the Supreme Court approved its use. Courts must be careful with such charges, but they are not violative of the U.S. Constitution. However, some states have banned the *Allen* charge.

In the event of a **hung jury,** the court will declare a mistrial and set a new trial date. Due to the expense and inconvenience of trying cases a second time, plea bargains are often reached.

If a verdict is reached, the parties are summoned to the courtroom and the jury verdict is read. The parties may request that the jury be polled. **Polling the jury** involves asking each juror how he or she voted. If there has been an error, the judge may order the jury to return to deliberations or may declare a mistrial.

Jurors have an obligation to follow the law, as interpreted by the trial judge, when rendering a verdict.[28] Trial judges instruct jurors in this obligation. Further, the trial judge is not to instruct the jury, nor the parties to encourage the jury in closing arguments, to disregard the law. This rule affects defense, not prosecution. That is, if a law (defining a crime or punishment) is harsh or unfavorable, defendants have an interest in arguing that a jury should disregard the law and acquit, notwithstanding guilt. This is not permitted in most, if not all, jurisdictions. Accordingly, a defendant has no right to insist that a jury be instructed that it has the authority to nullify the law.[29]

In 2012 a professor in Manhattan was charged with obstructing justice for standing outside a courthouse with a sign that read "Jury Information" and distributed pamphlets encouraging jurors who disagree with a law to disregard it and acquit the defendants charged under it. The charges were dismissed by the trial court, finding that his general pleas were not intended to influence jurors in specific cases, as required by the statute.[30] The case also raises First Amendment Free Speech questions.

In reality, though, juries can and may disregard the law—even though unlawful. When a jury retires, its deliberations are secret; and each juror, while feeling bound by the law, also feels bound by personal conscience. A jury does not have to support its verdict with a statement of its findings and conclusions. An acquittal, even if the result of nullification, is valid. Accordingly, although the trial judge may comment on the evidence to the jury before it retires to deliberate, a judge may not instruct a jury that the government has met its burden and that the jury must return a guilty verdict.[31]

hung jury
■ A jury that cannot reach a verdict (decision) because of disagreement among jurors.

polling the jury
■ Individually asking each member of a jury what his or her decision is. Polling is done by the judge, at the defendant's request, immediately after the verdict.

JNOV/New Trial

If the jury returns a verdict of guilty, the defendant may move for a judgement notwithstanding the verdict, or **JNOV.** This is similar to a directed verdict, in that the defendant is asserting that the evidence is insufficient to support a guilty verdict.

In addition to JNOV, a defendant may file a motion for a new trial. The common-law equivalent of a motion for a new trial was the *writ of error coram nobis*. *Coram nobis* is still recognized in a few states.

JNOV
■ A request by a defendant convicted by a jury for the court to set aside the verdict as unsupported by the evidence.

The motion for a new trial is different from the JNOV because the defendant is not claiming that the evidence was insufficient, but rather that the trial was flawed. For example, if a defendant believes that evidence was admitted that should have been excluded and that he or she was denied a fair trial because of the admission of the evidence, he or she may file a motion for new trial. A motion for new trial may also be made because of new evidence discovered after trial.

> **Web Links**
>
> **Famous Trials**
>
> Professor Linder of the University of Missouri at Kansas City has an interesting and fun Web site. Information on famous trials can be found there, as can legal jeopardy and golf! http://www.law.umkc.edu/faculty/projects/ftrials/ftrials.htm

Key Terms

beyond a reasonable doubt
challenged for cause
hung jury
in limine

JNOV
objections
peremptory challenge
polling the jury

sidebar
voir dire examination

Review Questions

1. What rights are encompassed by the Confrontation Clause?
2. What is the standard of proof in criminal cases? Define that standard.
3. How soon after arrest must a defendant be tried to comply with the Sixth Amendment's speedy trial clause?
4. What is jury nullification? May a prosecutor ask a jury to nullify? May defense counsel?
5. Distinguish challenging a prospective juror for cause from using a peremptory challenge.
6. Does a defendant have a right to self-representation?
7. What must a defendant show on appeal to be successful with a claim of ineffective assistance of counsel at trial?

Problems & Critical Thinking Exercises

1-4. Does each of the following defendants have a right to a jury trial? Explain your answer.

1. A juvenile delinquency proceeding has been initiated against John because of his involvement with drugs. For more than a year he has been dealing drugs, a crime punishable by as much as five years in prison in his state.
2. Jane is charged with simple assault. In her state that crime is punishable by a maximum fine of $2,500 and 12 months imprisonment. However, the judge assigned to her case has never sentenced a person to more than four months and customarily suspends that sentence to probation.
3. Nick is 16 years old. He is charged with murder in state trial court. Murder in his state is punished with life imprisonment or death.
4. Norm, an officer in the military, has been charged with raping a female officer. Rape is punished with 10 years to life imprisonment in the military.

Endnotes

1. *Baldwin v. New York*, 399 U.S. 66 (1970).
2. *McKeiver v. Pennsylvania*, 403 U.S. 528 (1971).
3. *Williams v. Florida*, 399 U.S. 78 (1970).
4. *Burch v. Louisiana*, 441 U.S. 130 (1979).
5. *Smith v. Illinois*, 390 U.S. 129 (1968).
6. *Maryland v. Craig*, 497 U.S. 836 (1990).
7. *Cumbie v. Singletary*, 991 F.2d 715 (11th Cir. 1993).
8. *Crawford. v. Washington*, 541 U.S. 36 (2004).
9. 564 U.S. ___ (2011).
10. 567 U.S. ___ (2012).
11. *Brooks v. Tennessee*, 406 U.S. 605 (1972).
12. *Johnson v. Louisiana*, 406 U.S. 356 (1972).
13. *Estelle v. Williams*, 425 U.S. 501 (1976).
14. See *Carey v. Musladin*, 549 U.S. ___ (2006).
15. *Stewart v. Corbin*, 850 F.2d 492 (9th Cir. 1988).
16. *Barker v. Wingo*, 407 U.S. 514 (1972).
17. *United States v. Marion*, 404 U.S. 307 (1971).
18. 18 U.S.C. § 3161.
19. 18 U.S.C. § 3162.
20. *Betts v. Brady*, 316 U.S. 455 (1942).

21. *Argersinger v. Hamlin*, 407 U.S. 25 (1972).
22. *Burgett v. Texas*, 389 U.S. 109 (1962).
23. *Batson v. Kentucky*, 476 U.S. 79 (1986).
24. Fed. R. Crim. P. 24(b).
25. *Batson v. Kentucky*, 476 U.S. 79 (1986) and *J.E.B. v. Alabama*, 511 U.S. 127 (1994).
26. *United States v. Locascio*, 6 F.3d 924 (2d Cir. 1993).
27. 570 U.S. __ (2013).
28. *See United States v. Avery*, 717 F.2d 1020 (6th Cir. 1983).
29. *United States v. Newman*, 743 F. Supp. 533 (M.D. Tenn. 1990).
30. Benjamin Weiser, Jury Statute Not Violated By Protestor, Judge Rules, *The New York Times*, April 19, 2012.
31. *See Sparf v. United States*, 156 U.S. 51 (1895); *United States v. Martin Linen Supply Co.*, 430 U.S. 564 (1977).

CHAPTER 7

SENTENCING AND APPEAL

Chapter Outline

Sentencing
  Sentencing Procedure
  Forms of Punishment
  Habitual Offender Statutes
Postconviction Remedies
  Appeal
  Habeas Corpus

Chapter Objectives

After completing this chapter you should be able to:

- describe and apply to fact scenarios the laws of punishment, including the constitutional limitations of punishment.
- describe the sentencing process and identify the constitutional rights defendants possess at sentencing.
- connect and apply the various forms of punishment to the objectives of criminal justice.
- identify and describe the law of appeals and postconviction relief.
- identify the material facts and legal issues in nearly all of the cases you read, describe the courts' analyses and conclusions in the cases, and demonstrate the ability to synthesize and think critically about the law of the subject.

SENTENCING

After conviction, sentence must be imposed. For many misdemeanors and nearly all infractions, sentence is imposed immediately. For felonies and some misdemeanors, a future sentencing date is set.

In most cases, sentence is imposed by the trial judge. A few jurisdictions provide for a jury sentence recommendation, and even fewer actually permit the jury to impose sentence. Juries always plays a role in deciding whether death should be imposed. In some states, a jury recommendation is required before death can be imposed. In all jurisdictions, due process and jury trial right empower juries to find the facts, called an aggravating factor, that are required in capital cases.

The legislature determines how a crime should be punished. Legislatures normally set ranges within which judges may punish violators. In recent years there has been a substantial movement to limit the discretion of judges. This has been done in the federal system and many states.

The right of the legislative branch in this area is curbed by the Eighth Amendment, which prohibits "cruel and unusual punishment." The protection of the Eighth Amendment has been extended to state proceedings through the Fourteenth Amendment. However, legislatures enjoy wide discretion in deciding how to punish criminals.

Sentencing Procedure

The Presentence Investigation/No Right to Counsel

After a defendant is determined guilty, a sentencing date is set. For most felonies and misdemeanors the date will be set far enough in the future to permit the probation officer to complete a presentence investigation.

The investigation typically begins with an interview of the defendant. Information concerning the defendant's drug habits, criminal history, family, employment history, education, medical and psychological problems, and personal finances is obtained. The defendant is also permitted to give his or her version of the facts surrounding the offense. There appears to be no right to counsel during this interview,[1] although most courts and probation officers permit attorneys to attend. The Seventh Circuit Court of Appeals held that the Sixth Amendment right to counsel does not apply at presentence interviews by probation officers. The court reasoned that because probation officers are neutral judicial employees, and not law enforcement officers, interviews conducted by them are not critical stages of an *adversarial* proceeding.[2] The Seventh Circuit, like other courts that have considered the issue, thus determined that the presentence interview is a neutral, nonadversarial meeting between the probation officer and the defendant. This is so even though the defendant may be in custody and admissions could lead to greater punishment.

Three facts support the conclusion that there is no right to counsel during a presentence investigation interview. First, the objective of the interview is to gather information to assist the sentencing court, not to establish that the defendant committed a crime. Second (and related to the first), a probation officer is not, strictly speaking, a law enforcement officer. Third, the questions asked at the interview are routine, and defense counsel can properly advise the client of his or her rights before the interview occurs.

In addition to conducting an interview of the defendant, the probation officer will obtain copies of vital documents, such as the defendant's "rap sheet" and relevant medical records. The probation officer will attempt to verify the information provided by the defendant through these documents and other investigatory processes.

When the probation officer has completed the investigation, a presentence report is prepared. This report reflects the information discovered during the investigation and is used by the court in determining what sentence should be imposed. Often, the prosecutor and law enforcement officers involved in prosecuting the defendant, family members of the defendant, and the victim of the crime are permitted to make statements that are incorporated into the report.

There is no constitutional right to the preparation of a presentence report; however, most jurisdictions have followed the lead of the federal government, which requires a presentence report unless the record contains information sufficient to enable the meaningful exercise of sentencing discretion.[3]

In the federal system, the defendant is entitled to review the presentence report prior to sentencing. This is true in most states as well, but the right is not absolute. For example, the recommendation of the probation officer may be kept confidential.[4]

At the sentencing hearing, the defendant may disprove factual statements contained in the report. To this end witnesses may be called and exhibits introduced.

The Sentencing Hearing

The next stage in the process is the sentencing hearing. Sentencing hearings are adversarial. Witnesses may be called, other evidence introduced, and arguments made. In most instances the hearing is before a judge, not a jury, and accordingly the rules of evidence are relaxed. When the hearing is before a jury, such as in capital cases, the rules of evidence are fully effective. This is a critical stage under the Sixth Amendment, and therefore there is a right to counsel. As is true for defendants at earlier stages of the process, convictees are entitled to more than a warm body; they are entitled to effective assistance of counsel. To prove ineffective assistance of counsel, it must be shown that the attorney's representation fell below an objective standard of reasonableness and that the defendant was actually prejudiced. The following case, which involves the sentencing of a man for a brutal rape and murder, is an example of ineffective counsel at sentencing.

In most instances, sentencing facts are established by preponderance of the evidence and are found by the sentencing judge. In rare instances, however, clear and convincing evidence or proof beyond a reasonable doubt is required. Death cases are an example. This issue has also arisen in the context of sentence enhancements. For example, due process requires that any fact that increases the penalty for a crime beyond the prescribed statutory maximum, other than the fact of a prior conviction, must be submitted to a jury and proved beyond a reasonable doubt. So, a sentencing scheme that increases the punishment for racially motivated second-degree murder beyond the limits set by the second-degree murder statute is invalid unless the racial motive is proved to the jury beyond a reasonable doubt.[5]

One issue that has received considerable attention, and contradictory treatment, from the Supreme Court in recent years is the use of **victim impact statements** at

victim impact statement

■ At the time of sentencing, a statement made to the court concerning the effect the crime has had on the victim or on the victim's family.

sentencing. A *victim impact statement* is an oral or written statement to the sentencing judge explaining how the crime has affected the victim and, possibly, the victim's family. In 1987 the Supreme Court handed down *Booth v. Maryland,* 482 U.S. 496 (1987), wherein it invalidated a state statute requiring sentencing judges to consider victim impact statements in capital cases. The Court determined that the use of victim impact statements could prejudice the proceeding by injecting irrelevant, but inflammatory, evidence into the sentencing determination.

Only four years later, though, the Supreme Court overruled *Booth* in *Payne v. Tennessee.* Thus, victim impact evidence may be admitted, even if it is not related to the facts surrounding the crime. The decision concerning admissibility must be made on a case-by-case basis, and it is a violation of due process to admit evidence that is so prejudicial that the sentencing becomes fundamentally unfair.

On the other side of the coin, defendants are generally allowed to present nearly any evidence at sentencing. This right is constitutionally mandated in capital cases; the Supreme Court has said that a state cannot preclude a defendant from proffering evidence in support of a sentence less than death.[6]

Punishing Acquitted Crimes

Historically, judges have held considerable discretion in sentencing. The rules of evidence are relaxed, and judges may hear evidence that is otherwise inadmissible. Victim impact evidence, family history, medical history, mental health history, employment history, and criminal history are examples of the type of evidence that is considered at sentencing.

Additionally, the nature of the crime committed and the particular manner in which it was committed are considered. In some cases, evidence concerning the nature and manner of the offense may include evidence of other crimes that were committed in conjunction with the offense under sentence. An interesting question concerns whether a defendant may have a sentence increased for acquitted crimes. This issue was before the Supreme Court in *United States v. Watts* (1997).[7] Police discovered both cocaine and guns in a search of Watts's property, and he was subsequently charged and tried for possession of cocaine and possession of a gun in relation to a drug offense. The jury convicted him of the former charge and acquitted him of the latter charge. At sentencing, however, the trial judge found that Watts did use the gun in relation to a drug offense and, accordingly, increased his sentence for the cocaine possession conviction.

On appeal, the Supreme Court affirmed the sentence enhancement. The Court stressed that judges have historically had significant discretion in sentencing and that the enhancement was not punishment for an acquitted offense, but instead was an enhanced punishment for the manner in which the defendant committed the crime of conviction. Also important are the differing standards of proof between conviction and sentencing. Conviction requires a finding beyond a reasonable doubt, while sentencing requires proof by preponderance of the evidence. The high standard of proof for conviction, according to the Court, means that an acquittal cannot be interpreted as a finding of fact. An acquittal means that the government has not proved its case, not that the defendant did not commit the act in question. However, for reasons to be discussed, the status of *Watts* is unknown.

Proving Facts for Sentencing

In a practice similar to that of using acquitted crimes to enhance a sentence, judges have historically used facts not presented to the trial jury to increase sentences. If there is a plea of guilty, the judge must find that the essential elements of the crime were committed. This usually involves a recitation of the facts by the defendant. If there has been a trial, the judge is armed with the findings of the jury; or in the case of a bench trial, of the trial judge. Once the facts have been established at trial, whether by confession or a finding of fact, additional evidence must be received at sentencing. However, that evidence is limited to the facts that are relevant to the sentencing decision. For over 150 years, trial judges routinely found facts, often by a preponderance of the evidence, at sentencing hearings. Judges have always been restricted by jury decisions. That is, they cannot refind facts that have been decided by trial juries. For example, if a jury finds a defendant guilty of possession of a specific amount of cocaine, a sentencing judge is prohibited from increasing the sentence because the judge finds that the defendant possessed a greater amount of cocaine.

However, judges would commonly find other facts that affected the final sentence—for example, whether a defendant possessed a weapon while engaged in a drug deal in a case where the defendant was charged only with dealing drugs, not possession of the weapon. Often these facts were proved by the preponderance standard.

In recent years, however, a new body of law has developed around the Sixth Amendment's jury trial right. In short, these cases require that all findings that are used to support the sentence must be heard by a jury and found to be true beyond a reasonable doubt.[8] In *Blakely*, the defendant had been charged with first-degree kidnapping. He and the state reached a plea agreement that reduced the charges to second-degree kidnapping involving domestic violence and the use of a firearm. Pursuant to the plea agreement, the state recommended a sentence of between 49 and 53 months. The judge, however, found that the crime involved deliberate cruelty and enhanced the sentence to 90 months. After the defendant objected, the judge conducted a three-day fact hearing on the deliberate cruelty question. The judge again sentenced the defendant to 90 months, having found deliberate cruelty following the hearing.

The Supreme Court reversed, finding that it was not possible for the judge to justify the enhanced sentence solely because of the facts admitted in the guilty plea. While the defendant admitted to kidnapping and the use of a gun, he did not provide evidence that he acted with deliberate cruelty. Accordingly, the judge had to find facts the trial jury was not charged with determining. This effort is proved by the judge's need to conduct a three-day sentencing hearing. Because the Sixth Amendment guarantees individuals the right to have all facts essential to sentencing heard by a jury, using the reasonable doubt standard, the trial judge erred. Whether the judge had charged the trial jury to make the deliberate cruelty finding or had empaneled a jury at sentencing to make the finding, the sentence would not have violated the Sixth Amendment.

Similarly, in the 2007 *Cunningham* case, the Court invalidated a California law that created an upper range of 12 years in prison for the crimes covered by the jury's verdict but allowed the judge to sentence the offender to an additional four years for facts the judge could find, by preponderance of the evidence, at a sentencing hearing. Later, in the discussion of the federal sentencing guidelines, you may read an excerpt of the Supreme Court's decision *United States v. Booker* wherein the right to have facts decided by a jury under the Sixth Amendment was used to invalidate the mandatory nature of the federal sentencing guidelines. The relationship between *Booker* and *Watts* is not clear. *Watts* may be overruled altogether. At the least, *Booker* demands that the conduct for which the defendant was acquitted be found by a jury before a judge may rely upon them at sentencing.

In capital cases the Supreme Court has specifically held that the aggravating circumstances that must be found to impose death have to be found by a jury and beyond a reasonable doubt.[9] Judges may still be empowered to decide whether to impose death or another punishment, but death is only an option to the judge if the jury finds an aggravating factor. Some states have delegated only the aggravating factor decision to juries, as required, and others have handed the jury both the aggravating factor and the sentencing decision.

Forms of Punishment

The legislature determines what type of sentence may be imposed; judges impose sentences.

Capital Punishment

Clearly the most controversial punishment is the death penalty. In early American history, capital punishment was commonly used. During the nineteenth century, use of the death penalty greatly declined. Today, more than half the states provide for the death penalty, and its use has regained popular support. Although the number of inmates actually executed every year is small, the number is increasing.

The contention that the death penalty is inherently cruel and unusual and therefore violative of the Eighth Amendment has been rejected. However, the Court has struggled, as have state courts and legislatures, with establishing standards for its use.

In *Furman v. Georgia*, 408 U.S. 238 (1972), the Court held that the death penalty cannot be imposed under a sentencing procedure that creates a substantial risk of being implemented in an arbitrary manner. It found that Georgia's law permitted arbitrary decisions and so declared it void. *Furman* required that the sentencer's discretion be limited by objective standards to eliminate unfairness—specifically, to eliminate racial and other bias from death sentence decisions.

States responded to *Furman* in various ways. Some chose to eliminate discretion entirely by mandating capital punishment for certain crimes. The Supreme Court invalidated mandatory capital punishment laws in *Locket v. Ohio*, 438 U.S. 586 (1978). In *Locket* the Court held that individualized sentencing was constitutionally required. The Court stated that any law prohibiting a sentencer from considering "as a mitigating factor, any aspect of a defendant's character or record and any circumstances of the offense that the defendant proffers as a basis for a sentence less than death" creates an unconstitutional risk that the "death penalty will be imposed in spite of factors which may call for a less severe penalty."[10]

However, Georgia's new death penalty legislation was upheld in *Gregg v. Georgia*, 428 U.S. 153 (1976). The new law provided that the jury must find, in a sentencing hearing separate from the trial, an aggravating circumstance before the death penalty could be imposed. The statute enumerated possible aggravating circumstances. By requiring a jury to find an aggravating circumstance, arbitrariness is believed to be lessened. Indeed, today the decision to impose death must be made by a unanimous jury, and defendants must be given the opportunity to present mitigating evidence. A statute that mandates death in all cases is invalid. A statute may, however, require death if a jury finds that the mitigating factors do not outweigh the aggravating factors.[11]

Furman, Gregg, Locket, and their progeny stand for the principle that a sentencing statute cannot totally eliminate discretion, nor grant so much discretion that the death penalty can be imposed arbitrarily. These concepts of individualized sentencing and minimized discretion in sentencing are somewhat antithetical. The Supreme Court itself recognizes that a tension exists between the two goals and has struggled to establish procedures and standards to successfully implement them. "Experience has shown that the consistency and rationality promised in *Furman* are inversely related to the fairness owed the individual when considering a sentence of death. A step toward consistency is a step away from fairness."[12]

The death penalty issue has been divisive to the Court. Some justices have so strongly believed that the death penalty is unconstitutional (either inherently or as administered) that they have refused to acquiesce to notions of stare decisis on the issue. Justice Thurgood Marshall, for example, dissented in every capital punishment case, including both denials of petitions of certiorari and cases under review, because of his firmly held belief that capital punishment was unconstitutional.

Until 1994, Justice Harry Blackmun held that the death penalty was not inherently unconstitutional. However, in *Callins v. Collins*, he made the following statement.

> Courts are in the very business of erecting procedural devices from which fair, equitable, and reliable outcomes are presumed to flow. Yet, in the death penalty area, this Court, in my view, had engaged in a futile effort to balance these constitutional demands, and now is retreating not only from the *Furman* promise of consistency and rationality, but from the requirement of individualized sentencing as well. Having virtually conceded that both fairness and rationality cannot be achieved in the administration of the death penalty . . . the Court has chosen to deregulate the entire enterprise, replacing, it would seem, substantive constitutional requirements with mere aesthetics, and abdicating its statutorily and constitutionally imposed duty to provide meaningful judicial oversight to the administration of death by the States. From this date forward, I no longer shall tinker with the machinery of death. For more than 20 years I have endeavored—indeed, I have struggled—along with a majority of this Court, to develop procedural and substantive rules that would lend more than the mere appearance of fairness to the death penalty endeavor. Rather than continue to coddle the Court's delusion that the desired level of fairness has been achieved and the need for regulation eviscerated, I feel morally and

intellectually obligated simply to concede that the death penalty experiment has failed. It is virtually self-evident to me now that no combination of procedural rules or substantive regulations ever can save the death penalty from its inherent constitutional deficiencies. The basic question—does the system accurately and consistently determine which defendants "deserve" to die?—cannot be answered in the affirmative. It is not simply that this Court has allowed vague aggravating circumstances to be employed . . . relevant mitigating evidence to be disregarded . . . and vital judicial review to be blocked. . . . The problem is that the inevitability of actual, legal, and moral error gives us a system that we know must wrongly kill some defendants, a system that fails to deliver the fair, consistent, and reliable sentences of death required by the Constitution. . . . Perhaps one day this Court will develop procedural rules or verbal formulas that actually will provide consistency, fairness, and reliability in a capital-sentencing scheme. I am not optimistic that such a day will come. I am more optimistic, though, that this Court eventually will conclude that the effort to eliminate arbitrariness while preserving fairness "in the infliction of [death] is so plainly doomed to failure that it—and the death penalty—must be abandoned altogether." . . . I may not live to see that day, but I have faith that eventually it will arrive. The path the Court has chosen lessens us all. I dissent.[13]

One decision that bothered Justice Blackmun was *McCleskey v. Kemp*, 481 U.S. 279 (1987), wherein the Court refused to set aside a death sentence even though the defendant presented reliable statistical data supporting the conclusion that race continues to be a significant factor in the application of capital punishment. The Court held that statistical evidence could not be used to invalidate an entire sentencing scheme; rather, the burden falls on each individual defendant to prove that race was a factor in his or her sentence. Justice Blackmun argued that the Court was thereby abandoning the *Furman* requirement of consistency and rationality.

The definition of cruelty is an evolving concept. Electrocution, lethal injection, hanging, and shooting are all approved methods of executing a prisoner. Other methods, such as starvation, would not pass constitutional muster. In 2008, the Supreme Court decided that Kentucky's lethal injection process was constitutional in *Baze v. Rees*.[15]

The Eighth Amendment has been interpreted to prohibit sentences that are disproportionate to the crime committed. In this vein, the Supreme Court has held that capital punishment may not be imposed for the crime of raping an adult woman.[16] In *Kennedy v. Louisiana*, 558 U.S. 1 (2008) the long-standing question whether child rapists could be put to death was answered in the negative.

Although the text was included in your excerpt, be aware that the Court was careful to note that the decision was limited to crimes against the person, not crimes against the State (e.g., terrorism, treason).

In another case it was decided that a person may not be put to death for aiding in a felony that results in murder, unless there was an intent to kill.[17] In 2005, the Supreme Court extended the protection from capital punishment to individuals who are under the age of 18 when they commit their capital crimes.[18]

In 1986, the Supreme Court stated that defendants who are incapable of understanding why they are being executed because of insanity may not be executed until they regain their faculties.[19] In *Atkins v. Virginia*[20] (2002) the Court applied similar reasoning to reach the same conclusion about individuals who are cognitively disabled.

Corporal/Physical Punishment

The Eighth Amendment limits the use of physical punishment. Punishment is not, however, unconstitutional simply because it involves pain. The issue is whether the pain is excessive. Pain is excessive when it exceeds the quantity necessary to achieve a legitimate penological purpose, such as rehabilitation or retribution. Generally, hard labor is not per se cruel.[21] If the labor is beyond the physical limits of the inmate, or involves unnecessary pain, it is unconstitutional.

Whipping has been held both constitutional[22] and unconstitutional[23] by lower courts. The Supreme Court has not decided the issue.[24]

Solitary confinement may be used in some circumstances, such as when a prisoner is disruptive or is highly dangerous. The use of prolonged solitary confinement for other prisoners is of questionable constitutionality.

The basic medical and nutritional needs of inmates must be satisfied by the government. Deliberately disregarding the medical or nutritional needs of inmates, or in some other manner imposing cruel or unusual punishment, can lead to liability under 42 U.S.C. § 1983.

The Supreme Court has said that the Eighth Amendment is to be interpreted consistent with society's evolving standards of decency. Therefore, although some courts have approved sterilization, and many states are considering chemical castration of men who commit sexual assault, there is a possibility that such practices could be found inconsistent with the Eighth Amendment.

Incarceration

Restraint is an effective method of dealing with dangerous persons. Incarceration serves this purpose, and in some cases the offender is also rehabilitated. Regrettably, because rehabilitation is rare and (contrary to popular belief) prison conditions are often poor, many offenders leave prison angry, no more educated or employable, and occasionally more dangerous.

Nevertheless, incarceration continues to be the most common method of punishing violent offenders. Offenders may be committed to prisons, camps, or local jails. Those sentenced to short terms (one year or less) are usually housed in a local jail. Individuals sentenced to longer terms are committed to prisons.

Like capital punishment, the Eighth Amendment's prohibition of cruel and unusual punishments establishes boundaries. The cruelty provision impacts the conditions of confinement. This subject is discussed later, in this book.

The principle of keeping punishments proportional to crimes is not significant to incarceration as a form of punishment. The Court has given legislatures wide berth when setting terms of imprisonment for all crimes. Some justices, such as

Antonin Scalia, reject the notion of proportionality altogether and as was famously suggested by Justice Stevens, Justice Scalia would permit life imprisonment for a parking ticket. *Harmelin v. Michigan*[26] is an example. The Court, in a divided opinion, upheld life imprisonment with no possibility of parole for possession of cocaine.

The Court has recognized a few limits for defendants of special populations. In the 2010 case *Graham v. Florida*, for example, the Court held that a juvenile may not be sentenced to life imprisonment without parole for a non-homicide crime. The Court extended this reasoning to murder by juveniles in *Miller v. Alabama*.

Shaming

Using shame to punish has a long history, memorialized in the Nathaniel Hawthorne book, and film of the same name, *The Scarlet Letter*. Shaming was a common punishment in colonial America but declined in popularity in favor of imprisonment. Judges, citizens, and sometimes offenders, disillusioned with prison as a form of punishment, are increasingly returning to shaming. Consider the following examples:

- A federal judge ordered a mail thief to stand in front of a post office in San Francisco for 8 hours wearing a sign that read "I stole mail. This is my punishment." The sentence was upheld on appeal.[27]
- A woman who regularly drove onto a sidewalk to avoid a school bus was ordered to stand on a public street wearing a sign that read "Only an idiot would drive on a sidewalk to avoid a school bus."[28]
- Drunk drivers have been required to put license plates on their cars that identify them as having been convicted of DUI.
- Sexual offenders are required to register with local law enforcement after release and their locations are made known to the general public.
- A woman was required to place an advertisement in her local newspaper declaring that she purchased drugs in the presence of her children.
- One judge offered thieves probation is they permitted their victims to take one item each from the offenders' homes.
- A man who was convicted of assaulting his wife was ordered to allow her to spit in his face.[29]

Indeterminate and Determinate Sentencing

The **indeterminate sentence** gives corrections officials the greatest amount of control over an inmate's sentence. Under an indeterminate sentence, the judge sets a minimum and maximum period to be served, and the corrections agency determines the actual date of release. Once common in the United States, indeterminate sentencing has fallen into disfavor.

In **determinate sentencing** schemes, the sentencing judge is given discretion to set a fixed sentence from within a range set by the legislature. The determinate sentence is fixed, and there is no possibility of early release.

indeterminate sentence

▪ A sentence having a minimum and maximum, with the decision of how long the criminal will serve depending on the criminal's behavior in prison and other things.

determinate sentence

▪ An exact penalty set by law.

Definite and Indefinite Sentencing

Unlike determinate sentencing, with definite sentencing the sentencing judge has no discretion. Rather, the legislature establishes the specific penalty to be imposed for each crime, and there is no possibility of early release. Definite sentencing reduces sentencing disparity. However, it is criticized for not allowing the particular facts of each case to be taken into consideration.

Indefinite sentencing incorporates both judicial and corrections agency discretion. It is the antithesis of definite sentencing. The sentencing judge is given a range from which to impose sentence, and the corrections agency is delegated the authority to grant early releases.

Presumptive Sentencing

In many instances, when a legislature gives the sentencing judge discretion, it also establishes a *presumptive sentence*. That is, the legislature states what sentence should be imposed from within a range, absent **aggravating circumstances** or **mitigating circumstances.** Circumstances upon which the judge relies to increase the presumptive sentence are aggravating; those used to justify a sentence below a presumption are mitigating.

If a judge deviates from a presumptive sentence, the aggravating or mitigating circumstances justifying the departure must be made part of the record. For example, an assault statute may call for one to three years' punishment with a presumptive sentence of 18 months. If the judge sentences the defendant to more or less than 18 months, the reasons must be reflected on the record. Of course, even when deviating from a presumption, the sentencing judge must remain within the statutory limits.

What constitutes an aggravating or mitigating circumstance is often expressed in the statute. Examples of aggravating circumstances are injury, torture, or death of the victim; use of a weapon during commission of the crime; whether the crime involved a child; and whether the defendant violated a trust. Examples of mitigating circumstances are physical disability of the defendant; the defendant's having dependents; a crime committed in a non-violent manner; and the defendant's acting in good faith.

aggravating circumstances

■ Actions or occurrences that increase the seriousness of a crime, but are not part of the legal definition of that crime.

mitigating circumstances

■ Facts that provide no justification or excuse for an action, but that can lower the amount of moral blame and thus lower the criminal penalty or civil damages for the action.

Suspended Imposition of Sentence

For some misdemeanors and infractions, judges are sometimes permitted to *suspend imposition of sentence* (SIS), also known as *diversion*. SIS is one of many forms of community-based correction, a term that refers to several varieties of nonincarceration correctional programs, such as probation, restitution, halfway houses, and parole. (Some of these other forms of community-based correction are discussed later.)

SIS is different from suspended sentencing. In SIS, a judge not only withholds sentencing the defendant but also refrains from entering a judgement of conviction until some future date. If the defendant complies with imposed conditions until that date, the prosecution is dismissed and the defendant is freed from having a criminal record. Suspended sentences, in contrast, involve conviction and imposition of sentence, but the defendant is relieved of actually serving the sentence so long as conditions are satisfied.

Where available, SIS is usually limited to non-violent misdemeanors and infractions and is available to first-time offenders only.

Concurrent and Consecutive Sentencing

If a defendant is already serving a sentence for another crime, or is convicted of two related crimes, the sentencing judge may impose **concurrent sentences** or **consecutive sentences.** If two sentences are concurrent, it is said that they "run together." That is, a defendant who receives two 5-year sentences will actually spend 5 years incarcerated. If the sentences are consecutive, the defendant will spend a total of 10 years incarcerated.

Parole

After committing a defendant to a correctional institution, the judge loses control and responsibility over that defendant, unless a statute provides otherwise. In many states, **parole** is available to prison inmates. *Parole*, an early release from prison, is used to encourage inmates to stay out of trouble and engage in rehabilitative efforts while in prison. Parole decisions are made by corrections officials (i.e., a parole board). Similar to probation, an offender must comply with certain conditions while on parole. Conditions routinely include not possessing a gun; not contacting witnesses, judge, jurors, or prosecutors associated with the offender's conviction; and not becoming involved in further criminal activity. Violation of a condition of parole may result in recommitment to prison.

Parole has fallen into disfavor in recent years. The result has been to limit the availability of parole in many situations. Parole has been eliminated for those convicted of crimes against the United States.

The Federal Guidelines

In November 1987, the Federal Sentencing Guidelines became effective. The guidelines are a milestone in federal criminal law. Their purpose is twofold: (1) to reduce sentencing disparity and (2) to achieve "honesty in sentencing."[30] Prior to the Guidelines, judges were given a large penalty range from which a defendant could be sentenced. The result of this discretion was that defendants similarly situated were often sentenced very differently. One goal of the Guidelines is to reduce such disparity in sentencing.

The second goal, honesty in sentencing, concerns parole. Prior to the Guidelines, defendants could be released on parole, in some cases, after only one-third of the imposed sentence had been served. In addition, prisoners complained that parole was arbitrarily and inconsistently applied. Accordingly, Congress eliminated parole, and the guidelines now reflect the time that will be served, less 54 days of good time that may be earned yearly (after the first year).

To achieve the first goal—the reduction of sentencing disparity—the Guidelines greatly limit the discretion of the judge in sentencing. To determine what sentence should be imposed, the offender's criminal history category and offense level must be determined. The criminal history category is simply determined by the number of prior convictions of the offender.

Finding an offender's offense level is more complex. First, the crime is assigned a base offense number. That number is then increased by "specific offense characteristics." Adjustments to this figure are then made for mitigating or aggravating circumstances. This final figure is the offense level.

concurrent sentences

▪ Prison terms that run at the same time.

consecutive sentences

▪ An additional prison term given to a person who is already convicted of a crime; the additional term is to be served after the previous one is finished.

parole

▪ Early release from prison or jail. Parole is usually granted with conditions such as requiring the parolee to refrain from communicating with the victim of the crime that led to the confinement and remaining free of criminality while on parole. If the conditions of parole are violated, parole may be revoked and the parolee may be returned to confinement to complete the original sentence.

Once the criminal history category and offense level are determined, the court looks to the sentencing table. This table provides a small range (the top figure never exceeds 25 percent of the bottom figure) from which the judge is to sentence the defendant. Only in rare instances may a judge deviate from the proscribed sentencing range.

The Guidelines continue to permit judges to suspend sentences to probation for offenses at the low end of the sentencing table. For offenses just above the probation cutoff, judges may sentence an offender to probation, provided some form of confinement is ordered, such as house arrest or community confinement. There is also a third layer of offenses, for which the judge may order a "split sentence." This is where one-half or more of the sentence must be served in prison, and the remaining amount may be served in another form of confinement.

The Guidelines have been the subject of much controversy. Federal judges themselves have been very critical of the Guidelines. Many contend that the reason judges are complaining is simply their loss of authority. Though this may be true, there also appear to be problems caused by the rigidity of the Guidelines.

The drafters of the Guidelines knew that all factors that should be considered in sentencing could not be anticipated (or quantified). As such, provisions are made to permit deviation from the Guidelines. However, deviation is rarely permitted. This practice has led to some absurd results. For example, one 21-year-old honor student, with no prior record, was sentenced to 10 years in prison for his involvement in one drug transaction.[31] At least one federal district judge has resigned because of dissatisfaction with the guidelines.

The guidelines were mandatory for nearly 20 years, surviving many constitutional challenges. Then, in 2005, the Supreme Court decided that the mandatory nature of the guidelines violated the Sixth Amendment's jury trial requirement in *United States v. Booker*.

The impact of *Booker* on sentencing has not been significant. The vast majority of convictees have continued to be sentenced within the ranges established by the guidelines after *Booker* was decided. The patterns of sentencing, even within the guidelines, were largely unchanged. Also, differences in sentencing (e.g., by region) that existed before *Booker* continued post-*Booker*.[32]

The federal government was not the first to enact sentencing guidelines. At least two states, Minnesota and Washington, were using guidelines when the federal version became law. It is probable that more jurisdictions will contemplate similar reform in the future.

Probation and Revocation

A popular alternative to incarceration is probation, also known as a **suspended sentence**. Probation is not always an alternative and is rarely available for crimes that are punished with life imprisonment or death. While on probation, the defendant is released from custody, but must comply with conditions imposed by the court during the probationary period. Each defendant is placed under the supervision of a probation officer during this period. The probation officer is an officer of the court, not of the corrections system.

Typical conditions of probation include a requirement of steady employment, refraining from other unlawful conduct, not carrying a firearm or other weapon, and not

suspended sentence

■ A sentence (usually "jail time") that the judge allows the convicted person to avoid serving (usually if the person continues on good behavior, completes community service, etc.).

leaving the jurisdiction of the court. A judge may tailor conditions to fit the circumstances of each case. For example, a child molester may be prohibited from obtaining employment that requires working around children.

Some judges make consent to search by a probation officer a condition of probation. This may include search of the person as well as property. In some cases, judges impose the search requirement independently; in others, the defendant and prosecutor stipulate to the searches through a plea agreement. In either situation, are there limits to this authority? May a probation officer search a probationer at any time, in any manner, and without any cause to believe that mischief is afoot? Further, can a defendant who is facing incarceration as an alternative give meaningful consent to such a condition? This is the subject of the *Consuelo-Gonzalez* case, in which the court decided that probationers are entitled to full Fourth Amendment protection as to law enforcement officers generally. Searches by police officers of probationers must satisfy the usual Fourth Amendment requirements.

Probationers are also protected by the Fourth Amendment's reasonableness requirement in regard to searches by probation officers. However, the standards are lowered, as the public has a greater interest in searching the probationer and the probationer has a lessened expectation to privacy. Also, probation officers do have a penal objective; in fact, they should have the welfare of their probationers in mind.

Therefore, probation officers may search a probationer's person or property with reasonable grounds; no warrant is required, although the search must be conducted in a reasonable manner. These conclusions have also been reached by the Supreme Court.[33] As a condition of probation, a search condition must be reasonably related to the probation, or it is invalid. Therefore, if a person is convicted of embezzlement, a condition providing for searches of the person would be unreasonable. The result would, of course, be different if the offense were possession of a firearm or drugs.

Finally, any other condition of probation that encroaches upon a constitutional guarantee is suspect. For example, a condition that restricts free speech is unconstitutional in most circumstances.[34] However, the right to travel freely and to bear arms are examples of constitutionally preserved rights that are commonly restricted during probation and parole.

A defendant who violates a condition of probation may be disciplined. Generally, the decision about whether any action should be taken for a violation is made by the probation officer. If a violation is extreme, the probation officer may file a petition to revoke probation. The sentencing court then holds a **revocation hearing.** If the petition is granted, the defendant is taken off probation and incarcerated.

At the revocation hearing, the defendant may be entitled to counsel. As a general rule, the right is not found in the Sixth Amendment, as the "critical stages" of trial have passed. In one rare case, the Supreme Court held that a Sixth Amendment right to counsel did exist at a revocation hearing. In *Mempa v. Rhay*, 389 U.S. 128 (1967),

revocation hearing

■ The due process hearing required before the government can revoke a privilege it has previously granted.

the trial judge withheld sentencing, placed the defendant on probation, and did not pronounce sentence until after the defendant violated his probation and then had it revoked. Because the revocation hearing turned out to be the defendant's sentencing hearing, where there is a right to counsel under the Sixth Amendment, the Court found that the Sixth Amendment applied.

The Due Process Clauses of the Fifth and Fourteenth Amendments may also provide a right to counsel at a revocation hearing. If a substantial question of law or fact must be resolved at the hearing, counsel must be appointed for the indigent defendant so that the issues can be fully explored and developed. If revocation is obvious, though, counsel need not be allowed.

Community Service

One alternative to incarceration for non-violent offenders is community service. In such a program, a defendant's sentence is suspended and the completion of a stated number of community service hours is a condition of the defendant's probation.

In most instances, the probation officer works with the probationer to find an appropriate job. However, the judge may require that a specific job be performed.

The requirements of community service range from unskilled to professional. For example, a judge may require that a professional, such as a physician or attorney, work in a clinic that provides services to the poor. The same person may be expected to pick up trash from local roads. Clearly, the former makes best use of the defendant's skills and benefits the community the most.

Restitution

The purpose of restitution is to compensate the victim, not to punish the offender. As such, restitution is not a substitute for other forms of punishment.

Restitution is limited to the actual amounts resulting from the offenses convicted.[35] Said another way, restitution is limited to losses resulting from the specific conduct that formed the basis of the conviction.[36] However, an agreement between the government and the defendant to pay a higher amount may be constitutional.[37]

Restitution may be made a condition of probation. A probationer's refusal to pay restitution can result in a revocation of probation. However, when a fine or restitution is imposed as a condition of probation, and "the probationer has made all reasonable efforts to pay . . . yet cannot do so through no fault of his own, it is fundamentally unfair to revoke probation automatically without considering whether adequate alternative methods of punishing the defendant are available."[38]

Fines

Unlike the goal of restitution, the purpose of a fine is to punish the offender. Accordingly, restitution monies are paid to victims, and fines end up in the public treasury. Fines are a common method of punishing misdemeanants. Serious crimes are frequently punished with both a fine and incarceration. Any fine imposed must be reasonable; that is, the amount must be within the financial means of the offender. Excessive fines are prohibited by the Eighth Amendment.

It is a violation of equal protection to sentence individuals without means to pay a fine to longer periods of incarceration than those received by individuals who can pay a fine. In *Williams v. Illinois*,[39] a defendant was sentenced to a maximum one year in prison and a $500 fine for petty theft. Illinois statute provided that if at the end of the year, the fine (and court costs) were not paid, the defendant was to remain in jail for a time to satisfy the debt. This sentence was calculated at $5.00 per day. The Court found that because Williams was indigent, the statute violated the Equal Protection Clause by improperly sentencing defendants according to economic status. Of course, a defendant who has the financial means to pay a fine, and does not, may have probation revoked or incarceration increased.

Forfeiture

Forfeitures are similar to fines in that they involve the taking of property and money to punish defendants. A forfeiture is, however, not directed at the defendant's pocketbook in general, as is a fine. Rather, forfeiture focuses on taking the property owned by a defendant that is in some manner connected with the crimes. Automobiles, airplanes, or boats used to transport drugs are an example. Forfeiture has become an increasingly popular tool amongst law enforcement agencies.

Procedurally, forfeiture may occur within and as part of a criminal proceeding. In addition, many laws permit forfeiture to occur in a separative in rem civil proceeding. Most statutes allow law enforcement officers to make seizures based upon probable cause, to be immediately followed by the filing of a forfeiture proceeding.[40] Of course, seizure can also occur later in the proceedings. Under federal law, if a seizure was proper (i.e., based upon probable cause), the burden of proof falls on a claimant to establish that the property is not subject to seizure. The claimant must prove this by a preponderance of the evidence.[41]

Under federal law, forfeiture is provided for in several instances, including violations of the Racketeer Influenced and Corrupt Organizations Act (RICO) and under the so-called drug kingpin statute, the Continuing Criminal Enterprise law.[42]

There are limits to the use of forfeiture. In *United States v. James Daniel Good Real Property*,[43] the Supreme Court determined that the Due Process Clause requires the government to provide notice and a preseizure hearing when it intends to forfeit real property, unless exigent circumstances justify an immediate seizure. There is no requirement of preseizure notice in cases where property can disappear. The Court stated that in cases where property is movable, immediate seizure, without notice or a hearing, is necessary to "establish the court's jurisdiction over the property" and to guard against someone absconding with the property.

A critical issue concerns the relationship between the crime and the property forfeited. Forfeiture of all property associated with a crime can be troubling. Forfeiting a boat that was purchased with drug money and is used to transport drugs from Colombia to the United States is not problematic. But is it constitutionally sound to forfeit a home because one joint of marijuana is discovered inside? Does the Eighth Amendment's Excessive Fines Clause limit the use of forfeitures? In *Austin*, the Supreme Court examined this issue.

The *Austin* Court held that the Eighth Amendment's Excessive Fines Clause applies to civil in rem forfeiture proceedings. Accordingly, a forfeiture must be proportional to the offense. A fine or forfeiture that is grossly larger than the underlying offense is excessive and violative of the Eighth Amendment. The fine at issue in *United States v. Bajakajian* is an example of an excessive fine.

Similarly, even though forfeiture may be characterized as civil, the exclusionary rule applies to bar illegally seized evidence in quasi-criminal forfeiture cases.[44] This is contrary to the rule that the exclusionary rule is not applied in civil and administrative cases.

Modern Sentencing Alternatives

In recent years, many new alternatives to incarceration have been developed. Such alternatives are actually forms of probation, and, as such, are administered by courts and probation officers.

For the non-violent criminal, work release is an alternative. While in these programs the offender lives in a jail, but is permitted to leave jail to work. Work release has many advantages. The defendant continues to earn a living. This is particularly important if the defendant has dependents. Also, it is good for the self-esteem of offenders; they continue to feel a useful part of the community. The final advantage is true of many sentencing alternatives: the cost to the public is lower because the offender is often required to pay, in whole or part, for participation in the program.

For those convicted of some alcohol and drug offenses, courts have turned to alcohol and drug treatment over imprisonment. These programs vary greatly. For first-time drunk driving convictions, offenders may be required to do one or more of the following, in addition to traditional conditions of probation:

1. Participate in an alcohol treatment program, such as Alcoholics Anonymous.
2. Report for periodic urine or blood tests to detect the presence of alcohol.
3. Take a drug such as Antabuse, which makes a person ill if alcohol is ingested.
4. Participate in a defensive/safe-driving school.

If a defendant has a previous drunk driving conviction, he or she is likely to receive some "executed time" or jail time, in addition to some or all of the previously listed conditions. A few courts have tried a form of shock treatment. For example, a defendant may be required to meet with drunk drivers who are responsible for killing someone and discuss that experience. In another example, at least one judge has required that a drunk driver work in a hospital emergency room so that the defendant would be exposed to alcohol-related injuries and deaths.

First-time drug users may also be placed on probation, subject to conditions similar to those previously listed: periodic urinalysis or blood screening and drug counseling and treatment. This form of probation is not available to drug dealers.

Two other forms of probation that may be used independently or mixed with one or more of the others are house arrest and halfway houses. If a defendant is sentenced to house arrest, he or she may not leave the home without prior permission of the probation officer, except in emergencies.

Today, the use of electronic shackles makes enforcement of house arrests easier. These devices are attached to the probationer's leg; and through the transmission of a radio signal, it can be determined if the defendant is at home.

Halfway houses are minimum security homes located in the community. Generally they serve two groups of offenders: those making the transition from prison to the community and those who need some confinement, but not jail or prison.

Halfway houses are commonly used in conjunction with work release programs. The residents are given some freedom to leave the home but are restricted in their travel. Often such homes provide drug and alcohol counseling and treatment and vocational training.

Yet another community-based correction program is the boot camp or "shock incarceration" program. Boot camps are gaining in popularity as a method of reforming youthful offenders. As of early 1994, nearly 30 states were operating prison boot camps.[45]

The typical boot camp experience involves 90 to 180 days of "rigid military-training atmosphere followed by intensive community supervision." Boot camp programs are usually limited to first-time offenders who have been sentenced to a term of imprisonment. Most programs are designed to accommodate individuals sentenced to prison, but a growing number of jails are using boot camps as an alternative to traditional confinement.[46]

This is not by any means an exhaustive list of alternative punishments. The list is limited only by the U.S. Constitution and the imagination of judges. For example, one Florida judge required those convicted of drunk driving to place bumper stickers on their cars warning of their convictions. This requirement was upheld by the Florida Court of Appeals.[47]

Habitual Offender Statutes

The career criminal or repeat offender is now subject to extreme penalty in most jurisdictions. These statutes are referred to as *recidivist* or **habitual offender laws.**

Most statutes provide for an increased penalty if a defendant has been convicted of a stated number of felonies, often three, within a certain period of time, such as 10 years. These are popularly known as the "three strikes and you're out" laws.

To prevent unfair prejudice to the defendant, the jury usually does not know about the habitual criminal charge until it has reached a verdict in the underlying charge. So, if Pam is charged with murder and of being a habitual criminal, the jury would initially know only of the murder charge. If the jury comes back with an acquittal, the habitual criminal charge is dismissed. If the verdict is guilty, the jury is then told that it must also determine if the defendant is an habitual criminal. This is known as a bifurcated procedure.

To prove the habitual criminal charge, the prosecutor will introduce court records reflecting the prior convictions and, in some instances, call the prosecutors involved in the prior convictions to attest that the defendant was indeed convicted.

Habitual criminal laws have been attacked as violative of the Double Jeopardy Clause. Such claims have not been successful, as they are not considered a second punishment of one of the earlier offenses. Rather, evidence of a criminal record provides a reason to increase the penalty for the most recent offense.

halfway house
■ A facility in which persons recently discharged from a rehabilitation center or prison live for a time and are given support and assistance in readjusting to society at large.

habitual offender statutes
■ Laws that may apply to a person who has been convicted of as few as two prior crimes (often violent or drug-related crimes) and that greatly increase the penalties for each succeeding crime.

POSTCONVICTION REMEDIES

Technically, motions for new trials are postconviction remedies. Other than such motions, there are two major methods of attacking a conviction or other decision at the trial level: appeal and habeas corpus.

Appeal

The Constitution of the United States does not expressly confer a right to appeal.[48] Regardless, every state provides for appeal either through statute or constitution. Once a state establishes a right to appeal, the U.S. Constitution requires that appellate procedure not violate the Fourteenth Amendment's Due Process or Equal Protection Clauses.

Appeals from federal district courts go to the U.S. Courts of Appeals (circuit courts). From there, appeal is taken to the Supreme Court of the United States. In state cases, appeal is taken to the state intermediate appellate court, if any. Appeal from that court is taken to the state high court, usually named the Supreme Court of the state. All issues, federal and state, are heard by those courts. Issues of state law may not be appealed any further. If the defendant wishes to appeal a decision of the state high court concerning an issue of federal law, the appeal is taken to the United States Supreme Court.

Filing the Appeal

Because the right to appeal is purely statutory, it may be lost if it is not timely filed. The federal rules require that appeals be filed within 10 days of the date of judgement.[49] The government is given 30 days in those instances where it may appeal. Appeals from state courts to the United States Supreme Court must be filed within 90 days of the entry of judgement.[50]

Procedures vary, but it is common to require the appellant to file several documents to begin the appeal. The first document is a notice or petition of appeal. This simply informs all the parties, as well as the trial judge, that the case is being appealed. A designation of record will also be filed by the parties. Through this document, the parties select the portions of the trial record that they desire to be sent to the appellate court. A statement of issues that must be resolved on appeal may also be filed by the appellant. Finally, a filing fee must be paid. Appellants who cannot afford it may seek relief from the filing fee requirement.

After the necessary documents are filed, the parties brief the issues for the appellate court. The appellate court, in its discretion, may hear oral arguments.

Because the penalty for untimely filings is harsh (dismissal of the appeal), most courts recognize constructive filings. This is particularly true for incarcerated defendants who rely on counsel or prison officials in preparing or filing an appeal.

Note that most jurisdictions provide for the possibility of bail pending appeal. This is most often available in misdemeanor cases; however, it may be granted in felony cases also.

The Scope of Review

To avoid unnecessary delay, only **final orders** may be appealed. Therefore, erroneous pretrial decisions are not corrected until appeal is taken, after the case is completed. Orders that may not be reviewed until after final judgement are those relating to the suppression of evidence, discovery, and the sufficiency of the charging instruments.

There are a few exceptions to the final judgement rule. The most prominent exception is the collateral order doctrine. Under this doctrine, orders that are independent of the criminal case may be immediately appealed. The appeal proceeds concurrently with the underlying criminal case.

Appeals taken from ongoing litigation (where no final order has been issued) are called **interlocutory appeals.** Orders holding a defendant incompetent to stand trial, denying bail, and denying a defendant's double jeopardy claim have been held collateral and immediately appealable.[51] Certain orders that occur after judgement, such as revocation of probation, are also immediately appealable.

Remember, cases are not retried on appeal. Appellate courts review the record for errors of law, not fact. That means the appellate court will not examine the evidence and substitute its judgement for that of the trial court (or jury). However, the court will examine the record to make sure that sufficient evidence exists to support the judgement. So long as sufficient evidence can be found, the appellate court will not reverse, even if it would have decided the case differently. Issues of law are reviewed anew (de novo).

Not every error warrants reversing the trial court. Only when an error prejudices the defendant is reversal required. An error is prejudicial if there is a possibility that it changed the outcome of the case. If not, it was **harmless error.** The appellant bears the burden of proving that he or she was prejudiced by the error of the trial court.

Some error is so violative of the Constitution that it is irrebuttably presumed prejudicial, so reversal is automatic. An order denying defense counsel at trial is never harmless error.[52]

Prosecution/Defense Appeals

Because of the Double Jeopardy Clause, defendants have a broader right to appeal than does the government. A defendant who is tried and convicted is free to appeal any factual or legal error. However, this right may be limited by a requirement of *preservation*. To satisfy this rule, the defendant must raise the issue at the trial level. This gives the trial judge an opportunity to avoid error.

Failure to raise the issue results in a waiver. For example, a defendant who does not challenge the sufficiency of an indictment at the trial level may not raise the issue for the first time before the appellate court. The same is true of evidentiary matters. The defendant must object to the admission of evidence that he or she believes should be excluded, so as to preserve the issue for appeal.

The prosecution has a limited right to appeal. Because of the prohibition on trying a person twice for the same offense, the government has no right to appeal acquittals. However, most states permit the government to appeal certain orders issued before jeopardy attaches. Orders dismissing charging instruments, suppressing evidence prior to

final judgement (order)

■ The last action of a court; the one upon which an appeal can be based.

interlocutory appeal

■ The *Interlocutory Appeals* Act (28 U.S.C. 1292 (1948)) is a federal law that provides for an appeal while a trial is going on if the trial judge states in writing: (1) A legal question has come up that directly affects the trial. (2) There are major questions as to how that point of law should be resolved. (3) The case would proceed better if the appeals court answers the question.

harmless error

■ A trivial mistake made by a judge in the procedures used at trial, or in making l-egal rulings during the trial.

trial, and releasing the defendant before trial may be appealed. These interlocutory appeals do not violate the Fifth Amendment's Double Jeopardy Clause, because jeopardy does not attach until a jury has been impaneled or the first witness is sworn in a nonjury trial. See Chapter 14 for a more thorough discussion of double jeopardy and appeals.

The Right to Counsel on Appeal

There is no Sixth Amendment right to counsel on appeal. The Sixth Amendment right begins once a defendant is charged and continues, at all critical stages, through trial and sentencing. In some instances, it is in effect at probation revocation. It does not ever include appeals.

The right to counsel on appeal can be found, however, in the Equal Protection Clause of the Fourteenth Amendment. The Supreme Court said, in *Douglas v. California*,[53] that indigent defendants convicted of a felony have a right to appointed counsel on appeal, provided that the appeal is by right. *By right* means that the defendant's appeal must be heard by the appellate court. Most, if not all, states have provided for appeal by right.

If an appeal is discretionary, the Equal Protection Clause of the Fourteenth Amendment does not compel the state to provide counsel.

As is true at trial, the defendant is entitled to effective counsel. The appointed attorney has an ethical obligation to zealously pursue the defendant's appeal. Because of the large number of frivolous appeals, the Supreme Court has stated that an appointed attorney may be allowed to withdraw. However, the following must be done: first, the attorney must request withdrawal from the appellate court; second, a brief must be filed explaining why the attorney believes the appeal to be wholly without merit. In that brief, all potential issues must be outlined for the court's review. If the appellate court agrees that there are no valid issues, the attorney may withdraw. If the court finds an issue that has some merit, the lawyer must continue to represent the defendant.

Habeas Corpus

Both the states and federal governments have habeas corpus relief. Here we discuss federal habeas corpus relief, particularly federal habeas corpus in state criminal proceedings. Although habeas corpus relief is available at any stage of a criminal proceeding, most habeas corpus petitions are filed after conviction. The discussion here is limited to such postconviction petitions.

Through habeas corpus proceedings, an individual may attack the lawfulness of confinement, whether it be substantive or procedural in nature. Further, the conditions of confinement and the lawfulness of an imposed punishment may be reviewed by a habeas court.

History

Translated, *habeas corpus* means "you have the body." In action, the writ is used to order someone who has custody of another to bring that person before the court. Any person who believes that he or she is being detained illegally may use the writ to gain his or her freedom. Because of the significant power of the writ, it has come to be known as the "Great Writ of Liberty."

The writ has ancient origin, dating back as far as the twelfth century. Habeas corpus was often used to enforce provisions of the Magna Carta. The success of the writ in protecting liberty in England influenced the drafters of the U.S. Constitution. The result is Article I, § 9, clause 2, which states: "The Privilege of the Writ of Habeas Corpus shall not be suspended unless when in Cases of Rebellion or Invasion the Public Safety may require it."

Federal habeas corpus is important in criminal law because it is used to challenge state court convictions. That is, if a defendant believes that his or her federal constitutional rights were violated in a state court, he or she may attack the conviction through federal habeas corpus.

Habeas corpus has had congressional authorization since 1789. The first statute made habeas corpus available only to federal prisoners. This was changed by the Habeas Corpus Act of 1867, which extended habeas corpus to any person "restrained of his or her liberty in violation of the constitution, or of any treaty or law of the United States." The 1867 act continues to be in effect, with some modifications.

Scope of Review

The current habeas corpus statutes are found at 28 U.S.C. §§ 2241–2255. Section 2254 provides habeas corpus relief to state prisoners. Under § 2255, federal prisoners are to move to vacate or set aside their sentences, in a procedure nearly identical to § 2254. Relief under this section must be sought before a federal prisoner can bring habeas corpus. Even then, the statute states that habeas corpus shall not be issued if the prisoner was unsuccessful with a § 2255 claim, unless that proceeding was "inadequate or ineffective." A biased judge is an example of when habeas corpus may be issued after a § 2255 motion has been denied.

The federal courts continued to have little involvement with state proceedings, even after the 1867 act extended the reach of federal habeas corpus to state prisoners. This was largely due to Supreme Court decisions limiting the review of federal habeas corpus to questions of jurisdiction.

The scope of review was enlarged in *Brown v. Allen*, 344 U.S. 443 (1953), in which it was held that federal habeas corpus could be used to relitigate all issues of federal law. This decision significantly increased the power of federal habeas corpus and resulted in increased intervention of federal courts in state criminal proceedings.

The Supreme Court has since narrowed habeas corpus relief by decision. For example, a state prisoner may not use federal habeas corpus to relitigate Fourth Amendment claims (search and seizure), provided the defendant was provided a "full and fair litigation" in state court. Also, the Court has emphasized that the purpose of habeas corpus is to provide relief to persons imprisoned in violation of the laws of the United States, not to relitigate or correct factual errors. Accordingly, a claim of innocence, even when supported by new evidence, is not alone sufficient to confer habeas jurisdiction upon a court. An independent constitutional claim must be made for a court to examine such a petition.[54]

Exhaustion of Remedies

Before a state prisoner can seek the aid of a federal court, he or she must satisfy certain procedural requirements. First, the defendant must use all means available in the state system to correct the alleged error. This is the doctrine of **exhaustion of remedies**. Section 2254(b) states:

> An application for a writ of habeas corpus in behalf of a person in custody pursuant to the judgment of a State court shall not be granted unless it appears that the applicant has exhausted the remedies available in the courts of the State, or that there is either an absence of available corrective process or the existence of circumstances rendering such process ineffective to protect the rights of the prisoner.

The remedies that must be exhausted depend on what is available in the state system, such as motions for new trial, state habeas corpus relief, and appeals. Of course, if no remedy is available, the defendant may immediately petition for habeas corpus relief.

If a remedy is available, but it would be futile to exhaust it, habeas corpus may be brought without exhaustion. For example, assume State Supreme Court has previously addressed the legal issue raised by the defendant, and its decision is contrary to the defendant's claim. Unless there is reason to believe that the court will reconsider its decision, there is no need to exhaust this remedy. Excessive delay in the state proceedings may also be a basis for bringing habeas corpus before the state remedies have been exhausted, provided the state does not have a remedy for such delays (e.g., mandamus).

The fact that a defendant has failed to timely appeal (or file a motion for new trial, etc.) does not mean that habeas corpus is unavailable. The question is: Are state remedies available? If a defendant has missed the right to appeal under state law, and no other remedy is available, then habeas corpus may be used to resolve his or her federal constitutional claims. However, defendants who deliberately bypass state procedures may be denied habeas relief.[55]

The Custody Requirement

The Habeas Corpus Act speaks of prisoners "in custody." However, this has been interpreted to include all wrongful restraints of liberty. The Supreme Court has said that persons who are subject to "restraints not shared by the public generally" are entitled to habeas corpus protection, even though they may not be in the physical custody of the government.

Under this interpretation, persons placed on probation and parole have been held to be in custody, as have defendants released on bail.[56] Habeas corpus protection is also available to a defendant who has served his or her entire sentence, because the restraint of liberty includes not only incarceration but also collateral loss of civil liberties (e.g., right to carry a weapon), injury to reputation, and the possibility of an increased penalty for a later conviction.

A defendant who is lawfully detained may use habeas corpus to challenge his or her sentence if he or she believes it is excessive. Also, if he or she was convicted of several crimes and was sentenced to consecutive sentences, he or she need not wait until

---

exhaustion of remedies

■ A person must usually take all reasonable steps to get satisfaction from a state or federal government before seeking judicial relief.

the lawful sentence expires before petitioning for habeas corpus. It appears that an invalid sentence may be attacked even though it runs concurrently with a valid sentence. Again, the collateral effects of the conviction are the rationale.

Procedure

The following rules were established by the United States Supreme Court to implement 22 U.S.C. § 2254.[57] The petition for habeas corpus relief is filed in the federal district within which the prisoner is being held. The petition shall name the person who has custody of the applicant as the respondent. Indigent persons may file a motion to proceed in forma pauperis, which relieves such persons from paying the filing fee.

Immediately after the petition is filed, the district judge will examine the petition. If the petition is "plainly" invalid, the court will dismiss it. If not, the court will direct the respondent to answer the petition.

Counsel may be appointed and discovery is available, with leave of the district court. After the petition has been answered and appropriate discovery conducted, the district court may hold an evidentiary hearing and issue an opinion or rule from the record without a hearing. Habeas corpus decisions may be appealed.

The Right to Counsel

To date, the Supreme Court has not found a constitutional right to the assistance of counsel in preparing and presenting a petition for habeas corpus.

In some instances the district court may have to hold an evidentiary hearing. It is possible that in such instances a due process right to counsel exists to assure that the hearing is fair. The issue is not of critical importance presently, because federal habeas corpus rules require the appointment of counsel for such hearings. Additionally, the rules give the district court the discretion to appoint counsel earlier, if necessary.

Although there may be no right to counsel, there is a right to "access to the courts." Therefore, prisoners must be furnished with paper, pens, stamps, and access to a law library. Further, unless a prison provides adequate legal assistance to its prisoners, so-called jailhouse lawyers may not be prohibited from assisting other inmates in the preparation of legal documents.

Web Links

Punishment and Sentencing

Information and documents about trials, sentencing, appeals, and punishment can be found at *http://truTV.com*

There is much information about the death penalty on the Internet. Here are a few sites:

http://www.deathpenaltyinfo.org/

http://www.prodeathpenalty.com/

http://www.aclu.org/capital/

http://web.amnesty.org/

Chapter 7: Sentencing and Appeal

Key Terms

aggravating circumstances
commutation of sentence
concurrent sentences
consecutive sentences
determinate sentencing
exhaustion of remedies
final orders

habitual offender laws
halfway houses
harmless error
indeterminate sentence
interlocutory appeals
mitigating circumstances
pardon

parole
reprieve
revocation hearing
suspended sentence
victim impact statement

Review Questions

1. What is a presentence investigation? Who conducts the investigation, and what is its purpose?
2. What are aggravating and mitigating circumstances in sentencing?
3. What is the final judgement rule?
4. Does a defendant have a right to appointed counsel on appeal?
5. What is habeas corpus?
6. Distinguish harmless from prejudicial error.
7. May victim impact evidence be considered by sentencing courts?
8. Which of the following punishments has the Supreme Court held to be inherently cruel and unusual?
   a. Death by hanging
   b. Death by starvation
   c. Flogging
   d. Solitary confinement
   e. Imprisonment without lighting or a bed
9. Differentiate a suspended imposition of sentence from a sentence suspended to probation.

Problems & Critical Thinking Exercises

1–4. Kevin, an attorney, has been indicted for embezzlement. After his preliminary hearing, he filed a motion to suppress a confession he believes was illegally obtained. A hearing was conducted and the trial court granted his motion. The evidence was vital to the prosecution.

Kevin's attorney has also requested that the trial be continued because he claims that Kevin is not competent to stand trial. The judge ordered a mental evaluation, held a hearing, and found Kevin competent to stand trial.

The defense also requested that the court order a number of police officers to submit to depositions prior to trial. The court denied the motion.

At trial, the defendant objected to the introduction of a document that he believed was unconstitutionally obtained during a search of his office. The judge overruled the objection and admitted the confession into evidence.

Answer the following questions using these facts.

1. The prosecution strongly believes that the documents that were suppressed are admissible. The prosecutor objects on the record to the judge's order and then appeals the issue after Kevin is acquitted. What should be the outcome on appeal?
2. Kevin disagrees with the trial court finding of competency. What is his remedy?

3. Believing that Kevin cannot have a fair trial without the depositions, his attorney filed an interlocutory appeal seeking an order from the appellate court requiring the trial judge to provide for the depositions. What should be the outcome?

4. Kevin appealed the trial court's decision denying his motion to suppress the document. The appellate court affirmed the trial court, and Kevin filed a habeas corpus petition in federal court claiming that his federal constitutional rights were violated by admission of the evidence. What should be the outcome?

Endnotes

1. The Supreme Court has not yet answered this question. *See also United States v. Rogers*, 921 F.2d 957 (10th Cir. 1990), *cert. denied*, 111 S. Ct. 113 (1991).
2. *United States v. Jackson*, 886 F.2d 838 (7th Cir. 1989).
3. Fed. R. Crim. P. 32(c)(1).
4. Fed. R. Crim. P. 32(c)(3).
5. *Apprendi v. New Jersey*, 530 U.S. 466 (2000).
6. *Eddings v. Oklahoma*, 455 U.S. 104 (1982).
7. *United States v. Watts*, 519 U.S. 148 (1997).
8. *See Apprendi v. New Jersey*, 530 U.S. 466 (2000); *Blakely v. Washington*, 542 U.S. 296 (2004); *United States v. Booker*, 543 U.S. 220 (2005); and *Cunningham v. California*, _____ U.S. (2007).
9. *Ring v. Arizona*, 536 U.S. 584 (2002).
10. *Locket v. Ohio*, 438 U.S. at 604–05.
11. *See Kansas v. Marsh*, 548 U.S. (2006).
12. *Callins v. Collins*, 510 U.S. 1141 (1994) 114 S. Ct. 1127, 1132 (1994) (Blackmun, J., dissenting).
13. 114 S. Ct. at 1129–30.
14. All the data appearing before this endnote in this sidebar was taken from Jeffrey Kirchmeier, "Another Place Beyond Here: The Death Penalty Moratorium Movement in the United States," *73 U. Colo. L. Rev.* 1 (2002).
15. 553 U.S. 35 (2008).
16. *Coker v. Georgia*, 433 U.S. 584 (1977).
17. *Enmund v. Florida*, 458 U.S. 782 (1972).
18. *Ford v. Wainwright*, 477 U.S. 399 (1986).
19. *See Roper v. Simmons*, 543 U.S. 551 (2005).
20. 536 U.S. 304.
21. *Pervear v. Commonwealth*, 72 U.S. (5 Wall) 475 (1867); *Wing Wong v. United States*, 163 U.S. 228 (1896); *Kehrli v. Sprinkle*, 524 F.2d 328 (10th Cir. 1975).

22. *Delaware v. Cannon*, 55 Del. 587, 190 A.2d 574 (1963).
23. *Jackson v. Bishop*, 404 F.2d 571 (8th Cir. 1968).
24. For a thorough discussion of the constitutionality of whipping, *see* Daniel E. Hall, "When Caning Meets the Eighth Amendment: Whipping Offenders in the United States," 4 *Widener J. Pub. L.* 403 (1995).
25. 21 *U.S.C.* 841(b)(1).
26. 501 U.S. 957 (1991).]
27. United States v. Gementera, 379 F.3d 596 (9th Cir. 2004).
28. Laura Edwins, *10 Weird Criminal Sentences*, The Christian Science Monitor. Found on May 15, 2013 at csmonitor.com
29. All the examples with the exception of the first and second come from Jan Hoffman, *Crime and Punishment: Shame Gains Popularity*, The New York Times. January 16, 1997. Found at http://www.nytimes.com/1997/01/16/us/crime-and-punishment-shame-gains-popularity.html?pagewanted=all&src=pm
30. Breyer, "The Federal Sentencing Guidelines and the Key Compromises Upon Which They Rest," 17 *Hofstra L. Rev.* 4 (1988).
31. Federal Judges Association, *In Camera* (Dec. 1990).
32. Final Report on the Impact of the *United States v. Booker* on Federal Sentencing, United States Sentencing Commission, March 2006.
33. *Griffin v. Wisconsin*, 483 U.S. 868 (1987).
34. *Porth v. Templar*, 453 F.2d 330 (10th Cir. 1971).
35. *United States v. Green*, 735 F.2d 1203 (9th Cir. 1984).
36. *Hughey v. United States*, 495 U.S. 411 (1990).
37. *Phillips v. United States*, 679 F.2d 192 (9th Cir. 1982).
38. *Bearden v. Georgia*, 461 U.S. 660, 668–69 (1983).
39. 399 U.S. 235 (1970).
40. *See*, for example, 21 U.S.C. § 881.
41. 19 U.S.C. § 1615.
42. *See* 21 U.S.C. § 853.
43. 114 S. Ct. 492 (1993).
44. *One 1958 Plymouth v. Pennsylvania*, 380 U.S. 693 (1965).
45. *The Growing Use of Jail Boot Camps: The Current State of the Art* (Washington, DC: National Institute of Justice, October 1993).
46. Belinda McCarthy & Bernard McCarthy, *Community-Based Corrections*, 2nd ed. (Belmont, CA: Brooks/Cole, 1991), p. 128.
47. *Goldschmitt v. State*, 490 So. 2d 123 (Fla. Dist. Ct. App.), *review denied*, 496 So. 2d 142 (Fla. 1986).
48. *McKane v. Durston*, 153 U.S. 684 (1894).
49. Fed. R. Crim. P. 37.

50. Supreme Ct. R. 11.1.
51. W. Lafave & J. Israel, *Criminal Procedure* § 26.2(c). (Hornbook Series; St. Paul, MN: West, 1985).
52. *Gideon v. Wainwright*, 373 U.S. 335 (1963).
53. 372 U.S. 353 (1963).
54. *Herrera v. Collins*, 113 S. Ct. 853 (1993).
55. *Fay v. NOIA*, 372 U.S. 391 (1963).
56. *Jones v. Cunningham*, 371 U.S. 236 (1963); *Hensley v. Municipal Court*, 411 U.S. 345 (1973).
57. *See Rules Governing Section 2254 Cases in the United States District Courts* (February 1989). These rules also contain the forms necessary to petition for habeas corpus relief in the district court of the United States.

CHAPTER 8

THE TWO ESSENTIAL ELEMENTS

Chapter Outline

Mens Rea
    Mens Rea and the Common Law
    General, Specific, and Constructive Intent
    Strict Liability
    Vicarious Liability
    Corporate Liability
    Current Approaches to Mens Rea
    Proving Mens Rea
    Motive
Actus Reus
    Voluntariness
    Thoughts and Statements as Acts
    Personal Status as an Act
    Possession as an Act
    Duty Imposed by Statute
    Duty by Relationship
    Duty by Contract
    Assumption of Duty
    Creating Danger
    Causation
    The "Year-and-a-Day Rule"
    Possession as an Act
    Omissions as Acts
    Causation

Chapter Objectives

After completing this chapter you should be able to:

- identify and define the two basic elements of most crimes, mens rea and actus reus.
- describe the evolution of mens rea and actus reus from the early common law to modernity, particularly as found in the Model Penal Code.
- be challenged to reflect on what it means to have a guilty mind, from both a psychological and a legal perspective.
- define and describe corporate and vicarious liability.

- apply and compare the historic and modern law of mens rea and actus reus to real life scenarios.
- define and apply element analysis to statutory definitions of crimes.
- read and identify the major elements of a judicial opinion.
- identify the major elements of a case brief.

MENS REA

Nearly every crime consists of two essential elements: the mental and the physical. This chapter begins by addressing the mental element and concludes by examining the physical element.

It is common to distinguish between acts that are intentional and those that occur accidentally. Everyone has caused injury to another person or another person's property accidentally. That the injury was accidental (not intended) often leads to a statement such as, "I'm sorry. I didn't mean to hurt you." In these situations, people often feel a social obligation to pay for any injuries they have caused, or to assist the injured party in other ways, but they probably do not expect to be punished criminally. As the late Supreme Court Justice Holmes stated, "Even a dog distinguishes between being stumbled over and being kicked." As this statement implies, to make such a distinction between accidental and intentional acts that injure others appears to be natural. For humans, it is consistent with common notions of fairness. Indeed many of the earliest laws known to humanity, dating back thousands of years, distinguish intentional from intentional behavior, treating the latter as less serious. Modern criminal law follows this model; that is, people are often held accountable for intentional behavior and not for accidental, even though the consequences may be the same. However, this is not always so. Under some circumstances, accidental behavior (negligent or reckless) may be the basis of criminal liability.

Mens rea is the mental part, the state of mind required to be criminally liable. It is often defined as "a guilty mind" or possessing a criminal intent. It is best defined as the state of mind required to be criminally liable for a certain act. It is sometimes the case that no intent whatsoever is required to be guilty of a crime, although most criminal laws require intent to some degree before criminal liability attaches to an act.

Mens rea is an important concept in criminal law. It is also a confusing one, largely because of the inconsistency and lack of uniformity between criminal statutes and judicial decisions. One author found 79 words and phrases in the U.S. Criminal Code used to describe mens rea.[1] Often, when courts or legislatures use the same term, they do so assuming different meanings for the term. For this reason, the drafters of the Model Penal Code attempted to establish uniform terms and definitions for those terms. The Model Penal Code approach is examined later. First, you will learn how mens rea was defined at the common law.

mens rea

■ (Latin) A state of mind that produces a crime.

Mens Rea and the Common Law

One principle under the common law was that there should be no crime if there was no act accompanied by a guilty mind. The Latin phrase that states this principle is: "actus non facit reum nisi mens sit rea." Today, under some statutes, no intent is required to be guilty of a crime. Despite this, the principle that "only conscious wrongdoing constitutes crime is deeply rooted in our legal system and remains the rule, rather than the exception."[2]

Many terms have been used to describe a guilty mind. Malicious, mischievous, purposeful, unlawful, intentional, with specific intent, knowing, fraudulent, with an evil purpose, careless, willful, negligent, and reckless are examples of terms and phrases used to describe the mental state required to prove guilt.

General, Specific, and Constructive Intent

general intent
■ The desire to commit a prohibited act but not the outcome of that act.

specific intent
■ An intent to commit the exact crime charged or the precise outcome of the act, not merely an intent to commit the act without an intention to cause the outcome.

One common law distinction is between **general intent** and **specific intent.** The distinction turns on whether the defendant intended to cause the consequences of the act. If the defendant had a desire or purpose to cause the *result* of the act, then the defendant possessed specific intent. If the defendant intended only the act, and not the result of that act, then the defendant possessed general intent. For example, Don Defendant throws a large rock at Victoria Victim, inflicting a fatal wound. If Defendant only intended to injure Victim, not kill her, then he possessed general intent. However, if Defendant threw the rock hoping it would kill Victim, then he possessed specific intent. The distinction between general and specific intent is often an important one, as many statutes require specific intent for a higher-level crime and general intent for a lower crime. In this example, many state statues would allow Defendant to be responsible to be charged with first-degree murder if he intended to kill Victim, but with second-degree murder if he only intended to injure Victim under many contemporary state statutes.

So long as a defendant intends to cause the result, it is irrelevant that the means used to achieve the result are likely to fail. For example, assume Defendant desires to cause the death of Victim. One day, while walking down a street, Defendant notices Victim far away. Defendant picks up a rock and hurls it toward Victim, hoping it will strike Victim and kill her, although because of the distance, he does not expect the rock to strike its intended target. However, all of those afternoons practicing his baseball pitch paid off, and the rock hits Victim in the head, killing her instantly. The fact that Defendant threw the rock with an intent to kill is enough to establish Defendant's specific intent. The fact that the act is unlikely to be successful is no defense.

scienter
■ (Latin) Knowingly; with guilty knowledge. [pronounce: si-*en*-ter]

Specific intent may also be proved, in some jurisdictions, by showing that the defendant possessed knowledge of a particular fact or illegality. This requirement of knowledge is known as **scienter.** Although scienter and mens rea are commonly treated as synonyms, they are not. Scienter is a specific form of mens rea. If an individual commits a crime with a scienter element while believing that the act engaged in is lawful or without the specific knowledge required, then specific intent is lacking, and only general intent can be proven.[3] Scienter often does not require proof of subjective knowledge (what was actually in the defendant's mind), but can be established if the prosecution can prove that the defendant should have known the fact in question. For example, assume that Abina recently emigrated to the United States. In her home country uniforms are common. Security guards, cab drivers, and hotel employees all wear uniforms that are difficult to distinguish from police. Not fully acclimated to the

United States, she ignored the warning of a police officer to not cross a street against a red pedestrian light. She didn't give the office much thought because she was accustomed to ignoring people in uniform. The officer approached her, threatened to arrest her, and she struck the officer in the face. She was arrested and charged with battery of a peace officer, a felony. A jury Returning to our police officer example, a jury could find that a reasonable person should have known that the individual was an officer because heshe was wearing a police uniform, for example, and find the defendant guilty of assault on a police officer, even if the jury believes that the defendant didn't subjectively know the assaulted individual was a police officer.

Consider the crime of receiving stolen property. If an individual received stolen property, but did so without knowledge that it was stolen, then no crime has been committed. For some crimes that require scienter, the absence of scienter may leave a general-intent crime. If a man strikes a person whom he believes is obstructing traffic, he has committed an assault. If he knew, or should have known, that the person was a police officer attempting to direct traffic, then he may be accountable for the higher crime of assault on a police officer. However, if the police officer was not wearing a uniform and did not announce himself as an officer, then the defendant is liable only for simple assault. Possession of burglary tools and obstruction of justice are also examples: the former requiring knowledge of the tools' character and the latter requiring knowledge of obstruction.

At common law, specific intent could be found in a third type of situation, whenever **constructive intent** could be proven. That is, although the defendant does not intend to cause the result, it is so likely to occur that the law treats the act as one of specific intent. If John fires a handgun at close range at Sally, aiming at her torso, and kills her as a result, it is possible that he could be charged with the specific-intent crime of first-degree murder, even though he only intended to injure her. This is because the possibility of killing someone under those circumstances is significant. However, liability may not exist if he had aimed at her leg and the weapon discharged improperly, causing the bullet to strike her in the torso. This is because the likelihood of killing someone with a gunshot to the leg is much less than with a gunshot to the upper body. The bullet entered the victim's torso as a result of the malfunction of the gun; it was not Defendant's desire to shoot her in the upper body. As to the amount of probability necessary to prove constructive intent, only "practical or substantial" probability is required, not absolute.[4]

constructive

■ Inferred, implied, or presumed from the circumstances.

Specific intent can be found in a fourth situation, whenever a defendant intends a result beyond the act taken. This refers to situations when a criminal act is uncompleted. For example, if a man attacks a woman intending to rape her, but she is able to free herself and escape, he may be charged with assault with intent to rape. To prove this charge, the prosecution must show that he assaulted the victim with the specific intent of raping her. Proving that the defendant had a specific intent to assault her is not enough to sustain the intent-to-rape charge, although it would justify a conviction for assault, a lesser crime.

Another example is the crime of breaking and entering with the intent to burglarize. Again, the prosecution must prove that the defendant intended to steal from the home after the entry and did not complete the burglary for some reason. Proving that the defendant broke in and entered, but had no intent to steal, will support a conviction for breaking and entering, but not intent to commit burglary.

General intent is much easier to define, as it is simply the desire to act. In most situations, if the prosecution can show that a defendant intended to take the act that resulted in the prohibited outcome, then general intent is proved. Generally, no desire to cause a particular consequence is required. So, if you fire a gun without a desire to kill someone, but the bullet does kill a person, you possess a general intent and may be prosecuted for a general-intent homicide.

Some jurisdictions require more than simply a desire to act to prove general intent. In those states, some level of negligence must be proven. Consider the following two examples:

Rural Defendant has lived on a farm for more than 20 years. Defendant's nearest neighbor is over three miles away, and Defendant routinely target shoots in his backyard. He has never encountered anyone in the area where he shoots, and everyone who lives in the community knows of his practice. One day, while target shooting, he accidentally shoots and kills a trespasser he did not know was on his property. In the second example, Metro Defendant likes to hunt on weekends. One weekend, Metro and his friend were hunting and Metro lost sight of his friend. Eager to capture his first deer of the season, Metro fired into a bush in which he observed some movement. But Metro's friend was in the bush, and Metro's gunshot inflicted a fatal wound.

In both examples, the defendants had no desire to harm the individuals who were shot, and both possessed the intent to fire the weapon. A strict construction of general and specific intent results in both defendants committing a general-intent murder. However, In some jurisdictions, Rural may be free from liability because he appears to have been less reckless or negligent than Metro, who should have considered the possibility that it could have been his friend who was causing the disturbance in the bush.

This discussion has not exhausted the many definitions and distinctions that exist for specific and general intent. In the *Carson* case, it appears that the Court of Appeals for the District of Columbia has created a hybrid general-specific intent for the crime of cruelty to children.

Malum in Se and Malum Prohibitum

Often, crimes are characterized as either malum in se or malum prohibitum. If a crime is inherently evil, it is malum in se. If a crime is not evil in itself, but is only criminal because declared so by a legislature, then it is malum prohibitum. Examples of crimes that are malum in se are murder, rape, arson, and mayhem. Failure to file your quarterly tax report or to get the proper building permit are both crimes malum prohibitum.

The distinction between malum in se and malum prohibitum is used throughout criminal law, but the importance of the distinction is in how it affects intent. Crimes malum in se are treated as requiring an evil intent, and crimes malum prohibitum are not. Some crimes may be both malum in se and malum prohibitum, depending upon the degree of violation. For example, speeding "a little over the limit may be malum prohibitum, but speeding at high speed malum in se."[5] Whether an act is malum prohibitum or in se often determines what crime may be charged. This decision usually revolves around the issue of foreseeability of harm.

In the preceding example, speeding slightly over the limit is not likely to cause another's death, whereas racing through a city at 30 miles over the speed limit can foreseeably cause a fatal accident. If while driving four miles over the speed limit, the defendant strikes and kills a pedestrian who walks into the driver's path from behind another car, the act is likely to be determined malum prohibitum, and no resulting manslaughter charge will follow. However, the same may not be true if the driver is traveling at 30 miles over the speed limit when the accident occurs.

Transferred Intent

Whenever a person intends a harm, but because of bad aim or other cause, the intended harm befalls another, the intent is transferred from the intended victim to the unintended victim. This is the doctrine of **transferred intent.** If John Defendant observes a neighbor burning the American flag and in anger shoots at him, missing him but killing William, the doctrine of transferred intent permits prosecution of Defendant as if he intended to kill William.

There are limits on the doctrine of transferred intent. First, the harm that actually results must be similar to the intended harm. If the harms are substantially different, then the intent does not transfer. For example, if A throws a baseball at B's window, hoping to break it, and the ball instead hits C in the head and kills him, it cannot be said that the intent to break the window transfers to C and that A can be punished for intentionally killing C. Person A may be criminally liable for a lesser crime, such as involuntary manslaughter, depending upon the amount of negligence involved, but he is not responsible for intentionally causing C's death.

A second limitation on the doctrine is that the transfer cannot increase the defendant's liability. In other words, any defenses the defendant has against the intended victim are transferred to the unintended victim. For example, A shoots at B in self-defense but hits C, inflicting a fatal wound. Because A had a valid defense if B had been killed by the shot, then A also has a defense as to C. In this case, A has committed no crime.

In some situations a defense may only limit a person's criminal liability to a lesser charge. You will learn later that certain defenses negate specific intent, but not general intent. One such defense is intoxication. Assault is a general-intent crime, whereas assault with an intent to kill is a specific-intent crime. Intoxication may be a defense to the higher assault with an intent to kill, but not assault. So if A, while intoxicated, hurls a knife at B but hits C, A may be charged with assault because intoxication would be no defense if she hit B. Person A would have a defense against the specific-intent crime of assault with intent to kill, so the same defense is available for harm to C.

transferred intent

■ The principle that if an unintended illegal act results from the intent to commit a crime, that act is also a crime.

Strict Liability

At the beginning of this chapter, it was noted that some acts are criminal although no mens rea accompanies the prohibited act. These crimes are proven simply by showing that the act was committed, and no particular mental state has to be proved at all. This

strict liability

■ Guilt of a criminal offense even if you had no criminal intention (mens rea).

strict liability crimes

■ Crimes or offenses in which mens rea or criminal intent is not an element. Such offenses include regulatory crimes, petty offenses, and infractions.

is **strict liability,** or liability without fault, and is an exception to the common-law requirement that there be both an evil mind and an evil act to have a crime. The term *strict liability* is not used in all jurisdictions. Further, the term also has a tort meaning. Do not confuse criminal liability without fault with tort strict liability. However, for convenience, the term "strict liability" is used in this text.

Strict liability crimes usually are minor violations, punished by fines and not incarceration. However, strict liability is permitted as the mental element, or lack thereof, for felonies and may be punished with incarceration.

Most traffic violations, such as running a stoplight and speeding, are examples of strict liability crimes. Laws intended to protect minors are often silent on knowledge of the age of the victim. Statutory rape, for example, is treated as a strict liability crime in most states; therefore, a mistaken belief, even if it is the result of a fraudulent representation of age by the victim, does not relieve the defendant of criminal responsibility for having sexual intercourse with a minor. Similarly, selling drugs or alcohol or otherwise contributing to the delinquency of minors often does not have a mens rea requirement, at least in regard to the age of the victim. It is common for crimes that are malum prohibitum to be strict liability, whereas crimes malum in se usually require proof of some mental state. It is also generally true that violation of crimes malum prohibitum is not punished as severely as violation of crimes malum in se.

Often, "public offenses" or "regulatory offenses" are strict liability. The term "regulatory" is often used because the criminal prohibition has been established by an administrative agency through rulemaking, is enforced by an administrative agency, or is part of a comprehensive regulatory scheme established by a legislature. In many cases, strict liability laws deal with potential, rather than actual, harms. For example, a murder statute can be applied only after someone has been murdered. However, many strict liability offenses deal with violations and no harm. As examples, running a stoplight, speeding, or failing to have adequate fire extinguishers in your business may or may not result in an injury. Regardless of whether harm results, you are liable for the offense.

This approach is considered regulatory because the purpose is to induce compliance (using the easy-proof standard) with the law, rather than to punish for caused harm. Increased compliance is a result of an awareness by people that violation alone means liability; hence, they are more cautious and less likely to engage in the prohibited conduct. Of course, this argument can be made to justify making all crimes strict liability. The idea of not requiring any intent for acts to be criminal is contrary to the American values of fairness and justice, and this is probably the reason that the strict liability standard has not been extended to all crimes.

Strict liability is available only for crimes defined by legislatures. With little restriction, legislatures may define an act as criminal without requiring proof of intent. However, in jurisdictions that continue to recognize common-law crimes, mens rea must be an element.

There are an increasing number of regulatory offenses in the United States. Indeed, there has been a significant in the number of strict liability crimes, both regulatory and other, in recent decades. According to one study, 40% of nonviolent federal offenses created during a two-year period had no, or weak, mens rea requirements.[6]

Strict liability crimes, particularly those that impose serious penalties, have been challenged on many grounds. Some jurists believe that the expansion of strict liability beyond infractions and regulatory violations threatens democracy itself. In constitutional terms, these concerns manifest as due process challenges, and many lower courts have stricken strict liability laws under this theory. But the United States Supreme Court has upheld strict liability statutes in most instances, affording legislatures wide latitude in defining criminality.[7] Even so, there are limits, and if a legislature eliminates proof of mens rea for a crime that has traditionally required proof of specific intent or purpose or omits mens rea for a crime that is punished severely, due process is implicated and may be the basis for invalidating the change.

In the *Morissette* case, the Supreme Court addressed the omission of mens rea for the traditional crime of converting (theft) spent bomb casings The defendant was convicted at the trial level, but the United States Supreme Court reversed the conviction.

Strict Liability and Statutory Construction

The problem addressed by the Supreme Court in *Morissette* occurs often: What is the mens rea requirement when a statute does not provide for such? That decision depends on many factors. First, the **legislative history** of the statute may indicate whether the crime was intended to have a mens rea requirement. The statements of members of legislatures while debating the law (before it became law and was a bill), reports of committees of Congress, and other related materials may indicate whether the legislature intended a mens rea requirement. Second, courts look to whether the crime existed under the common law. If so, the mens rea used under the common law may be adopted by the court. Other factors include the seriousness of the harm to the public; mens rea standards for other related crimes; the punishment imposed upon conviction; the burden that would be placed on the prosecution if mens rea were required; and rules of statutory construction.

Generally, the greater the potential harm to the public and the more difficult it is for prosecution to prove mens rea, the more likely a court is to find that strict liability is to be imposed.[8] Although not a significant factor, the amount of penalty can play a role. The greater the penalty, the more likely that some intent will be read into the statute. Also, courts will look to other related statutes for guidance. If a state legislature has consistently required proof of intent for all crimes of larceny and theft, then if a new statute is enacted dealing with a particular theft (i.e., theft of computer information), and that law does not specify the mental state that must be proven, the court will fill in the missing element with intent.

Finally, courts have rules that must be followed when interpreting a statute. These are known as *canons* of **statutory construction.** You previously learned one of these rules; that is, whenever a statute can be construed as either constitutional or unconstitutional, it must be read as constitutional. Some jurisdictions follow the rule, either by judicial rule (canon) or by statute, that if a criminal statute does not specifically impose strict liability, then the court is to impose a mens rea requirement. This is what the Supreme Court did in *Morrisette*. And *Troiano* is a case from New York, a state jurisdiction where such a rule is applied. See Exhibit 8–1 for examples of other canons that are applied in criminal cases.

legislative history

■ The background documents and records of hearings related to the enactment of a bill.

statutory construction

■ Guidelines employed by judges in the interpretation of statutes that have developed and evolved over hundreds of years.

There is an important exception to the presumption of mens rea when a statute is silent on the subject, public welfare cases. The Supreme Court has long recognized that public welfare, or regulatory, laws are often intended to impose strict liability because of the large risk that legislatures and administrative agencies are attempting to manage. In such cases, courts are not to impose mens rea when the law, statute or administrative regulation, is silent on state of mind. For example, strict liability for corporate officials

Exhibit 8-1 EXAMPLES OF CANONS OF CONSTRUCTION THAT APPLY IN CRIMINAL CASES

Canon	Description
Narrow Construction	Criminal statutes are to be narrowly construed by courts.
Ambiguous Language	Ambiguous language in a statute is to be construed in the defendant's favor or, if too ambiguous, the statute is void.
Legislative Prerogative	Courts are to be mindful that the source of penal law should be legislatures, not courts. Criminal statutes are to be narrowly construed. This is also known as the Rule of Lenity.
Constitutionality Presumption	Statutes are presumed constitutional, and if a court can construe a statute as constitutional or unconstitutional without causing unfairness to the defendant, the statute is to be construed as constitutional.
Plain Meaning	The plain meaning of a statute shall be enforced unless the result is absurd. If absurd, the court may turn to other evidence (e.g., legislative intent) to assist in interpreting the statute.

who injure consumers who purchased misbranded drugs was upheld.[9] Similarly the Court refused to impute mens rea for the crime of possessing a hand grenade because of the public safety rationale of the law.[10] For a law to qualify as a public welfare statute, the harm that it seeks to prevent or control must seriously threaten health or life. In addition, the history of how the act as regulated is important. If the threat is not widespread and significant, the law will not be characterized as public welfare and a court will be more likely to impose mens rea.[11]

Another factor is implicit in the public welfare cases—the nature of the act regulated. If the act was a crime at the common law that required the government to prove state of mind, as opposed to being a recent regulatory creation, it is more likely that a court will want to impose mens rea.

Vicarious Liability

The term **vicarious liability** refers to situations in which one person is held accountable for the actions of another. Under vicarious liability, there is no requirement of mens rea as there is for strict liability, and in addition, there is no requirement for an act, at least not by the defendant. The person who is liable for the actions of another need not act, encourage another to act, or intend any harm at all. As is true with vicarious liability in tort law, this situation is most common between employers and employees.

Employers may be liable for the actions of their employees when criminal laws relating to the operation of the business are violated. For example, the owner of a business may be prosecuted for failure to comply with product safety regulations, even though that was a duty delegated to an employee and the owner had no knowledge that the products manufactured were substandard. Vicarious liability is often imposed on those who market food and drugs.[12] This is because of the significant public welfare interest in the quality of these products.

Corporate Liability

Corporate liability is a form of vicarious liability. Under the common law, corporations could not be convicted of crimes. However, this is no longer the law.

Corporations, partnerships, and other organizations can be held criminally accountable for the acts of their employees and agents under traditional respondeat superior theory. Agents must be working within the scope of their employment for the company to be liable. If an employee of Starbucks strikes an enemy while on break in the parking lot of the store, the company is not liable for battery. However, if officers of a corporation send employees into a workplace knowing that it is dangerous and represent to the employees that it is safe, the company may be liable for battery to the employee, or even manslaughter, if death results.

One legal scholar identified three theories under which corporations can be found criminally liable today. The first is traditional principal-agent theory, which developed at the common law. Second, corporations should be liable for the actions of their policymakers but not their employees. The third theory holds that corporations are liable for their agents and employees when corporate policy or practices fail to prevent the crime from happening.[13]

The Model Penal Code provides for corporate liability when the agent is acting within the scope of employment. In addition, it must be shown that the corporation had a duty under the law to act, and the act was not done or the act taken by the agent was authorized, requested, commanded, performed, or recklessly tolerated by the board of directors or other high management.[14]

Today, in most jurisdictions, corporations can be held criminally liable for any act that is criminal for a natural person. This includes crimes against the person, such

vicarious liability
▪ Legal responsibility for the acts of another person because of some relationship with that person.

corporate liability
▪ The liability of a corporation for the acts of its directors, officers, shareholders, agents, and employees.

as rape, murder, and battery. *People v. Warner-Lambert Co.,* which appears later in this chapter, is an example of when a company was charged with negligent homicide. In a subsequent case in Illinois, a corporation was convicted of involuntary manslaughter and several of its officers were convicted of murder for the death of an employee that could have been prevented.[15] The most common criminal actions against corporations, however, are not crimes against person. They are property and regulatory crimes.[16]

Obviously, companies cannot be incarcerated, so fines are usually imposed. In some instances, **injunctions** may be imposed or a company's status may be altered, suspended, or terminated. Finally, note that corporate liability does not free the agent from criminal liability. In most cases, the agents or employees remain criminally liable for their acts. Indeed, proving corporate mens rea can be more difficult than proving individual mens rea. Two prominent cases illustrate this point.

One of the most famous cases of alleged corporate crime involved Ford Motor Company. In the late 1960s, Ford designed a new subcompact car, the Pinto. To maximize trunk space, the Pinto's fuel tank was located behind the rear axle rather than above it, which was the common design. However, this new design made the car more vulnerable to fire and explosions in rear-end accidents. Other design decisions, including lack of reinforcement of the rear of the car and a poorly designed fuel filler pipe, accentuated the risk. Following several deaths from fires resulting from rear-end collisions, civil suits were filed against Ford in different states. During discovery in one of those actions, a report that detailed the costs of correcting the problem ($11 per car, 12.5 million cars, totaling $137 million) in comparison to the costs of the expected number of deaths and injuries (180 deaths, 180 injuries, totaling $49.5 million) was produced. This and other evidence led prosecutors in Indiana to charge Ford with negligent homicide.[17]

Many civil actions also were filed by individuals who were harmed. Ultimately, Ford was not convicted of the charged crime but was found liable in several civil actions. Although an unsuccessful criminal prosecution, the Ford case continues to be prominent in discussions of corporate criminal liability because the underlying premise of the prosecution—namely, that a corporation can be charged with traditional crimes—was generally accepted.

The 2002 Enron debacle is another example. As a result of misrepresentations about Enron's financial status by Enron officers and Enron's accounting firm, Arthur Andersen, LLP, investors were not aware of Enron's financial distress. Employees and investors lost millions of dollars when the company went bankrupt in December 2001. In addition to criminal charges against Enron officials, Enron's accounting firm, Arthur Andersen, LLP, was charged with obstruction of justice for destroying Enron documents and computer files that were sought by federal authorities. The government alleged that Andersen employees destroyed files containing unfavorable information about Enron that had not been made available to investors. Andersen, a top-five accounting firm, had 85,000 employees and offices the world over at the time of its indictment. Many commentators were critical of the indictment, asserting that the focus of corporate crime should be the responsible individuals, not companies. A conviction of Andersen, it was alleged, could lead to more than a fine (as provided for by statute). Andersen faced demise by losing its Securities and Exchange status and its corporate status. This would result in 85,000 unemployed individuals, most of whom were not parties to the crime.

injunctions

■ A judge's order to a person to do or to refrain from doing a particular – thing.

Ultimately, Andersen was convicted of obstruction of justice and was sentenced to 5 years' probation and a $500,000 fine. The terms of its probation included additional fines if it committed new crimes, and the firm was required to obtain approval before it sold its assets. Andersen appealed, and in 2005 a unanimous Supreme Court set aside the conviction.[18] However, as a result of the scandal, Andersen had lost nearly all of its clients, had surrendered its license to practice before the Securities and Exchange Commission, had its license revoked in many states, its total staffing had fallen to just a few hundred, and the firm was defending against more than a hundred civil actions by the time the Supreme Court issued its decision in 2005. When this text went to press in 2014, Arthur Anderson LLP was still in business, although it surrendered its license to practice before the Securities and Exchange Commission, lost its right to practice in many states, and was conducting little accounting work.

Current Approaches to Mens Rea

The Model Penal Code and States of Mind

The drafters of the Model Penal Code chose to reject most of the common law terms when they addressed mens rea. The result is that the Model Penal Code recognizes four states of mind: purposeful; knowing; reckless; and negligent (see Exhibit 8–2).[19]

Exhibit 8–2 MENS REA UNDER THE MODEL PENAL CODE

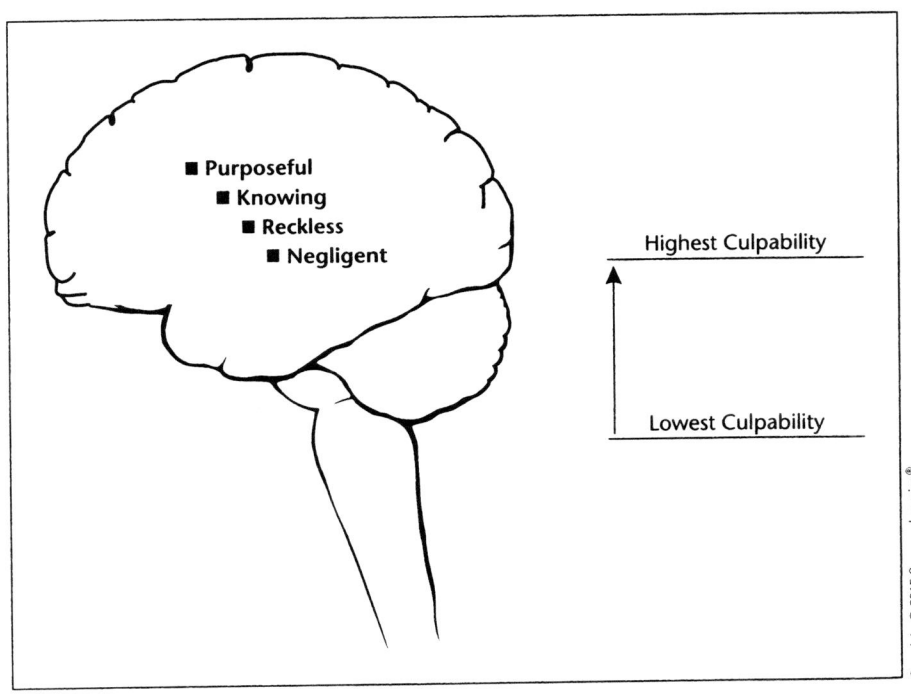

purposely
- Intentionally; knowingly.

knowingly
- With full knowledge and intentionally; willfully.

recklessness
- Indifference to consequences; indifference to the safety and rights of others. Recklessness implies conduct amounting to more than ordinary negligence.

negligence
- Under the MPC, a defendant acts negligently when the resulting harm or material element of a crime occurs because of the defendant has taken a substantial and unjustifiable risk, even if the risk is not perceived, so long as the risk involves a gross deviation from the standard of conduct that a law-abiding person would observe.

element
- A basic part. For example, some of the *elements* of a cause of action for battery are of an intentional, unwanted physical contact. Each of these things ("intentional," "unwanted," etc.) is one element.

To act **purposely,** a defendant must have a desire to cause the result. *Purposely* most closely equates with what the common law called *specific intent.*

To act **knowingly,** a defendant must be aware of the nature of the act and be practically certain that his or her conduct will cause a particular result—which is not the defendant's objective. The difference between purposeful acts and knowing acts is that to be purposeful, one must act intending to cause the particular result. To act knowingly, the defendant must be practically certain (nearly 100% positive) that the result will occur, but the defendant is not taking the act to cause that result. For example, if a legitimate moving company owner leases a van to an illegal drug dealer knowing that the van will be used to transport drugs across the country, the owner has acted knowingly. He has not acted with purpose, because it is not the owner's objective to transport the contraband.

The third state of mind recognized by the Model Penal Code is **recklessness.** Individuals act recklessly when they consciously disregard a substantial and unjustifiable risk that the result will occur. The difference between a knowing act and a reckless act is in the degree of risk. "A person acts 'knowingly' with respect to a result if he is nearly certain that his conduct will cause the result. If he is aware only of a substantial risk, he acts 'recklessly' with respect to the result."[20] The Code says that the risk taken must be one that involves a "gross deviation from the standard of conduct that a law-abiding person would observe in the actor's situation."[21]

The final state of mind is **negligence.** The definition of negligence is similar to recklessness; that is, there must be a "substantial and unjustifiable risk" taken by the defendant. However, a person acts negligently when there is no conscious awareness of the risk, when there should have been. To act recklessly, one must take a risk that amounts to a "gross deviation from the standard of conduct that a law-abiding person would observe in the actor's situation." When defendants have acted negligently, they have failed to perceive (be aware of) the risk altogether, and that failure is a gross deviation from a law-abiding person's standard.

Element Analysis

So far, the discussion of culpable states of mind has been limited to one state of mind for each individual crime. For example, under the common law, a specific intent to kill must have been proven to establish first-degree murder. This was true of all offenses under the common law; that is, only one state of mind had to be shown. This was true even if the crime had many different elements.

Elements are the parts of a crime. The prosecution must prove all the elements of a crime beyond a reasonable doubt to gain a conviction. For example, the common-law elements of larceny were (1) the taking and carrying away (2) of personal property (3) of another (4) with an intent to steal. The prosecution has the burden of proving all four elements. If the prosecution fails to prove any element, the defendant must be acquitted. At common law, only one mental state had to be proved: intent to steal. Additionally, the prosecution had to show that the other four elements occurred without reference to mental state. This is known as *offense analysis,* as the entire offense is thought of as requiring one mental state.

The Model Penal Code (MPC), as well as some specific statutes, recognizes that the various acts of a crime may involve differing mental states. As such, each element of a crime may have a different mens rea.[22]

Assume that state law prohibits (1) notary publics (2) from notarizing documents (3) of known blood relatives (4) of the third degree or closer (degrees define closeness of family relationship). Under the Code, the first two elements appear to require no mental state—just the act of a notary notarizing a document. Hence, it would be no defense for the notary to claim that he was signing the document as a witness and not as a notary. The third element requires specific knowledge that the person for whom he notarizes the document is a blood relative. If the notary can prove that there was no reason for him to have known of the relationship, then his knowledge is negated. The last element is likely to be treated as a negligence element. It would be a valid defense for the notary to show that she made a reasonable error as to the degree of the relationship. Attempt to apply element analysis when examining penal statutes in your state or in your criminal law class.

Proving Mens Rea

At trial, the prosecution has the burden of establishing that the defendant possessed the required mental state when the act was committed. Proof of intent can be troublesome to prosecution, especially when the prosecution has to prove subjective intent. *Subjective intent* refers to the motives, intentions, and desires that were in the defendant's mind at the time the act took place. Subjective intent is a defendant's actual intent.

Objective intent is not the defendant's actual intent; rather, it is a legal imposition upon defendants of what they should have known or believed at the time the act occurred. Generally, the law imposes a reasonable person standard. That means that the defendant is expected to have known or believed what a reasonable person would have known at the time of the act. Objective intent is easier to prove than is subjective intent. This is because the prosecution does not have to probe directly into a defendant's mind to prove that an intent to harm existed; rather, all that has to be shown is that the defendant should have known that the harm would result.

In most cases, defendants do not admit to committing the acts in question. Even when defendants do admit to some acts, they commonly deny intent. For crimes that require intent, admission of the act is not enough to sustain a conviction. The question is: How does a prosecutor gain a conviction for a crime that requires showing of intent when the defendant denies possessing the required intent? The answer is by using **inferences**.

An *inference* is a conclusion that a judge or jury is permitted to make after considering the facts of a case. Imagine that a man walks up to another man and strikes him in the head with a hammer, using great force in his swing. The wound is fatal, and the attacker is charged with first-degree murder. To sustain a first-degree murder charge in this jurisdiction, it must be shown that the man intended to cause the victim's death. The defendant disavows such intent, admitting only that he intended to hit and injure the victim. In such a case, the jury would be permitted to infer the defendant's intent to kill the victim from the seriousness of the act. In a jurisdiction that uses the objective standard, the jury could conclude that a reasonable person would have known that the

inference

■ A fact (or proposition) that is *probably* true because a true fact (or proposition) leads you to believe that the *inferred* fact (or proposition) is also true.

blow from a hammer would cause the victim's death, and the subjective intent of the defendant would not matter.

A **presumption** is a conclusion that must be made by a judge or jury. Most people have heard of the presumption of innocence in criminal law. This presumption is a *rebuttable presumption*. Rebuttable presumptions are conclusions that must be made by a judge or jury, unless disproven by the facts. Hence, defendants are innocent until proven guilty. *Irrebuttable presumptions* are conclusions that must be made by the judge or jury and cannot be disproved. Regardless of what the evidence shows, an irrebuttable presumption stands as a fact.

presumption

■ A presumption *of law* is an automatic assumption required by law that whenever a certain set of facts shows up, a court must automatically draw certain legal conclusions.

motive

■ The reason why a person does something.

Motive

The reason a person commits a crime is **motive.** More particularly, the reason that leads a person to a desired result or particular action is motive.

Motive is different from mens rea. Motive leads to mens rea. Motive is concerned with why people act. Mens rea, in contrast, is concerned with whether a person intended to act. For example, greed is a motive for many acts. A bank robber's motive for robbing a bank is greed (or even, possibly, the challenge). The robber's mens rea is neither greed nor the emotional thrill resulting from the risk; rather, it is the intent to take money using force or threat. Said another way, the robber's mens rea (intent) is used to satisfy the motive (greed).

Motive is not an element of crimes. Therefore, prosecutors do not have to prove motive to be successful in a prosecution. As a practical matter, however, the trier of fact will want to know why the defendant committed the alleged crime. In many crimes, the motive will be apparent. Greed is easily understood and is imputed by juries to accused thieves. In other crimes, such as murder, there may be no apparent motive, and the prosecutor may need to introduce evidence explaining why a defendant would commit such a heinous crime. Was the murder motivated by greed (e.g., to gain an inheritance), or by passion (e.g., in revenge for infidelity), or by some other emotion? Usually, the prosecutor will prove motive; but in a case in which the defendant has pleaded insanity, the defendant bears the burden of providing either that there was no motive (e.g., the defendant did not want this to happen, but a mental disease or defect made her do it), or that the motive was the product of insanity (e.g., he believed the decedent was Godzilla).

A bad motive does not make an otherwise lawful act criminal. Conversely, a good motive does not excuse the commission of a crime. The issue is simply whether the prosecution has proven, beyond a reasonable doubt, that all the elements of the crime were committed.

Motive plays a role at sentencing. A good motive may justify a mitigation of sentence, whereas a bad motive may act in the reverse.

In some instances, a good motive may prevent charges from being filed at all. Police and prosecutors do not pursue some cases, even though a crime has been committed, when a person acted with good intentions. Conversely, law enforcement officials may pursue a case more passionately if the defendant acted from an evil motive. Exhibit 8–3 summarizes mens rea versus motive.

Exhibit 8–3 MENS REA V. MOTIVE

	Mens Rea	**Motive**
Defined	The level of intentionality to commit an act that is required to prove a crime.	The reason a person acted.
Trial	An element of nearly all crimes that must be proven at trial beyond a reasonable doubt.	Not an element of any crime and doesn't have to be proved. However, a prosecutor may need to establish voluntariness motive in order to persuade a fact finder to convict.
Sentencing	May be considered in mitigation or aggravation.	May be considered in mitigation or aggravation.

Copyright © 2015 Cengage Learning®.

ACTUS REUS

Earlier in this chapter you learned the Latin phrase "actus non facit reum nisi mens sit rea." The phrase expresses the common-law requirement that two essential elements must be present to have a crime: a guilty mind and a guilty act. **Actus reus** is the physical part of a crime; it is the act engaged in by the accused. An act is a physical movement. If Mrs. X shoots and kills Mrs. T, the act is pulling the trigger of the gun.

The Model Penal Code states that a "person is not guilty of an offense unless his liability is based on conduct that includes a voluntary act."[23]

Voluntariness

To be held criminally liable for one's actions, those actions must be voluntary. To be voluntary, an act must occur as a result of the actor's conscious choice. The person accused must have acted freely, or no liability attaches. The Model Penal Code requires that acts be voluntary and specifically lists the following as being involuntary:

1. reflexes and convulsions;
2. bodily movements during unconsciousness or sleep;
3. conduct during hypnosis or resulting from hypnotic suggestion; and
4. other movements that are not a product of the effort or determination of the actor.[24]

Do not confuse the concepts of mens rea and actus reus. All that is required to have an act is a choice by the defendant to act. No evil intent is required to have an act; that is a question of mens rea. Say that Jim chooses to swing his arm. As a result, he hits Tom. What intent is required to prove battery and whether Jim possessed that

actus reus

■ (Latin) An act. For example, an *actus reus* is a "wrongful deed" (such as killing a person) which, if done with mens rea, a "guilty mind" (such as *malice aforethought*), is a crime (such as *first-degree murder*).

intent are questions of mens rea. For actus reus, all that need be known is whether Jim voluntarily chose to swing his arm. His swing would be involuntary if Bill grabbed Jim's arm and moved it, causing it to strike Tom.

In the *Cogdon* case, a woman was acquitted of murdering her daughter because it was determined that her acts were not voluntary.[25] No defense of insanity was raised in this case. If it had been, the analysis would have been different. In most jurisdictions, one cannot claim lack of a voluntary act if insanity is also claimed. In those situations, the rules of the insanity defense apply See Chapter 13 for a complete discussion of insanity as a defense.

Thoughts and Statements as Acts

Thoughts alone are not acts that can be made criminal. People may think evil thoughts, but if there is no act furthering such a thought, there is no crime.

Generally, people are also free to speak. The First Amendment to the U.S. Constitution protects freedom of speech. When the First Amendment applies, speech may not be made criminal. There are, however, limits to First Amendment protection of speech. Inciting riots, treason, solicitation, conspiracy, and causing imminent harm to others are examples of speech that may be prohibited. You will learn more about the First Amendment protection of speech later.

Personal Status as an Act

Generally, a person's status cannot be declared criminal. Illness, financial status, race, sex, and religion are examples of human conditions. Some conditions are directly related to illegal behavior. For example, being addicted to illegal narcotics is a condition that cannot be punished. This is because status is generally believed not to be an act. However, using and selling prohibited narcotics are acts and may be punished.

Vagrancy is one area over which there is a split in legal opinion. Some courts have held that vagrancy may be prohibited; others have determined that vagrancy is a condition and does not constitute a crime. One author noted that there is a "growing body of authority" holding such statutes unconstitutional.[26]

In *Robinson v. California*, [Shouldn't this info should go within endnote 27? Maybe not because it's within a feature.] the United States Supreme Court was called upon to review a California statute that made it a crime "either to use narcotics, or to be addicted to the use of narcotics." The Court reversed Robinson's conviction, and in the opinion stated:

> This statute, therefore, is not one which punishes a person for the use of narcotics, for their purchase, sale or possession, or for antisocial or disorderly behavior resulting from their administration. It is not a law which even purports to provide or require medical treatment. Rather, we deal with a statute which makes the "status" of narcotic addiction a criminal offense, for which the offender may be prosecuted "at any time before he reforms." California has said that a person can be continuously guilty of this offense, whether or not he has ever used or possessed any narcotics within the state, and whether or not he has been guilty of any antisocial behavior there.

It is unlikely that any State at this moment in history would attempt to make it a criminal offense for a person to be mentally ill, or a leper, or to be afflicted with a venereal disease. A State might determine that the general health and welfare require that the victims of these and other human afflictions be dealt with by compulsory treatment, involving quarantine, confinement, or sequestration. But in the light of contemporary human knowledge, a law which made a criminal offense of such a disease would doubtless be universally thought of to be an infliction of cruel and unusual punishment in violation of the Eighth and Fourteenth Amendments. . . .

We cannot but consider the statute before us as of the same category . . . . We hold that a state law which imprisons a person thus afflicted as a criminal, even though he has never touched any narcotic drug within the State or been guilty of any irregular behavior there, inflicts a cruel and unusual punishment in violation of the Fourteenth Amendment. . . .[27]

While personal status may not be criminalized, it may be subject to the regulatory authority of the state. Individuals who are mentally ill and who pose a danger to themselves or others may be civilly committed, for example. This includes the commitment of sexual predators. This topic is discussed more fully in Chapter 9.

Possession as an Act

Possession of certain items, such as narcotics or burglary tools, may be made criminal. Possession of deadly weapons is both a federal and a state crime. Following the terrorist attacks of September 11, 2001, for example, Congress made it unlawful to possess biological agents or delivery systems for biological agents that are intended to be used as weapons.[28] Possession is not, strictly speaking, an act. Possession does not involve an active body movement; rather, possession is a passive state of being. Even so, most possession laws have been upheld.

Jurisdictions differ in what is required to prove possession. Some require that actual possession be shown, whereas others allow proof of constructive possession. Constructive possession is used to extend criminal liability to those who never exercised actual possession but had dominion and control over the contraband. A person who is the owner and driver of a car may have never possessed the cocaine that his passenger is using, but the law says that the driver is in constructive possession because the dominion and control over the auto belong to the driver. In essence, the law imposes a duty on people to remove illegal items from the area over which they have dominion and control. Failure to comply with such a duty is treated as an act and can lead to criminal liability.

One problem with crimes of possession is the possibility of convicting people who had no knowledge of the existence of illegal items in an area under their dominion and control. An owner of a house has dominion and control over the guest room but may not be aware that a guest has brought illegal items into the room. Most jurisdictions have remedied this problem by requiring knowledge of the presence of the goods. The Model Penal Code also uses such a test. The Code states that possession is an act as long as the "possessor knowingly procured or received the thing possessed or was aware of his control thereof for a sufficient period to have been able to terminate his possession." Under the Code, possession can be actual or constructive. However, if constructive, the possessor must have known of the items for a period of time long enough to permit the possessor to terminate possession. So, if the owner of the house discovered the cocaine only minutes before the police arrived to search the premises, no possession could be found on the owner's behalf.

Finally, one person or many people can be in possession of items. Using the preceding example, assume that two or more people jointly owned the home in question. All of the owners could be liable, if it was determined that all had constructive possession and adequate time to remove the cocaine from the house. It is possible that fewer than all of the owners knew of the cocaine and, as such, did not have constructive possession. Each person who is alleged to have dominion and control (constructive possession) must be examined individually, and separate decisions as to their individual liability must be made.

Omissions as Acts

In 2011 allegations of sexual abuse of children by former Penn State assistant football coach Jerry Sandusky went viral. Sandusky was convicted and sentenced in 2012 to 30 to 60 years in prison for abusing many young men.[29] But this wasn't the end of the story. Several other Penn State officials were charged with crimes resulting from Sandusky's crimes, including perjury and failure to report abuse of a minor. Rape and perjury are acts. Failing to report a crime does not involve an act. It is just the opposite—failure to act. Generally, only acts are prohibited by criminal law. Rarely does criminal law require a person to act. However, in some situations, people have a duty to act, and failure to act is criminal. An **omission** is a failure to act when required to do so by criminal law.

omission
■ Failing to do something that should be done.

It is often the case that a person who may have a moral duty to act does not have a legal duty to act. In most instances, people do not have a legal duty to assist one another in times of need. It would not be criminal in most jurisdictions for an excellent swimmer to watch another drown. Nor would it be criminal to watch another walk into a dangerous situation, such as a bank robbery in progress, if the observer had no connection with the criminal event. There are exceptions to this rule. To be liable for a failure to act, a person must have a "duty" to act. The duty to act can come about in many different ways.

At common law, several exceptions to the "no duty to assist people in danger" rule evolved. Many of these are discussed in the following paragraphs. Bear in mind that many legislatures have codified one or more of these exceptions. In those instances, the duty is imposed by statute and not the common law.

Duty Imposed by Statute

Under the common law, in most instances people had no duty to assist others whose lives were in danger. Today, criminal statutes may impose liability for failure to assist someone in danger. A few states have enactments that directly change the common-law rule and require people to assist others who are in danger. However, even in those jurisdictions, rescue need not be attempted if the rescuer's life would thereby be endangered. Imposing criminal liability for not rescuing someone in danger of losing life or limb continues to be the exception and not the rule. However, no legal reason prevents all jurisdictions from requiring people to rescue one another when there is no danger associated with the rescue.

Setting aside the common law doctrine that one doesn't have a duty to act, many contemporary statutes impose a duty to act in specific circumstances. The Penn State sex abuse crimes are an example. At one point, a Penn State employee witnessed a rape of a youth by Sandusky in Penn State's showers. The employee reported the incident to Joe Paterno, who was Penn State's football coach at the time. Paterno is alleged to have passed on the report to his superiors, Tim Curley and Gary Schultz. Pennsylvania law required knowledge of sexual abuse by an employee to be reported to the "person in charge," who had an obligation to pass the report along to "authorities." Questions were raised about whether Paterno reported all that he knew, whether he should have reported the incident to authorities, and whether Curley and Schultz made the required reporting to authorities. At the time of this writing in 2013, the two men were awaiting trial for perjury and failure to report.

Failing to report child abuse is one of many examples of omissions as crimes today. State and federal laws require businesses that store or dispose of toxic materials to file certain documents, taxpayers are required to file tax returns, drivers of automobiles involved in accidents are required to stop at their accident scenes, and some states require individuals to report wild animals that are loose.

Some states go further than others in creating statutory obligations that did not exist at the common law. For example, Ohio criminalizes the failure to report any felony that has, or is being, committed. The same law requires health care professionals to report stab wound, gunshot wounds, and burn injuries that appear to be the result of violence.[30]

Duty by Relationship

A duty to assist another can be created by the existence of a personal relationship. The most common examples are parent-to-child and spouse-to-spouse. In such personal relationships, a level of dependence exists that gives rise to criminal liability for failure to assist the party who is in danger. There is no bright-line rule for determining if a duty is owed. The more that one party becomes dependent upon another party or the parties become dependent upon one another, the more likely that a duty to assist is created.

Generally, any time a joint enterprise is undertaken by two or more parties, it can be assumed that a duty to assist one another during that enterprise is created. For example, if two people decide to go river rafting, they must rescue one another during that rafting trip, provided that the rescuer is not endangered by attempting the rescue.

In the parent–child relationship, a parent can be guilty of manslaughter if the child dies as a result of the parent's failure to seek medical attention for the child when the child is sick, or for failing to pull the child out of a pool when the child is drowning. The same would be true of a spouse. If a wife permitted her husband to die when she could have saved his life by summoning medical attention, she could be criminally liable. In addition, it has been held that employers owe a duty to assist their employees. For example, the master of a ship must attempt to rescue a seaman who has fallen overboard.??

Duty by Contract

A duty to act can be created in a third way—by contract. For example, physicians are hired to care for the health of their patients. If a doctor watches as a patient slowly dies, doing nothing to save the patient's life when there were measures that could have been taken, the doctor is liable for homicide. The same is true of a lifeguard. The lifeguard is hired to save those who are drowning, and if a lifeguard sits and watches a swimmer drown when the swimmer could have been saved, the lifeguard is liable for homicide.

Remember, the general rule is that people owe no duty to rescue others. So, if an expert swimmer happens to be on the beach when another person is drowning, the expert swimmer can watch the person drown without risking criminal liability.

Assumption of Duty

Even though the general rule is that people do not have a duty to rescue strangers, it is possible, either expressly or by one's actions, to make an *assumption of duty*. The assumption is express if it is stated orally or in writing. Assumption is different from duty premised on contract, in that assumptions are gratuitous. If Sidney is at a pool and agrees to care for another's child, Sidney has assumed the duty expressly. If the child falls into the pool, and Sidney takes no action to save the child, Sidney is liable for murder if the child drowns.

It is possible through one's actions to assume the duty to rescue someone. Assume that Sidney is now at a lake. One person, David, is swimming, and three other people are relaxing on the beach. David begins to scream for help. Sidney jumps up and dives into the water to rescue David. Halfway out to David, she changes her mind and returns to shore. By the time she returns to shore, it is too late for someone else to make the swim to David, and David dies. In this case, Sidney assumed the duty of the rescue by beginning the rescue attempt. However, whether Sidney is liable for murder depends on what condition the drowning person was left in after Sidney changed her mind. If Sidney's actions caused the other three people on the beach to fail to attempt a rescue, Sidney's actions left David in a worse condition than he would have been in had Sidney not begun the rescue. However, if Sidney's actions did not prevent anyone else from attempting a rescue, Sidney's action did not put David in a worse situation and Sidney is not liable for murder, even if the other person fails in the rescue attempt.

Finally, note that we can easily change this last example into an express assumption. All that has to be added is a statement by Sidney to the others on the beach that she will swim out and rescue David. Such a statement, if it caused others to forgo a rescue attempt, is an express assumption of duty.

Creating Danger

Any time a person creates the circumstance that endangers a stranger, a duty to save the stranger is created. This is true whether the danger was caused intentionally or negligently. So, if an arsonist sets fire to a house that is believed to be empty and is discovered not to be, the arsonist must attempt to save anyone inside. If not, the arsonist is also a murderer. The same would be true of a negligently caused fire. If an electrician begins a fire in a home and does nothing to warn the inhabitants, the electrician is also liable for murder.

Causation

Some acts are criminal even though the prohibited result does not occur. For example, it is a crime to lie when testifying in court (the crime of perjury). Assume that the purpose of the lie is to deceive the jury and change the outcome of the case. Even if no juror—or anyone else, for that matter—believes the lie and the purpose is not achieved, it is a crime. Causation is not an issue in such crimes.

For crimes that do require a particular result, the act must be the "cause" of the result. In criminal law, two forms of causation exist: factual and legal. If either of these "causes" is missing, then a defense as to the intent of the crime exists. Even if so, the actor may be convicted of a lower, non-intent crime.

An act is the *cause in fact* of the result if the result would not have occurred unless the act occurred. This is known as the *sine qua non* test, which means that "but for" the conduct, the harm would not have resulted.

Legal cause must also be proved. Legal causation focuses on the degree of similarity between the defendant's intended result and the actual result. It also examines the similarity between the intended manner used to bring about a result and the actual manner that caused the result. Generally, the greater the similarity between the purpose and the result, and the manner intended and the manner that actually caused the result, the more likely that the defendant is the legal cause. Legal cause is also commonly referred to as **proximate cause**. *Proximate* means "nearly, next to, or close." In the context of criminal causation, it refers to the relationship between the act and the result. The result must be a consequence of the act, not a coincidence. A happening is proximately caused by an act if a reasonable person would have foreseen and expected the result. This is called **foreseeability.**

Most problems raised in this area involve legal causation, not factual causation. This is because, to prove factual causation, it must be shown that the defendant's action set into motion the events that led to the prohibited result. The question that should be asked is, had the defendant not acted, would the result have happened? If the answer is no, then the defendant is the factual cause. Determining legal causation is more troublesome, however.

Let us examine a few examples. Hank shoots Mark, intending to kill him. Mark dies from the gunshot wound. Hank is the factual cause of the murder because it was

legal cause
- The proximate cause of an injury; probable cause; cause that the law deems sufficient.

foreseeable
- The degree to which the consequences of an action *should* have been anticipated, recognized, and considered beforehand. *Not* hindsight.

proximate cause
- The "legal cause" of an accident or other injury (which may have several actual causes). The *proximate cause* of an injury is not necessarily the closest thing in time or space to the injury, and not necessarily the event that set things in motion, because "proximate cause" is a legal, not a physical concept.

his conduct that caused Mark to die. To state it another way, "but for" Hank's act, Mark would not have died." Hank is also the legal cause of Mark's death because the resulting death is identical to Hank's intention.

Now assume that Hank intended only to injure Mark, not to kill him. Accordingly, he shot Mark in the arm. Mark then contacted a hospital, which dispatched an ambulance. The paramedics who arrived to assist Mark negligently administered a dangerous medication, which caused his death. Hank continues to be the factual cause of Mark's death, because if he had not injured Mark, the medical attention that ended Mark's life would not have been necessary. However, Hank is not the legal cause of Mark's death. This is because the result greatly differs from Hank's intent. There is not enough similarity between Hank's purpose when he shot Mark (to cause an injury) and the resulting harm (Mark's death).

Note that it is common for legal cause to be lacking when an **intervening cause** exists, as it does in the previous example. An *intervening cause* is a happening that occurs after the initial act and changes the outcome. Intervening causes function to block the connection between an act and the result, because the intervening cause changes what would have been the result if the result had flowed freely from the act. Intervening causes can negate or lower criminal liability for the particular result. However, lower crimes may continue to be punishable. In the preceding example, the intervening cause is the negligent medical care of the paramedics. Hank's intent was not to cause Mark's death, and, as such, he was not the legal cause of Mark's death. Of course, Hank may also have a mens rea defense.

Assume that Hank shot Mark intending to kill him, but because Hank is a poor shot, he only injured Mark. As before, the paramedics who treat Mark negligently administer the wrong medication and cause his death. Again, Hank is the factual cause of Mark's death. Whether he is the legal cause is debatable. Even though the intended result occurred, it occurred in a manner entirely unintended. If the manner in which the result occurs differs significantly from the manner that was intended, the defendant may not be liable. This appears consistent with common notions of fairness: Why should Hank be liable for murder when at least part of the blame belongs to the paramedics? Courts are split on this issue. Some would find that Hank is liable for intent murder, whereas others would hold Hank liable for a lower murder.

If a victim suffers the intended injury while attempting to avoid the injury, the defendant is liable for the crime, even though the manner is entirely different than intended. So if Mark is struck and killed by a bus while running from Hank, who intends to stab Mark to death, Hank is considered both the legal and the factual cause of Mark's death. There is a limit to this theory; that is, there must be some nexus between the unintended manner and the act. If a reasonable person would not have expected the result to occur, the defendant is not liable. So, if Mark was not killed by a passing bus but, rather, by a hit on the head by a piano accidentally dropped by movers, Hank is not the legal cause of his death. This is true even though Mark would not have happened to be under the piano if he were not running from Hank.

---

intervening cause

■ A cause of an accident or other injury that will remove the blame from the wrongdoer who originally set events in motion.

In the rare instance where two events happen simultaneously, and both could be the legal cause of the outcome, both are treated as the legal cause. This is true even if only one event was the actual cause. For example, if two people shoot a victim at the same moment, both are liable for murder. However, it is possible that only one actually caused the death. If it is not possible to determine which bullet was the actual cause of death, both people are liable. If it can be determined which bullet was responsible for killing the victim, the other party is relieved of responsibility for murder (although not attempted murder).

Even though the preceding examples dealt with purposeful crimes, remember that the principle applies to all crimes that require a particular result. The result need not be one that comes about purposefully or intentionally. Crimes of recklessness and negligence may require a specific result to be criminal. Reckless homicide requires that the behavior that is reckless actually cause a death.

The Model Penal Code also requires that the conduct in question be the actual result or cause of the result. Section 2.03 of the Model Penal Code also, if a particular result is necessary to prove a crime, the "element is not established unless the actual result is a probable consequence of the actor's conduct." Further, the Code states that the crime is not proven if the actual result is different from the defendant's purpose, unless:

1. The resulting harm is the same; however it occurred to the wrong person or thing (transferred intent).
2. The actual harm is not as great or as serious as intended.
3. The actual harm involves the same kind of injury or harm as intended and is not *too remote or accidental* in its occurrence to have a bearing on the actor's liability.

These requirements apply to all levels of culpability under the Code—that is, purposeful, knowing, reckless, and negligent—and must be adjusted accordingly. So, if the crime is one of recklessness or negligence, then the Code's criteria should be viewed in light of risks and probable results and not purpose.

The phrase "too remote or accidental" is the Code's proximate cause requirement. It is the same as discussed earlier, except that the drafters of the Code chose not to use the phrase "proximate cause." In *People v. Warner-Lambert Co.*, a company and some of its officers were indicted for manslaughter and negligent homicide. The charges stemmed from an industrial accident at one of Warner-Lambert's plants. The high court of New York dismissed the indictments, finding that the defendants were not the proximate cause of the plant employees' deaths because the explosion that caused their deaths was not foreseeable.

The "Year-and-a-Day Rule"

At common law, a person could not be charged with murder if the victim did not die within one year and one day after the act took place. The rule was one of causation. It was developed to prevent a conviction for murder at a time in history when medical science could not precisely determine the actual cause of a person's death. If a person lived for more than a year and a day after being injured by a defendant's acts and then died, it was assumed that medical science could not pinpoint the exact cause of death and that to hold the defendant liable would be unjust. It is questionable, in light of the advances in medicine, whether the rule should continue to exist. It has been abolished in many states. In *Rogers v. Tennessee* (2001) the Supreme Court reviewed a conviction in Tennessee that was allowed to stand because the Tennessee courts announced the abrogation of the rule in the case. The court was asked to invalidate the conviction as *ex post facto* and contrary to due process.

Concurrence

In this chapter you have learned that there are two primary components of crimes—the mental and the physical. Although a showing of mens rea is not required for every crime, there must be a showing of some act or omission for all crimes.

For crimes that have both a mental and a physical element, an additional requirement of concurrence must be proved. *Concurrence* is the joining of mens rea and the act. The mens rea must be the reason that the act was taken. Stated another way, the mental state must occur first and set into motion the act. For example, Sandira hates Andy and desires to see him dead. Because of this feeling, Sandira waits for Andy to leave the house one night and runs him down with her car. In such a case, Sandira's mens rea set into motion the act that caused Andy's death. Now imagine that Sandira accidentally kills Andy in an auto accident. After the accident, she exclaims his happiness over Andy's demise. In this case, the mens rea occurred after the act. It was not the catalyst for the act that killed Andy, and, as such, there was no concurrence.

The mere fact that the mental state happens before the act does not mean that there is concurrence. There must be a connection between the intent and the act; the mens rea must set the act into motion. So if Doug forms the desire to kill Andy today but takes no action to further the desire, he cannot be charged with murder a year later when he accidentally shoots Andy while hunting.

As stated by the Court of Appeals of Indiana:

> Unless statutorily stated otherwise, it is black letter law that in order to constitute a crime "criminal intent" . . . must unite with an overt act, and they must concur in point of time. There must be a criminal act or omission as well as criminal intent. A felonious intent unconnected with an unlawful act constitutes no crime. . . . A person can only be punished for an offense he has committed and never for an offense he may commit in the future. A crime cannot be predicated upon future acts or upon contingencies or the taking effect of some future event.[31]

Web Links

American Bar Association

The American Bar Association's home page *http:www.abanet.org* has considerable law-related information, including criminal law, legal education, and legal ethics topics. It also contains links to other sources of legal information.

Key Terms

actus reus
constructive intent (to match specific intent]
corporate liability
elements
foreseeability
inferences
injunctions
intervening cause

knowingly
legal cause
legislative history
mens rea
motive
negligence
omission
presumption
proximate cause

purposely
recklessness
scienter
specific intent
statutory construction
strict liability
strict liability crimes
transferred intent
vicarious liability

Review Questions

1. In criminal law, causation is broken down into two forms. Name and briefly describe each.
2. Can a person be prosecuted for failing to save a stranger from danger? Why or why not?
3. What is concurrence?
4. What is an omission?
5. The Model Penal Code recognizes four types of mens rea. Name and briefly describe each.
6. What is vicarious liability?
7. What is a rebuttable presumption? An irrebuttable presumption?
8. Can corporations and other associations be guilty of crimes?
9. Distinguish mens rea from motive.

Problems & Critical Thinking Exercises

1-6. Many prisoners in the state and federal correctional systems are held at minimum-security "farms." Only inmates considered not to be dangerous are housed at these facilities because of the minimal security. In fact, in many cases it is possible for inmates to simply walk off. Of course, most do not leave the premises, because to do so results in an increased sentence (either due to a conviction for escape or a decrease in "good time") and a likelihood that the sentence will be spent in prison rather than the more desirable farm. Despite this practice, prisoners of these facilities do escape. Problems 1 through 6 present several different sets of facts involving a fictitious inmate, Spike Vincelli. Read each problem and discuss the defenses, if any, that Spike may have against a charge of escape. Discuss each in light of the following two statutes:

Statute I
It shall be unlawful for any person committed to any correctional facility to escape from that facility. Escape is defined as passing beyond the borders of a facility with an intent to never return or being lawfully beyond the borders of the facility and not returning when required to do so with an intent to never return. Violation of this statute constitutes a felony.

Statute II
It shall be unlawful for any person committed to any correctional facility to leave the premises of the facility. Leaving is defined as passing over the boundary lines of the facility. Violation of this statute constitutes a misdemeanor.

1. On June 21, Spike Vincelli received a telephone call from a hospital informing him that his mother had been involved in a serious accident. That evening, Spike left to see his mother, intending to return in the morning.

2. On June 21, Spike Vincelli had his first epileptic seizure. The seizure caused Spike to fall outside the boundary line surrounding the facility.

3. On June 21, Spike Vincelli decided that he was bored with living on the farm. That night he walked off the premises and fled for a friend's house 300 miles away, intending never to return.

4. On June 21, Spike Vincelli became involved in a fight with Ben Ichabod. In a fit of rage, Ben picked Spike up and threw him over the fence surrounding the farm. Spike was caught outside the fence by a guard before Spike had an opportunity to return.

5. In early April, Spike Vincelli decided that he was going to escape. He developed a plan that called for him to leave in July and meet his brother, who was passing through the area. As part of the plan, Ben Ichabod, a fellow inmate, was enlisted to pick Spike up off the ground and throw him over the fence that surrounded the facility. However, Ben, who is not very bright, threw Spike over the fence on June 21.

6. On June 21, Spike Vincelli became involved in a fight with Ben Ichabod. Ben, in a fit of rage, picked Spike up and threw him over the fence surrounding the facility. While outside the fence, Spike became overcome with a sense of freedom and ran from the facility.

7. Fred failed to show up for a date he had made with Penni. Penni, who was angered by Fred's actions, decided to vent her anger by cutting the tires of Fred's automobile. However, Penni did not know what make of automobile Fred drove and mistakenly cut the tires of a car owned by Fred's neighbor, Stacey. Penni is now charged with the "purposeful destruction of personal property." Penni claims that her act was not purposeful because she did not intend to cut the tires of Stacey's car. Discuss this defense.

8. William, an experienced canoeist, was hired by a Boy Scout troop to supervise a canoe trip. While on the trip, two boys fell out of their canoe and began to drown. William watched as the boys drowned. Is William criminally liable for the deaths?

9. Sherri, who was near bankruptcy, decided to burn her house down and make an insurance claim for the loss. Sherri started the fire, which spread to a neighbor's house located 20 feet from Sherri's home. Unknown to Sherri, her neighbor was storing massive quantities of dynamite in the home. The fire at the neighbor's house spread to the room where the explosives were being stored, and the resulting explosion caused such vibrations that a construction worker one block away fell off a ladder and subsequently died from the fall. Sherri is charged with arson and murder. She has pled guilty to arson but maintains that she is not liable for the death of the worker. Is she correct?

10. The following statute was enacted by State Legislature:

    It shall be unlawful for any person to be a pedophile. Pedophilia is defined as a condition where a person over the age of 17 years possesses a sexual desire for a person under the age of 8 years.

    While attending a group therapy session, Jane admitted that she had sexual interest in boys under 8 years of age. A member of the group contacted the local police and reported Jane's statement. Jane was subsequently arrested and charged with violating the quoted statute. Discuss her defenses, if any.

11. Ashley, Amy, and Karen are roommates in college. They occupy a four-bedroom apartment, and all share in the bills and household duties. One weekend, a friend of Karen's, Janice, came to visit. Janice arrived on Thursday and was scheduled to stay until Monday. She stayed in the extra bedroom. On Thursday evening, Ashley discovered, while she was watching Janice unpack, that Janice had a significant amount of cocaine in one suitcase. Later that night, Ashley discussed this matter with Karen, who stated, "I'm sure she does—why does it matter to you?" Ashley immediately confronted Janice and told her that she would have to remove the cocaine from the premises or Ashley would call the police. Janice picked up the suitcase, carried it to her car, and placed it in the trunk. The next morning, when Karen learned what Ashley had done, Karen encouraged Janice to bring the suitcase back into the apartment. On Sunday morning, the police arrived with a warrant to search the apartment. The search uncovered the suitcase in the extra bedroom. Later, at the police station, the suitcase was opened and the drugs were discovered. All four women were charged with possession. Do Amy, Ashley, or Karen have a defense? The jurisdiction where they live applies the Model Penal Code.

12. In some nations, vicarious criminal liability is much broader than in the United States. For example, parents may be vicariously liable for the criminal acts of their children until the children reach adulthood. Should such laws be adopted in the United States? Explain your answer.

13. Develop your own fact scenarios, one demonstrating specific intent and another demonstrating general intent. Explain why each is an example of specific intent or general intent.

14. Using the two fact scenarios you created in problem 13, change the facts so the general-intent crime becomes a specific-intent crime and the specific-intent crime becomes a general-intent crime.

Endnotes

1. J. Goldstein, et al., *Criminal Law: Theory and Process* (New York: Free Press, 1974).
2. 21 Am. Jur. 2d, *Criminal Law* 129 (1981).
3. See *United States v. Birkenstock*, 823 F.2d 1026 (7th Cir. 1987); *United States v. Pompanio*, 429 U.S. 10 (1976).
4. LaFave & Scott, *Criminal Law* (Hornbook Series, St. Paul: West, 1986), at 217.
5. LaFave & Scott at 34.
6. Gary Fields and John R. Emshwiller, *As Federal Crime List Grows, Threshold of Guilt Declines, The Wall Street Journal*, September 27, 2011.
7. See *Lambert v. California*, 355 U.S. 225 (1957), in which the United States Supreme Court found that a strict liability statute was violative of the due process clause of the United States Constitution.
8. LaFave & Scott at 244–45.
9. *United States v. Dotterweich*, 320 U.S. 277 (1943).
10. *United States v. Freed*, 401 U.S. 601 (1971).
11. For a thorough discussion of mens rea and public welfare rationale see J. Manly Parks, The Public Welfare Rationale: Defining Mens Rea in RCRA, 18 Wm. & Mary Envtl. L.& Pol'y Rev. 219 (1993), http://scholarship.law.wm.edu/wmelpr/vol18/iss1/6
12. *United States v. Dotterweich*, 320 U.S. 277 (1943).
13. Jeffrey P. Cogin, *Corporations Can Kill Too: After Film Recovery, Are Individuals Accountable for Corporate Crimes*, Loyola of Los Angeles Law Review 19 (1986): 1411, 1413-1414, http://digitalcommons.lmu.edu//llr/vol19/iss4/12
14. Model Penal Code § 2.07 deals with liability of corporations and unincorporated associations.
15. For more on the original cases, see Cogin, *infra*. For the reversals, see *People v. O'Neil, 194 Ill. App.3d 79*, 550 N.E.2d 109 (1990). The convictions of the individuals were reversed and remanded for retrial on appeal. The defendants pled guilty to involuntary manslaughter to avoid retrial. William Presecky, *2 Bosses Plead Guilty in 83 Death of Plant Worker*, Chicago Tribune, September 8, 1993, http://articles.chicagotribune.com/1993-09-08/news/9309080122_1_charles-kirschbaum-job-related-death-film-recovery-systems
16. See Jeffrey S. Parker, "Criminal Sentencing Policy for Organizations: The Unifying Approach of Optimal Penalties," 26 *Am. Cr. Law R.* 513 (1989).
17. For more on this case, see Francis T. Cullen, William J. Maakestad, and Gray Cavender, *Corporate Crime under Attack: The Ford Pinto Case and Beyond* (Cincinnati: Anderson Publishing, 1987). See also G. Schwartz, "The Myth of the Ford Pinto Case," 43 *Rutgers Law R.* 1013 (1991).

18. Arthur Andersen v. United States, 544 U.S. 696 (2005)
19. Model Penal Code § 2.02, General Requirements of Culpability.
20. Kaplan & Weisberg, *Criminal Law* (Boston: Little, Brown, 1986).
21. Model Penal Code § 2.02(2)(c).
22. The Model Penal Code actually recognizes three "objective elements" that may have differing culpability levels. Those are circumstance, result, and conduct. Also, the Code provides, at § 2.02(4), that one mental state shall apply to an entire offense, unless a contrary intent is plain.
23. Model Penal Code § 2.01.
24. *Id.*
25. *King v. Cogdon* (Vict. 1950).
26. A. Loewy, *Criminal Law*, 2nd ed. (Nutshell Series) (St. Paul: West, 1987).
27. *Robinson v. California,* 370 U.S. 660 (1962).
28. Model Penal Code §2.01(4).
29. Tim Rohan, *Sandusky Gets 30 to 60 Years For Sexual Abuse, New York Times*, October 8, 2012, http://www.nytimes.com/2012/10/10/sports/ncaafootball/penn-state-sandusky-is-sentenced-in-sex-abuse-case.html
30. O.R.C. sec. 2921.22.
31. *Gebhard v. State*, 484 N.E.2d 45, 48 (Ind. Ct. App. 1985).

CHAPTER 9

CRIMES AGAINST THE PERSON

Chapter Outline

Studying Crimes
Homicide
    Homicide and the Common Law
    Statutory Approaches to Homicide
    Manslaughter
    The Model Penal Code Approach to Homicide
    Life, Death, and Homicide
    Suicide
    Corpus Delicti
Assault and Battery
    Aggravated Assault and Battery
Mayhem
Sex Crimes
    Rape
    Nonforcible Rape
    Sodomy
    Rape Shield Laws
    Incest
    Sex Offenses Against Children
    Megan's Laws, Commitment, and Castration
Kidnapping and False Imprisonment
    Kidnapping
    Parental Kidnapping
    False Imprisonment
Stalking
    Cyberstalking
Civil Rights and Hate Crimes

Chapter Objectives

After completing this chapter you should be able to:

- list, explain, and compare the elements of common law and contemporary crimes against the person, such as murder, rape, and assault.
- list, explain, and compare the common defenses to charges of crimes against the person, such as self-defense.
- identify and analyze contemporary legal issues concerning death and suicide.
- identify the material facts and legal issues in 1/3 of the cases you read.

STUDYING CRIMES

In the next three chapters you will learn about many crimes. It would be impossible to include a discussion of all crimes. The federal government and each city and state have their own unique laws. What follows is a discussion of the major crimes recognized, in some form, in most jurisdictions. The crimes have been categorized as crimes against the person, crimes against property, and crimes against the public. Although it is common to make these distinctions, do not concern yourself with understanding why these classifications have been made; they are used only for organizational purposes. In a sense, all crimes are offenses against the public in the United States. That is why the public prosecutes crimes, and private individuals may not. Also, any offense "against property" is actually injuring a person, not the property. A stolen iPod set does not long to be returned to its rightful owner. However, the rightful owner does feel wronged and desires the return of the stolen item. In a sense, the classifications are often accurate in that they describe the focus of the criminal conduct. The focus of a thief's act is property; hence, a crime against property. The focus of a rapist's attack is a human; hence, a crime against a person.

All of the following crimes have been broken into parts. Each part of a crime is an **element** of that crime. At trial, every element of a crime must be proven beyond a reasonable doubt by the prosecution. If any element is not proven beyond a reasonable doubt, the accused must be found not guilty. The rule requires that each element be proved individually. That is, if a crime consists of six elements, and a jury is convinced that five have been proven, but cannot say that the sixth has been proven beyond a reasonable doubt, then there must be a not-guilty verdict. This is true even if the jury was solidly convinced that all the other elements were true and generally believed that the defendant committed the crime. Later you will learn more about the standard for determining guilt beyond a reasonable doubt.

Finally, you may notice that, often, if one crime has been proven, all the elements of a related lesser crime can also be proved. For example, if a defendant is convicted of murdering someone with a hammer, he has also committed a battery of the victim. In such circumstances, the lesser offense merges into the greater offense. This is the **merger** doctrine. Under this doctrine, both crimes may be charged; but if the defendant is convicted of the more serious crime, the lesser is absorbed by the greater, and the defendant is not punished for both. If acquitted of the greater charge, the defendant may be convicted of the lesser.

HOMICIDE

Homicide is the killing of one human being by another. Not all homicides are crimes. It is possible to cause another person's death accidentally, that is, accompanied by no mens rea. For example, if a bridge builder lost her balance and fell against a coworker, causing the coworker to fall to his death, no crime has been committed, but there has been a homicide.

Criminal homicide occurs when a person takes another's life in a manner proscribed by law. The law proscribes more than intentional killings. Under the Model Penal Code, purposeful, knowing, negligent, and reckless homicides may be punished.

element

▪ A basic part. For example, some of the *elements* of a cause of action for battery are an intentional, unwanted physical contact. Each of these things ("intentional," "unwanted," etc.) is one "element."

merger of offenses

▪ When a person is charged with two crimes (based on exactly the same acts), one of which is a lesser included offense of the other. The lesser crime *merges* because, under the prohibition against double jeopardy, the person may be tried for only one crime.

Exhibit 9-1 CRIME CLOCK 2011

2011 CRIME CLOCK STATISTICS

A Violent Crime occurred every	**26.2 seconds**
One Murder every	36.0 minutes
One Forcible Rape every	6.3 minutes
One Robbery every	1.5 minutes
One Aggravated Assault every	42.0 seconds
A Property Crime occurred every	**3.5 seconds**
One Burglary every	14.4 seconds
One Larceny-theft every	5.1 seconds
One Motor vehicle Theft every	44.1 seconds

Source: US FBI, Uniform Crime Reports (2012)

The mens rea part of homicide is important. The determination of what mens rea was possessed by the defendant (actually, what mens rea can be proven by the prosecution) will usually determine what crime may be punished. At common law, various forms of murder were developed. This is where we begin.

Homicide and the Common Law

Initially, at common law, all murders were punished equally: the murderer was executed.[1] Over time, the value of proportional punishment developed and homicides were eventually divided into murder and manslaughter with differentiated punishment. Manslaughter was punished by incarceration, not death.

Murder, at common law, was defined as (1) the unlawful killing of a (2) human being with (3) malice aforethought. It was the requirement of malice aforethought that distinguished murder from manslaughter. Although malice aforethought was defined differently among the states, the following types of homicide became recognized as murder under the common law:

1. When the defendant intended to cause the death of the victim.
2. When the defendant intended to cause serious bodily harm, and death resulted.

3. When the defendant created an unreasonably high risk of death that caused the victim's death, regardless of the defendant's mens rea. This was known as "depraved-heart murder."
4. When the doctrine of felony-murder was applicable.

All criminal homicides that did not constitute murder were treated as manslaughter. Today, nearly every jurisdiction further divides murder into degrees, and most divide manslaughter into voluntary and involuntary. Few jurisdictions rely on the common-law definition of malice aforethought. However, many states continue to recognize felony-murder.

The Felony-Murder Doctrine

Cole Allen Wilkins committed a burglary of a home that was under construction. He loaded several appliances stolen during the burglary into the bed of a pickup truck. Sixty-two miles away from the burglarized home, a stove that Wilkins' had loaded into the truck fell onto the interstate. Wilkins left the stove on the road, and later a driver was killed when he swerved into the path of an oncoming vehicle in an attempt to avoid hitting the stove. Wilkins was charged and convicted of a crime that developed a long time ago, first-degree felony murder. You will learn more about his appeal in a moment, after you are introduced to this old crime.

At common law, one who caused an unintended death during the commission (or attempted commission) of any felony was guilty of murder. This became known as **felony-murder**. Under the early common law all felonies were punished by death. Generally, most of the crimes that were felonies under the common law posed a threat to human life. This threat was one justification for the harshness of the rule. However, as the common law developed, many new crimes were created, many of which did not involve serious threat to human life. For this reason the felony-murder doctrine was very harsh, as it applied to all felonies regardless of their relative dangerousness to human life. In time, courts began to limit the application of the rule to specified felonies—those perceived as posing the largest threat to human life. It was common to apply the rule to rape, mayhem, arson, kidnapping, and robbery.

For example, Grace and Eva decided to rob the First National Bank. They agreed to use whatever amount of violence is necessary to carry out the robbery. During the robbery a bank teller summoned the police by use of a silent alarm. As Grace and Eva were leaving the bank, the police shouted to them, ordering their surrender. Grace then fired a shot from her gun and fatally wounded a police officer. Using the felony-murder rule, both Grace and Eva are criminally liable for the death of the police officer, even though Eva did not fire the weapon or conspire with Grace to kill the officer.

The felony-murder rule acts to impute the required mens rea to the defendant and to create a form of vicarious liability between cofelons. The rule imputes mens rea because it applies in situations of unintended death; however, murder in the first degree is a specific-intent crime. The rationale is that one who engages in inherently dangerous crimes should be aware of the high risk to human life created by the crime. Vicarious liability is also imposed in some states; that is, all the individuals involved in the perpetration of the crime may be criminally liable for the resulting death.

felony-murder rule
■ The principle that if a person (even accidentally) kills another while committing a felony, then the killing is murder.

Today, most states have felony-murder statutes. Generally, the following requirements must be proven to establish a felony-murder:

1. The defendant must have been engaged in the commission, or attempted commission, of a named felony, and
2. during the commission, or attempted commission, of that felony a death occurred, and
3. there is a causal connection between the crime and the death.

In most jurisdictions the legislature has specified the crimes that must be committed, or attempted, for the rule to apply. A few jurisdictions have limited the application of the rule to crimes that were felonies at common law, and others have limited the rule to felonies that involve a threat to human life.

To satisfy the second requirement, it must be determined when the commission of the crime began and when it concluded. This appears to be an easy task, and it is in most cases, but in some instances it is not clear. Suppose that a robber knew that a large sum of money was being transferred between a bank and an armored car at a particular time and intended to steal the money during that transfer. Also assume that on the day of the robbery, the traffic was heavier than anticipated by the robber and, in an effort to arrive at the bank on time, the robber ran a stop sign. While passing through the intersection, the robber struck another vehicle, killing the driver. Was this death during the commission, or attempted commission, of the robbery? What if a police officer were to chase an individual from the scene of a felony and get shot 15 minutes and one mile away from the scene of the crime? Is this during the commission, or attempted commission, of the felony? It is likely that no felony-murder would be found in the first example, because the death was too far removed from actual commission of the crime. The result would be different if the robber struck and killed the motorist while fleeing from the police immediately after commission of the holdup. This answers the second question. Courts have generally held that deaths that occur during the flight of a felon are "during the commission of the felony." However, the chase must be immediate, and the rule does not apply if there is a gap between the time the crime occurred, or was attempted, and the time the chase begins. The third element can be troublesome. In many ways this requirement is similar to the causation requirement discussed in Chapter 8 regarding actus reus. That is, the commission, or attempted commission, of the felony must be the legal cause (proximate cause) of the death. The death must be a "consequence, not coincidence" of the act; the resulting death must have been a foreseeable consequence of the act. So, if a patron of a store suffers a heart attack during a robbery, which was precipitated by the crime, the robbers are guilty of felony-murder if the patron dies. However, if a patron who is unaware of an ongoing robbery suffers a heart attack and dies, the robbers are not liable for the death. The mere fact that the death and the crime occurred simultaneously does not mean that the robbers were the legal cause of the death.

Returning to Defendant Wilkins and the stolen stove, he won reversal of his conviction in 2013 because the Supreme Court of California found the nexus between the death of the motorist and the burglary to be too distant in time and lacking in nexus.[2]

In some states, the act that causes the death of the victim need not be taken by one of the perpetrators of the crime. For example, if Grace and Eva become involved in a shoot-out with the police after they rob the First National Bank, and the police accidentally shoot an innocent bystander, then Grace and Eva are guilty of felony-murder. This is because they began the series of events that led to the death of the bystander. However, if a police officer (or another) kills one of many felons who are jointly involved in the commission of the crime, it is generally held that the other felons are not guilty of felony-murder.[3]

Although the felony-murder rule does impose vicarious liability between cofelons, this aspect is limited. If a defendant can prove that he did not commit the act that caused the death; did not authorize, plan, or encourage the act of his cofelon; and had no reason to believe that his cohort would commit the act, he has a defense to felony-murder in some jurisdictions. Note that the rules concerning parties (principals and accomplices) to crimes may create liability independent of the felony-murder rule. (See Chapter 12 for a discussion of parties to crimes.)

Finally, note that in most jurisdictions that continue to recognize felony-murder, the murder is treated as first-degree murder for the purpose of sentencing. Other statutes provide that felony-murders that occur during named felonies are to be treated as first-degree murder and that murders during "all other felonies" are to be treated as second-degree murder. Even if the statute that creates this "all other felony" category does not expressly state that the felony must involve a danger to human life, it is common for courts to impose the requirement.

In the *Losey* case, a defendant appealed his conviction of involuntary manslaughter and aggravated burglary. The Ohio Court of Appeals applied a statute that read, "No person shall cause the death of another as a proximate result of the offender's committing or attempting to commit a felony." The statute named the crime involuntary manslaughter. The case is interesting from a causation perspective. Read the case and decide for yourself if the defendant should be punished for the death that occurred.

Misdemeanor Manslaughter

Similar to the felony-murder rule, one may be guilty of misdemeanor manslaughter if a death results from the commission of a misdemeanor, not a felony. Conviction of misdemeanor manslaughter results in liability for manslaughter, often involuntary manslaughter, and not murder.

Just as the felony-murder doctrine has been limited in recent years, so has the crime of misdemeanor manslaughter. This is due largely to the significant increase in the creation of nonviolent crimes by legislatures and administrative bodies. Many states require that the misdemeanor be *malum in se*, and crimes that are *malum prohibitum* cannot be a basis for misdemeanor manslaughter. Requiring that the misdemeanor have a mens rea element is another limitation; that is, strict liability crimes may not be the basis for misdemeanor manslaughter. There is a trend to reject the misdemeanor manslaughter rule (as there is with the felony-murder rule) and require that one of the four types of culpability recognized by the Model Penal Code (purposeful, knowing, negligent, or reckless) be present before imposing liability.

Statutory Approaches to Homicide

first-degree murder

■ The highest form of homicide. The killing of another person with malice and premeditation, cruelty, or done during the commission of a major felony is typically murder in the first degree.

second-degree murder

■ Murder without premeditation.

Although the common law recognized only one form of murder, most states now divide murder into degrees; most often into first and second degrees. **First-degree murder** is the highest form of murder and is punished more severely than second-degree murder. **Second-degree murder** is a higher crime than manslaughter.

First- and Second-Degree Murder

For a murder to be of the first degree, the highest crime, it must be shown that the homicide was willful, deliberate, and premeditated. Generally, first-degree murder applies whenever the murderer has as a goal the death of the victim. *Willful,* as used in first-degree murder, is a specific-intent concept. To be willful, the defendant must have specifically intended to cause the death.

Deliberate is usually defined as "a cool mind, not acting out of an immediate passion, fear, or rage." The term *premeditated* means "to think beforehand." Similar to *deliberate*, it eliminates impulsive acts from the grasp of first-degree murder. It is commonly said that there must be a gap in time between the decision to kill and the actual act. Of course, the length of the gap is the critical issue. Most courts hold that the gap in time must be "appreciable." Again, this term does little to define the length of time. The fact is that courts differ greatly in how they define *appreciable*. There are many reported cases where a lapse of only seconds was sufficient.[4] Some courts have held that all that need be shown is that the defendant had adequate time to form the intention before taking the act; the length of time is not determinative of the question.[5]

In *State v. Snowden*, the defendant appealed his conviction of first-degree murder, claiming that he lacked premeditation. As such, he should have been convicted of second-degree murder, not first-degree. Decisions such as this obscure the difference between first- and second-degree murder. Do you agree with the Idaho Court that there can be premeditation even if there is "no appreciable space of time between the intention to kill and the act of killing"? Note that the facts of this case did not require mention of the prior case where it was held that "no appreciable" time has to be shown. The fact that the autopsy evidenced that the murder occurred after the victim suffered torture would justify a murder conviction under the statute.

Note that the statute mentioned in *Snowden* to describe first-degree murder is used by many jurisdictions. Those murders that result from poisoning, follow torture, or are traditional felony-murders are often designated first-degree murder. Following the attacks of September 11, 2001, some states amended their statutes to include deaths resulting from terrorist activity in the classification of first degree murders.[6] Second-degree murder is commonly given the negative definition "all murders that are not of the first degree are of the second." Second-degree murders differ from first in that the defendant lacked the specific intent to kill or lacked the premeditation and deliberation element of first-degree murder.

Intent to Do Serious Bodily Harm and the Deadly Weapon Doctrine

One method of reducing a murder from the first-degree to the second-degree is by proving that the defendant did not intend to kill but only intended to cause the victim serious bodily harm. Note that if the defendant intended less than serious bodily harm, the crime is either manslaughter or a form of reckless or negligent homicide.

In this area, inferences are important. Juries (or judges, if the court is acting as the finder of fact) are permitted to view the facts surrounding the murder and determine what the defendant's state of mind was when the act occurred. A jury may conclude from the facts that the defendant did intend to cause the death of the victim and convict the defendant of first-degree murder. If a jury concludes that the defendant did not intend to cause the death of the victim, but that the defendant did intend to cause serious bodily injury, then the crime is second-degree murder.

A related inference used in murder cases is the *deadly weapon doctrine*. This rule permits juries to infer that a defendant intended to kill his or her victim if a **deadly weapon** was used in the killing. Being an inference, this conclusion does not have to be drawn; it is a decision for the fact finder. If a jury were to conclude that a defendant's use of a deadly weapon indicated that murder was intended, then a first-degree murder conviction would be warranted. So, if Gwen intended only to injure Fred by shooting him, but Fred died because of the wound, then a jury could convict Gwen of first-degree murder. Of course, the jury could reject the inference if they believed that Gwen did not intend to kill Fred, and in that case either second-degree murder (if her intent was to inflict serious bodily injury) or manslaughter would be appropriate.

Any device or item may be a deadly weapon if, from the manner used, it is calculated or likely to produce death or serious bodily injury.[7] The Model Penal Code defines a deadly weapon as "any firearm, or other weapon, device, instrument, material, or substance, whether animate or inanimate, which in the manner it is used or is intended to be used is known to be capable of producing death or serious bodily injury."[8] Under these definitions, some items that are not normally considered deadly may be deadly weapons if their use is calculated to cause serious bodily injury or death. The opposite is also true; some items that are normally considered deadly may not be, if used

deadly weapon

■ Any instrument likely to cause serious bodily harm under the circumstances of its actual use. Such things as a fan belt used to choke a man and a fire used to burn an occupied house have been called *deadly weapons* by courts.

Exhibit 9-2 CIRCUIT COURT/CRIMINAL DIVISION

```
                        CIRCUIT COURT
STATE OF WISCONSIN      CRIMINAL DIVISION              MILWAUKEE COUNTY
-----------------------------------------------------------------------
STATE OF WISCONSIN, Plaintiff            INFORMATION

      vs.                                CRIME(S):
                                         See Charging Section Below
Jeffrey L. Dahmer    05/21/60            STATUTE(S) VIOLATED
924 N. 25th St.                          See Charging Section Below
Milwaukee, WI                            COMPLAINING WITNESS:
                                         Donald Domagalski
                  Defendant              CASE NUMBER:
                                         F-912542
-----------------------------------------------------------------------
```

I, E. MICHAEL MC CANN, DISTRICT ATTORNEY FOR MILWAUKEE COUNTY, WISCONSIN, HEREBY INFORM THE COURT THAT THE ABOVE NAMED DEFENDANT IN THE COUNTY OF MILWAUKEE, STATE OF WISCONSIN,

COUNT 01: FIRST DEGREE MURDER

COUNT 12: FIRST DEGREE INTENTIONAL HOMICIDE

on or about June 30, 1991, at 924 North 25th Street, City and County of Milwaukee, did cause the death of another human being, Matt Turner a/k/a Donald Montrell, with intent to kill that person contrary to Wisconsin Statutes section 940.01(1).

Upon conviction of each count of First Degree Intentional Homicide and each count of First Degree Murder, Class A Felonies, the penalty is life imprisonment.

DATED   E. MICHAEL MC CANN
                                         DISTRICT ATTORNEY

        9/10/91   _E. Michael McCann_
                                         District Attorney

                                         Jeffrey L. Dahmer
                                         9.10.91

Jeffrey L. Dahmer 9.10.91
* The statement on page (3)
1 is accurate as it applies
to this day
        Jeffrey L. Dahmer
             9.10.91

Source: http://law2.umkc.edu/faculty/projects/ftrials/mcveigh/mcveighcertif.html

in a manner that does not pose a threat of serious harm or death. Hence, a bowling ball may be transformed from a recreational device into a deadly weapon when it is used to crush a person's skull. A gun, probably the most obvious example of a deadly device, may not be deemed deadly if used to hit someone over the head. A person's hands and feet are not normally deadly weapons. However, if it can be shown that the victims were significantly smaller than the defendants or that the defendants were especially expert in the use of their hands to cause injury, then the hands may constitute deadly weapons.

In the *Labelle* case, the inference created by the deadly weapon doctrine was used to affirm a trial court conviction of attempted murder.

Communicable Diseases and Murder

Communicable diseases, such as acquired immunodeficiency syndrome (AIDS) and anthrax, raise interesting criminal law situations. First, the intentional transmission of a disease can be criminal. For example, passing a disease to another, if intentional, is either attempted murder, if the disease is not passed to the victim, or murder, if the disease is successfully passed to, and causes the death of, the victim. This was what happened following the September 11, 2001, terrorist attacks on the World Trade Center and Pentagon. One week after the attacks, letters containing deadly anthrax spores were mailed to two U.S. senators and several media outlets. Five people were killed and many more were injured. The attacks led to the largest bioterrorism investigation in U.S. history. The key suspect in the case committed suicide in 2008, as the filing of charges against him became imminent. Although no one was ever charged, the highly contagious nature of the material and the obvious intentionality of the act would have easily supported a high mens rea homicide charge.[9]

Second, the unintentional but criminally negligent or reckless passing of such a disease may also be criminal under negligent manslaughter statutes. Sharing a needle with another, knowing that it has been used by an HIV-infected individual, falls into this category, as does the passing of the disease by a prostitute who knows of her infection to a client.

Third, due to the nature of the disease, it is often not discovered until long after it is contracted, and death may not occur for many years. This poses problems in jurisdictions that continue to follow the year-and-a-day rule or other similar rules.

Fourth, in some situations, defendants have claimed that, because of the low probability of infecting another person, it is a factual impossibility to commit murder using AIDS. Fifth, AIDS may be characterized as a deadly weapon, and therefore, a charge of assault may be elevated to assault with a deadly weapon. Similarly, attacks leading to death may be treated as murder under the deadly weapon doctrine.

In most states, preexisting laws (e.g., murder, attempted murder, and intentional transmission of venereal disease) are relied upon to prosecute AIDS-related crimes. However, a few states have enacted statutes specifically directed at the intentional or negligent transmission of AIDS.

Manslaughter

manslaughter

- A crime, less severe than murder, involving the wrongful but nonmalicious killing of another person.

At common law, murder was an unlawful killing with malice aforethought. **Manslaughter** was an unlawful killing without malice aforethought. Just as was the case with murder, the common law did not divide manslaughter into degrees. Whenever the states began codifying homicides, it was common for manslaughter to be divided into degrees, commonly referred to as voluntary and involuntary, although a few jurisdictions used first- and second-degree language. Today, many jurisdictions continue to recognize two forms of manslaughter.

The important fact is that manslaughter is a lesser crime than murder; accordingly, it is punished less severely. It is a lesser crime because some fact or facts exist that make the defendant less culpable than a murderer in the eyes of the law. The most common fact that mitigates a defendant's culpability is the absence of a state of mind that society has decided should be punished as murder. Even though society has decided that, because of such extenuating circumstances, a defendant should not be punished as a murderer, it has also decided that some punishment should be inflicted.

Provocation

provocation

- An act by one person that triggers a reaction of rage in a second person. *Provocation* may reduce the severity of a crime.

Provocation of the defendant by the victim can reduce a homicide from murder to manslaughter. In jurisdictions that grade manslaughter, a provoked killing is treated as the higher manslaughter, whether that provoked killing is called first-degree or voluntary.

The theory of provocation, also known as "heat-of-passion manslaughter," is that a defendant was operating under such an anger or passion that it was impossible for the defendant to have formed the desire to kill, which is required for both first- and second-degree murder. The defense of provocation applies to instances in which people act without thinking, and their impulsive act is the result of the victim's behavior.

Again, an objective test is used when examining the defense of provocation. To prove provocation, it must be shown that the provoking act was so severe that a reasonable person may also have killed. It does not require that a reasonable person would have killed, only that a reasonable person would have been so affected by the act that homicide was possible. A few states have enumerated the acts that may function to negate intent to kill (and reduce the homicide to manslaughter) in their manslaughter statutes. Any act not included may not be used by a defendant to reduce a murder charge.

Catching one's spouse in the act of adultery is an example of an act that is considered adequate provocation to reduce any resulting homicide to manslaughter. This rule applies only to marriages and not to other romantic relationships. Generally, serious assaults (batteries) may constitute adequate provocation.

If two people are engaged in "mutual combat," then any resulting death may be reduced from murder to voluntary manslaughter. The key to this defense is mutuality. If it can be shown that the victim did not voluntarily engage in the fight, then the defense of mutual combat is not applicable, and the defendant is responsible for murder.

It is widely held that words and gestures are never adequate provocation. This is true regardless of how vile or vicious a statement or gesture is to the defendant. However, some recent cases have distinguished statements that are informational from those that are not. In such situations, if a statement provides information of an act, and that act would be sufficient provocation, if witnessed, then the statement may also be provocation.

In the *Schnopps* case, the trial judge refused to instruct the jury on the alternative of manslaughter, as opposed to murder. The trial judge followed the rule that statements are never adequate provocation. The appellate court reversed the judge, holding that the statements made by the defendant's wife directly before he killed her may have been adequate provocation for a jury to find voluntary manslaughter and not murder.

Usually, when claiming adultery as provocation, one must actually have caught his or her spouse in the act. Also, the general rule is that words are not adequate provocation. What did the court do in the *Schnopps* case? It appears that the court attempted to sidestep those rules, in a manner that would permit the benefit of the defense without changing the rules. It did this by holding that in adulterous situations, an admission of adultery to one's spouse, when uttered for the first time, is as shocking as finding one's spouse engaged in the act.

Finally, the defense will not be available if there was a sufficient "cooling-off" period. That is, if the time between the provocation and the homicide was long enough for a defendant to regain self-control, then the homicide will be treated as murder and not manslaughter.

Imperfect Self-Defense and Defense of Others

If Aryana harms Ita while defending herself from Ita's attack, Aryana is said to have acted in self-defense. Self-defense, when valid, normally works to negate criminal liability entirely. So, if Aryana kills Ita to avoid serious bodily harm or death, she has committed an excused homicide. What happens if Aryana was incorrect in her belief that her life was endangered by Ita? This is known as an imperfect self-defense and does not negate culpability entirely. It may, however, reduce liability. Thus, Aryana may be liable only for voluntary manslaughter and not murder. For Aryana to be successful in her claim, she must prove that she had a good-faith belief that her life was in danger and that the killing appeared to be necessary to protect herself.

A person may also have an imperfect self-defense when an excessive amount of force is used as protection. So, if Aryana was correct in her belief that she needed to use force for her protection, but used excessive force, she receives the benefit of reduced liability. Again, there must be a reasonable, although incorrect, belief that the amount of force used was necessary.

The concept of self-defense is extended to the defense of others. So, if Aryana kills Ita while defending Thea and Haris from apparent imminent harm, Aryana is no more liable than if she were defending herself. Just as with an imperfect self-defense, if individuals have a mistaken, but reasonable, belief that another is in danger, and they kill as a result of that belief, they are responsible for voluntary manslaughter rather than murder. Also, if one uses deadly force when a lesser amount of force would have been sufficient to stay the attack, liability is limited to manslaughter, provided that the belief that deadly force was necessary was reasonable under the circumstances.

Involuntary Manslaughter

The lowest form of criminal homicide in most jurisdictions is involuntary manslaughter, sometimes named second-degree manslaughter. In most instances involuntary manslaughter is a form of negligent or reckless manslaughter.

You have already learned the misdemeanor manslaughter rule. In jurisdictions that recognize the rule, the person who commits the misdemeanor that results in an unintended death is responsible for the lowest form of criminal homicide.

Involuntary manslaughter also refers to negligent homicide, vehicular homicide, and similar statutes that punish for unintended, accidental deaths. The classic vehicular homicide is when a motorist runs a red light, strikes another car, and causes the death of the driver or passenger of that automobile. Some states, such as Illinois, make vehicular homicide a separate crime from involuntary manslaughter and impose a lesser punishment for vehicular homicide.[10]

Be aware that many states now have specific statutes dealing with deaths caused by intoxicated drivers. Often the punishment is greater if the death is the result of a drunk or otherwise impaired driver.

The term *negligent* has a different meaning in criminal law than in civil law. In tort law, any unreasonable act that causes an injury creates tort liability. In criminal law, more must be shown. The risk taken by the defendant must be high and pose a threat of death or serious bodily injury to the victim. In addition, some jurisdictions require that the defendant be aware of the risk before liability can be imposed. Of course, knowledge can be inferred from the defendant's actions. Some jurisdictions do not require knowledge of the risk (scienter).

The Model Penal Code Approach to Homicide

The Model Penal Code states, "A person is guilty of criminal homicide if he purposely, knowingly, recklessly, or negligently causes the death of another human being."[11] The Code then classifies all criminal homicides as murder, manslaughter, or negligent homicide. This is done by taking the four mens rea elements (purposeful, knowing, reckless, and negligent) and setting them into one of the classifications. There is some overlap; for example, under some conditions a reckless homicide is murder, and under other conditions it is manslaughter. Let us look at the specifics of the Code.

It is unsurprising that, all purposeful and knowing homicides are murder under the Model Penal Code. Additionally, a reckless homicide is murder when committed "under circumstances manifesting extreme indifference to the value of human life." The Code then incorporates a "felony-murder" type rule, by stating that recklessness and indifference to human life are presumed if the accused was engaged in the commission or attempted commission of robbery, rape, arson, burglary, kidnapping, or felonious escape. So, if the accused are involved in one of those crimes, and a death results, they may be charged with murder under the Code. Note that the Code creates only a presumption of recklessness and indifference, which may be overcome at trial. Murder is the highest form of homicide, and the Code declares it to be a felony of the first degree.

Manslaughters are felonies of the second degree under the Code. All reckless homicides, except those previously described, are manslaughters. As at common law, the Code contains a provision that reduces heat-of-passion murders to manslaughter.

Specifically, the Code states that a homicide, which would normally be murder, is manslaughter when it is

committed under the influence of extreme mental or emotional disturbance for which there is reasonable explanation or excuse. The reasonableness of such explanation or excuse shall be determined from the viewpoint of a person in the actor's situation under the circumstances he believes them to be.

Last, negligent homicides are entitled just that. They are felonies of the third degree.

Life, Death, and Homicide

The actus reus of murder and manslaughter is the taking of a human life. Determining when life begins and ends can be a problem in criminal law, especially when dealing with fetuses.

At common law it was not a crime to destroy a fetus, unless it was "born alive." To be born alive, the fetus must leave its mother's body and exhibit some ability to live independently. Some courts have required that the umbilical cord be cut and that the fetus show its independence thereafter before it was considered a human life. Breathing and crying are both proof of the viability of the child.

Today, many states have enacted feticide statutes that focus on the viability of the fetus. Once it can be shown that the fetus is viable—that is, could live independently if it were born—then anyone who causes its death has committed feticide. Of course, this does not apply to abortion. Since the United States Supreme Court decision in *Roe v. Wade,* 410 U.S. 113 (1973), a woman possesses a limited right to abort a fetus she carries. Thus, states may not prohibit abortions that are protected under that decision. The primary purpose of feticide statutes is to punish individuals who kill fetuses without the mother's approval, as occurred in the *Keeler* case (see Chapter 2).

At the other end of the life continuum is death. Medical advances have made the determination of when death occurs more complex than it was only years ago. For a long time, people were considered dead when they ceased breathing and no longer had a heartbeat. Today, artificial means can be used to sustain both heart action and respiration. That being so, should one be free of criminal homicide in cases where the victim is being kept "alive" by artificial means and there is no reasonable hope of recovery? Should a physician be charged with murder for "pulling the plug" on a patient who has irreversible brain damage and is in a coma? Using the respiration and heart-function test, it would be criminal homicide to end such a treatment. However, many states now use brain death, rather than respiration and heartbeat, to determine when life has ended. In states that employ a brain death definition, it must be shown that there is a total cessation of brain function before legal death exists. The importance of defining death is illustrated by the *Fierro* case.

Suicide

Successful suicide was a crime under the common law of England. The property owned by the one who committed suicide was forfeited to (taken by) the Crown. In early

American common law, attempted suicide was a crime, usually punished as a misdemeanor. Today suicide is not treated as a crime. However, it is possible to restrain and examine individuals who have attempted to commit suicide under civil psychiatric commitment laws.

It continues to be criminal to encourage or aid another to commit suicide. In most situations such a commission is treated as murder. Assisting suicide may be treated as murder, or, as in Michigan, it may be a separate crime that is punished less severely.

The most well-known suicide cases involve Dr. Jack Kevorkian of Michigan. Dr. Kevorkian, a physician, assisted 20 terminally ill persons in committing suicide between 1990 and 1994, earning him the nickname Dr. Death.

Dr. Kevorkian's license to practice medicine was suspended in 1991 for his behavior, and criminal charges have been filed against him on several occasions. The first three cases were dismissed because the statute under which he was charged was held unconstitutional.

The Michigan legislature enacted a law in February 1993 that provided for as much as 4 years' imprisonment and a $2,000 fine for providing the physical means by which another attempts or commits suicide or participates in a physical act by which another attempts or commits suicide. The person charged must have had knowledge that the other person intended to commit suicide.[12]

In 1999 Dr. Kevorkian allowed the news program *60 Minutes* to nationally broadcast his act of assisting Thomas Youk to die. However, Dr. Kevorkian went further than he had in previous cases. Rather than providing a machine to the patient that could assist in death, Dr. Kevorkian administered a lethal injection to Mr. Youk. He then challenged Michigan prosecutors to charge him again. They did, and Dr. Kevorkian was convicted of murder and sentenced to 10 to 25 years in prison. He was paroled in 2007 after serving 8 years in prison and died 4 years later.

While Dr. Kevorkian may have gone too far in committing euthanasia, his first three acquittals suggest that there is public support for physician-assisted suicide. In 1997 Oregon enacted the Death With Dignity Act. This law, which decriminalizes physician-assisted suicide under certain circumstances, is the first law of its type in U.S. history.[13] Whether other states will follow Oregon's lead remains to be seen. It will take individual state action to pave the way for physician-assisted suicide, however, since the Supreme Court handed down *Washington v. Glucksberg* (1997).[14] In *Glucksberg* the Court found that terminally ill patients do not possess a privacy or due process right in having physicians assist them in committing suicide. Accordingly, state action is required to recognize the right.

Corpus Delicti

corpus delicti

▪ (Latin) "The body of the crime." The material substance upon which a crime has been committed; for example, a dead body (in the crime of murder) or a house burned down (in the crime of arson).

Corpus delicti is a Latin phrase that translates as "the body of a crime." Prosecutors have the burden of proving the corpus delicti of crimes at trial. Every crime has a corpus delicti. It refers to the substance of the crime. For example, in murder cases the corpus delicti is the death of a victim and the act that caused the death. In arson, the corpus delicti is a burned structure and the cause of the fire.

A confession of an accused is never enough to prove corpus delicti. There must be either direct proof or evidence supporting a confession.

In murder cases the corpus delicti can usually be proved by an examination of the victim's corpse. After an autopsy a physician is usually prepared to testify that the alleged act either did, or could have, caused the death. In some instances, the body of a victim cannot be located. Such "no body" cases make the job of the prosecution harder. Even so, if evidence—such as blood stains and discovered personal effects—establishes that the person is dead, then murder may be proven. Of course, the prosecution must also show that the defendant caused the death. So, if a defendant confesses to a murder, or makes other incriminating statements, and no other evidence is found, then no corpus delicti exists, and the defendant cannot be convicted. However, if blood matching the victim's is discovered where the defendant stated the murder occurred, then a murder conviction can be sustained.

ASSAULT AND BATTERY

Assault and **battery** are two different crimes, although they commonly occur together. As with homicide, all states have made assaults and batteries criminal by statute.

A *battery* is an intentional touching of another that is either offensive or harmful. The mens rea element varies among the states; however, most now provide for both intentional and negligent battery. Of course, negligence in criminal law involves a greater risk than in civil law. To be negligent in criminal law, there must be a disregard of a high risk of injury to another; in tort law, one need only show a disregard of an ordinary risk. The Model Penal Code provides for purposeful, knowing, and reckless batteries. In addition, if one uses a deadly weapon, negligence may give rise to a battery charge. Otherwise, negligence may not provide the basis for a battery conviction.

The actus reus of battery is a touching. An individual need not touch someone with his or her actual person to commit a battery. Objects that are held are considered extensions of the body. If Sherry strikes Doug with an iron, she has battered him even though her person never came into contact with his. Likewise, items thrown at another are extensions of the person who took the act of propelling them into the air. If Doug were to injure Sherry with a knife he threw at her, then he has battered her.

A touching must be either offensive or harmful to be a battery. Of course, any resulting physical injury is proof of harm. The problem arises when one touches another in a manner found offensive to the person being touched, but there is no apparent physical injury. For example, a man who touches a woman's breast without her consent has committed a battery because the touching is offensive. If a person touches another in an angry manner, a battery has been committed, even though the touching was not intended to injure the party and in fact does no harm.

There are two varieties of assault. First, when a person puts another in fear or apprehension of an imminent battery, an assault has been committed. For example, if Gary attempts to strike Terry, but Terry evades the swing by ducking, Gary has committed an assault. The rule does not require that the victim actually experience a physical

assault

■ An intentional threat, show of force, or movement that could reasonably make a person feel in danger of physical attack or harmful physical contact. It can be a crime or tort.

battery

■ An intentional, unconsented to, physical contact by one person (or an object controlled by that person) with another person. It can be a crime or a tort.

blow; apprehension of an impending battery is sufficient. Apprehension is simply an expectation of an unwanted event. Also, the threat must be imminent to rise to the level of an assault. A threat that one will be battered in the future is not sufficient. So, if Terry told Gary that he was "going to kick the shit out of him in one hour," there is no assault.

Because an apprehension by the victim is required, there is no assault under this theory if the victim was not aware of the assault. For example, if X swings his arm at Y intending to scare Y, but Y has her back turned and does not see X's behavior, then there is no assault. This is not true of batteries. If X strikes Y, a battery has been committed, regardless of whether Y saw the punch coming.

The second type of assault is an attempted battery. This definition remedies the problem just discussed. Any unsuccessful battery is an assault, regardless of the victim's knowledge of the act. Of course, it must be determined that the act in question would have been a battery if it had been completed.

To prove battery, it must be shown that a contact was made. Making contact is not necessary to prove an assault. However, it is possible to have both an assault and a battery. If John sees Henry swing the baseball bat that strikes John, there has been an assault and battery. However, due to the doctrine of merger, the defendant will be punished only for the higher crime of battery.

Aggravated Assault and Battery

Under special circumstances, an assault or battery can be classified as aggravated. If aggravated, a higher penalty is imposed. The process of defining such crimes as more serious than simple assaults and batteries varies. Statutes may call such crimes aggravated assault or battery; or they may refer to specific crimes under a special name, such as assault with intent to kill; or they may simply use the facts at the sentencing stage to enhance (increase) the sentence; or they may refer to such crimes as a higher assault, such as felony assault rather than misdemeanor assault. In any event, the following facts commonly aggravate an assault or battery.

The assault is aggravated if the assault or battery is committed while the actor is engaged in committing another crime. So, if a man batters a woman while possessing the specific intent to rape her, he has committed an aggravated battery. This is true regardless of whether the rape was completed. If a defendant is stopped before he has committed the rape, but after he has assaulted or battered the victim, there has been an aggravated battery. Hence the crime may be titled "assault with intent to commit rape" or "assault with intent to murder."

It is also common to make assault and battery committed on persons of some special status more serious. Law enforcement officers or other public officials often fall into this category. Of course, the crime must relate to the performance or status of the officer to be aggravated. For example, if an off-duty police officer is struck by an angry neighbor over a boundary dispute, the battery is not aggravated. Examples of other protected classes of individuals are minors and the mentally disabled.

The extent of injury to the victim may also lead to an increased charge. Usually a battery may be aggravated if the harm rises to the level of "serious bodily injury." Some statutes specifically state that certain injuries aggravate the crime of battery, such as the loss of an eye. Mayhem, a related crime, is discussed next.

MAYHEM

Mayhem, originally a common-law crime, is the crime of intentionally dismembering or disfiguring a person. The crime has an interesting origin. In England, all men were to be available to fight for the king. It was a serious crime to injure a man in such a manner as to make him unable to fight. Early punishments for mayhem were incarceration, death, and the imposition of the same injury that had been inflicted on the victim. Originally, only dismemberment that could prevent a man from fighting for the king was punished as mayhem. As such, cutting off a man's leg or arm was punishable, whereas cutting off an ear was not. Of course, causing a disfigurement was not mayhem.

Today, both disfigurement and dismemberment fall under mayhem statutes. Many jurisdictions specifically state what injuries must be sustained for a charge of mayhem. Causing another to lose an eye, ear, or limb are examples, as is castration.

Some states no longer have mayhem statutes. They have chosen to treat such crimes as aggravated batteries.

mayhem
■ The crime of violently, maliciously, and intentionally giving someone a serious permanent wound. In some states, a type of aggravated assault. Once, the crime of permanently wounding another (as by dismemberment) to deprive the person of fighting ability.

SEX CRIMES

This section deals with crimes that involve sex. Keep in mind that crimes such as assault and battery may be sexually motivated. For example, if a man touches a woman's breast, he has committed a battery (provided that the touching was unwelcome).

The term "sex crimes" actually encompasses a variety of sexually motivated crimes. Rape, sodomy, incest, and sexually motivated batteries and murders are included. Obscenity, prostitution, abortion, distribution of child pornography, and public nudity are examples of other sex-related offenses.

Although certain offenses are universally prohibited, other offenses vary among the states. For example, rape is criminal in all states, but prostitution is not.

Rape

At common law, the elements of **rape** were (1) sexual intercourse with (2) a woman, not the man's wife (3) committed without the victim's consent and by using force. Many problems were encountered with this definition. First, the common-law definition required that the rapist be a man. Hence, women and male minors could not be convicted of rape. Also, the *marital rape exception* provided that men could not be convicted of raping their wives. Similarly, a man could not be charged with battering

rape
■ The crime of imposing sexual intercourse by force or otherwise without legally valid consent.

his wife if the battery was inflicted in an effort to force sex. This exception was founded upon the theory that when women married they consented to sex with their husbands upon demand. Additionally, many courts wrote that to permit a woman to charge her husband with such a crime would lead to destruction of the family unit. Finally, the last requirement, with force and without consent, led many courts to require victims to resist the attack to the utmost and to continue to resist during the rape.

States have changed the common-law definition of rape to remedy these problems. First, most states have worded their statutes to permit minors and women to be charged with rape. While there are few cases of women actually raping men, or other women, there are several cases where women have been convicted as principals to the crime.[15] The Model Penal Code is gender neutral regarding all sex crimes except rape.[16]

The marital rape exception has been abolished in most states. A few states have retained the rule in modified form; Ohio, for example, provides immunity to a husband except when he is separated from his wife.[17]

Finally, the last requirement has changed significantly. A person need not resist to the extent required under the common law. What is required now is proof that the victim did resist. However, a victim need not risk life or serious bodily injury in an attempt to prevent the rape. So, if a woman simply tells a man on a date, "I don't want to," there has been inadequate resistance. The result would be different if the man produced a gun and told the woman he would kill her if she resisted.

So, the elements of rape, under new statutes, are (1) sexual intercourse (2) with another against that person's will or without that person's consent and (3) by the use of force or under such a threat of force that a reasonable person would have believed that resistance would have resulted in serious bodily harm or death.

Note that one element has not changed—namely, the definition of sexual intercourse. Generally, the contact must be penis-vagina; anal sex, fellatio, and other acts are usually punished under sodomy statutes. The requirement is the same today as it was under the common law. The "slightest penetration" of the woman's vulva is sufficient. The man need not ejaculate.

Some states grade rape according to the extent of injuries that the victim received and whether the victim knew the rapist. The Model Penal Code punishes rape as a felony in the second degree, unless serious bodily injury occurs or the victim was not a social companion of the rapist, in which case the rape is of the first degree.

Nonforcible Rape

statutory rape

■ The crime of having sexual intercourse with a person under a certain state-set age, regardless of consent.

Under some circumstances, one may commit a rape even though the other party consented to the sexual contact. So-called **statutory rape** is such a crime. The actus reus of statutory rape is sexual intercourse with someone under a specified age, commonly 16. The purpose of the law is to protect those the law presumes are too young to make a mature decision concerning sex. Hence, consent is not relevant. So, a rape has occurred when a girl under age 16 consents to sexual intercourse with a male aged 18 or older.

In most states, statutory rape is a strict liability crime. The act of having sex with someone below the specified age is proof alone of guilt. No showing of mens rea is required. A few states impose a knowledge requirement. In those states, if the accused can convince the jury that there was reason to believe that the other party was "of age," then the accused is acquitted. For example, if a 15-year-old girl tells a boy that she is 17, she indeed looks 17, and she shows the boy a falsified identification bearing that age, he would have a defense to statutory rape.

In many states, only females are protected by statutory rape laws. If a boy of 15 years has sex with a girl of 17 years, the law will not punish her as they would the boy if the ages were turned around. It has been alleged that such treatment is violative of the Equal Protection Clause of the U.S. Constitution. The United States Supreme Court has rejected that claim by reasoning that a goal of such statutes is the prevention of teenage pregnancy. Because females can be impregnated, states have a legitimate interest in prosecuting males who have sex with females who are under the age of consent.[18] Using this analysis a state may prosecute males only, as females cannot impregnate young men or women. However, many acts by adult females (or adult males to young males) may be prosecuted under another law, such as child molestation or criminal deviate conduct.

Similar to statutory rape, having sex with those who are incapable of consenting due to mental or emotional disability is also rape.

Sodomy

Sodomy has traditionally been defined as noncoital sex with a member of the opposite sex, sex with a member of the same sex, or sex with an animal. Many statutes now include sodomy in "criminal deviate conduct" statutes. Sodomy is prohibited in most states; and in most jurisdictions fellatio, cunnilingus, bestiality, homosexual activity, anal sex, and sometimes masturbation are included. There is substantial disagreement concerning whether such acts should be prohibited between consenting adults. Those who support sodomy laws usually do so for religious reasons. Those who oppose such laws contend that two adults should be permitted to engage in any sexual conduct they desire, provided that no one is injured. In any event, one practical problem exists; enforcement of sodomy laws is nearly impossible. Determining what sexual acts people engage in privately is not an easy task. Additionally, law enforcement appears to have no incentive to enforce such laws when there appears to be no resulting injury, and there is substantial noncompliance with many sodomy laws, such as fellatio and cunnilingus.

Those who oppose enforcement of sodomy laws between consenting adults do not oppose punishment of those who force acts of sodomy on others. At common law, a man had to have penile-vulva contact to commit rape. If a man forced oral or anal sex on a woman, he committed sodomy. Sodomy was also punished severely. Some states continue to prohibit sodomy, even in marriage. And the Supreme Court upheld such laws until 2003, when it found the prohibition of sex, in any form, between consenting adults in private to be violative of the inherent right to privacy found in the Due Process Clauses in *Lawrence v. Texas*.[19]

Rape Shield Laws

So-called **shield laws** were enacted in the 1970s and 1980s in an effort to protect rape victims from harassment by defense attorneys at trial. Before such laws existed, defense attorneys often would use evidence of a victim's prior sexual conduct to infer that the victim

sodomy
■ A general word for an "unnatural" sex act or the crime committed by such act. While the definition varies, *sodomy* can include oral sex, anal sex, homosexual sex, or sex with animals.

shield laws
■ A state law that prohibits use of most evidence of a rape (or other sexual crime) victim's past sexual conduct at trial.

had consented to the act. It is thought that the humiliation of the rape itself, matched with the threat of harassment at trial, accounted for the nonreporting of many rapes.

To protect victims from unwarranted abuse at trial, rape shield laws were enacted. Evidence of prior sexual conduct, except with the defendant, is not permitted at trial. Also, evidence of a victim's reputation in the community is inadmissible.

Incest

Sex between family members is *incest*, which is a crime. Generally, law enforcement is concerned with abuse of children, although it is also a crime for two consenting adult family members to engage in sex. Often, when an adult family member is involved with a child, other statutes, such as child molestation laws, will also apply.

The actus reus of incest is intercourse, or other sexual conduct, between family members. Normally, incest laws parallel marriage laws for a definition of *family*. That is, if two people are permitted to marry under state law, then they are also permitted to engage in sex, regardless of marriage. It is common for states to prohibit marriage of individuals of first cousin affinity and closer.

If the incestuous party is a parent, courts often attempt to seek family counseling and therapy rather than incarceration. However, in extreme situations criminal penalties can be severe, and civil remedies allow removal of the child from the home, as well as termination of parental rights.

Sex Offenses Against Children

Most states have a number of statutes specifically aimed at protecting children from sexual abuse and exploitation. Indiana has five statutes that directly pertain to sexual activity with children. Those statutes are as follows:

Indiana Code § 35-42-4-3 Child Molesting

(a) A person who, with a child under twelve (12) years of age, performs or submits to sexual intercourse or deviate sexual conduct commits child molesting, a Class B felony. However, the offense is a Class A felony if it is committed by using or threatening the use of deadly force, or while armed with a deadly weapon, or if it results in serious bodily injury.

(b) A person who, with a child under twelve (12) years of age, performs or submits to any fondling or touching, of either the child or the older person, with intent to arouse or to satisfy the sexual desire of either the child or the older person, commits child molesting, a Class C felony. However, the offense is a Class A felony if it is committed by using or threatening the use of deadly force, or while armed with a deadly weapon.

(c) A person sixteen (16) years of age or older who, with a child of twelve (12) years of age or older but under sixteen (16) years of age, performs or submits to sexual intercourse or deviate sexual conduct commits child molesting, a Class C felony. However, the offense is a Class A felony if it is committed by using or threatening the use of deadly force, or while armed with a deadly weapon.

(d) A person sixteen (16) years of age, or older who, with a child twelve (12) years of age or older but under sixteen (16) years of age, performs or submits to any fondling or touching, of either the child or the older person, with intent to arouse or to satisfy the sexual desires of either the child or the older person, commits child molesting, a Class D felony. However, the offense is a Class B felony if it is committed by using or threatening the use of deadly force, or while armed with a deadly weapon.

(e) It is a defense that the accused person reasonably believed that the child was sixteen (16) years of age or older at the time of the conduct.

(f) It is a defense that the child is or has ever been married.

Indiana Code § 35-42-4-4 Child Exploitation

(b) Any person who knowingly or intentionally:

   (1) manages, produces, sponsors, presents, exhibits, photographs, films, or videotapes any performance or incident that includes sexual conduct by a child under sixteen (16) years of age; or

   (2) disseminates, exhibits to another person, offers to disseminate or exhibit to another person, or sends or brings into Indiana for dissemination or exhibition matter that depicts or describes sexual conduct by a child under sixteen (16) years of age; commits child exploitation. . . .

(c) A person who knowingly or intentionally possesses:

   (1) a picture;
   (2) a drawing;
   (3) a photograph;
   (4) a negative image;
   (5) undeveloped film;
   (6) a motion picture;
   (7) a videotape; or
   (8) any pictorial representation; that depicts sexual conduct by a child who is, or appears to be, less than sixteen (16) years of age and that lacks serious literary, artistic, political or scientific value commits possession of child pornography. . . .

Indiana Code § 35-42-4-5 Vicarious Sexual Gratification

(a) A person eighteen (18) years of age or older who knowingly or intentionally directs, aids, induces, or causes a child under the age of sixteen (16) to touch or fondle himself or another child under the age of sixteen (16) with intent to arouse or satisfy the sexual desires of a child or the older person commits vicarious sexual gratification. . . .

(b) A person eighteen (18) years of age or older who knowingly or intentionally directs, aids, induces, or causes a child under the age of sixteen (16) to:

(1) engage in sexual intercourse with another child under sixteen (16) years of age;
(2) engage in sexual conduct with an animal other than a human being; or
(3) engage in deviate sexual conduct with another person . . . commits vicarious sexual gratification. . . .

Indiana Code § 35-42-4-6 Child Solicitation

A person eighteen (18) years of age or older who knowingly or intentionally solicits a child under twelve (12) years of age to engage in:

(1) sexual intercourse;
(2) deviate sexual conduct; or
(3) any fondling or touching intended to arouse or satisfy the sexual desires of either the child or the older person; commits child solicitation. . . .

Indiana Code § 35-42-4-7 Child Seduction

(e) If a person who is:

(1) at least eighteen (18) years of age; and
(2) the guardian, adoptive parent, adoptive grandparent, custodian . . . of a child at least sixteen (16) years of age but less than eighteen (18) years of age; engages in sexual intercourse or deviate sexual conduct with the child, the person commits child seduction. . . .

Note that statutory rape falls under the child molestation statute in Indiana. Also, the defense of a good-faith and reasonable belief that a child is of statutory age is recognized by statute.

The number of people charged with committing sex crimes against children is increasing. Many of those charged are nonbiological guardians. This trend has led to statutes such as Ind. Code § 35-42-4-7, "Child seduction," which was added to Indiana's sex offenses statutes in 1987.

Megan's Laws, Commitment, and Castration

In New Jersey in 1994, Megan Kanka, a 7-year-old girl, was kidnapped, raped, and murdered by a recidivist sex offender who had been released from prison. In response, New Jersey enacted what has become known as **Megan's Law**. The statute requires sex offenders to register with local law enforcement agencies. These agencies, in turn, make the registration information available to the public.

Today, every state has some form of Megan's Law.[21] In some states, registration is required and the information is not generally available. In other states, the public may request the information. And in others, law enforcement officials are required to disseminate the information. The rapid adoption of such laws by the states is due in part to the federal government. In 1996 a federal statute became effective that encouraged the states to adopt such laws and threatened loss of federal funds to those states that did not participate.[22]

In addition to registration and notification laws, some states have turned to civil or regulatory law to control sex offenders. Kansas law, for example, provides for the civil commitment of sexual predators who are "mentally abnormal" or suffer a "personality disorder," who lack control over their behavior, and who pose a danger to others. The law may be applied to any individual who meets these standards, regardless of whether charged, convicted, or previously punished. The Supreme Court found this law constitutional in *Kansas v. Hendricks* (1997).[23]

Subsequently in the 2002 case *Kansas v. Crane*,[24] the Court again reviewed the Kansas law against a challenge that it violates due process to require anything less than total loss of control. The Court rejected this theory while reaffirming the *Hendricks* requirement of some loss of control.

A similar Washington state statute was upheld by the Supreme Court in *Seling v. Young* (2001).[25] The Court reasoned that the law is not criminal in nature, it is regulatory, and there is a long history of civil detention of individuals who are both mentally ill and dangerous. Federal law also provides for the civil commitment of sex offenders who are released from federal prison. The Supreme Court upheld the law against federalism challenges in 2010 in *United States v. Comstock*.[26]

Critics allege that these laws are unconstitutional efforts by states to bypass the criminal justice system by using civil commitment to punish sexual offenders. They also contend that individuals are not being punished for their actual behaviors but for their status. While the Supreme Court rejected these claims in the *Hendricks* case, it also emphasized that only individuals who are both mentally ill and dangerous may be committed and that the state must prove these elements in an adversarial hearing by at least clear and convincing evidence.

California has one of the most aggressive offender mental illness programs in the nation. The California Mentally Disordered Offender program (MDO) requires all corrections inmates to be screened for illness. If illness is found, inmates receive treatment while in prison. At the end of a prison term, an inmate is examined, and if determined to have a severe mental disorder that poses a danger to others, treatment is ordered as a condition of parole. Treatment is residential until an offender is determined to be no longer dangerous. Parolees in the MDO program are entitled to annual review and a hearing to determine dangerousness.

So-called chemical castration is also used to control sex offenders. Drugs such as Depo-Provera are used to inhibit the sex drive and sexual function of male sex offenders. Actual surgical castration is provided for by Texas law in lieu of taking the drugs. Texas leaves the choice to the offender. Castration is criticized for not addressing the underlying motivation of sex crimes—the need to control others. It is argued that castration will only lead to the commission of some other form of violent crime.[27]

KIDNAPPING AND FALSE IMPRISONMENT

Kidnapping

kidnapping

■ Taking away and holding a person illegally, usually against the person's will or by force.

Kidnapping was a misdemeanor at common law, although it was regarded as a very serious crime, often resulting in life imprisonment. Felonies were often punished by death at the early common law. Today kidnapping is a felony and carries a harsh penalty in most states. Additionally, if the kidnapping takes the victim across state lines, the crime is a violation of the Federal Kidnapping Act.[28] The federal government, usually the Federal Bureau of Investigation, may become involved in any kidnapping 24 hours after the victim has been seized, by virtue of the Federal Kidnapping Act, which creates a presumption that the victim has been transported across state lines after that period of time.[29]

The elements of kidnapping are (1) the unlawful (2) taking and confinement and (3) asportation of (4) another person (5) by use of force, threat, fraud, or deception.

The taking of the victim must be unlawful. Thus, arrests made by police officers while engaged in their lawful duties are not kidnappings. Neither is it kidnapping for a guardian to take a ward from one place to another, as long as the action is lawful. However, when officers, or others, act completely without legal authority, they may not be shielded from liability.

There must be a taking and confinement. Confinement is broadly construed. If Pat puts a gun to Craig's back and orders him to walk a half mile to Pat's home, there has been a confinement. Generally, there must be a restriction of the victim's freedom to take alternative action.

This taking and confinement must occur as a result of threat, force, fraud, or deception. Of course, Pat's gun in the example is ample threat to satisfy this requirement. Deception may also be used to gain control over the victim. For example, if Jon convinces his estranged wife to enter a house under the pretense of discussing their marital difficulties and then locks the door, he has fraudulently gained control over her.

Finally, there must be an asportation of the victim. *Asportation* means movement. The issue of the amount of movement necessary to meet this requirement is the most controversial question concerning kidnapping as a crime. The Model Penal Code and most states now hold that if the kidnapping is incidental to the commission of another crime, there is insufficient asportation; some courts speak in terms of a movement of a "substantial distance."[30] To be incidental, a kidnapping must simply be a product of an intent to commit another crime. If a bank robber orders a teller to move from her window to the safe to fill a bag with money, four of the elements of kidnapping are present; however, the third element, asportation, has not been established because the movement was only incidental to the robbery. The result may be different if the teller was ordered to move to the safe for the purpose of raping her. The issue of substantial distance was raised in *Commonwealth v. Hughes*. In that case the court focused on whether the movement substantially increased the risk of harm to the victim.

Many statutes specifically state that if the acts of asportation and confinement occur in furtherance of named crimes, then there is a kidnapping. Such statutes commonly include kidnapping for ransom, political reasons, rape, and murder. It is also common to upgrade kidnappings for these reasons. One type of kidnapping that is usually graded low is the taking of a child by a parent in violation of a court order.

Parental Kidnapping

With a dissolution of marriage comes the separation of property owned by the couple, as well as a custody order if the couple has children. Often, costly and bitter custody disputes are also the result of divorce. In recent years "childnapping," or kidnapping of one's own child in violation of a custody order, has received much public attention.

Due to the rise in the number of such acts, new statutes specifically aimed at parental kidnapping have been adopted. The federal government entered this arena in 1980 by enacting the Parental Kidnapping Prevention Act.[31] Although this statute does not concern itself with criminal sanctions for childnapping, it does require that all states respect child custody orders of other states. That is, a person cannot escape a court order concerning custody of the child by kidnapping the child and fleeing to another jurisdiction. Interestingly, the federal government has left the actual punishment of parental kidnapping to the states. The federal kidnapping act specifically excludes such acts from its reach. Thus, kidnapping by a parent must be punished in a state court. This may occur in the state from which the child is taken or in any state where the parent takes the child.

Kidnapping of one's own child is often punished less severely than other kidnappings. This is sensible because many childnappings do not create a risk to the child's welfare; rather, they are the result of an overzealous, loving parent or a parent who is trying to hurt the other parent. Obviously, the crime should be punished because of the harm to the custodial parent, but the crime does not have the same evil motive a kidnapping with an intent to rape or murder does.

False Imprisonment

The crime of **false imprisonment** is similar to kidnapping, and in fact all kidnappings involve a false imprisonment. The opposite is not true. Not all false imprisonments are kidnappings. A false imprisonment occurs when (1) one person (2) interferes (3) with another's liberty (4) by use of threat or force (5) without authority. The primary distinction between the two crimes is the absence of asportation as an element of false imprisonment.

Today, some states have one statute that encompasses both false imprisonment and kidnapping. Such statutes are drafted so that the crime is graded, often elevating the crime if the motive is ransom, rape, serious bodily injury, or murder.

false imprisonment
■ The unlawful restraint by one person of the physical liberty of another.

stalking
■ The crime of repeatedly following, threatening, or harassing another person in ways that lead to a legitimate fear of physical harm. Some states define *stalking* more broadly as any conduct with no legitimate purpose that seriously upsets a targeted person, especially conduct in violation of a protective order.

STALKING

In recent years, **stalking** has been the subject of considerable media, public, and legislative attention. Public awareness of stalking increased when prominent public figures who were the victims of stalkers, including politicians, actors, and law enforcement officials, began to speak out.

Stalking posed unique problems to law enforcement officials, prosecutors, and judges. Before 1990, no state had a law specifically aimed at combating stalking. Therefore, preexisting criminal laws, such as assault, battery, and threats, as well as the use of restraining orders, were relied upon in dealing with stalkers. But these laws proved ineffective. Often there is no assault, battery, or provable threat until the victim has been injured or murdered. Even when one of these crimes could be proven, sentences were short. Restraining orders also proved to give victims little protection.

In response to the growing public interest in stalking, California enacted the nation's first stalking law in 1990. By 1993, another 46 states had enacted similar laws.[32]

Stalking laws vary in their elements, but most include a list of acts that satisfy the actus reus of the crime. These include following, harassing, threatening, lying in wait, or conducting surveillance of another person. Usually, one act does not amount to stalking; rather, there must be a pattern or scheme of acts. The first statutes had as a mens rea element a specific intent to cause emotional distress, or to invoke fear of bodily injury or death. However, this has proven ineffective, as stalkers, who are often suffering from emotional or mental illness, often do not have a specific intent to cause fear or harm, even though either or both of these are likely to result. Many states, such as Washington, have remedied this by lowering the mens rea to actual or constructive knowledge. As long as the stalker should have known that the victim would suffer distress or fear, the mens rea satisfies this breed of stalking law. Through these laws, the police may intercede before violence occurs.

Even before stalking laws, many states criminalized harassment. Personal harassment, telephone harassment, and other specific forms of harassment are commonly included in these laws. However, as mentioned earlier, these statutes were not effective in stopping stalkers, primarily because of the short sentences violators usually received.

Cyberstalking

Cyberstalking

■ Cyberstalking is the crime of using communication technology to transmit obscene, abusive, or harrassing language intended to harass or threaten another person.

A new type of stalker has emerged in the recent past, the cyberstalker. **Cyberstalking** is the crime of using communication technology to transmit obscene, abusive, or harassing language intended to harass or threaten another person. Because of the impersonal and seemingly anonymous nature of electronic communications, it is both easier and safer to harass other persons than it has been in the past. In recent years, stalking using another person's identity has increased. Known as "spoofing," this crime has two victims: the individual receiving the messages and the individual whose identity has been stolen.

Both state and federal statutes exist that criminalize cyberstalking. For example, the Communications Decency Act, 47 U.S.C. § 223(a)(1)(A), provides for criminal prosecution of any person who "by means of a telecommunications device knowingly makes, creates, or solicits, and initiates the transmission of any comment, request, suggestion, proposal, image, or other communication which is obscene, lascivious, filthy, or indecent, with the intent to annoy, abuse, threaten or harass another person." Another federal statute, 18 U.S.C. § 875(c), makes it a federal crime to "transmit [ ] in interstate or foreign commerce any communication containing any threat to kidnap any person or any threat to injure the person of another." Other federal and state laws that were originally intended to apply to telephone harassment may apply as well.

The federal government extended its reach over stalking in 18 U.S.C. §2261(A) to include "harassment" and the use of computers to commit stalking. That statute makes criminal the act "to kill, injure, harass, or place under surveillance with intent to kill, injure, harass, or intimidate, or cause substantial emotional distress to a person" using "mail, any interactive computer service, or any facility of interstate or foreign commerce. . . ."

However, any time speech is criminalized, there is a First Amendment free speech issue. Statute 47 U.S.C. § 223(a)(1)(A) and similar statutes have been challenged as overbroad because they prohibit not only obscene speech, which clearly may be regulated, but also "indecent" speech that is intended to annoy. The jury is still out on this question.[33]

Although the Supreme Court has not spoken on the issue, lower courts have. In *United States v. Cassidy*, a federal trial court found the defendant's offensive tweeting to be protected by the First Amendment's free speech guarantee.

CIVIL RIGHTS AND HATE CRIMES

The federal and state governments have enacted laws criminalizing acts that encroach upon an individual's civil liberties. It is a crime against the United States for two or more persons to conspire to injure, oppress, threaten, or intimidate a person for exercising a federally secured right.[34]

In addition, any person acting pursuant to state law or authority (under color of law) who deprives a person of a federally secured right due to alienage, race, or color is guilty of a federal civil rights crime.[35] Because of the "color of law" requirement, defendants are usually state or local officials. It was under this statute that the police officers who beat Rodney King in Los Angeles were tried and convicted in federal court. In addition to criminal remedies, victims may seek civil remedies under a separate civil rights statute.[36] States have similar civil rights laws.

So-called hate crimes laws have become popular in recent years. By 1993, 49 states had enacted hate crimes statutes.[37] Although commonly referred to as hate crime laws, most of these statutes do not actually declare an act criminal; rather, they are sentence enhancements for crimes in which the motive was the victim's race, ethnicity, religion, or other factor.

Florida's hate crime law reads as follows:

Evidencing prejudice while committing offense; enhanced penalties

(1) The penalty for any felony or misdemeanor shall be reclassified as provided in this subsection if the commission of such felony or misdemeanor evidences prejudice based on the race, color, ancestry, ethnicity, religion, sexual orientation, or national origin of the victim:

  (a) A misdemeanor of the second degree shall be punishable as if it were a misdemeanor of the first degree.

  (b) A misdemeanor of the first degree shall be punishable as if it were a felony of the third degree.

(c) A felony of the third degree shall be punishable as if it were a felony of the second degree.

(d) A felony of the second degree shall be punishable as if it were a felony of the first degree.

[The statute then provides for civil remedies to victims in subsection 2.]

(3) It shall be an essential element of this section that the record reflect that the defendant perceived, knew, or had reasonable grounds to know or perceive that the victim was within the class delineated herein.[38]

Hate crimes laws have been attacked on First Amendment grounds as violating a person's right to expression. Clearly, a statute that makes a person's beliefs, and the expression of those beliefs, criminal is unconstitutional. But the Supreme Court has upheld statutes that enhance sentences when otherwise prohibited acts are taken because of a prejudicial motive. For example, a state cannot make it illegal to hate a particular ethnic group. Further, with few exceptions (e.g., fighting words), the state may not regulate a person's First Amendment right to express hatred of a particular group. But if the person's beliefs motivate a criminal act, such as a trespass or battery, then the sentence for that crime may be enhanced. See Chapter 4 for a more thorough review of the First Amendment aspects of hate crime legislation.

Web Links

Legislative Information

Washburn Law School maintains a comprehensive site that includes state and federal legislative information. Enter through http://www.washlaw.edu. The U.S. Library of Congress also has legislative information on its page at http://thomas.loc.gov.

Key Terms

assault
battery
corpus delicti
cyberstalking
deadly weapon
element
false imprisonment

felony-murder
first-degree murder
kidnapping
manslaughter
mayhem
merger of offenses
provocation

rape
second-degree murder
shield laws
sodomy
stalking
statutory rape

Review Questions

1. What is the primary distinction between first- and second-degree murder?
2. What is felony-murder?
3. What is the difference between an assault and a battery?
4. What is the marital rape exception?
5. John caught his wife having sex with another man. In a fit of rage, he killed his wife. What crime has been committed?
6. What is meant by the phrase "imperfect self-defense"?
7. What is the primary distinction between false imprisonment and kidnapping?
8. Under the common law, if a person cut another's limb off, what crime was committed?
9. Give an example of a nonforcible rape.
10. What was the common-law definition of murder?

Problems & Critical Thinking Exercises

1. State statute reads: "Any act of 1. sexual intercourse 2. with another person 3. against that person's will and 4. by use of force or under such a threat of force that resistance would result in serious bodily injury or death, is rape." Explain how this statutory definition of rape differs from the common-law definition.

2. On May 5, Mark and Sam, who had been neighbors for three years, argued over Sam's construction of a ditch, which diverted water onto Mark's property. Mark told Sam to stop construction of the ditch or he "would pay with his life." The following day, Mark and Sam met again in Sam's garage. Within minutes Mark became very angry and cut Sam's leg with an ax he found in Sam's garage. After cutting Sam he panicked and ran home. Sam attempted to reach a telephone to call for help, but the cut proved fatal.

    Mark has been charged with first-degree murder. He claims that he had no intent to kill Sam; rather, he only intended to hit him on the leg with the dull, flat side of the axe in an effort to scare Sam. Discuss the facts and explain what crimes could be proved and why.

3. On July 1, 2013, Jeff shot Megan during a bank robbery. Megan remained on life-support systems until September 4, 2014. At that time the systems were disconnected and she ceased breathing. On June 15, 2014, her physician had declared her brain dead. It was not until September 4, 2014, that her family decided to stop the life-support system. Jeff is charged with murder. Discuss any defenses he may have.

4. Penelope and Brenda had been enemies for years. One evening Penelope discovered that Brenda had attempted on many occasions to "pick up" Penelope's boyfriend. Penelope told a friend that she was "going to fix Brenda once and for all—that she was going to mess her face up bad." That evening Penelope waited for Brenda outside her home and attacked her with a knife. Penelope slashed her in the face four times and cut off one ear. Brenda reported the event to the police, who have turned it over to the county prosecutor's office. As the office legal assistant, you have been assigned the task of determining what crime can be charged.

5. State Statute reads: "It shall be a felony for any person to purposefully, knowingly, or recklessly cause the death of another person by the use of poison or other toxins." Eddie Farmer spread a toxic insecticide on his crops, which eventually

mixed with rainwater and made its way into his neighbor's well. The insecticide was new, but it had been recommended by other farmers who had used it successfully. His neighbor's seven-year-old son, Mikey, died from the poisons in the water. Eddie has been charged with violating the state statute. Is he liable?

6. One evening after a play Tracy was approached by a woman who pointed a pistol at her and ordered her to "give me all your money and jewelry." Tracy removed her jewels and handed them over, but told the robber that her money was in her purse, which was in the trunk of her car. The robber asked her where her car was parked, and Tracy pointed to a car 30 feet away. Tracy was then ordered to go to the automobile, remove the purse, and give it to the robber. She complied, and the woman ran off. The thief was eventually captured and tried for aggravated robbery and kidnapping. She was convicted of both and has appealed the kidnapping conviction. What do you think her argument would be to reverse the kidnapping conviction?

7. Do you believe that prostitution and solicitation of prostitution are victimless crimes? If so, does the threat of AIDS and other communicable diseases change your decision?

8. Make your best argument in support of legalizing (decriminalizing) prostitution.

9. Consider your life experiences. Have you ever committed a technical stalking (such as repeatedly seeking the affection of an uninterested person)?

Endnotes

1. A. Loewy, *Criminal Law*, 2d ed. (Nutshell Series; St. Paul: West, 1987).
2. **People v. Wilkins, Case** No. S190713, Supreme Court of California (March 7, 2013).
3. *See Commonwealth v. Redline*, 391 Pa. 486, 137 A.2d 472 (1958).
4. *See* LaFave & Scott, *Criminal Law* § 7.7 (Hornbook Series; St. Paul: West, 1986).
5. *State v. Corn*, 278 S.E.2d 221 (N.C. 1981).
6. *See,* for example, N.Y. Penal Law § 125.27(a)(xiii).
7. *Labelle v. State*, 550 N.E.2d 752 (Ind. 1990); *see also* LaFave & Scott at § 7.2(b).
8. Model Penal Code § 210.0(4).
9. The Federal Bureau of Investigation's prime suspect in the case committed suicide before he was charged. A microbiologist with a Ph.D. from the University of Cincinnati, Bruce Ivins had been employed by the United States Army Medical Research Institute of Infectious Diseases. See *http://www.fbi.gov/about-us/history/famous-cases/anthrax-amerithrax/amerithrax-investigation*
10. *See* Ill. Rev. Stat. ch. 38, para. 9–3.
11. The Model Penal Code addresses homicide at § 210.0 *et seq.*
12. Mich. Comp. Laws Ann. § 752.1027.
13. Robert Hardaway, Miranda Peterson, and Cassandra Mann, "The Right to Die and the Ninth Amendment: Compassion and Dying After *Glucksberg* and *Vacco*," 7 George Mason L. Rev. 313 (1999).

14. 521 U.S. 702 (1997).
15. See 65 Am. Jur. 2d *Rape* 28 (1976).
16. Model Penal Code § 213.
17. Ohio Rev. Code § 2907.
18. *Michael M. v. Superior Court*, 450 U.S. 464 (1981).
19. The Court upheld a sodomy law in *Bowers v. Hardwick*, 478 U.S. 186 (1986) but explicitly reversed that decision in *Lawrence v. Texas*, 539 U.S. 558 (2003).
20. Louise Elaine Ellison (July 1997), *A Comparative Study of Rape Trials in Adversarial and Inquisitorial Criminal Justice Systems,* Dissertation: University of Leeds, Faculty of Law.
21. Steven I. Friedland, "On Treatment, Punishment, and the Civil Commitment of Sex Offenders," 70 *U. Colo. L. Rev.* 73 (1999).
22. 42 U.S.C. § 14071.
23. 117 S. Ct. 2072 (1997).
24. 534 U.S. 407 (2002).
25. 531 U.S. 250 (2001).
26. 560 U.S. 126 (2010).
27. Jean Peters-Baker, "Challenging Traditional Notions of Managing Sex Offenders: Prognosis Is Lifetime Management," 66 *U. Mo. at Kansas City L. Rev.* 629 (1997).
28. 18 U.S.C. § 1201.
29. 18 U.S.C. § 1201(b).
30. Model Penal Code § 212.1.
31. 28 U.S.C. § 1738A.
32. Karen Brooks, "The New Stalking Laws: Are They Adequate to End Violence?" 14 *Hamline J. Pub. L. & Pol'y.* 259 (1993).
33. *ApolloMedia v. Reno*, 19 F. Supp. 2d 1081 (1998), aff'd, 119 S. Ct. 1450 (1999); and *ACLU v. Reno* 521 U.S. 844 (1997).
34. 18 U.S.C. § 241.
35. 18 U.S.C. § 242.
36. 42 U.S.C. § 1983.
37. *People v. Superior Court*, 15 Cal. App. 4th 1593, 1599 (1993).
38. Fla. Stat. Ann. § 775.085.

CHAPTER 10

CRIMES AGAINST PROPERTY AND HABITATION

Chapter Outline

Arson
Burglary
Theft Crimes
    Introduction to Theft Crimes
    Larceny
    Embezzlement
    False Pretenses
    Receiving Stolen Property
    Robbery
    Extortion
    Consolidated Theft Statutes
    Identity Theft
    The Model Penal Code Consolidation
    Destruction of Property
    Computer Theft Crimes

Chapter Objectives

After completing this chapter you should be able to:

- list the elements of historic and contemporary crimes involving property and habitation, such as arson, burglary, and larceny.
- identify the crimes of arson, burglary, and larceny in given fact scenarios.
- describe how computers and the Internet have given rise to new ways to commit old crimes and how the law is changing to deal with these developments.
- identify the material facts and legal issues in one-third of the cases you read, and describe the court's analyses and conclusions in the cases.

ARSON

Michael Marin, former Wall Street trader, Yale University School of Law graduate, and believed-to-be a millionaire, called the Phoenix, Arizona emergency line on July 5, 2009, to report that his estate mansion was ablaze. He reported having escaped the fire by wearing scuba gear to avoid the inhalation of smoke, and scaling down a rope ladder from the second floor. Later it was discovered that Marin was broke and unable to pay his bills. Police also discovered, thanks in part to a well-trained canine, that the fire was set intentionally. Marin was charged with arson and convicted in 2012. Moments after the verdict was read, Marin was seen on a court television monitor taking a drink from a sports bottle. He collapsed and died. Subsequent testing revealed that he ingested the poison cyanide. Oddly, the day Marin set fire to his home is the day of the greatest number of arsons in U.S. history, according to one source.[1]

arson

■ The malicious and unlawful burning of a building.

Arson is a crime against property. In addition, it is a crime against habitation. Crimes against habitation developed because of the importance of peoples' homes. In England and the United States, the concept that a "man's home is his castle" has great influence. A home is not merely property but, rather, a refuge from the rest of the world. As such, special common-law crimes developed that sought to protect this important sanctuary. Arson and burglary are such crimes.

At common law, arson was defined very narrowly. It was the (1) malicious (2) burning of a (3) dwelling house of (4) another. This definition was so narrowly construed that owners could burn their own property with an intent to defraud their insurers and not be guilty of arson, because they did not burn the dwelling of another.[2] In addition, the structure burned had to be a *dwelling*, which was defined as a structure inhabited by people. This definition did include outhouses and the area directly around the home (*curtilage*), as long as the area was used frequently by people. However, the burning of businesses and other structures was not arson.

To be a burning, the dwelling must actually sustain some damage, although slight damage was sufficient. If the structure is simply charred by the fire, there is a burning. However, if the structure is only smoke-damaged or discolored by the heat of a fire that never touched the building, there is no arson. Finally, causing a dwelling to explode is not arson, unless some of the dwelling is left standing after the explosion and is then burned by a fire caused by the explosion.

At common law, malice was the mens rea of arson. As was true of murder at common law, *malice* meant evil intent. However, an intentional or extremely reckless burning would suffice.

Today, the definition of arson has been broadened by statute in most, if not all, states. It is now common to prosecute owners of property for burning their own buildings, if the purpose was to defraud an insurer or to cause another injury. Be aware that the fraud may constitute a separate offense: defrauding an insurance carrier. Also, the structure burned need not be a dwelling under most statutes, though most statutes aggravate the crime if a dwelling is burned. Although the common law did not recognize explosions as a burning, the Model Penal Code and most statutes do.[3]

The mens rea for arson under the Model Penal Code is purposeful and reckless. If a person starts a fire or causes an explosion with the purpose of destroying the building or defrauding an insurer, a felony of the second degree has been committed. It is a felony of the third degree to purposely start a fire or cause an explosion and thereby recklessly endanger a person or structure.[4] Note that under the Model Penal Code the fire need not touch the structure, as was required by the common law. Setting the fire is enough to satisfy the burning requirement.

Arson is often graded. The burning of dwellings is usually the highest form of the crime. The burning of uninhabited structures is usually the next highest form of arson, and arson of personal property, if treated as arson, is the lowest.

BURGLARY

The (1) breaking and entering (2) of another's dwelling (3) at night (4) for the purpose of committing a felony once inside, was **burglary** at common law. A burglary, or entry of a dwelling, may be for the purpose of theft, rape, murder, or another felony. For that reason, burglary is a crime against habitation, as well as against property and person.

The first element, the actus reus, a breaking, can be satisfied by either an actual break-in or by a constructive breaking. If one enters a dwelling by simply passing through an open door or window (a trespass), there is no breaking. Generally, there has to be some act by the defendant to change the condition of the house so as to gain entry. For example, opening an unlocked door or window is a breaking, while passing through an open door or window is not a breaking. Of course, picking a lock and breaking a window or door are breakings.

A burglar may also gain entry by a constructive breaking. A constructive breaking occurs when one uses fraud or force to gain entry. So, if a burglar poses as a telephone repair worker to gain entry, then the breaking element has been satisfied. The same is true if the owner consents to the burglar's entry under threat or the use of force.

Once the breaking occurs, there must be an entry of the home. The burglar does not need to fully enter the structure; an entry occurs if any part of the burglar's body enters the house. So, the individual who breaks a window and reaches in to grab an item has entered the house.

Modern statutes have eliminated the breaking requirement, although most still require some form of "unlawful entry." Because trespasses, frauds, and breakings are unlawful, they satisfy modern statutory requirements.

The second element required is that the breaking and entry be of another person's dwelling. As with arson, at common law the structure had to be a dwelling. The person who lives in the dwelling does not have to be the owner, only an occupant. As such, rental property is included. Interestingly, at least one court has held that churches are dwellings, regardless of whether a person actually resides in the church, premised on the theory that churches are God's dwellings.[5] The dwelling had to belong to another person, so one could not burglarize one's own property. No jurisdiction continues to require that the structure be a dwelling. Most statutes now refer to all buildings or other structures.[6] However, if the structure burglarized is a dwelling, most states punish the crime more severely than if it was another type of building.

burglary
■ Unlawfully entering the house of another person with the intention of committing a felony (usually theft).

Exhibit 10-1

Actual breaking through the door

Entry through a closed unlocked door is considered a breaking

Entry through an open door is not a breaking

Gaining entry by threatening or coercing occupant to open door is a constructive breaking

Gaining entry through fraud is a constructive breaking

The third element was that the burglary occur at night. Although this is no longer an element of burglary, many states do aggravate the crime if it happens at night.

The fourth element is that the person entering must have as a purpose the commission of a felony once inside. This is the mens rea of the crime. If the person's intent is only to commit a misdemeanor, there is no burglary. If Jay's intent is to murder Mark, there is a burglary. It is not a burglary if Jay's intent is to punch Mark in the nose.

Of course, many breakings and enterings with an intent to commit a burglaries are not completed. A burglar may be caught by surprise by someone who was not known to be inside and flee from the property. It also happens that burglars are caught in the act by occupants who return to the building. In any event, what is important is that the intended felony need not be completed. All that needs to be proven is that the accused entered with an intent to commit a felony. As is always true, proving a person's subjective mental state is nearly impossible. Thus, juries are permitted to infer intent from the actions of the defendant. A jury did just that in the *Lockett* case.

Some statutes now provide that intent to commit any crime is sufficient, whether misdemeanor or felony. However, many continue to require an intent to commit either felony or any theft.

In summary, most jurisdictions have changed burglary in such a way that the following elements are common: (1) an unlawful entry (2) of any structure or building (3) for the purpose of committing a felony or stealing from the premises (4) once inside.

As mentioned, burglary may be graded and higher penalties imposed if the act occurred at night; involved a dwelling or was perpetrated at a dwelling that was actually inhabited at the time of the crime; or was committed by a burglar with a weapon. See Exhibit 10-1 for a summary illustration of burglary.

THEFT CRIMES

Introduction to Theft Crimes

There are many types of theft. It is theft to take a pack of gum from a grocery store and not pay for it; for a lawyer to take a client's trust fund and spend it on personal items; for a bank officer to use a computer to make a paper transfer of funds from a patron's account to the officer's with an intent to later withdraw the money and abscond; and to hold a gun on a person and demand that property and money be surrendered. However, they are all fundamentally different crimes.

Some thefts are more violative of the person, such as robbery, and others are more violative of a trust relationship, such as an attorney absconding with a client's money. The crimes also differ in the methods by which they are committed. A robbery involves an unlawful taking. Embezzlement, however, involves a lawful taking with a subsequent unlawful conversion.

Larceny was the first theft crime. It was created by judges as part of the common law. The elements of larceny were very narrow and did not cover most thefts. Larceny began as one crime, but developed into many different crimes. This was not a fluid, orderly development, for two reasons. First, when larceny was first created, well over 600 years ago, the purpose of making it criminal was more to prevent breaches of the peace (fights over possession of property) than to protect ownership of property. Larceny did not prohibit fraudulent takings of another's property. The theory was that an embezzlement or other theft by trick was less likely to result in an altercation (breach of the peace) between the owner and the thief, because the owner would not be aware of the theft until after it was completed. Using this theory, many courts were reluctant to expand the scope of larceny. Second, at early common law, larceny was punishable by death. For this reason, some judges were reluctant to expand its reach.[7]

Eventually, two other theft crimes were created, embezzlement and false pretenses. Despite the creation of these crimes, many theft acts continued to go unpunished because they fell into the cracks that separated the elements of the three common-law theft crimes. Some courts attempted to remedy this problem by broadening the definitions of the three crimes. However, computers, electronic banking, and other technological advances have led to new methods of stealing money and property, posing problems not anticipated by the judges who created the common-law theft crimes. Some states have changed their definitions of larceny, false pretenses, and embezzlement to be more contemporary. Other states have simply abandoned the common-law crimes and have enacted consolidated theft statutes. The common-law theft crimes, modern consolidated theft statutes, and the Model Penal Code approach to theft are discussed here.

Larceny

At common law the elements of **larceny** were (1) the trespassory taking (2) and carrying away (*asportation*) (3) of personal property (4) of another (5) with an intent to permanently deprive the owner of possession. The actus reus of larceny was the taking and carrying away of personal property of another. The mens rea was the intent to permanently deprive the owner of possession.

larceny

■ Stealing of any kind. Some types of larceny are specific crimes, such as *larceny by trick* or grand larceny.

To have had a common-law larceny, there must have been a "taking" of property. A taking alone would not have sufficed; the taking must have been unlawful or trespassory. That is, the property must be taken by the defendant without the owner's consent. This element is concerned only with the method that the defendant used in acquiring possession. For example, if Mandy takes Sean's wallet from his hand, she has committed a taking. However, if Sean were to give Mandy his wallet with the understanding that she is to return it at a specified time, there is no unlawful taking when she does not return it; she lawfully acquired possession of the wallet. Taking property from another without that person's consent was a trespass under the common law, but failing to return property was not.

In an effort to protect employers (masters) from theft by their employees (servants), the theory of *constructive possession* was created. This theory held that when an employee received actual possession of the employer's property as part of the job, the employer maintained "constructive possession" while the employee had custody of the property. If this theory had not been developed, employees would have been free to steal property entrusted to them, as larceny required a trespassory taking. Of course, if an employee took property that was not under his or her care, there was a trespassory taking.

Interestingly, the theory of constructive possession was never extended to other relationships. This led to the creation of a new crime—embezzlement.

Once the taking has been effected, the defendant must carry away the property. This carrying away is called *asportation*. Generally, any asportation, even slight movement, will satisfy this requirement. The term *asportation* is deceiving, as not all property has to be "carried away" to satisfy this requirement. Riding a horse away will satisfy the requirement, as will driving another's automobile. Most states have done away with the asportation requirement by statute.

Third, the item stolen must be personal property. Land and items attached to land (e.g., houses) are considered real property. Theft of such property was not larceny. All other property is personal property. Objects that are movable property are personal property. In the early years of larceny, there was a further requirement that the item stolen be tangible personal property. Tangible personal property includes most items, such as automobiles, books, electronic equipment, and the like. Documents, such as stocks, bonds, and promissory notes, which represent ownership of something, are considered intangible property. It was not larceny to steal intangible personal property. Under modern statutes, most states have broadened theft to include all types of property.

The fourth element is that the personal property taken and carried away must be owned by another. One cannot steal from oneself. However, the rule was extended to prohibit prosecution of a partner for taking partnership assets and joint tenants from taking each other's things; also, because husband and wife were one person under the common law, it was not possible for spouses to steal from one another.

Finally, the mens rea element: It is required that the defendant intend to permanently deprive the owner of possession of the property. In short, to be a thief one must have an intent to steal. If Jack takes Eddie's lawn mower, intending to return the mower when he has completed his mowing, he has not committed larceny, as he did not possess an intent to permanently deprive Eddie of his possession of the mower. Also, the accused must intend to deprive an owner (or possessor) of property to be guilty of larceny. If an accused had a good-faith belief that he had lawful right to the property, the requisite mens rea did not exist, and there was no larceny.

Although proving "an intent to permanently deprive the owner of possession" is the common method of proving the mens rea of larceny, it is not the only method. Courts have held that if the property is held so long that it causes the owner to lose a significant portion of its value, a larceny has occurred. Some cases have held that if the property is taken with an intent to subject the property to substantial risk, there is a larceny. Of course, the intent must exist at the time of taking. To illustrate this last method, imagine a thief who steals a plane intending to use it in a daredevil show. In such a case the thief is subjecting the property to a substantial risk, and even though the intent was to return the plane when the show was over, there is a larceny.

Embezzlement

The definition of larceny left a large gap that permitted people in some circumstances to steal from others. That gap was caused by requiring a trespassory taking of the property. For various reasons, people entrust money and property to others. The intent is not to transfer ownership (title), only possession. A depositor of a bank gives possession of money to the bank; a client may give an attorney money to hold in a trust account; a stockbroker may keep an account with a client-investor's money in it. In all of these situations, the money is taken lawfully; there is no trespassory taking. So, what happens if the person entrusted with the money *converts* (steals) it after taking lawful possession? At the early common law, it was not a crime. However, the thief could have been sued for recovery of the stolen money.

This theory was carried to an extreme in a case in which a bank teller converted money handed to him by a depositor to himself, by placing the money in his own pocket. It was held that there was no larceny, because the teller acquired the money lawfully. The court also determined that there was no larceny under the theory of constructive possession, because the employer (bank) never had possession of the money. If the teller had put the money in the drawer and then taken it, the bank would have had constructive possession, and he would have committed larceny. The result was that the teller was guilty of no crime.[8] Unsatisfied with this situation, the English Parliament created a new crime: **embezzlement**.

The elements of embezzlement are (1) conversion (2) of personal property (3) of another (4) by one who has acquired lawful possession (5) with an intent to defraud the owner.

To prove embezzlement, the prosecution must first show that an act of **conversion** occurred. Conversion is the unauthorized control over property with an intent to permanently deprive the owner of its possession or which substantially interferes with the rights of the owner.

embezzlement
■ The fraudulent and secret taking of money or property by a person who has been trusted with it. This usually applies to an employee's taking money and covering it up by faking business records or account books.

conversion
■ Any act that deprives an owner of property without that owner's permission and without just cause.

As was the case with larceny, only tangible personal property was included. Today, nearly all forms of personal property may be embezzled. Also, the property had to belong to another. One could not embezzle one's own property.

The element that distinguished embezzlement from larceny was the taking requirement. Whereas larceny required a trespassory taking, embezzlement required lawful acquisition. Accountants, lawyers, bailees, executors of estates, and trustees are examples of those who can commit embezzlement.

To satisfy the mens rea requirement of embezzlement, it must be shown that the defendant possessed an "intent to defraud." Mere negligent conversion of another's property is not embezzlement. Because the mens rea requirement is so high, bona fide claims of mistake of fact and law are valid defenses. If an accountant makes an accounting error and converts a client's money, there is no embezzlement. This is a mistake of fact. If a friend you loaned money to keeps the money with the mistaken belief that he is allowed to in order to offset damage you caused to his property last year (when the law requires that he sue you for the damage), there is no embezzlement. This is a mistake of law and negates the intent required, as does a mistake of fact.

Embezzlement is prohibited in all states. Some states have retained the name *embezzlement;* others have named it theft and included it in a consolidated theft statute. Embezzlement, which occurs in interstate commerce, federally insured banks, and lending institutions, or involves officers and agents of the federal government, is also made criminal by the statutes of the United States.[9] Statute 18 U.S.C. § 641 is the embezzlement of public monies, property, and records statute. Violation of that provision, if the property embezzled has a value of $100 or greater, results in a fine of up to $10,000 and 10 years in prison. The remainder of that statute deals with embezzlement of nonpublic property that occurs in interstate commerce or by federal officials. The penalties vary for each provision.

False Pretenses

At common law, it was not larcenous to use lies (false representations) to gain ownership of property. For example, if Brogan were to sell Sean a ring containing glass, while representing to Sean that the ring contained a diamond, it was not larceny under the early common law, even though Brogan knew that the ring contained glass. The early judges believed strongly in the concept of *caveat emptor,* which translates as "let the buyer beware."

As it had done with embezzlement, Parliament decided to make such acts criminal. It did so by creating the crime of **false pretenses**. The elements of false pretenses are (1) a false representation of (2) a material present or past fact (3) made with knowledge that the fact is false (4) and with an intent to defraud the victim (5) thereby causing the victim to pass title to property to the actor.

To prove the first element, it must be shown that the actor made a false representation. This representation may be made orally or by writing, or may be implied by one's actions. The law does not require that people disclose all relevant information during a business transaction—*caveat emptor* still exists in that regard. The law does, however,

false pretenses

■ A lie told to cheat another person out of his or her money or property. It is a crime in most states, though the precise definition varies.

require that any affirmative statements (or implications from actions) be true. So, if a buyer fails to ask if property has a lien against it, there is no false pretense if the seller does not inform the buyer of such. The opposite is true if the buyer inquires about existing liens and encumbrances and is told there are none.

The false representation must be important to the transaction. If the statement is important, the law says that it is *material*. Generally, a representation is material if it would have had an impact on the victim's decisionmaking had the victim known the truth at the time the transaction took place. For example, if Connie represents to Pam that the lighter in a used car she is selling works, when it does not, she has not committed false pretenses. However, if she states to Pam that the automobile recently had its engine replaced, that would be material and she would be liable for false pretenses if she knew that the statement was untrue.

The fact conveyed by the actor must not only be material, but it must also concern a present fact or past fact. In this context, *present* refers to the time of the transaction. Statements of expected facts, promises, predictions, and expectations cannot be the basis of false pretenses. So, if Aaron buys an automobile from Kathy and promises to pay her in 6 months, it is no crime if he fails to pay because he loses his source of income during that period. To permit breaches of such promises to be criminal would be the same as having a debtor's prison, which is not recognized in the United States. The same is not true if Aaron made the promise but had no intent of paying the debt. Some states treat this as false pretenses under the theory that his state of mind at the time of the sale was fraudulent. Some states do not treat his action as criminal and place the burden on Kathy to seek her own remedy in a civil cause of action. It is also necessary that the representation be one of fact. Accordingly, opinions are not included. Of course, the line between fact and opinion is often unclear.

It must also be proved that the defendant knew the statement was false. An unintentional misrepresentation is not sufficient to establish this element in most jurisdictions, although most jurisdictions will find knowledge if the lower mens rea standard, recklessness, is proved.

The defendant must have the additional mens rea of "intent to defraud." As with other theft crimes, if persons have a bona fide belief that a particular property belongs to them, there is a defense. In addition to intending to defraud the victim, it must also be shown that the victim was defrauded. Hence, if the victim was aware of the falsity of the statement and entered into the bargain anyway, there has been no crime.

Finally, the misrepresentation must be the cause of the victim passing title to property to the defendant. *Title* is ownership. Transferring possession to the defendant is not adequate. However, causing one to transfer possession of property by use of fraud was a type of larceny, known as *larceny by trick*. Just as with larceny and embezzlement, only tangible personal property was included within the grasp of the prohibition at early common law. Today, false pretenses usually includes all property that is subject to the protection of larceny—in most instances, this includes all personal property.

Fraudulent Checks

Related to the crime of false pretenses is the crime of acquiring property or money by writing a check (draft) from an account that has insufficient funds to cover the draft. The act appears to fall into the category of false pretenses. Some theorize that a check is a promise of future payment, and, accordingly, the check does not meet the "representation of present or past fact" requirement of false pretenses. Courts have rejected that theory and held that at the time one drafts a check, a representation is made that there are adequate funds in the account to pay the amount drafted.

Today, most states have bad-check statutes. Conviction of these laws, for the most part, results in a less serious punishment than conviction on false pretenses.[10] Three common material elements are found in bad-check statutes. First, the mens rea may be proven by showing either an intent to defraud the payee or knowledge that there were insufficient funds in the account. Second, the check must be taken in exchange for something of value; third, there must have been insufficient funds in the account.

Mail Fraud

Another crime related to false pretenses is mail fraud.[11] Mail fraud is a crime against the United States, because the mail system is run by a federal agency. Using the U.S. mail system with an intent to defraud another of money or property is mail fraud. The intended victim need not be defrauded; the act of sending such mails with the intent to defraud is itself criminal.

Mail fraud has become increasingly important in recent years, because it often is the foundation of a RICO count.

Racketeer Influenced and Corrupt Organizations Act

racketeer influenced and corrupt organizations act

■ (19 U.S.C. 1961). A broadly applied 1970 federal law that creates certain "racketeering offenses" that include participation in various criminal schemes and conspiracies, and that allows government seizure of property acquired in violation of the act.

Another federal statute that deals with fraud is the **Racketeer Influenced and Corrupt Organizations Act**, commonly known as RICO.[12] The United States Congress enacted RICO in the early 1970s in an attempt to curb organized crime.

Judicial interpretation of RICO has led to much controversy in recent years. Some people contend that the effect of court opinions has been to extend the prohibition of RICO beyond Congress's original intent. Today, all businesses, not just traditional organized crime, are subject to RICO.

To establish a RICO violation, the United States must prove that the (1) defendant received money or income (2) from a pattern of racketeering activity and (3) invested that money in an enterprise (business), (4) which is in interstate commerce or affects interstate commerce.

The second element is the key to proving a RICO violation. The term *pattern* means "two or more acts," referred to as the predicate acts. Those acts must fall into the definition of a "racketeering activity." The statute provides a list of state and federal crimes that are considered to be racketeering. Murder, kidnapping, extortion, and drug sales and transportation are examples of the state crimes included in the list. Mail fraud, wire fraud, "white slave traffic" or the transport of women across state boundaries for immoral purposes, securities fraud, and bribery are a few examples of the federal crimes included. Mail fraud is often the basis of a RICO violation, because the mails are often used by such enterprises.

For example, the Supreme Court announced in a 1994 decision that RICO could apply to a coalition of antiabortion groups that were alleged to have conspired, through a pattern of racketeering, to shut down abortion clinics.[13] In that case, extortion, including alleged threats of assault, was used to satisfy this element.

Violation of RICO can result in serious criminal penalties. In addition, victims of such activity may sue civilly and receive treble damages, costs, and attorney fees. RICO also provides for **forfeiture** of property in criminal proceedings. *Forfeiture* is the taking of property and money of a defendant by the government. Many crimes have forfeiture provisions. A forfeiture is not the same as a fine. Forfeitures and fines are both levied as punishment, but the focus of a fine is generally to hurt a defendant's pocketbook. Forfeitures are specifically aimed at getting the property or money connected to the crime for which the individual was convicted. So, in a RICO situation, a convicted party could stand to lose the enterprise itself, as well as all profits from that activity.

forfeiture
■ A deprivation of money, property, or rights, without compensation, as a consequence of a default or the commission of a crime.

However, many aspects of civil RICO are identical to criminal RICO. One such aspect is the pattern requirement. Whether the case is civil or criminal, a pattern of racketeering must be proven. The United States Supreme Court addressed the pattern question because the various appellate courts of the United States were divided on how to define that phrase. In *H.J., Inc. v. Northwestern Bell Telephone Co.*, 492 U.S. 229 (1989), the Supreme Court defined a pattern as more than one predicate act that are related to one another and the facts pose a threat of continued racketeering activity. *H.J.* is also a good illustration of how "legitimate businesses" are subject to RICO.

Forgery

Another crime related to fraud is **forgery**. *Forgery* is the (1) making of (2) false documents (or the alteration of existing documents making them false) (3) and passing the document (4) to another (5) with an intent to defraud.

forgery
■ Making a fake document (or altering a real one) with intent to commit a fraud.

The purpose of forgery statutes is both to prevent fraud and to preserve the value of written instruments. These functions are important because if forgery were to become common, people would no longer trust commercial documents, such as checks and contracts. The effect that would have on commerce is obvious.

The actus reus of forgery is the making of the document. That involves the actual writing and drafting of the document, as well as passing the document (*uttering*) to a potential victim. The mens rea of forgery is knowledge of the falsity of the document and an intent to defraud.

In many jurisdictions, forgery and uttering are separate crimes. In those states one must only make the false instrument and possess an intent to defraud. The defendant need not present the document (utter) to the victim. That act, when accompanied with an intent to defraud, is the crime of *uttering*.

Receiving Stolen Property

Not only is it a crime to steal another's property, but it is also a crime to receive property that one knows is stolen, if the intent is to keep that property. In essence, one who buys or receives as a gift property that is known to be stolen is an accessory (after the fact) to the theft. Although the law applies to anyone who violates its prohibitions, the primary focus of law enforcement is *fences,* people who purchase stolen property with the intent of reselling the property for a profit. They act as the retailers of stolen property, with the thieves acting as suppliers.

The elements of **receiving stolen property** are (1) receiving property (2) that has been stolen (3) with knowledge of its stolen character (4) with an intent to deprive the owner of the property.

Receipt of the property may be shown by showing either actual possession or constructive possession of the property. Constructive possession occurs any time the defendant has control over the property, even though the defendant does not have actual possession. For example, if one makes arrangements for stolen property to be delivered to one's home, there is receipt once the property is in the house, even if the defendant was not present when the property was delivered. Receiving includes not only purchases of stolen property but also other transfers, such as gifts.

The property in question must have been stolen. In this context, stolen property includes that property acquired from larcenies, robberies, embezzlement, extortion, false pretenses, and similar crimes.

The final two elements deal with the mens rea of the crime of receiving stolen property. It is necessary that the defendant knew of the property's stolen character at the time of acquiring the property. Actual knowledge that the property was stolen is required. However, if it can be proven that the defendant had a subjective belief that the goods were stolen, but lacked absolute proof of that fact, the crime has still been committed. The fact that a reasonable person would have known that the property was stolen is not enough to convict for receiving stolen property. If persons receive property under a bona fide belief that they have claim to the property, they are not guilty of receiving stolen property, even though that belief was unfounded.

The last element requires that the receiver of the property intends to deprive the owner of the property. Of course, if a defendant intends to keep the property, then this requirement is met. The language of the crime is broader, however, and includes any intent to deprive the owner of the use, ownership, or possession of the property. Thus, if one receives the property intending to destroy it or to give it as a gift, this element has been satisfied.

Not only do the states prohibit receiving stolen property, but the federal government also makes it a crime to receive stolen property that has traveled in interstate commerce or to receive stolen property while on lands controlled by the United States.[14]

receiving stolen property
■ The criminal offense of getting or concealing property known to be stolen by another.

Robbery

The material elements of **robbery** are (1) a trespassory taking (2) and carrying away (asportation) (3) of personal property (4) from another's person or presence (5) using either force or threat (6) with an intent to steal the property.

robbery
■ The illegal taking of property from the person of another by using force or threat of force.

Robbery is actually a type of assault mixed with a type of larceny. Because of the immediate danger created by the crime of robbery, it is punished more severely than either larceny or simple assault. Robbery was a crime under the common law and is a statutory crime in all states today.

The elements of trespassory taking—asportation, intent to steal, and that the property belongs to another—are the same as for larceny. However, robbery also requires that the property be taken from the victim's person or presence. So property taken from another's hands, off another's body, or from another's clothing is taken from the person. Property that is taken from another's presence, but not from the person, also qualifies. For example, if a bank robber orders a teller to stand back while the thief empties the cash drawer, there has been a robbery. The states differ in their definitions of "from another's presence," but it is generally held that property is in a victim's presence any time the victim is in control of the property. This is true in the bank robbery example, as the teller was exercising control over the cash drawer at the time of the robbery.

It is also necessary that the crime be committed with the use of force or threat. This element is the feature that most distinguishes robbery from larceny. As far as force is concerned, if any force is used beyond what is necessary to simply take the property, there is robbery. For example, it is larceny, not robbery, if a pickpocket steals a wallet free of the owner's knowledge. Only the force necessary to take the wallet was used. It is robbery, however, if the victim catches the pickpocket, and an altercation ensues over possession of the wallet. The same result is true when dealing with purse snatchers. If the snatcher makes a clean grab and gets away without an altercation, it is larceny from the person. If the victim grabs the bag and fights to keep it, then it is robbery. A threat of force may also satisfy this requirement. So, if the robber states to the victim, "Give me your wallet or I'll blow your head off," there is a robbery, even though there was no physical contact.

In most jurisdictions, the threatened harm must be immediate; threats of future harm are not adequate. It is also possible that the threat will be to someone else, such as a family member. The thief who holds a man's wife and threatens to harm her if the man does not give up his money is not free from the charge of robbery just because the person giving up the money is not the one threatened.

The mens rea of robbery is the specific intent to take the property and deprive the owner of it. As with the other theft crimes, a good-faith, but incorrect, claim of right to the property is a defense. In *Richardson v. United States*, 403 F.2d 574 (D.C. Cir. 1968), a defendant's claim of right to money was a gambling debt. The trial court did not permit the illegal debt to be used as a defense, but the appellate court reversed. It stated in its opinion that:

> The government's position seems to be that no instruction on a claim of right is necessary unless the defendant had a legally enforceable right to the property he took. But specific intent depends upon a state of mind, not upon a legal fact. If the jury finds that the defendant believed himself entitled to the money, it cannot properly find that he had the requisite specific intent for robbery.

Robbery is a crime pursuant to state law, and the United States has also prohibited certain robberies. Robbery of a federally insured bank is an example.[15]

Robbery is usually, if not always, graded. Robbery is graded higher if it results in serious injury to the victim or is committed using a deadly weapon.

Extortion

extortion

■ To compel, force, or coerce; for example, to get a confession by depriving a person of food and water. To get something by illegal threats of harm to person, property, or reputation. The process is called *extortion*.

Extortion is more commonly known as *blackmail*. Extortion is similar to robbery because both acts involve stealing money under threat. However, the threat in a robbery must be of immediate harm. Extortion involves a threat of future harm. At common law, extortion applied only against public officers. Today, extortion is much broader. The elements of extortion are (1) the taking or acquisition of property (2) of another (3) using a threat (4) with an intent to steal the property. In a few jurisdictions, the extortionist must actually receive the property, whereas others require only that the threat be made.

A threat of future physical harm satisfies the threat element, as do threats to injure another's reputation, business, financial status, or family relationship. As in the case of robbery, the threat may be directed at one person and the demand for property made on another. For example, if a thief states to John, "Give me $100,000 or I will kill your wife," he is an extortionist, even though he has not threatened John.

The threatened conduct itself need not be illegal to be extortion. For example, if Stacy tells Lisa that she is going to inform the authorities of Lisa's involvement in illegal drug trade unless Lisa pays her $10,000, she is an extortionist, even though informing the police of the activity is not only legal but is encouraged by society.

The federal government has made it a crime for federal officers to extort the public, to be involved in an extortion that interferes with interstate commerce, and to extort another by threatening to expose a violation of federal law.

The *Dioguardi* case deals with extortion in the labor relations area. In most situations it is proper for unions and employees to threaten to picket an employer. In this case the threats were not part of usual labor–management relations; they were made with the purpose of extorting corporate money. Accordingly, the threats were found to be extortion, not protected labor activity.

Consolidated Theft Statutes

The distinctions among the three common-law crimes of theft, larceny, embezzlement, and false pretenses are often hard to draw. This fact, matched with the belief that there is no substantive difference between stealing by fraud or by quick use of the hands, has led many jurisdictions to do away with the common-law crimes of larceny, false pretenses, and embezzlement and to replace them with a single crime named theft. Exactly what crimes are included in such statutes differs, but larceny, false pretenses, and embezzlement are always included. Many jurisdictions also add one or more of the following: fraudulent checks, receiving stolen property, and extortion.

These statutes often use the language of the common law in defining theft. For example, Florida's statute reads:

> A person is guilty of theft if he knowingly obtains or uses, or endeavors to obtain or to use, the property of another with intent to, either temporarily or permanently: (a) Deprive the other person of a right to the property or a benefit therefrom or Appropriate the property to his own use or to the use of any person not entitled thereto.[16]

This statute includes the three common-law theft crimes. The primary change of consolidated theft statutes is that prosecutors no longer need to charge which specific crime has occurred. At trial, if the jury decides that a defendant has committed a larceny and not an embezzlement, they can convict. At common law, if the defendant was charged with embezzlement, not larceny, the jury would be forced to acquit if they determined that the defendant committed larceny rather than embezzlement.

Robbery is usually not included in consolidated theft statutes because of its significant threat of harm. Consolidation usually includes only misappropriations of property that do not pose serious risks to life.

Of course, those crimes that are included in consolidation statutes are not always punished equally. Grading of such offenses based on the amount of property appropriated, the nature of the theft, and the type of property stolen is common.

Identity Theft

It is possible to steal a person's identity as well as a person's property. The advent of the computer has made identity theft more common. Identity theft occurs whenever an individual uses a victim's name, social security number, e-mail address, or other identifying items in an effort to represent himself or herself as the victim. The mens rea of most identity theft statutes is an intention either to gain something of value through the deceit or to commit any other crime. This is the text of the Washington identity theft statute:

RCW 9.35.020 Identity theft.

(1) No person may knowingly obtain, possess, use, or transfer a means of identification or financial information of another person, living or dead, with the intent to commit, or to aid or abet, any crime.

(2) (a) Violation of this section when the accused or an accomplice uses the victim's means of identification or financial information and obtains an aggregate total of credit, money, goods, services, or anything else of value in excess of one thousand five hundred dollars in value shall constitute identity theft in the first degree. Identity theft in the first degree is a class B felony.

(b) Violation of this section when the accused or an accomplice uses the victim's means of identification or financial information and obtains an aggregate total of credit, money, goods, services, or anything else of value that is less than one thousand five hundred dollars in value, or when no credit, money, goods, services, or anything of value is obtained shall constitute identity theft in the second degree. Identity theft in the second degree is a class C felony.

(3) A person who violates this section is liable for civil damages of five hundred dollars or actual damages, whichever is greater, including costs to repair the victim's credit record, and reasonable attorneys' fees as determined by the court.

(4) In a proceeding under this section, the crime will be considered to have been committed in any locality where the person whose means of identification or financial information was appropriated resides, or in which any part of the offense took place, regardless of whether the defendant was ever actually in that locality.

(5) The provisions of this section do not apply to any person who obtains another person's driver's license or other form of identification for the sole purpose of misrepresenting his or her age.

(6) In a proceeding under this section in which a person's means of identification or financial information was used without that person's authorization, and where there has been a conviction, the sentencing court may issue such orders as are necessary to correct a public record that contains false information resulting from a violation of this section.

An offender may be charged and convicted of both identity theft and the underlying crime. The defendant in the following case was convicted under the Washington statute. On appeal she alleged that her conviction of both identity theft and forgery put her in double jeopardy.

identity theft

▪ The act of assuming another person's identity by fraud.

The federal government also has an **identity theft** statute, the Identity Theft and Assumption Deterrence Act of 1998 (Identity Theft Act). Specifically, the Act[17] makes it a federal crime when anyone

> knowingly transfers or uses, without lawful authority, a means of identification of another person with the intent to commit, or to aid or abet, any unlawful activity that constitutes a violation of Federal law, or that constitutes a felony under any applicable State or local law.

The Model Penal Code Consolidation

The Model Penal Code contains a comprehensive consolidation of theft offenses.[18] Provided that a defendant is not prejudiced by doing so, the specification of one theft crime by the prosecution does not prohibit a conviction for another. So if defendants are specifically charged with larceny, they may be convicted of false pretenses or embezzlement by a jury.

The Code recognizes the following forms of theft:

1. Theft by taking (includes common-law larceny and embezzlement).
2. Theft by deception (includes common-law false pretenses).
3. Theft by extortion.
4. Theft of property known to be mislaid, misdelivered, or lost, and no reasonable attempt to find the rightful owner is made.
5. Receiving stolen property.
6. Theft of professional services by deception or threat.
7. Conversion of entrusted funds.
8. Unauthorized use of another's automobile.

The Code declares that thefts are felonies of the third degree if the amount stolen exceeds $500 or if the property stolen is a firearm, automobile, airplane, motorcycle, motorboat, or other vehicle; and, in cases of receiving stolen property, if the receiver of the property is a fence, then it is a felony of the third degree regardless of the value of the property. The Code makes all unauthorized uses of automobiles misdemeanors.

Because the crime of robbery involves a danger to people, it is treated as a separate crime.[19] If during the commission of a theft the defendant inflicts serious bodily injury upon another, threatens serious bodily injury, or threatens to commit a felony of the first or second degree, there is a robbery. It is a felony of the second degree unless the defendant attempts to kill or cause serious bodily injury, in which case it is a felony of the first degree.

Forgery is also treated as a separate offense.[20] Forgery is treated as a felony of the second degree if money, securities, postage stamps, stock, or other documents issued by the government are involved. It is a felony of the third degree if the forged document affects legal relationships, such as wills and contracts. All other forgeries are misdemeanors.

Destruction of Property

Every year a significant amount of financial loss is the result of destruction of property. Arson accounts for much of this total, but not all. Most states have statutes making the destruction of another's property criminal. These laws may be part of the statute covering arson or may be a separate section of the criminal code.

Destruction of property, commonly called **criminal mischief**, is normally a specific-intent crime and includes all types of destruction that affect the value or dignity of the property. For example, defacing a Jewish tombstone by painting a swastika on it would be criminal mischief, even though the paint can be removed and the tombstone is left physically unharmed.

Mischief is often graded so that the most heavily penalized offenses against public property are those resulting in damage in excess of a stated dollar amount or involving a danger to human life. The most serious mischiefs are usually low-grade felonies, and the rest are misdemeanors. For example, the Kentucky mischief statutes read:

malicious (criminal) mischief

■ The criminal offense of intentionally destroying another person's property.

Ky. Rev. Stat. § 512.020

(1) A person is guilty of criminal mischief in the first degree when, having no right to do so or any reasonable ground to believe that he has such right, he intentionally or wantonly defaces, destroys, or damages any property causing pecuniary loss of $1,000 or more.

(2) Criminal mischief in the first degree is a Class D felony.

Ky. Rev. Stat. § 512.030

(1) A person is guilty of criminal mischief in the second degree when, having no right to do so or any reasonable ground to believe that he has such a right, he intentionally or wantonly defaces, destroys, or damages any property causing pecuniary loss of $500 or more.

(2) Criminal mischief in the second degree is a Class A misdemeanor.

Ky. Rev. Stat. § 512.040

(1) A person is guilty of criminal mischief in the third degree when:

  (a) Having no right to do so or any reasonable ground to believe that he has such right, he intentionally or wantonly defaces, destroys, or damages any property; or

  (b) He tampers with property so as knowingly to endanger the person or property of another.

(2) Criminal mischief in the third degree is a Class B misdemeanor.

At common law, hairline distinctions existed among the three crimes against property: larceny, embezzlement, and false pretenses. Today, statutes in most states have consolidated theft crimes so that the focus is now on whether a theft occurred, not whether the correct crime has been charged. These consolidation statutes include larceny, false pretenses, and embezzlement. Although it varies, often such statutes will also include receiving stolen property, various forms of fraud, and extortion. Robbery and forgery are treated as separate crimes.

Arson and burglary are separate crimes because they involve more than a threat to property. At common law, only residences were protected by arson and burglary laws. As noted at the beginning of the chapter, because of the sanctity that our culture attaches to dwellings and because of the danger to human life created by arson and burglary, these crimes received special attention. Today, arson and burglary have been broadened to include more than just dwellings.

In addition to criminal remedies for these crimes, victims often have civil remedies available. As previously discussed, victims are responsible for filing and proving such a civil case. However, a prior admission of guilt (or conviction) may prevent defendants from relitigating their innocence in a civil trial.

Computer Theft Crimes

Computer-related crimes are costly and are on the rise. According to a report issued in 2008 by the Computer Security Institute, 50% of the respondent corporations reported having experienced virus attack, 44% reported insider abuse, 29% reported unauthorized access, 42% reported laptop theft, 27% experienced an attack specifically targeted at it or a small number of like organizations, 17% theft/loss of data, 13% system penetration, 6% website defacement, 2% sabotage, among other offenses. The total costs of these crimes is in the hundreds of billions of dollars each year.[21]

Computer crimes take two general forms. First, computers can be the target of a crime. Theft of hardware and software is an example. Destruction and vandalism of computers is another crime where the computer is itself the target of an unlawful act. Viruses are also used to destroy computer programs.

A second form of computer crime involves using a computer as a tool in the commission of a crime. Violating privileges by improperly obtaining confidential information, threat and harassment through cyberspace, and the illegal distribution of obscenities fall into this category. Computers can also be used to steal. Obtaining illegal entry into a bank's computer records from a personal computer in order to steal money is an example, as is using another person's personal identification number and bank card to access an automatic teller machine.

Many computer-related crimes are punishable without special computer crimes laws. Existing penal laws such as theft, larceny, and criminal mischief may include computer activity. For example, stealing funds from a bank through a computer can usually be prosecuted under existing theft laws if a special computer theft statute has not been enacted. Similarly, criminal mischief statutes could be used to prosecute the intentional destruction of computer programs by viruses.

In addition to existing laws, the federal government and 49 states had enacted special legislation to deal with computers and crimes by 1998. The Federal Counterfeit Access Device and Computer Fraud and Abuse Act became law in 1984 and was amended in 1986 by the Computer Fraud and Abuse Act. That law prohibits:

1. A knowing, unauthorized access to information contained in a federal interest computer.
2. An intentional, unauthorized access to financial information held by a financial institution or credit agency.
3. An intentional, unauthorized access of a computer of the United States that would affect the government's operation of the computer.
4. Thefts of property by use of computer as a result of a knowing and intentional scheme to defraud.

5. Knowingly altering, damaging, or destroying information within a federal interest computer or preventing the authorized use of such a computer.
6. Knowingly trafficking in any password without authorization if the trafficking affects interstate commerce or is used by or for the U.S. government.

Some of these crimes are misdemeanors, and others are felonies. The federal government regulated computer crime further through the **Computer Abuse Amendments Act of 1994**.[22] This statute criminalizes the transmission of any data intended to cause damage to a computer used by the federal government or a financial institution. It also prohibits "trafficking in passwords" that provide access to government computers or that interfere with interstate or foreign commerce.

In addition, there is a federal electronic espionage statute. Statute 18 U.S.C. § 1831 protects corporate propriety information. It reads, in part:

> In General—
> Whoever, intending or knowing that the offense will benefit any foreign government, foreign instrumentality, or foreign agent, knowingly—
> (1) steals, or without authorization appropriates, takes, carries away, or conceals, or by fraud, artifice, or deception obtains a trade secret;
> (2) without authorization copies, duplicates, sketches, draws, photographs, downloads, uploads, alters, destroys, photocopies, replicates, transmits, delivers, sends, mails, communicates, or conveys a trade secret;
> (3) receives, buys, or possesses a trade secret, knowing the same to have been stolen or appropriated, obtained, or converted without authorization;
> (4) attempts to commit any offense described in any of paragraphs (1) through (3); or
> (5) conspires with one or more other persons to commit any offense described in any of paragraphs (1) through (3), and one or more of such persons do any act to effect the object of the conspiracy, shall, except as provided in subsection (b), be fined not more than $500,000 or imprisoned not more than 15 years, or both.

The private sector expends considerable resources in the prevention and detection of computer crimes. Law enforcement agencies have been forced to hire investigators and consultants with computer expertise to effectively investigate claims and educate the public in preventing computer crimes. As computer use and dependence increase, so will computer crimes.

On the other side, computer technology has advanced law enforcement in some respects. The *Briggs* case is an illustration of the application and complexity of computer crimes.

The **National Crime Information Center** (NCIC) is used by law enforcement agencies nationwide in the reporting and detection of wanted persons. Computers are used to organize and manage case files. Graphics programs are used to recreate crimes and to project a fugitive's appearance after donning a disguise or after having aged. These are but a few of the uses computers play in law enforcement. The use of computers by law enforcement raises interesting search and privacy questions. This topic is discussed in Chapter 12.

National Crime Information Center

■ Computerized records of criminals, warrants, stolen vehicles, etc.

Web Links

Crime Data

Two excellent sites will provide a huge amount of data on crime. Reports on crime-related issues may also be found in these locations. The first is the National Institute of Justice, at http://www.ojp.usdoj.gov/nij/, and the second is the Bureau of Justice Statistics, at http://www.ojp.usdoj.gov/bjs/. Both are U.S. Department of Justice offices

Key Terms

arson
burglary
conversion
criminal mischief
embezzlement
extortion

false pretenses
forfeiture
forgery
identity theft
larceny

National Crime Information Center
Racketeer Influenced and Corrupt Organizations Act
receiving stolen property
robbery

Review Questions

1. What is "constructive breaking," when referring to the crime of burglary?
2. Define larceny.
3. What is criminal mischief?
4. Embezzlement is often punished more severely than simple larceny. Why?
5. What does the acronym RICO represent? What are the basic elements of RICO?
6. What are "fences?" At common law, what crime do fences commit?
7. How is destruction of a building by explosion treated by the Model Penal Code? At common law?
8. Brogan runs by a woman on the street and grabs her purse as he passes her. The purse is easily pulled from her arm, and Brogan's intent is to keep the contents. What crime has been committed?
9. Brogan runs by a woman on the street and grabs her purse as he passes her. The woman catches the strap and fights to keep the purse; however, the strap breaks, and Brogan is successful. He keeps the contents of the purse. What crime has been committed?
10. What is the difference between forgery and uttering?

Problems & Critical Thinking Exercises

1. Arson is quite different today than it was at common law. What are the major differences?
2. Burglary is quite different today than it was at common law. What are the major differences?
3. Doug and Sherri are an elderly couple who are retired and residing in Florida. Both have suffered substantial physical deterioration, including vision loss and poor memory. Ned, who had coveted their 1962 Corvette for years, told the couple that they should trust him with their financial affairs, including giving him title to their vehicle. He told the two that he would drive them to the places they needed to go, but that state law required that his name appear on the title of the car, as he would be the sole driver. Doug and Sherri complied with his request, believing that his statement concerning Florida law was correct.

    Subsequently, the couple created a trust account and named Ned as trustee. The purpose of the account was to provide Ned with a general fund from which he was to pay the household bills. Ned withdrew all the money and placed it into his personal account. When this occurred, the couple contacted Ned, who claimed to know nothing of the account. Sherri contacted the local prosecutor, who conducted an investigation. Through that investigation, it was discovered that Ned held title to the Corvette.

    You work for the prosecutor. Your assignment is to determine what crimes have been committed, if any. Your state has no theft statute, but recognizes common-law theft crimes.

4. Gary and Paige were friends until they discovered that they shared an interest in Tracy. After Paige won her affection, Gary became enraged and took a key and ran it down the side of Paige's car. He then poured gasoline over the car and set it on fire. Gary has been arrested. What crimes should be charged?

5. Kevin was walking down the sidewalk that passed in front of Sean's home. As he passed Sean's house, he looked in a front window and noticed a carton of soft drinks sitting in the kitchen. As he was thirsty, Kevin broke the front window and crawled into Sean's house. Once inside, he poured himself a glass of cola and sat down at the dining room table. While seated at the table, he picked up a ring with a value in excess of $1,000, and put it into his pocket. When he finished his drink, he placed the empty glass in the sink and left. He later sold the ring and bought a stereo with the proceeds. What crimes have been committed, using common-law theft crimes?

6. Brogan has an affair with Janice, who is married. After Janice ends the affair, Brogan threatens to tell Janice's husband about their sexual involvement unless Janice pays Brogan $5,000. Janice complies. What crime has been committed?

7. Penni is working the night shift at a local convenience store when Craig and Guido come in. Craig states to Penni, "Give us all the money in the register and we will not hurt you. Give us any trouble and we will knock the #?!@ out of you!" Penni complies. What crime has been committed? What if they had been brandishing weapons?

8. Discuss what crimes you think should be included in consolidated theft statutes and why. Explain why particular crimes should be left out of such a statute.

Endnotes

1. Davenport, P., *Michael Marin, Ex-Wall Street Trader, Took Cyanide After Arson Guilty Verdict*. Huffington Post, July 27, 2012, found at http://www.huffingtonpost.com/2012/07/27/michael-marin-cyanide_n_1710731.html and *Arson in America*: The odd tale of Michael Marin, IndependentMail.com (April 23, 2013).
2. 5 Am. Jur. 2d *Arson* 2 (1962).
3. Model Penal Code § 220.1.
4. Model Penal Code § 220.1(1) and (2).
5. *People v. Richards*, 108 N.Y. 137, 15 N.E. 371 (1988).
6. LaFave & Scott, *Criminal Law* 797 (Hornbook Series; St. Paul: West, 1986).
7. A. Loewy, *Criminal Law*, 2d ed. (Nutshell Series; St. Paul: West, 1987).
8. *Bazeley's Case,* 2 East P.C. 571 (Cr. Cas. Res. 1799); *see* LaFave & Scott, *Criminal Law* § 8.1 (Hornbook Series; St. Paul: West, 1986).
9. 18 U.S.C. § 641 *et seq.*
10. LaFave & Scott, *Criminal Law* § 8.9 (Hornbook Series; St. Paul: West, 1986).
11. 18 U.S.C. § 1341.
12. 18 U.S.C. § 1961 *et seq.*
13. *N.O.W. v. Scheidler*, 114 S. Ct. 798 (1994).
14. 18 U.S.C. § 2311 *et seq.*
15. 18 U.S.C. § 2113.
16. Fla. Stat. Ann. § 812.012 *et seq.*
17. 18 U.S.C. § 1028.
18. Model Penal Code § 223 *et seq.* deals with theft offenses.
19. *Id.* § 222.1.
20. *Id.* § 224.1.
21. 2008 Computer Crime and Security Survey, Computer Security Institute (2008), http://gocsi.com/sites/default/files/uploads/CSIsurvey2008.pdf
22. 18 U.S.C. §§ 1029–30.

CHAPTER 11

CRIMES AGAINST THE PUBLIC

Chapter Outline

Defining a "Crime Against the Public"
Crimes Against Public Morality
    Prostitution and Solicitation
    Deviate Sexual Conduct
    Marriage, Contraception, and Abortion
    Indecent Exposure and Lewdness
    Obscenity
    Regulating the Internet
Crimes Against the Public Order
    Riot and Unlawful Assembly
    Disturbing the Peace
    Incitement/Advocacy of Unlawful Conduct
    Threats
    Vagrancy and Panhandling
    Crimes Involving Firearms
    Drug and Alcohol Crimes
Crimes Against the Administration of Government
    Perjury
    Bribery
    Tax Crimes
    Obstruction of Justice
    Contempt
Crimes Against Sovereignty and Security
    Treason
    Sedition and Espionage
    Terrorism
Crimes Against the Environment
    Clean Water Act
    Clean Air Act
    Comprehensive Environmental Response, Compensation, and Liability Act
    Resource Conservation and Recovery Act
    Occupational Safety and Health Act
    Toxic Substances Control Act
    Federal Insecticide, Fungicide, and Rodenticide Act
    Emergency Planning and Community Right-to-Know Act
    Endangered Species Act
    Marine Mammal Protection Act

Chapter Objectives

After completing this chapter, you should be able to

- describe historic and contemporary crimes against the public, including crimes against the public order, against the administration of government, against public morality, and against the environment.
- critically examine and discuss the laws of terrorism, especially those laws enacted in response to the September 11, 2001, attacks on the United States.
- explain the tension between national security and freedom and how the war on terror confounds the historic distinction between the law of war and criminal law
- explain what role that morality has, and what you believe it should play, in penal law.
- identify the material facts and legal issues in one-third of the cases you read and describe the court's analyses and conclusions in the cases.

DEFINING A "CRIME AGAINST THE PUBLIC"

Chapters 9 and 10 were concerned with crimes that victimize individuals or entities, such as corporations and other business organizations. This chapter examines crimes that do not have individual victims. These are crimes involving the public welfare, social order, and society's morals. Many, if not most, of these crimes are malum prohibitum in nature, not malum in se.

Historically religion has played a role in the "criminalization" of "victimless" crimes. Of course, religious groups do not dictate such policy—this would violate the First Amendment's Establishment Clause. Religion does, however, influence the moral values of the members of a society. In the United States this influence is predominantly Christian. This is the reason that some acts that directly harm no one are prohibited.

Some critics call for an end to "victimless crimes." Despite this opposition, many victimless crimes exist and are likely to continue to be prohibited. However, in a democracy such as the United States, it is important to avoid an unwarranted infringement of civil liberties. The more a law is premised upon a moral judgement, the greater the scrutiny of, and reasons justifying, such laws should be.

Some of the crimes discussed here bear directly upon the administration of government and justice and less upon moral determinations. For example, contempt of court is a crime against the public, and the premise of its prohibition is the theory that if society punishes offenders, others will comply with court orders, and the administration of justice will be enhanced. Prostitution is an example of a crime that is prohibited more for moral reasons than any other.

The crimes included in this chapter have been divided into five subsections: crimes against public morality; crimes against the public order; crimes against the administration of government; crimes against sovereignty and security; and crimes against the environment.

CRIMES AGAINST PUBLIC MORALITY

Prostitution and Solicitation

prostitution

■ A person offering her (in most states, his or her) body for sexual purposes in exchange for money. A crime in most states.

Often said to be the oldest profession, **prostitution** is prohibited in every state except Nevada, where each county is given the authority to determine whether it should be permitted.

Prostitution is defined as (1) providing (2) sexual services (3) in exchange for compensation. In a few states, only intercourse is included in the definition of sexual services. In most states, however, sexual services include sodomy, fellatio, cunnilingus, and the touching of another's genitals. The Model Penal Code includes homosexual and other deviate sexual conduct in its definition of sexual activity.[1]

The service must be provided in exchange for compensation. The person who is sexually promiscuous, but unpaid, goes unpunished. Compensation normally means money, but it can come in any form. Thus, the prostitute who accepts legal services from a lawyer in exchange for sexual services has received compensation. Where prostitution is illegal, it is common for prostitutes to use businesses, such as massage parlors and escort services, as fronts.

Solicitation is a related crime. Any person who engages in selling sex, buying sex, or attempting to buy sex is guilty of solicitation. Note that a prostitute may be guilty of both solicitation and prostitution, if the prostitute makes the first contact with the buyer. There need not be the actual sale of sex for solicitation—only an attempt to sell sexual services. The clients of prostitutes, when prosecuted, are charged with solicitation.

The Model Penal Code states that "[a] person commits a violation if he hires a prostitute to engage in sexual activity with him, or if he enters or remains in a house of prostitution for the purpose of engaging in sexual activity."[2]

Those who promote prostitution (*pimps*) are usually punished more severely than prostitutes and customers. The Model Penal Code makes knowingly promoting prostitution a felony of the third degree if a child under 16 years of age is prostituted; the defendant's wife, child, or other ward is prostituted; the defendant forces or encourages another to engage in prostitution; or the defendant owns, controls, or manages a house of prostitution. In all other cases promotion is a misdemeanor.

Nearly all sex-for-hire cases fall under state jurisdiction. However, the federal government may be involved in prosecution when a prostitute is transported in interstate commerce, or any other person is transported in interstate commerce for an immoral purpose.[3]

Deviate Sexual Conduct

Rape and related crimes were discussed in Chapter 9. That chapter focused on sexual behavior that results in harm to a victim. This discussion is different, as there is usually no victim other than society as a whole. Deviate sexual conduct has many definitions, but most states include fellatio, cunnilingus, anal sex, and all homosexual activity within the grasp of their deviate sexual statutes. Therefore, consenting adults, married or not, may be prosecuted for participating in such sexual activity under many older statutes.

The foundation of the prohibition of sodomy and related acts is morality. Adherents of many religions, including Christianity, believe that all sex other than vaginal intercourse between a man and woman is deviate. The reality is that many, if not most, people engage in sex that satisfies the definition of deviate sex. For this reason, many people argue that such acts are normal and should not be prohibited. Others argue that it does not matter if the behavior is normal or deviate—that sex between two consenting adults is private and involves no victims and, as such, is of no concern of the government. Regardless such laws continue to exist. Further, they have survived constitutional challenges in many instances.

Despite continued prohibition of sodomy, and related acts, in many states, the laws are seldom enforced. One reason is that law enforcement officials have shown a reluctance to enforce such laws, often because crimes perceived as more serious are time-demanding and leave little manpower and resources to enforce victimless crimes. In addition, there simply is the problem of discovering violations. Most sexual conduct occurs privately, and thus the police rarely discover violations independently. Of course, those who participate in prohibited sexual conduct are not likely to report their sex partners' acts to law enforcement. But it is possible for officers to discover violations, and several cases where it has happened have resulted in arrests, convictions, and appellate review.

In 1982, a local police officer discovered Michael Hardwick engaged in consensual oral sex with another man in Hardwick's bedroom. The officer was in the house to serve a warrant on Hardwick. The officer arrested both men for violating Georgia's sodomy statute. Although the prosecutor declined to file charges, Hardwick sued the Georgia attorney general, seeking an order of the court enjoining enforcement of the sodomy law. The case made its way to the Supreme Court of the United States, where the law was upheld. Hardwick's theory was that the right to privacy, found implicit in the Fourteenth Amendment's due process guarantee, shielded private consensual sexual conduct from governmental regulation. The Court rejected this argument, holding that the nation's long moral history of revulsion and prohibition of same-sex sodomy outweighed Hardwick's privacy concerns. The decision of the Court was 5–4. Justice Powell voted with the majority, and after his retirement he stated that he regretted his vote in the case. This is not the end of the story, however. In 1998, the Georgia Supreme Court found the statute to be violative of the privacy protections in the Georgia Constitution.[4] Then, the United State Supreme Court revisited the issue in *Lawrence v. Texas*.

Marriage, Contraception, and Abortion

Marriage is a state-coopted institution. States regulate marriage in a number of ways. All states specify how many people may marry, two in each union, who may marry (no close relatives), who has the authority to perform the marriage ceremony, when couples may marry (some states require a waiting period and/or blood tests), and the payment of a fee for the issuance of a license. Additionally, states and the federal government have built marriage into their tax schemes. There are limits, however, to the regulation of marriage. For example, for many years states prohibited and criminalized marriages between people of different races. As you will read in Chapter 14, the Supreme Court invalidated these laws as violating one's right to liberty, as protected by due process. Similarly, criminal prohibitions of the use of contraceptives and early term abortions were invalidated.

Due process and equal protection are evolving values and rights. Although a federalism and not a deviate sexual conduct case, the Supreme Court's 2013 decision *United States v. Windsor*, which invalidated a provision of the Defense of Marriage Act, contains sweeping equal protection and due process language that can be interpreted as foreshadowing a decision securing a right to same sex marriage in the near future. These topics are discussed more fully in Chapter 14.

Indecent Exposure and Lewdness

Indecent exposure, or the exposure of one's "private parts" in public, was a common-law misdemeanor. Today, the crime is usually criminalized by state statute or local ordinance.

Most indecent exposure laws require (1) an intentional exposure (2) of one's private parts (3) in a public place. In some jurisdictions, it is required that the exposure be done in an "offensive manner."

In 1991, the United States Supreme Court examined a public nudity statute in the context of nude barroom dancing. In *Barnes v. Glen Theater, Inc.*,[5] the Court upheld an Indiana statute that required dancers to wear pasties and G-strings. Although the court found that nude dancing was expressive conduct, it determined that states may require the dancers to cover their genitals. The court did say that erotic performances were protected by the First Amendment, provided the dancers wear a scant amount of clothing. The Court upheld the law because it determined that the state's objective was not to regulate expression, but to regulate for order and morality. Further, the Court held that the interference with expression was minimal.

The Model Penal Code prohibits public indecency. The Code goes further with a provision proscribing all lewd acts that the defendant knows are likely to be observed by others who would be "affronted or alarmed" by the acts.[6]

Obscenity

> Congress shall make no law respecting the establishment of religion, or prohibiting the free exercise thereof; *or abridging the freedom of speech*, or of the press; or the right of the people peaceably to assemble, and to petition the Government for a redress of grievances.

This is the First Amendment to the U.S. Constitution. Most, if not all, states have a similar provision in their constitutions. The italicized portion represents the only protection of speech in the Constitution. Because it is brief and broad, it is dependent upon a great amount of interpretation to give it meaning. Also, because of its brevity and broadness, courts often interpret it differently. Even the Supreme Court has changed its interpretation of the clause, in particular areas, on several occasions. Freedom of speech encompasses far more than will be examined in this chapter. What will be discussed here is the extent of governmental power to regulate conduct that it deems to be indecent. Specifically, this section addresses sexually explicit materials, including films, books, and erotic dancing. It is well established that the term *speech*, as used in the First Amendment, means more than spoken utterances. It includes all forms of expression.

Both the federal and state governments regulate conduct, speech, books, movies, and other forms of expression that are believed to be "obscene." State governments are the most involved with regulating obscenity, due to general police power (the power to regulate for the health, welfare, and safety of citizens). However, the federal government is also involved; for example, it has criminalized sending obscene materials through the mail.[7]

Not all indecencies may be criminalized. Simply because something strikes one person as indecent does not mean that it should be prohibited. People have differing values, and to allow governments to prohibit all conduct (or other things) that is found offensive by some member of society would be to allow our government to criminalize all aspects of life. In addition, people perceive things differently. For example, in 1990 the Cincinnati Arts Center was charged with obscenity for displaying photographs taken by a respected artist, Robert Mapplethorpe. Included in the photos were depictions of nude children. The prosecutor contended that the pictures were obscene. A jury did not agree. The Arts Center and its director were acquitted, and many of the jurors commented that the testimony of art experts convinced them that the pictures had serious artistic value and were not obscene.[8]

It is important that the First Amendment be flexible and tolerant of new ideas and methods of expression. Simply because the majority of citizens would not see value in a form of expression does not mean it has no value. If the opposite were true, then expression aimed at particular minority groups could be censored. This is not to say that there is no limit on the freedom of expression. When considering sexually oriented expression, that line is drawn when the expression becomes obscene.[9]

Obscenity has proven to be an elusive concept for the Supreme Court. Through a series of decisions, from 1957 to the present, the Court has attempted to define *obscenity*. The famous quotation from Justice Potter Stewart -"I shall not today attempt further to define [obscenity]; and perhaps I could never succeed in intelligibly doing so. But I know it when I see it."—*Jacobellis v. Ohio*,[10] is a testament to the difficulty in defining such a concept. It also reflects what many people believe—that they may not be able to define obscenity, but they recognize it when they see it.

In *Roth v. United States*,[11] it was held that because it lacks redeeming social importance, obscenity is not protected by the First Amendment. The Court then established a test for determining whether something was obscene, and, as such, not protected by the First Amendment. That test was "whether to the average person, applying contemporary community standards, the dominant theme of the material taken as a whole appeals to prurient interest." In addition, the material had to be "utterly without redeeming social value." Simply because "literature is dismally unpleasant, uncouth, and tawdry is not enough to make it 'obscene.'"[12]

In 1973 the Supreme Court reexamined the *Roth* obscenity test in *Miller v. California*.[13] In *Miller* the Court rejected the requirement that the material be "utterly without redeeming social value" and lowered the standard to lacking "serious literary, artistic, political, or scientific value." The test under *Miller* has three parts:

1. The average person, applying contemporary community standards, would find that the work, taken as a whole, appeals to the prurient interest and
2. the work must depict or describe, in a patently offensive manner, sexual conduct specifically defined by the applicable state law, and
3. the work, when taken as a whole, must lack serious literary, artistic, political, or scientific value.

The *Miller* test makes it easier for states to regulate sexual materials. An "average person" has been equated with a reasonable person, as used in tort law.[14] The material must appeal to "prurient interest." Materials that have a tendency to excite a lustful, "shameful or morbid interest in nudity, sex or excretion" meet the prurient interest element.[15] Material that provokes normal, healthy, sexual desires is not obscene because it does not appeal to prurient interest.[16]

The Court gave examples in *Miller* of "patently offensive" materials that included depictions or descriptions of "ultimate sex acts, normal or perverted, actual or simulated . . . of masturbation, excretory functions, and lewd exhibition of the genitals."

One area where the states have substantially more power to regulate obscenity is when minors are involved. The Court has held that all child pornography is unprotected because of the special need to protect children from exploitation.[17] Similarly, governments may prohibit the distribution and sale of erotic materials to minors, even if such materials are not obscene.[18] Also, in *Osborne v. Ohio*,[19] the Supreme Court held that a person may be convicted for possession of child pornography in the home. This is an exception to the general rule that a person may possess obscene material in the home.

As mentioned in *Miller*, governments may control the time, place, and manner of expression. Accordingly, certain restrictions may be valid that deal with expression in certain places, such as establishments that sell alcohol. (Chapter 13 addresses constitutional defenses to criminal accusations and discusses other time, place, and manner issues.)

One place where the authority of the government to regulate sexually explicit materials is lessened is in homes. In many respects, the law reflects the attitude that a "man's home is his castle" and deserves special protection. Thus, the United States Supreme Court struck down the conviction of a man for possession of obscene materials in his home.[20] However, as previously mentioned, a person is not privileged to possess child pornography in the home.

The Model Penal Code makes it a misdemeanor to knowingly or recklessly do any of the following:[21]

1. Sell, deliver, or provide (or offer to do one of the three) any obscene writing, picture, record, or other obscene representation.
2. Present or perform in an obscene play, dance, or other performance.
3. Publish or exhibit obscene materials.
4. Possess obscene materials for commercial purposes.
5. Sell or otherwise commercially distribute materials represented as obscene.

The Code presumes that anyone who distributes obscene materials in the course of business has done so knowingly or recklessly.

Material is considered obscene under the Code if "considered as a whole, its predominant appeal is to prurient interest, that is, a shameful or morbid interest, in nudity, sex, or excretion, and if in addition it goes substantially beyond customary limits of candor in describing or representing such matter." Note that the Code's definition is similar to the Supreme Court's definition. The Code does add the requirement that the material go beyond "customary limits of candor." The Code makes it an affirmative defense that the obscene material was possessed for governmental, scientific, educational, or other justified causes. It also is not a crime for a person to give such materials to personal associates in noncommercial situations. The Code focuses on punishing commercial dissemination of obscene material.

Obscenity is a complex area of law. Many different criminal prohibitions exist throughout the states and federal government that focus on the sale, distribution, and possession of sexually oriented materials, performance of erotic dance, and public nudity. So long as minors are not involved, the activity is protected unless it is obscene. To determine whether pornography is obscene (hardcore), one must apply the three-part *Miller* test. The states are free to regulate if children are involved, either as participants in the erotic materials (or performance) or as buyers of erotic materials, even if the material is not obscene.

In 2010, the Supreme Court invalidated a federal statute that regulated films that depicted animal cruelty on First Amendment grounds.

Regulating the Internet

> The ability of the World Wide Web to penetrate every home and community across the globe has both positive and negative implications—while it can be an invaluable source of information and means of communication, it can also override community values and standards, subjecting them to whatever more may or may not be found online. . . . [T]he Internet is a challenge to the sovereignty of civilized communities, States, and nations to decide what is appropriate and decent behavior.[22]

According to Internetworldstats.com, Internet use around the world exceeded 2.4 billion users in 2012. The greatest number of users are found in Asia, followed by Europe and North America. However, the greatest penetration is in North America, followed by Oceana/Australia and Europe. Evincing that the Internet is becoming a worldwide phenomenon, the greatest growth in users between 2000 and 2012 was in the Middle East, Africa, Latin America, and Asia. Some commentators believe it is reshaping the political identity of people all over the world. Others believe it is a great social equalizer, tearing down class, education, and economic barriers. Still others are concerned about the negative social impact the Internet may present. Many of the barriers that are being destroyed were in place to protect those individuals who are not capable or mature enough to protect themselves. To protect these people, state legislatures and Congress have acted to regulate the Internet.

Obscene and harmful information has been the primary source of regulation, although commercial transactions, gambling, and other subjects are also regulated. In 1998, 16 million children under the age of 18 were using the Internet. Over 6 million of the children using the Internet were under the age of 13. Simultaneous to the growth in child use of the Internet has been a growth in adult sites. In 1998, it was estimated that there were more than 30,000 adult sites on the Internet and that as much as 70 percent of all Web traffic was unsuitable for children.[23] The first major national attempt to protect children from adult-oriented information on the Internet was the Communications Decency Act of 1996.[24] This statute limited the transmission of "obscene" and "indecent" materials to children. However, this statute was held unconstitutional by the Supreme Court in *Reno v. ACLU* (1997).[25] "The Supreme Court held that the law was overbroad because it prohibited both protected speech (indecent materials) and unprotected speech (obscene materials)." Obscene material, as defined by *Miller* and other cases, may be regulated but indecent material may not. In addition, the Court found that the law was overbroad because it limited access, both adult and juvenile. While it is lawful to limit the access of children to indecent materials (even if not obscene), the law limited the access of everyone because under current technology there is not a way to create zones that children cannot enter. In real space, it is possible to create such zones. Adult bookstores, for example, are zones where children may not enter.

Congress attempted again to protect children from the dangers of the Internet in 1998 through the Child Online Protection Act.[26] This law limited regulation to material that is harmful to minors. The law specifically incorporates the *Miller* test into its definition of what is prohibited. In a narrowly drafted decision, the Supreme Court upheld this law in 2002.[27] The court made it clear, however, that other constitutional issues may need to be examined in an attempt to correct the error of the Communications Decency Act. It remains to be seen if this law is constitutional.

In addition to shielding minors from adult content, Congress and the states have attempted to protect children from being used in sexually explicit films. While there is no question that the use of children can be criminalized, as can the possession of child pornography itself, modern technology has changed the landscape considerably. Today, it is possible to have genuine photos of children and alter them to make it appear as if they are nude or engaged in sexual conduct. Photos of adults can be merged with those of children, and other computer graphic techniques can be employed to create virtual child pornography.

In the Child Pornography Prevention Act of 1996, Congress prohibited not only images of actual children in pornography but also "virtual" images created with the use of computers. As was true of the Communications Decency Act, the Supreme Court found the law to be contrary to First Amendment principles in *Ashcroft v. Free Speech Coalition*.

States also have laws regulating the Internet. Of course, these laws must be crafted to avoid First Amendment and state-law free speech barriers. Additionally, the interstate character of the Internet can create jurisdictional problems for states. In *American Library Association v. Pataki* (S.D. N.Y. 1997),[28] a New York statute that regulated the Internet in much the same manner as the federal Communications Decency Act was invalidated not on First Amendment grounds but on jurisdictional grounds. The federal court that heard the case ruled that New York was without the authority to regulate conduct outside its borders. Congress responded to the *Free Speech Coalition* decision by enacting an amended version of the law that was invalidated. The new statute, known as PROTECT, criminalizes soliciting, distributing, promoting, or presenting images with the belief, or that is intended to cause another to believe, that they are depictions of minors. To avoid the overbreadth problem of *Free Speech Coalition*, PROTECT did not include a ban on all virtual child pornography. The Court found the subtle distinction between banning all virtual child pornography and those depictions intended to convince others that they are actual minors adequate to uphold the law in *United States v. Williams*.[29]

Due to the plethora of cases addressing pornography and obscenity, it is strongly recommended that thorough research be conducted. There is a good chance that precedent with similar facts may be found. Beware, however, that this is an issue that often leaves courts split. Be sure that the opinions you find reflect the law of your jurisdiction.

CRIMES AGAINST THE PUBLIC ORDER

Crimes against the public order are crimes that involve **breaches of the peace**. The phrase *breaches of the peace* refers to all crimes that involve disturbing the tranquility or order of society. Breaches of the peace as a crime has its roots in early English common law. In England, breaches of the peace by individuals were criminal, as were breaches by groups.

Three groups of breaches were recognized; all were punished as misdemeanors. If three or more people met with an intention of causing a disturbance, they committed the common-law offense of unlawful assembly. If the group took some action in an attempt to breach the peace, they were guilty of rout; if they were successful, the crime was riot.

Today, all jurisdictions prohibit breaches of the peace in some form by statute. The names of statutory crimes include disorderly conduct, unlawful assembly, riot, inciting violence, unlawful threat, and vagrancy.

breachs of the peace

■ A vague term for any illegal public disturbance; sometimes refers to the offense known as "disorderly conduct." It is defined and treated differently in different states.

Riot and Unlawful Assembly

Most states now have legislation that prohibits groups of people from meeting with the purpose of committing an unlawful act or committing a lawful act in an unlawful manner. This crime may be named unlawful assembly or riot. A group, or "assembly," is a specified minimum number of people, often three or five. Some jurisdictions continue to recognize the distinctions between unlawful assembly, rout, and riot.

The Model Penal Code recognizes two related crimes: riot and failure to disperse. Both crimes require an assembly of two or more persons who are behaving in a disorderly manner. If the purpose of the assembly is to commit a crime (felony or misdemeanor), to coerce public officials to act or not act, or if a deadly weapon is used, then the crime is riot.[30]

Failure to disperse occurs when a law enforcement officer, or other official, orders the members of a group of three or more to disperse, and someone refuses. The disorderly conduct that the assembly is engaged in must be "likely to cause substantial harm or serious inconvenience, annoyance, or alarm," before an officer may order the group to disperse. This provision is included because the freedoms to associate and assemble are protected by the First Amendment to the U.S. Constitution, and such activity may be regulated only when it poses a threat to person, property, or society.

Most jurisdictions punish these crimes as misdemeanors. However, they may be elevated to felony if committed with a dangerous weapon, if someone is injured as a result of the activity, or if law enforcement officers are obstructed from performing their duties. The Model Penal Code makes rioting a felony of the third degree and failure to disperse a misdemeanor.

Disturbing the Peace

As mentioned, individuals may also commit crimes against the public order. Disturbing the peace is such a crime. This crime is also known as disorderly conduct, threat, excessive noise, and affray. In essence, any time the public order or tranquility is unreasonably interrupted by an individual, disturbance of the peace has occurred. States may have one law that encompasses all such acts or separate statutes for each.

Disturbances may occur in hundreds of forms. One may disturb the peace by making loud noises in a residential area at midnight, by attempting to cause fights with others, or by encouraging others to engage in similar conduct. Statutes often also prohibit indecent language and gestures.

These statutes are often broadly worded and are vague. As such, they are often attacked as being unconstitutional. The defenses of overbreadth and vagueness are discussed in Chapter 13 on defenses and are not covered here. One defense that will be examined is the First Amendment right to free speech and its relationship to offensive words and gestures.

As you have learned, the First Amendment protects all forms of expression. This protection prohibits government from making expression criminal. However, exceptions to the First Amendment have been created. Words that have a likelihood of causing a riot are such an exception. That is, even though the words are expression, they may be punished. The reason is obvious: riots lead to property damage, personal injuries, and sometimes death. As such, the interest of the government to control such behavior outweighs the First Amendment interest.

fighting words

■ Speech that is not protected by the First Amendment to the U.S. Constitution because it is likely to cause violence by the person to whom the words are spoken.

The **fighting words** doctrine is another exception. The Supreme Court has defined *fighting words* as those that inflict injury, tend to incite an immediate breach of the peace, or by their nature will cause a violent reaction by a person who hears them.[31] Laws that regulate speech that may be regulated, such as fighting words, must be drafted narrowly; that is, only the conduct intended must be prohibited. If a law is drawn so broadly that both fighting words and legitimate speech are criminalized, it is unconstitutional and void.

The defendant in the *Witucki* case was convicted of disorderly conduct. The court found that his speech was unprotected because he used fighting words.

Incitement/Advocacy of Unlawful Conduct

Whenever one person, acting independently, encourages another to commit an unlawful act or intends to cause a riot, the crimes of incitement of unlawful behavior or incitement of riot may be charged. Unlike riot, which requires a group, one person may commit this crime. Unlike disturbing the peace, it may be committed in a peaceful manner.

However, because the First Amendment applies, such statutes must be narrowly drawn. In fact, only speech that creates a **clear and present danger** may be controlled. The United States Supreme Court has said that "incitement of imminent lawless action" may be regulated.[32] Anything less may not be regulated. Hence, merely advocating unlawful conduct in the abstract is protected. Advocating future unlawful conduct is also protected, as it poses no imminent threat.

Threats

Finally, in the speech arena, threats are addressed. Threat statutes may make threatening individuals, groups, or even property, criminal. Threats to harm people are similar to assaults. However, threat is broader, as it often protects property and the people at large. The purpose of threat statutes is to preserve public order, and the purpose of assault statutes is to protect individuals.

For example, if a defendant were to call in a bomb threat to a public office, there would be no assault, but there is a threat. A person may be guilty of threat by making the prohibited statements, even if untrue. So, if a defendant makes a bomb threat, but has placed no bomb in the building, a crime has been committed. Threats are misdemeanors in most jurisdictions and are punished less severely than assaults. In the *Thomas* case, the defendant was convicted under the Kentucky threat statute.

Vagrancy and Panhandling

Vagrancy, as a criminal law issue, has received considerable attention. Most states and municipalities have statutes that forbid vagrancy. At common law, a *vagrant* was one who wandered from place to place with no means of support, except the charity of others. At one time, in early English law, vagrancy applied to disorderly persons, rogues (a dishonest wanderer), and vagabonds (a homeless person with no means of support).

Beginning in the 1880s, it was common in the United States for statutes to prohibit a wide range of behavior as vagrancy. These statutes were drafted broadly to allow law enforcement officers considerable discretion in their enforcement. This discretion was used to control the "undesirables" of society. Many statutes made the status of being homeless, a gambler, and a drug addict a crime.

Today, states may not make personal status, such as drug addiction or alcoholism, a crime. The United States held that doing so violates the Eighth Amendment's prohibition of cruel and unusual punishment.[33] However, until 1972, people found undesirable by the police could be arrested under broadly worded vagrancy statutes for "wandering," or walking around a city, because this was an act, not a status. This situation ended in 1972 when the United States Supreme Court handed down *Papachristou v. City of Jacksonville*, 405 U.S. 156 (1972). The Court announced in that case that vagrancy statutes that prohibit walking around, frequenting liquor stores, being supported by one's wife, and similar behavior, to be "too precarious for a rule of law" and violative of the Due Process and Cruel and Unusual Clauses of the Constitution.

clear and present danger

■ A test of whether or not speech may be restricted or punished. It may be if it will probably lead to violence soon or if it threatens a serious, immediate weakening of national safety and security.

The result of *Papachristou* has been more narrowly drawn vagrancy statutes. Today such laws focus on more particularized behavior, and in many instances a mens rea element has been added. This addition prevents simple acts, such as walking at night, from being criminal. For example, a vagrancy law may prohibit "loitering or standing around with an intent to gamble," or "loitering or standing in a transportation facility [e.g., bus station] with the intent of soliciting charity."

In recent years panhandling (begging) has increasingly become a problem for most cities. Panhandlers often choose to congregate in and near public transportation egresses and ingresses, because of the large number of people who use such facilities. Because panhandlers are sometimes aggressive and intimidating to patrons of such facilities, some jurisdictions have chosen to prohibit begging at public transportation sites.

As the number of homeless persons grows in the United States, so will the problems associated with vagrancy and panhandling. Examine statutes and ordinances that prohibit such activities with an awareness that they must be drawn carefully to avoid a First Amendment speech problem. Also be aware that other constitutional provisions may be implicated, such as the First Amendment's freedom of association and the Due Process and Equal Protection Clauses of the Fifth and Fourteenth Amendments.

Crimes Involving Firearms

A discussion of the regulation of firearms properly begins with the Second Amendment to the U.S. Constitution, which reads:

> A well regulated Militia, being necessary to the security of a free State, the right of the people to keep and bear Arms, shall not be infringed.

Despite the tireless efforts of firearms lobbyists to convince the nation that the Second Amendment was intended to protect the individual's right to possess arms, the Supreme Court of the United States as well as nearly all lower courts that have heard this issue have concluded that the Amendment is intended to preserve a collective right, the right to have a well-regulated militia. The second half of the clause, to keep and bear arms, is interpreted as conjunctive with the first half of the clause, which provides for a well-regulated militia.

In a 1939 Supreme Court decision, *United States v. Miller*,[34] a defendant who had been charged under a federal law prohibiting possession of short-barreled shotguns and rifles challenged the law as violating his Second Amendment right to possess a firearm. The Court stated:

> The Constitution as originally adopted granted to the Congress power—"To provide for calling forth the Militia to execute the Laws of the Union, suppress Insurrections and repel Invasions; To provide for organizing, arming, and disciplining, the Militia, and for governing such Part of them as may be employed in the Service of the United States, reserving to the States respectively, the Appointment of the Officers, and the Authority of training the Militia according to the discipline prescribed by Congress." U.S.C.A. Const. art. § 8. With obvious purpose to assure the continuation and render possible the effectiveness of such forces the declaration and guarantee of the Second Amendment were made. It must be interpreted and applied with that end in view.

The Militia which the States were expected to maintain and train is set in contrast with Troops which they were forbidden to keep without the consent of Congress. The sentiment of the time strongly disfavored standing armies; the common view was that adequate defense of country and laws could be secured through the Militia—civilians primarily, soldiers on occasion.

The signification attributed to the term Militia appears from the debates in the Convention, the history and legislation of Colonies and States, and the writings of approved commentators. These show plainly enough that the Militia comprised all males physically capable of acting in concert for the common defense. 'A body of citizens enrolled for military discipline.' And further, that ordinarily when called for service these men were expected to appear bearing arms supplied by themselves and of the kind in common use at the time.

The Supreme Court affirmed this interpretation of the Second Amendment in the 1980 case *United States v. Lewis*.[35] The Court did not pass on the question if the Second Amendment establishes an individual right, as opposed to connecting the right to arms to the militia right, again until 2008 when it invalidated a Washington, D.C., ordinance forbidding the possession of handguns in the home in *District of Columbia v. Heller*, 554 U.S. The Court explicitly found an independent, individual right to possess arms under the Second Amendment for the first time.

However, Washington, D.C., is federal territory. As such, *Heller* did not address whether the Second Amendment's right to possess firearms applies against the states. Indeed, several cases from the late 1800s stood for the principle that the Second Amendment, whatever its meaning, only limited federal authority. The Supreme Court accepted *certiorari* in a case involving state regulation of arms only a year following the *Heller* decision and issued a decision in 2010.

Possession, Sale, and Transfer Laws

McDonald and *Heller* apply to possession of handguns in the home. There is nothing in those decisions to limit the authority of government to require the registration of firearms, background checks prior to firearms purchases, or to more thoroughly regulate larger and more dangerous firearms, or the possession of any firearm outside of the home. One of the most common forms of weapons regulation is possession. Both federal and state laws prohibit a variety of possession-related offenses. These include improper possession of a weapon that is otherwise permitted, e.g., concealed possession; possession of altogether prohibited weapons, e.g., machine guns; and possession by certain classes of persons, e.g., possession by ex-felons, aliens, fugitives, mental incompetents, individuals who were dishonorably discharged from the military, those under stalking-related court orders, and individuals convicted of misdemeanor domestic violence. The possession of firearms is also prohibited in certain areas designated by statute. Near schools, in public buildings, in airports, in national and state parks, and on airplanes are examples.

One of the most significant federal firearms statutes is the National Firearms Act.[36] Enacted in reaction to the organized crime problem of the 1930s, this law prohibited the sale and possession of automatic weapons (machine guns). Another important federal law is the Gun Control Act of 1968. Among its many provisions are a prohibition of mail order guns and the prohibition of the possession, transfer, or receipt of firearms by felons, aliens, and certain other persons. Many of the limitations of the Gun Control Act were repealed or reduced in the Firearm Owners Protection Act of 1986,[37] such as lifting the ban on the interstate sales of long guns and the use of the U.S. Post Office mail to ship ammunition. The federal Brady Handgun Violence Prevention Act of 1993—named for President Ronald Reagan's White House Press Secretary James Brady, who was shot during an attempted assassination of the president—requires all federally licensed gun dealers to conduct background checks of firearms purchasers to ensure that purchasers do not fall into one of the categories of ineligible buyers under the Gun Control Act of 1968. Records checks are now being implemented through the National Instant Background Check System (NICS). Another federal statute, the Violent Crime Control and Law Enforcement Act of 1994, prohibits the sale of semiautomatic weapons and large ammunition magazines. Additionally, the Bureau of Alcohol, Tobacco, Firearms and Explosives, the federal agency charged with enforcing federal gun laws, has promulgated a large set of regulations interpreting and further regulating firearms.

Firearms Use Laws

Many jurisdictions forbid the discharge of firearms in urban areas, absent good cause. Arizona's unlawful discharge statute (A.R.S. § 13-3107) reads:

(A) A person who with criminal negligence discharges a firearm within or into the limits of any municipality is guilty of a class 6 felony. . . .

(C) This section does not apply if the firearm is discharged:

(1) As allowed pursuant to the provisions of Chapter 9 of this title.
(2) On a properly supervised range.
(3) In an area recommended as a hunting area by the Arizona game and fish department, approved and posted as required by the chief of police, but any such area may be closed when deemed unsafe by the chief of police or the director of the game and fish department.
(4) For the control of nuisance wildlife by permit from the Arizona game and fish department or the U.S. fish and wildlife service.
(5) By special permit of the chief of police of the municipality.
(6) As required by an animal control officer in the performance of duties as specified in section 9-499.04.
(7) Using blanks.
(8) More than one mile from any occupied structure as defined in section 13-3101.
(9) In self-defense or defense of another person against an animal attack if a reasonable person would believe that deadly physical force against the animal is immediately necessary and reasonable under the circumstances to protect oneself or the other person.

Other law forbids the use of certain weapons for hunting and fishing. For example, shotguns may not be permitted in the hunting of certain game. Some statues prohibit "aiming," "pointing," and otherwise threatening people with firearms.

The use of a weapon in the commission of a crime is sometimes a separate crime from the underlying offense. Nearly all jurisdictions require or permit enhancement of sentences for crimes committed while in possession of a firearm.

Registration and Licensing

In addition to background checks, many states require guns to be registered. In some instances, licenses must be obtained to carry or use weapons.

The National Firearms Act[38] requires national registration of all firearms manufactured or transferred in the United States, and it prohibits the sale of automatic weapons (machine guns).

Drug and Alcohol Crimes

Crimes that involve the use of narcotics and alcohol may be classified in many ways. In one sense, such activity offends many people in society and appears to be an offense against the public morality. Whenever a pimp uses a young woman's drug addiction to induce her to become involved in prostitution, it appears to be a crime against an individual. In the states, drug and alcohol crimes are universally regulated, although definitions and punishments vary considerably.

Drug and alcohol crimes are included in this section because of their impact on the order of society. Alcohol-related driving accidents are the cause of many fatalities. Drug addiction often is the cause of other crimes, such as theft, assaults, and prostitution. Police report that a number of domestic problems are caused by alcohol and drugs and that much of the violence directed toward law enforcement officers is drug related. Large cities, such as Detroit and Washington, D.C., have experienced a virtual drug boom, which has led to increased assaults, batteries, and drug-related homicides. Many addicts, desperate for a "fix," steal for drug money.

Drug and alcohol use are also expensive. Corporate America has recently awakened to the expenses associated with employee drug use. Employees who use drugs have high absenteeism and low productivity. Decreased performance caused by drug use can be costly, in both human and dollar terms. This is true especially in positions that require great concentration or pose risks to others, such as that of commercial pilots. In addition to business expenses, the high cost of rehabilitation can disable a family financially, and the price of drug-abuse detection and prosecution is high.

Alcohol Crimes

Let it not be mistaken, alcohol is a drug. However, the law treats alcohol differently than it does other drugs. Alcohol may be legally possessed, consumed, and sold, subject only to a few restrictions. Narcotics, on the other hand, are significantly restricted. Their sale, possession, and consumption are limited to specific instances, such as for medical use. The federal government, as well as every state, has statutes that spell out what drugs are regulated.

There are many alcohol-related crimes. Public drunkenness laws make it criminal for a person to be intoxicated in a public place. This crime is a minor misdemeanor and rarely prosecuted, as many law enforcement agencies have a policy of allowing such persons to "sleep it off" and then releasing them.

All states have a minimum age requirement for the sale or consumption of alcohol. Those below the minimum age are minors. Any minor who purchases or consumes alcohol is violating the law. Additionally, any adult who knowingly provides alcohol to a minor is also guilty of a crime, commonly known as contributing to the delinquency of a minor.

Merchants holding liquor licenses may be subject to criminal penalties for not complying with liquor laws, such as selling alcohol on holidays, Sundays, or election day, as well as for selling alcohol to minors. A merchant who violates liquor laws may also suffer the civil penalty of revocation of liquor license.

Alcohol and automobiles have proven to be a deadly and expensive combination. All states have laws that criminalize driving while under the influence of alcohol or drugs. Driving while under the influence of alcohol or drugs, driving while intoxicated, and driving with an unlawful blood-alcohol level are the names of these crimes.

These statutes are generally of two genres. One type of law generally prohibits the operation of a motor vehicle while under the influence of any drug, including alcohol. To prove this charge, the quantity of the drug or alcohol in the defendant's system is not at issue; the defendant's ability to operate the vehicle safely is. In such cases, field sobriety tests are often required of the suspect. These are tests that the suspect usually performs at the location where the police made the stop. Coordination, spatial relations, and other driving-related skills are tested by field sobriety tests.

The second type of law prohibits driving a motor vehicle any time a person's blood-alcohol level is above a stated amount. The states vary in the quantity required, although 8 hundredths of a percent (0.08) and 10 hundredths of a percent (0.10) are common. The effect of these laws is that an irrebuttable presumption is created. The law presumes that anyone with the stated blood-alcohol level or above cannot safely operate a motor vehicle. Under such statutes, evidence that a person can safely operate a motor vehicle with a blood-alcohol level greater than the maximum allowed is not permitted.

In recent years drunk driving has received considerable public and legislative attention. The result has been stricter laws and greater punishment for offenders. The once-common police practice of driving drunk drivers home is virtually nonexistent today.

First offenses are usually misdemeanors. Second or third offenses are felonies. In many jurisdictions, there has been a move toward alcohol treatment rather than incarceration. This often involves house arrest, alcohol treatment, and defensive driving education. Also, while in these programs, convicted persons are commonly required to submit to periodic blood or urine screening.

For first-time offenders, these programs have many advantages over prison. First, the focus is on curing the alcohol problem. If successful, the possibility of repetition is eliminated. Second, convicted persons are often permitted to continue to work and maintain family relationships. Finally, the cost of administration of alcohol programs is lower than the cost of incarceration. The value of such programs for repeat offenders is questionable, and in many jurisdictions jail time is required as early as a second conviction.

Drug Crimes

Unlike possession of alcohol, possession of other drugs is a crime. Every state and the federal government has enacted some variation of the Uniform Controlled Substance Act, a model act (similar to the Model Penal Code) drafted by the Commissioners on Uniform Laws. These statutes establish schedules of drugs that categorize drugs based on their danger, potential for abuse, and medical benefits. These factors then determine a drug's allowed usage. For example, one schedule exists for drugs that may not be used under any condition, and another schedule permits use for medical and research purposes only. There are three basic drug crimes: possession, sales/distribution, and use.

Possession of prohibited drugs is a crime. Of course, actual possession is sufficient actus reus, but some jurisdictions also make constructive possession criminal. Constructive possession permits conviction of those people who exercise dominion and control over property where the illegal drug is located, even though the person has no "actual physical possession" of the prohibited narcotic. However, the Model Penal Code[39] and most jurisdictions require knowledge that the drug was present before culpability is imposed. As such, if a guest stays in Robert's home, Robert is not criminally liable for any drugs the guest has stowed away, unless Robert is aware of their presence. Once Robert becomes aware, he must see that the drugs are removed within a reasonable time or risk a possession charge.

First-time conviction of possession, if the quantity is small, is a misdemeanor and normally results in probation. In many states, if a person pleads guilty, submits to a term of probation, and successfully completes the probation, then no adjudication of guilt is entered; so, no record of conviction exists. Probation terms usually include drug counseling, periodic drug testing, and no other arrests during the period. This type of procedure is known as *deferred sentencing or suspended imposition of sentence.* See Chapter 7 for a discussion of sentencing.

The sale or distribution of prohibited drugs is the second primary drug offense. Generally, it is punished more severely than possession. Not only are sales prohibited, but any "delivery" or "distribution" of drugs is also illegal. "Possession with an intent to deliver or sell" is similar to simple possession, except a mens rea of intending to sell must be proven. Possession with an intent to sell or deliver is punished more severely than possession; often, such possession is punished equally with actual sale or delivery.

The quantity of the drug involved affects the level of punishment for both possession and sale/distribution offenses. Other factors, such as selling to minors, may aggravate the sentence.

Unauthorized use of a controlled substance is also a crime. The mens rea is knowing use. So, if a person takes a pill containing a controlled substance that someone—who represented it to be an aspirin—gives him or her, there is no crime. Of course, the taking must be voluntary. If a person is forced down and injected with an illegal drug, he or she has committed no crime.

Recall from the earlier discussion of actus reus that addiction to controlled substances may not be made criminal. The United States Supreme Court has held that criminalizing a person's status as an addict is cruel and unusual punishment, as prohibited by the Eighth Amendment to the U.S. Constitution.[40] It is permitted, however, to punish a person for the act of taking a controlled substance.

RICO and CCE

You have already learned that the Racketeer Influenced and Corrupt Organizations Act (RICO) was enacted to fight organized crime in all its forms. Another federal statute, Continuing Criminal Enterprise (CCE),[41] was enacted specifically to combat drug trafficking. The statute is aimed at prosecuting the people at the top of the drug-dealing and smuggling pyramid, and, accordingly, it has become known as the "Drug Kingpin statute."

A person engages in a criminal enterprise if (1) he is an administrator, organizer, or other leader (2) of a group of five or more people (3) who are involved in a series of drug violations. A *series* of violations means three or more drug convictions.[42]

Conviction of CCE results in stern punishment. A general violation receives 20 years to life in prison. Second convictions carry 30 years to life. If a person is determined to be a "principal leader," the amount of drugs involved was enormous, or the enterprise made $10 million or more in one year from drugs, then life imprisonment is mandatory. Fines may also be imposed. Also, the statute provides for imprisonment or death when murder results from the enterprise.[43]

Finally, the Comprehensive Forfeiture Act of 1984[44] applies to both RICO and CCE violations. This statute permits the government to seize property and money that is used in the commission of the crimes and that is a product of the crimes. So, if a drug dealer uses a boat to smuggle drugs, the boat can be seized, even though it may have been purchased with "honest" money. Any items acquired with drug money may be seized, as can bank accounts and trusts.

Possession of Drug Paraphernalia

Another tool in the government's arsenal against drug use are laws that prohibit the sale, use, and possession of drug paraphernalia. These laws are often aimed at retailers who sell the devices that are used to take drugs. Needles, roach clips, and specialized pipes are examples of the type of paraphernalia that are proscribed.

These laws have been challenged on many fronts. One challenge asserts that such laws are vague because they do not adequately describe what is proscribed. In addition, it has been asserted that these laws are overly broad because they include devices that may be used for both legitimate and illegal purposes.[45] These issues were considered by the United States Supreme Court in the 1994 case, *Posters 'N' Things, Ltd. v. United States*.[46] In this case the Court held that a law proscribing items "primarily intended" or "designed for" drug use was neither too vague nor overly broad and, accordingly, found it constitutional.

CRIMES AGAINST THE ADMINISTRATION OF GOVERNMENT

Perjury

perjury

■ Lying while under oath, especially in a court proceeding. It is a crime.

Perjury was a crime at common law and continues to be prohibited by statute in all states.

The basic elements of perjury are (1) the making of a (2) false statement (3) with knowledge that it is false (4) while under oath. To gain a conviction, the prosecution has the tough burden of proving the mens rea: that the person who made the statement knew that it was false. As with other crimes, juries are permitted to infer a defendant's knowledge from surrounding facts.

In addition, the statement must be made while under oath. Be aware that this requirement includes far more than testifying in court. Most laws cover all statements made before a person authorized to administer oaths. Therefore, perjury laws apply to people who sign affidavits before notary publics and appear as witnesses before a court reporter (e.g., for deposition), a grand jury, and all others who have the authority to administer oaths. For those individuals who have a religious objection to "swearing," the law permits an affirmation. This is simply an acknowledgment by the witness that the testimony he or she renders is truthful. The law treats an affirmation in the same manner as it does an oath.

Some jurisdictions require that the false statement be "material," or important to the matter. This requirement prevents prosecutions for trivial matters. Some jurisdictions have defined *materiality* as any matter that may affect the outcome of a case. If a statement is not material, even if untrue, then a perjury conviction is not permitted.

A related crime is **subornation of perjury**. This crime occurs when one convinces or procures another to commit perjury. One who commits subornation is treated as a perjurer for the purpose of sentencing.

subornation of perjury
■ The crime of asking or forcing another person to lie under oath.

In addition to being a crime in every state, perjury has been made criminal by statute in the United States. 18 U.S.C. § 1621 reads:

> Whoever (1) having taken an oath before a competent tribunal, officer, or person, in any case in which a law of the United States authorizes an oath to be administered, that he will testify, declare, depose, or certify truly . . . is true, willfully and contrary to such oath states or subscribes any material matter which he does not believe to be true. . . .

Of course, truth is a complete defense to a charge of perjury. What is truthful is not always easy to determine, and in most questionable cases prosecutors choose not to pursue the matter. This decision is largely due to the mens rea element.

Bribery

As is true of perjury, **bribery** was a crime at English common law. Actually, bribery was initially a violation of biblical law, because it was wrong to attempt to influence judges, who were considered to be God's earthly representatives. Eventually, the crime was recognized by the courts of England.

bribery
■ The offering, giving, receiving, or soliciting of anything of value in order to influence the actions of a public official.

Today, bribery is a statutory crime in the states and in the United States. The essential elements of the crime are (1) soliciting or accepting (2) anything of value (3) with the purpose of (4) violating a duty or trust. Two primary forms of bribery are that of a public official and commercial bribery.

As mentioned, bribery began as a prohibition of influencing a judge. The crime was eventually extended to include bribery of all public officials and public servants. Statutes make it bribery to be the one accepting or giving the "thing of value." Hence, if a corporate official gives a public official money in exchange for awarding a contract to the company, both the corporate officer and the public official have committed bribery.

Most bribery statutes declare that unsuccessful offers are bribes. Thus, if the public official rejects the offer of the corporate officer, there is still a bribery violation. The offer need not be of money in exchange for a favor; anything of value is sufficient. Automobiles, tickets to a St. Louis Cardinals game, and a promise of sexual favors all satisfy this requirement.

The offer must be made to a *public official or servant*. Both terms are defined broadly. Further, the offeror must be seeking to influence the official in a matter over which the official has authority. Most courts have held that whether the officer actually had the authority to carry out the requested act is not dispositive; the issue is whether the offeror believes that the official possesses the authority. Awarding of government contracts, setting favorable tax assessments, and overlooking civil and criminal violations are examples of corrupt acts.

The offer alone makes the offeror guilty of bribery. For the public official to be convicted, there must be an acceptance. This usually means that the official does the requested act; however, it is widely held that an acceptance is all that is necessary to support a conviction.

Bribery has been extended beyond the public affairs realm to commercial life. Whenever a person who is engaged in business activities breaches a duty or trust owed to someone (or something, such as a business organization) in exchange for something of value, bribery has been committed.

The Model Penal Code declares that commercial bribery is a misdemeanor. The Code applies to people in specific positions, such as lawyers, accountants, trustees, and officers of corporations.[47] Anyone who makes an offer to someone in one of these positions to violate the trust or duty created by the position is guilty of bribery. Of course, any person holding such a position who accepts such an offer is also guilty of bribery. The Code specifically states that any person who holds himself or herself out to the public to be in the business of appraising the value of services or commodities is guilty of bribery if he or she accepts a benefit to influence the decision or appraisal. Knowing that one is violating the trust is the mens rea under the Code.

If a seller for the Widgcom Company were to offer the purchasing agent of Retailers, Inc., money in exchange for receiving the contract to supply Retailers with Widgets for the next year, commercial bribery has occurred. A corporate officer who accepts free personal air travel in exchange for buying all corporate airline tickets from the same airline has committed bribery.

Finally, note that there are statutes that prohibit "throwing" athletic contests for pay. That is, any player, coach, owner, or official who accepts a benefit to cause one participant to win or lose commits bribery. These laws often apply to both professional and amateur sports.

Tax Crimes

You have likely heard the quip, "In life, only two things are certain, death and taxes." Tax revenues are the lifeblood of government. In the United States, people are taxed at the federal, state, and local levels (county, municipal, and school district taxes). These taxes come in many forms, including income tax, gift and estate tax, sales tax, and excise taxes. Tax laws apply to individuals, estates, and business entities.

All taxing authorities have statutes that impose both civil and criminal penalties for violation of tax laws. Common violations of tax laws are tax evasion, failing to file a required tax return, filing a fraudulent return, and unlawful disclosure of tax information. These are not the only crimes related to taxes, however, as shown by the applicable federal statutes, which embody 16 tax-related crimes.[48]

Tax evasion involves paying less tax than required or underreporting one's income with the intent of paying less tax. The federal statute covering tax evasion reads:

26 U.S.C. § 7201 Attempt to evade or defeat tax

Any person who willfully attempts in any manner to evade or defeat any tax imposed by this title or the payment thereof shall, in addition to other penalties provided by law, be guilty of a felony and, upon conviction thereof, shall be fined not more than $100,000 ($500,000 in the case of a corporation), or imprisoned not more than 5 years, or both, together with the costs of prosecution.

Tax fraud, a crime closely related to evasion, involves using fraud or false statements to avoid a tax obligation. This crime may occur in many ways, including falsifying statements that are provided to a revenue agency, such as fraudulent receipts used for deductions. Filing false tax returns is also a form of tax fraud.

Failure to file a required tax return is also criminal. The relevant federal statute reads:

26 U.S.C. § 7203 Willful failure to file return, supply information, or pay tax

Any person required under this title to pay any estimated tax or tax, or required by this title or by regulations made under authority thereof to make a return, keep any records, or supply any information, who willfully fails to pay such estimated tax or tax, make such return, keep such records, or supply such information . . . [shall] be guilty of a misdemeanor and, upon conviction thereof, shall be fined not more than $25,000 ($100,000 in the case of a corporation), or imprisoned not more than 1 year, or both, together with the costs of prosecution.

Note that § 7203 applies to anyone who is required to file a tax return, pay a tax, or supply information. Therefore, this provision can be the basis of a prosecution of an employer who pays his or her employees in cash and makes no report to the Internal Revenue Service. Likewise, although some entities are not taxed, such as partnerships, they are required to file informational returns, and failure to do so violates this provision.

Tax evasion, filing fraudulent tax returns, and the unauthorized disclosure of information are crimes of commission. That is, an affirmative act is required to commit these crimes.

tax evasion
■ The deliberate nonpayment or underpayment of taxes that are legally due. Criminal tax evasion has higher fines than civil fraud and the possibility of a prison sentence upon the showing of "willfulness."

tax fraud
■ The deliberate nonpayment or underpayment of taxes that are legally due.

Failing to file a required return, or other information, is an act of omission. Proving such crimes requires not proof of an illegal act but that a required act was not taken. The quoted statutes require willful violations. Negligence in preparing a tax return or in filing the return is not criminal. However, such errors may lead to civil penalties.

The willfulness requirement was considered by the Supreme Court in *Cheek v. United States*.

Tax laws require the disclosure of all income and profits. This includes income from illegal sources. Gamblers are required to report their winnings, prostitutes their income, and drug dealers the profits derived from their sales. Failure to report income from illegal acts is the same as failure to report legally earned income. Because requiring people to report income from illegal activities raises a self-incrimination problem, tax laws require that all information obtained be kept confidential. Tax officials are not permitted to disclose such information to law enforcement authorities, and to do so is *unlawful disclosure*. The privilege against self-incrimination is discussed more thoroughly in Chapter 13.

Obstruction of Justice

Obstruction of justice refers to any number of unlawful acts. As a general proposition, any act that interferes with the performance of a public official's duties obstructs justice. However, the crime is most commonly associated with law enforcement and judicial officials.

The types of acts that fall under such statutes include tampering with witnesses or jurors, interfering with police officers, destroying evidence needed for a court proceeding, and intentionally giving false information to a prosecutor in an effort to hinder a prosecutorial effort. However, obstruction statutes are drafted broadly, thereby permitting creative prosecutions. For example, it is common for women who are physically abused by their husbands to contact the police during a violent episode and demand the husband's arrest, usually in an effort to get the man out of the house. Once the husband is arrested, many women lose interest in prosecuting and often refuse to testify against their husbands in court. In such a case, a prosecutor could charge the wife with obstruction of justice because of her refusal to testify.

Resisting arrest is a similar crime. At common law, one could resist an unlawful arrest. Although a few jurisdictions have retained this rule, this is not presently the law in most jurisdictions. Most states have followed the Model Penal Code approach, which prohibits even moderate resistance to any arrest.[49] It is a wise rule, considering the remedies that are available if a police officer makes an unlawful arrest. If the arrest is unlawful, but in good faith, the arrestee will be released either at the police station or after the first judicial hearing. If the arrest was unlawful and made maliciously, the arrestee not only will be released but also has a civil cause of action for false imprisonment and violation of civil rights.

Contempt

Failure to comply with a court order is contemptuous, as is taking any act with the purpose of undermining a court's authority or intending to interfere with its administration and process. Although statutes provide for contempt, it is widely accepted that the contempt power is inherent.

Contempt is broken down into direct and indirect criminal contempt and direct and indirect civil contempt. *Direct contempt* refers to acts that occur in the presence of the judge. Although contempt usually occurs in the courtroom, the judges' chambers and office area are included. *Indirect contempt* refers to actions taken outside the presence of a court but that are violative of a court order.

Criminal contempt is levied to punish a person for violating a court order. Civil contempt, in contrast, does not have punishment as its purpose. It is intended to coerce a person into complying with a court order. For example, if Mary refuses to testify at a trial despite an order to testify, the judge may order her confined until she complies. Once she testifies, she is free. It is often said that civil contemnors hold the keys to their jail cells, whereas criminal contemnors do not. In theory, one who has been held in civil contempt can be punished for criminal contempt after complying with the court order. In practice this punishment seldom occurs, presumably because judges and prosecutors feel that the civil punishment imposed is adequate.

The contempt power is significant. Indirect criminal contemnors are entitled to all the protections of other criminal defendants, such as a right to a trial, assistance of counsel, and proof beyond a reasonable doubt. Direct criminal contemnors have no such rights, as the act took place in the presence of a judge. However, any sentence imposed may be appealed and reviewed for fairness.

Civil contemnors have few rights. They do not possess the rights of those accused of crimes, because civil contempt is not considered a criminal action. In most instances they enjoy no right to appeal. A civil contemnor holds his or her own key; he or she must comply with the court's order. Of course, if an appellate court determines that the underlying order is unlawful, the civil contemnor is released. However, the individual may be charged with criminal contempt for failure to comply with the order before it was held unlawful by an appellate court. The fact that a court order may be nullified at some future date does not justify noncompliance. Court orders must be obeyed to assure the orderly administration of justice.

Legislatures also have the power to cite for contempt. Legislatures, usually through committees, conduct hearings and other proceedings when considering bills and amendments to statutes. The contempt power serves the same function for legislatures that it does for courts. It furthers the orderly performance of legislative duties. Refusal to testify before a legislative body (usually a committee) or to produce documents or other items, and disruption of a proceeding are examples of legislative contempt. Persons charged with legislative contempt possess the same rights as defendants charged with other crimes. In most instances, legislative bodies refer contempt cases to prosecutors, rather than adjudicating such cases themselves.

contempt

■ A willful disobeying of a judge's command or official court order. Contempt can be *direct* (within the judge's notice) or *indirect* (outside the court and punishable only after proved to the judge). It can also be *civil contempt* (disobeying a court order in favor of an opponent) or *criminal contempt*.

CRIMES AGAINST SOVEREIGNTY AND SECURITY

In the last section you read about crimes that interfere with public administration. Those crimes may—but not necessarily—be intended to destroy the government or to make a political statement. This section examines the very serious crimes of treason, sedition, espionage, and terrorism.

Treason

The United States has had law dealing with treason since its earliest years. The only crime mentioned in the Constitution is treason. Article III, section 3 reads:

> Clause 1: Treason against the United States, shall consist only in levying War against them, or in adhering to their Enemies, giving them Aid and Comfort. No Person shall be convicted of Treason unless on the Testimony of two Witnesses to the same overt Act, or on Confession in open Court.
>
> Clause 2: The Congress shall have Power to declare the Punishment of Treason, but no Attainder of Treason shall work Corruption of Blood, or Forfeiture except during the Life of the Person attainted.

Congress implemented Clause 1,[50] and the resulting elements of the offense are as follows:

1. A person who owes an allegiance to the United States,
2. *Levies* war or *Adheres* to an enemy of the United States and
3. commits an overt act and
4. possesses treasonable intent.

Interestingly, one does not have to be a citizen of the United States to commit treason. Persons living in the United States owe allegiance to the nation and may be charged with treason. Generally, speech is not an overt act, except when state secrets are revealed to an enemy. To satisfy the mens rea requirement, one must intend to betray the United States. Clause two requires two witnesses to the treasonous act. The two witnesses may testify to separate acts, so long as they support the same act of treason.

Sedition and Espionage

Sedition has been recognized as a crime since the first days of the Constitution. The Alien and Seditions Acts of the late eighteenth century made it a crime to write false, scandalous, or malicious stories about the government; increased the residency period required to become a citizen; and increased the president's authority to deport dangerous aliens.

The provisions of the sedition laws prohibiting free speech were controversial, and many prominent Americans opposed them—including Thomas Jefferson and James Madison. After the law expired by its own sunset provision, Congress reimbursed the paid fines for all those who had been convicted under its authority.[51]

Today there are several sedition laws, including a prohibition of seditious conspiracies to overthrow the government;[52] the Logan Act, which prohibits individuals from corresponding with foreign governments in relation to disputes such governments may have with the United States; and a prohibition of recruiting members of the U.S. armed forces to act against the United States.[53]

Many forms of espionage and subversive activities are made criminal in the federal statutes.[54] Most of these require either an intention or reason to believe the United States will be injured and an overt act in furtherance of the crime.

Terrorism

Prior to September 11, 2001, there were many terrorism statutes. Post-9/11, there are many more. This section examines a few of the federal statutes defining terrorism crimes. Other issues, such as the rights of detainees in the War on Terror and electronic eavesdropping in a post-9/11 environment, are discussed later in this book.

Recent acts of terrorism, however, have been the catalyst to new terrorism and sedition laws. The Foreign Intelligence Surveillance Act of 1978 (FISA) delegated substantial authority to federal law enforcement officials. FISA provided for secret court orders authorizing surveillance (without probable cause) of non-U.S. persons. The objective of such orders is not to build cases for criminal prosecution, but to gather foreign intelligence.

In 1995 Timothy McVeigh, with accomplices, bombed the federal building in Oklahoma City, Oklahoma, killing 167 people, including several children, and injuring over 600 others.[55] It would be the worst act of terror, in terms of loss of life, in modern United States until the attacks of September 11, 2001. McVeigh was eventually executed for the deaths resulting from the bombing. See Exhibit 11-1 for a copy of McVeigh's death certificate. Unhappy with the lack of rights of the victims during the trial of McVeigh and with the right of defendants to repeated habeas corpus appeals on the same subjects, Congress, with President Clinton's approval, enacted the Antiterrorism and Effective Death Penalty Act of 1996. Through this statute habeas corpus relief was limited, inter alia, by requiring petitions to be filed within one year and limiting the number of petitions that may be filed in any one case. The Act also requires victim compensation and requires courts to provide closed-circuit television access to victims in instances where the venue of trial is changed from the location of the crime.

Following the September 11 attacks, the Uniting and Strengthening America by Providing Appropriate Tools Required to Intercept and Obstruct Terrorism Act of 2001 was enacted. This law is commonly known as the Patriot Act. The Patriot Act was reauthorized, with amendments, in 2006. The Patriot Act changed existing law (including the Omnibus Crime Control and Safe Streets Act of 1968) in many ways, including the following:

* Federal law enforcement authority to monitor e-mail and other forms of communication was expanded. Examples include treating stored voice-mail messages like e-mail, not as telephone conversations. E-mail enjoys less protection than telephone conversations do.
* Federal court authority to issue pen register and trap orders (devices used to determine the origin of electronic communications) was broadened to include the entire nation.

Exhibit 11-1 OFFICIAL COPY, VIGO COUNTY HEALTH DEPARTMENT CERTIFICATE OF DEATH

Vigo County, Indiana Health Department Death Certificate for Timothy McVeigh, who was executed for the 1995 bombing of the Murrah Federal Building in Oklahoma City, OK.

Source: http://law2.umkc.edu/faculty/projects/ftrials/mcveigh/mcveighcertif.html

- Prior to the Patriot Act, law enforcement officers did not have to establish probable cause to obtain a court order to a telephone company to trace (using pen register/traps). Because the content of telephone conversations was not being intruded upon, law enforcement officers were only required to show that the data are "relevant to an ongoing investigation." The Patriot Act extended this procedure to obtaining a record of Web addresses a suspect visits, even though identification of a Web address also identifies content.
- The Patriot Act authorizes "roving wiretaps." A roving wiretap is authorization to move a wiretap from one telephone or form of communication to another in order to follow the communications of the person under surveillance.
- Several new crimes were created, including money laundering of cybercrime and terrorism, overseas use of fraudulent U.S. credit cards, terrorist attacks on mass transit, and harboring terrorists, and it increased the penalties for counterfeiting.
- The Attorney General of the United States was delegated greater authority to deport suspected alien terrorists.
- Law enforcement agencies were given the authority to share grand jury and wiretap information that constitutes "foreign intelligence" with intelligence agencies. Previously, this action was not permitted.

Also in response to the September 11 attacks, President Bush issued Military Order 1. This order empowered the Secretary of Defense to detain members of al Qaeda who have participated in, or planned, terrorist activity. The order also provided for military tribunals for terrorists with a two-thirds majority of each commission required for conviction. The Secretary of Defense then issued Military Commission Order 1, which was an elaboration of the responsibilities and authorities issued by President Bush in Military Order 1. This order established the procedures for implementing President Bush's order. For example, it permits the imposition of the death sentence, mandates a secret vote of the military judges, and allows for forfeiture of the property of those convicted.

In 2002, Congress created the Department of Homeland Security (DHS) through the Homeland Security Act. DHS is headed by a secretary, a cabinet-level officer. DHS is charged with preventing and responding to terrorism and with overseeing the other responsibilities of the agencies under DHS supervision. Much of the federal government's arsenal in the war on terror was consolidated under DHS. The Federal Emergency Management Agency, U.S. Coast Guard, Customs, Border Patrol, Secret Service, Transportation Security Administration, and Citizenship and Immigration Services (previously Immigration and Naturalization Service) are all units reporting to DHS. In total, DHS has nearly 200,000 employees under its umbrella.

These new laws are not without their critics. The most common criticism is that civil liberties are being lost in the effort to increase national security. To these critics, two threats are posed by terrorism. The first is terrorism. The second is the possible overreaction to terrorism. Proponents of these new laws believe that terrorism is substantially different from other crime and that the loss of some freedoms is needed to maintain security.

The Crimes of Terrorism

The Federal Terrorism statute, 18 U.S.C. § 2331, defines international terrorism as follows:

(1) the term "international terrorism" means activities that—

    (A) involve violent acts or acts dangerous to human life that are a violation of the criminal laws of the United States or of any State, or that would be a criminal violation if committed within the jurisdiction of the United States or of any State;

    (B) appear to be intended—

        (i) to intimidate or coerce a civilian population;

        (ii) to influence the policy of a government by intimidation or coercion; or

        (iii) to affect the conduct of a government by mass destruction, assassination, or kidnapping; and

    (C) occur primarily outside the territorial jurisdiction of the United States, or transcend national boundaries in terms of the means by which they are accomplished, the persons they appear intended to intimidate or coerce, or the locale in which their perpetrators operate or seek asylum;

(2) the term "national of the United States" has the meaning given such term in section 101(a)(22) of the Immigration and Nationality Act;

(3) the term "person" means any individual or entity capable of holding a legal or beneficial interest in property;

(4) the term "act of war" means any act occurring in the course of—

    (A) declared war;

    (B) armed conflict, whether or not war has been declared, between two or more nations; or

    (C) armed conflict between military forces of any origin; and

(5) the term "domestic terrorism" means activities that—

    (A) involve acts dangerous to human life that are a violation of the criminal laws of the United States or of any State;

    (B) appear to be intended—

        (i) to intimidate or coerce a civilian population;

        (ii) to influence the policy of a government by intimidation or coercion; or

        (iii) to affect the conduct of a government by mass destruction, assassination, or kidnapping; and

    (C) occur primarily within the territorial jurisdiction of the United States.

Another statute, 18 U.S.C. § 2332, prohibits the following acts:

(a) Prohibited acts.—

    (1) **Offenses.**—Whoever, involving conduct transcending national boundaries and in a circumstance described in subsection (b)—

        (A) kills, kidnaps, maims, commits an assault resulting in serious bodily injury, or assaults with a dangerous weapon any person within the United States; or

(B) creates a substantial risk of serious bodily injury to any other person by destroying or damaging any structure, conveyance, or other real or personal property within the United States or by attempting or conspiring to destroy or damage any structure, conveyance, or other real or personal property within the United States; in violation of the laws of any State, or the United States, shall be punished as prescribed in subsection (c).

(2) **Treatment of threats, attempts and conspiracies.**—Whoever threatens to commit an offense under paragraph (1), or attempts or conspires to do so, shall be punished under subsection (c).

(b) **Jurisdictional bases.**—

(3) **Circumstances.**—The circumstances referred to in subsection (a) are—

(A) the mail or any facility of interstate or foreign commerce is used in furtherance of the offense;

(B) the offense obstructs, delays, or affects interstate or foreign commerce, or would have so obstructed, delayed, or affected interstate or foreign commerce if the offense had been consummated;

(C) the victim, or intended victim, is the U.S. government, a member of the uniformed services, or any official, officer, employee, or agent of the legislative, executive, or judicial branches, or of any department or agency, of the United States;

(D) the structure, conveyance, or other real or personal property is, in whole or in part, owned, possessed, or leased to the United States, or any department or agency of the United States;

(E) the offense is committed in the territorial sea (including the airspace above and the seabed and subsoil below, and artificial islands and fixed structures erected thereon) of the United States; or

(F) the offense is committed within the special maritime and territorial jurisdiction of the United States.

(2) **Co-conspirators and accessories after the fact.**—Jurisdiction shall exist over all principals and co-conspirators of an offense under this section, and accessories after the fact to any offense under this section, if at least one of the circumstances described in subparagraphs (A) through (F) of paragraph (1) is applicable to at least one offender.

(c) **Penalties ...**

Yet another definition of terrorism can be found in the Homeland Security Act, 6 U.S.C. § 101(15):

(15) The term "terrorism" means any activity that—

(A) involves an act that—

(i) is dangerous to human life or potentially destructive of critical infrastructure or key resources; and

(ii) is a violation of the criminal laws of the United States or of any State or other subdivision of the United States; and

(B) appears to be intended—

   (i) to intimidate or coerce a civilian population;

   (ii) to influence the policy of a government by intimidation or coercion; or

   (iii) to affect the conduct of a government by mass destruction, assassination, or kidnapping.

In an attempt to strike at terrorist organizations, federal law authorizes the Secretary of State to designate any foreign group of two or more persons that commit terrorist activities or plan or prepare to commit terrorist activities. Once designated, those who support the organization are in violation of federal law, noncitizens who are members of these organizations are immediately deportable, and the financial resources of the organizations may be seized by the United States.

Additionally, other federal statutes address specific acts of terrorism, such as bioterrorism; bombing public places; attacking mass transportation systems; harboring terrorists; supporting and financing terrorism, terrorist organizations, and nations that support terrorism; and using weapons of mass destruction. For example, 18 U.S.C. § 2332(a) prohibits the use of a weapon for mass destruction

(1) against a national of the United States while such national is outside of the United States;

(2) against any person or property within the United States, and the mail or any facility of interstate or foreign commerce is used in furtherance of the offense; such property is used in interstate or foreign commerce or in an activity that affects interstate or foreign commerce; any perpetrator travels in or causes another to travel in interstate or foreign commerce in furtherance of the offense; or the offense, or the results of the offense, affect interstate or foreign commerce, or, in the case of a threat, attempt, or conspiracy, would have affected interstate or foreign commerce;

(3) against any property that is owned, leased or used by the United States or by any department or agency of the United States, whether the property is within or outside of the United States; or

(4) against any property within the United States that is owned, leased, or used by a foreign government. *Weapon of mass destruction* is defined as "any destructive device as defined in this law, any weapon that is designed or intended to cause death or serious bodily injury through the release, dissemination, or impact of toxic or poisonous chemicals, or their precursors, any weapon involving a biological agent, toxin, or vector (as those terms are defined in section 178 of this title), any weapon that is designed to release radiation or radioactivity at a level dangerous to human life."

Following the tragic attacks of September 11, 2001, Zacarias Moussaoui was charged with being the intended twentieth hijacker. Moussaoui could not board any of the hijacked flights on September 11 because he was in federal custody. Exhibit 11-2 is an excerpt of his indictment.

Exhibit 11-2 INDICTMENT OF THE TWENTIETH HIJACKER IN THE SEPTEMBER 11, 2001, ATTACKS ON THE UNITED STATES

IN THE UNITED STATES DISTRICT COURT FOR THE EASTERN DISTRICT OF VIRGINIA ALEXANDRIA DIVISION

UNITED STATES OF AMERICA

-v-

ZACARIAS MOUSSAOUI,
   a/k/a "Shaqil,"
a/k/a "Abu Khalid al Sahrawi,"

Defendant.

CRIMINAL NO:

Conspiracy to Commit Acts of Terrorism Transcending National Boundaries
(18 U.S.C. §§ 2332b(a)(2) & (c))
(Count One)

Conspiracy to Commit Aircraft Piracy
(49 U.S.C. §§ 46502 (a)(1)(A) and (a)(2)(B))
(Count Two)

Conspiracy to Destroy Aircraft
(18 U.S.C. §§ 32(a)(7) & 34)
(Count Three)

Conspiracy to Use Weapons of Mass Destruction
(18 U.S.C. § 2332a(a))
(Count Four)

Conspiracy to Murder United States Employees
(18 U.S.C. §§ 1114 & 1117)
(Count Five)

Conspiracy to Destroy Property
(18 U.S.C. §§ 844(f), (i), (n))
(Count Six)

DECEMBER 2001 TERM AT ALEXANDRIA INDICTMENT

THE GRAND JURY CHARGES THAT:

<u>COUNT ONE</u>

(Conspiracy to Commit Acts of Terrorism Transcending National Boundaries)

<u>Background: al Qaeda</u>

1. At all relevant times from in or about 1989 until the date of the filing of this Indictment, an international terrorist group existed which was dedicated to opposing non-Islamic governments with force and violence. This organization grew out of the "mekhtab al khidemat" (the "Services Office") organization which had maintained offices in various parts of the world, including Afghanistan, Pakistan (particularly in Peshawar), and the United States. The group was founded by Usama Bin Laden and Muhammad Atef, a/k/a "Abu Hafs al Masry,"

(continued)

Exhibit 11-2 (continued)

together with "Abu Ubaidah al Banshiri," and others. From in or about 1989 until the present, the group called itself "al Qaeda" ("the Base")....

2. Bin Laden and al Qaeda violently opposed the United States for several reasons. First, the United States was regarded as an "infidel" because it was not governed in a manner consistent with the group's extremist interpretation of Islam. Second, the United States was viewed as providing essential support for other "infidel" governments and institutions, particularly the governments of Saudi Arabia and Egypt, the nation of Israel, and the United Nations organization, which were regarded as enemies of the group. Third, al Qaeda opposed the involvement of the United States armed forces in the Gulf War in 1991 and in Operation Restore Hope in Somalia in 1992 and 1993. In particular, al Qaeda opposed the continued presence of American military forces in Saudi Arabia (and elsewhere on the Saudi Arabian peninsula) following the Gulf War. Fourth, al Qaeda opposed the United States Government because of the arrest, conviction and imprisonment of persons belonging to al Qaeda or its affiliated terrorist groups or those with whom it worked. For these and other reasons, Bin Laden declared a jihad, or holy war, against the United States, which he has carried out through al Qaeda and its affiliated organizations.

3. One of the principal goals of al Qaeda was to drive the United States armed forces out of Saudi Arabia (and elsewhere on the Saudi Arabian peninsula) and Somalia by violence. Members of al Qaeda issued *fatwahs* (rulings on Islamic law) indicating that such attacks were both proper and necessary.

4. Al Qaeda functioned both on its own and through some of the terrorist organizations that operated under its umbrella, ...

7. Since at least 1989, until the filing of this Indictment, Usama Bin Laden and the terrorist group al Qaeda sponsored, managed, and/or financially supported training camps in Afghanistan, which camps were used to instruct members and associates of al Qaeda and its affiliated terrorist groups in the use of firearms, explosives, chemical weapons, and other weapons of mass destruction. In addition to providing training in the use of various weapons, these camps were used to conduct operational planning against United States targets around the world and experiments in the use of chemical and biological weapons....

<u>The September 11 Hijackers</u>

9. On September 11, 2001, co-conspirators Mohammed Atta, Abdul Alomari, Wail al-Shehri, Waleed al-Shehri, and Satam al-Suqami hijacked American Airlines Flight 11, bound from Boston to Los Angeles, and crashed it into the North Tower of the World Trade Center in New York. (In this Indictment, each hijacker will be identified with the flight number of the plane he hijacked.)

10. On September 11, 2001, co-conspirators Marwan al-Shehhi, Fayez Ahmed, a/k/a "Banihammad Fayez," Ahmed al-Ghamdi, Hamza al-Ghamdi, and Mohald al-Shehri hijacked United Airlines Flight 175, bound from Boston to Los Angeles, and crashed it into the South Tower of the World Trade Center in New York.

Exhibit 11–2 (continued)

11. On September 11, 2001, co-conspirators Khalid al-Midhar, Nawaf al-Hazmi, Hani Hanjour, Salem al-Hamzi, and Majed Moqed hijacked American Airlines Flight 77, bound from Virginia to Los Angeles, and crashed it into the Pentagon.

12. On September 11, 2001, co-conspirators Ziad Jarrah, Ahmed al-Haznawi, Saaed al-Ghamdi, and Ahmed al-Nami hijacked United Airlines Flight 93, bound from Newark to San Fransisco, and crashed it in Pennsylvania.

The Defendant

13. ZACARIAS MOUSSAOUI, a/k/a "Shaqil," a/k/a "Abu Khalid al Sahrawi," was born in France of Moroccan descent on May 30, 1968. Before 2001 he was a resident of the United Kingdom. MOUSSAOUI held a masters degree from Southbank University in the United Kingdom and traveled widely.

The Charge

16. From in or about 1989 until the date of the filing of this Indictment, in the Eastern District of Virginia, the Southern District of New York, and elsewhere, the defendant, ZACARIAS MOUSSAOUI, a/k/a "Shaqil," a/k/a "Abu Khalid al Sahrawi," with other members and associates of al Qaeda and others known and unknown to the Grand Jury, unlawfully, wilfully and knowingly combined, conspired, confederated and agreed to kill and maim persons within the United States, and to create a substantial risk of serious bodily injury to other persons by destroying and damaging structures, conveyances, and other real and personal property within the United States, in violation of the laws of States and the United States, in circumstances involving conduct transcending national boundaries, and in which facilities of interstate and foreign commerce were used in furtherance of the offense, the offense obstructed, delayed, and affected interstate and foreign commerce, the victim was the United States Government, members of the uniformed services, and officials, officers, employees, and agents of the governmental branches, departments, and agencies of the United States, and the structures, conveyances, and other real and personal property were, in whole or in part, owned, possessed, and leased to the United States and its departments and agencies, resulting in the deaths of thousands of persons on September 11, 2001.

Overt Acts

In furtherance of the conspiracy, and to effect its objects, the defendant, and others known and unknown to the Grand Jury, committed the following overt acts:

MOUSSAOUI Trains at Al Qaeda Training Camp

14. In or about April 1998, ZACARIAS MOUSSAOUI was present at the al Qaeda-affiliated Khalden Camp in Afghanistan.

* * *

MOUSSAOUI Inquires About Flight Training

34. On or about September 29, 2000, ZACARIAS MOUSSAOUI contacted Airman Flight School in Norman, Oklahoma using an e-mail account he set up on September 6 with an internet service provider in Malaysia.

(continued)

Exhibit 11-2 (continued)

35. In or about October 2000, ZACARIAS MOUSSAOUI received letters from InfocusTech, a Malaysian company, stating that MOUSSAOUI was appointed InfocusTech's marketing consultant in the United States, the United Kingdom, and Europe, and that he would receive, among other things, an allowance of $2500 per month.

<u>MOUSSAOUI Comes to the United States</u>

46. Between on or about February 26, 2001, and on or about May 29, 2001, ZACARIAS MOUSSAOUI attended the Airman Flight School in Norman, Oklahoma, ending his classes early.

<u>MOUSSAOUI Contacts a Commercial Flight School</u>

51. On or about May 23, 2001, ZACARIAS MOUSSAOUI contacted an office of the Pan Am International Flight Academy in Miami, Florida via e-mail.

<u>Hijackers Open Bank Accounts</u>

52. In Summer 2001, Fayez Ahmed (#175), Saeed al-Ghamdi (#93), Hamza al-Ghamdi (#175), Waleed al-Shehri (#11), Ziad Jarrah (#93), Satam al-Suqami (#11), Mohald al-Shehri (#175), Ahmed al-Nami (#93), and Ahmed al-Haznawi (#93) each opened a Florida SunTrust bank account with a cash deposit.

<u>MOUSSAOUI Inquires About Aerial Application of Pesticides</u>

53. In or about June 2001, in Norman, Oklahoma, ZACARIAS MOUSSAOUI made inquiries about starting a crop dusting company.

<u>MOUSSAOUI Purchases Flight Training Equipment</u>

56. On or about June 20, 2001, ZACARIAS MOUSSAOUI purchased flight deck videos for the Boeing 747 Model 400 and the Boeing 747 Model 200 from the Ohio Pilot Store.

<u>MOUSSAOUI Pays for Flight Lessons</u>

60. On or about July 10 and July 11, 2001, ZACARIAS MOUSSAOUI made credit card payments to the Pan Am International Flight Academy for a simulator course in commercial flight training.

<u>MOUSSAOUI Purchases Knives</u>

68. On or about August 3, 2001, ZACARIAS MOUSSAOUI purchased two knives in Oklahoma City, Oklahoma.

<u>MOUSSAOUI Travels from Oklahoma to Minnesota</u>

70. On or about August 9 and August 10, 2001, ZACARIAS MOUSSAOUI was driven from Oklahoma to Minnesota.

<u>MOUSSAOUI Takes Commercial Flying Lessons in Minnesota</u>

71. On or about August 10, 2001, in Minneapolis, Minnesota, ZACARIAS MOUSSAOUI paid approximately $6,300 in cash to the Pan Am International Flight Academy.

Exhibit 11-2 (continued)

72. Between August 13 and August 15, 2001, ZACARIAS MOUSSAOUI attended the Pan Am International Flight Academy in Minneapolis, Minnesota, for simulator training on the Boeing 747 Model 400.

<u>MOUSSAOUI Possesses Knives and Other Items</u>

73. On or about August 16, 2001, ZACARIAS MOUSSAOUI possessed, among other things:

- two knives;
- a pair of binoculars;
- flight manuals for the Boeing 747 Model 400;
- a flight simulator computer program;
- fighting gloves and shin guards;
- a piece of paper referring to a handheld Global Positioning System receiver and a camcorder;
- software that could be used to review pilot procedures for the Boeing 747 Model 400;
- a notebook listing German Telephone #1, German Telephone #2, and the name "Ahad Sabet;"
- letters indicating that MOUSSAOUI is a marketing consultant in the United States for Infocus Tech;
- a computer disk containing information related to the aerial application of pesticides; and
- a hand-held aviation radio.

<u>MOUSSAOUI Lies to Federal Agents</u>

74. On or about August 17, 2001, ZACARIAS MOUSSAOUI, while being interviewed by federal agents in Minneapolis, attempted to explain his presence in the United States by falsely stating that he was simply interested in learning to fly.

<u>Final Preparations for the Coordinated Air Attack</u>

76. On or about August 22, 2001, Fayez Ahmed (#175) used his VISA card in Florida to obtain approximately $4,900 cash, which had been deposited into his Standard Chartered Bank account in UAE the day before.

77. On or about August 22, 2001, in Miami, Florida, Ziad Jarrah (#93) purchased an antenna for a Global Positioning System ("GPS"), other GPS related equipment, and schematics for 757 cockpit instrument diagrams. (GPS allows an individual to navigate to a position using coordinates pre-programmed into the GPS unit.)

(continued)

Exhibit 11-2 (continued)

78. On or about August 25, 2001, Khalid al-Midhar and Majed Moqed purchased with cash tickets for American Airlines Flight 77, from Virginia to Los Angeles, California, scheduled for September 11, 2001.

79. On or about August 26, 2001, Waleed al-Shehri and Wail al-Shehri made reservations on American Airlines Flight 11, from Boston, Massachusetts, to Los Angeles, California, scheduled for September 11, 2001, listing a telephone number in Florida ("Florida Telephone #1") as a contact number.

80. On or about August 27, 2001, reservations for electronic, one-way tickets were made for Fayez Ahmed and Mohald al-Shehri, for United Airlines Flight 175, from Boston, Massachusetts, to Los Angeles, California, scheduled for September 11, 2001, listing Florida Telephone Number #1 as a contact number.

81. On or about August 27, 2001, Nawaf al-Hazmi and Salem al-Hazmi booked flights on American Airlines Flight 77.

82. On or about August 28, 2001, Satam al-Suqami purchased a ticket with cash for American Airlines Flight 11.

83. On or about August 28, 2001, Mohammed Atta and Abdulaziz Alomari reserved two seats on American Airlines Flight 11, listing Florida Telephone #1 as a contact number.

84. On or about August 29, 2001, Ahmed al-Ghamdi and Hamza al-Ghamdi reserved electronic, one-way tickets for United Airlines Flight 175.

85. On or about August 29, 2001, Ahmed al-Haznawi purchased a ticket on United Airlines Flight 93 from Newark, New Jersey, to San Francisco, California, scheduled for September 11, 2001.

86. On or about August 30, 2001, Mohammed Atta (#11) purchased a utility tool that contained a knife.

87. On or about September 3, 2001, in Hamburg, Germany, Ramzi Bin al-Shibh, using the name "Ahad Sabet," received approximately $1500 by wire transfer from "Hashim Ahmed" in UAE.

88. On or about September 4, 2001, Mohammed Atta (#11) sent a FedEx package from Florida to UAE.

89. On or about September 5, 2001, Ramzi Bin al-Shibh traveled from Dusseldorf, Germany, to Madrid, Spain, and did not return to Germany.

90. On or about September 6, 2001, Satam al-Suqami (#11) and Abdulaziz Alomari (#11) flew from Florida to Boston.

<u>The September 11, 2001 Terrorist Attacks</u>

100. On or about September 11, 2001, the hijackers possessed a handwritten set of final instructions for a martyrdom operation on an airplane using knives.

Exhibit 11-2 (continued)

101. On or about September 11, 2001, Mohammed Atta (#11) and Abdulaziz Alomari (#11) flew from Portland, Maine to Boston, Massachusetts.

102. On or about September 11, 2001, Mohammed Atta (#11) possessed operating manuals for the Boeing 757 and 767, pepper spray, knives, and German travel visas.

103. On or about September 11, 2001, Ziad Jarrah (#93) possessed flight manuals for Boeing 757 and 767 aircraft.

104. On or about September 11, 2001, Mohammed Atta, Abdul Aziz Alomari, Satam al-Suqami, Waleed M. al-Shehri, and Waleed al-Shehri hijacked American Airlines Flight 11, a Boeing 767, which had departed Boston at approximately 7:55 A.M. They flew Flight 11 into the North Tower of the World Trade Center in Manhattan at approximately 8:45 A.M., causing the collapse of the tower and the deaths of thousands of persons.

105. On or about September 11, 2001, Hamza al-Ghamdi, Fayez Ahmed, Mohald al-Shehri, Ahmed al-Ghamdi, and Marwan al-Shehhi hijacked United Airlines Flight 175, a Boeing 767, which had departed from Boston at approximately 8:15 A.M. They flew Flight 175 into the South Tower of the World Trade Center in Manhattan at approximately 9:05 A.M., causing the collapse of the tower and the deaths of thousands of persons.

106. On or about September 11, 2001, Khalid al-Midhar, Majed Moqed, Nawaf al-Hazmi, Salem al-Hazmi, and Hani Hanjour hijacked American Airlines Flight 77, a Boeing 757, which had departed from Virginia bound for Los Angeles, at approximately 8:10 A.M. They flew Flight 77 into the Pentagon in Virginia at approximately 9:40 A.M., causing the deaths of 189 persons.

107. On or about September 11, 2001, Saeed al-Ghamdi, Ahmed al-Nami, Ahmed al-Haznawi, and Ziad Jarrah hijacked United Airlines Flight 93, a Boeing 757, which had departed from Newark, New Jersey bound for San Francisco at approximately 8:00 A.M. After resistance by the passengers, Flight 93 crashed in Somerset County, Pennsylvania at approximately 10:10 A.M., killing all on board.

<u>COUNT TWO</u>

(Conspiracy to Commit Aircraft Piracy)

1. The allegations contained in Count One are repeated.

2. From in or about 1989 until the date of the filing of this Indictment, in the Eastern District of Virginia, the Southern District of New York, and elsewhere, the defendant, ZACARIAS MOUSSAOUI, a/k/a "Shaqil," a/k/a "Abu Khalid al Sahrawi," and other members and associates of al Qaeda and others known and unknown to the Grand Jury, unlawfully, wilfully and knowingly combined, conspired, confederated and agreed to commit aircraft piracy, by seizing and exercising control of aircraft in the special aircraft jurisdiction of the United States by force, violence, threat of force and violence, and intimidation, and with wrongful intent, with the result that thousands of people died on September 11, 2001.

(continued)

Exhibit 11-2 (continued)

<u>Overt Acts</u>

3. In furtherance of the conspiracy, and to effect its illegal objects, the defendant, and others known and unknown to the Grand Jury, committed the overt acts set forth in Count One of this Indictment, which are fully incorporated by reference.

(In violation of Title 49, United States Code, Sections 46502(a)(1)(A) and (a)(2)(B).)

COUNT THREE

(Conspiracy to Destroy Aircraft)

1. The allegations contained in Count One are repeated.

2. From in or about 1989 until the date of the filing of this Indictment, in the Eastern District of Virginia, the Southern District of New York, and elsewhere, the defendant, ZACARIAS MOUSSAOUI, a/k/a "Shaqil," a/k/a "Abu Khalid al Sahrawi," and other members and associates of al Qaeda and others known and unknown to the Grand Jury, unlawfully, wilfully and knowingly combined, conspired, confederated and agreed to willfully destroy and wreck aircraft in the special aircraft jurisdiction of the United States, and to willfully perform acts of violence against and incapacitate individuals on such aircraft, so as likely to endanger the safety of such aircraft, resulting in the deaths of thousands of persons on September 11, 2001.

<u>Overt Acts</u>

3. In furtherance of the conspiracy, and to effect its illegal objects, the defendant, and others known and unknown to the Grand Jury, committed the overt acts set forth in Count One of this Indictment, which are fully incorporated by reference.

(In violation of Title 18, United States Code, Sections 32(a)(7) and 34.)

COUNT FOUR

(Conspiracy to Use Weapons of Mass Destruction)

1. The allegations contained in Count One are repeated.

2. From in or about 1989 until the date of the filing of this Indictment, in the Eastern District of Virginia, the Southern District of New York, and elsewhere, the defendant, ZACARIAS MOUSSAOUI, a/k/a "Shaqil," a/k/a "Abu Khalid al Sahrawi," and other members and associates of al Qaeda and others known and unknown to the Grand Jury, unlawfully, wilfully and knowingly combined, conspired, confederated and agreed to use weapons of mass destruction, namely, airplanes intended for use as missiles, bombs, and similar devices, without lawful authority against persons within the United States, with the results of such use affecting interstate and foreign commerce, and against property that was owned, leased and used by the United States and by departments and agencies of the United States, with the result that thousands of people died on September 11, 2001.

Exhibit 11–2 (continued)

<u>Overt Acts</u>

3. In furtherance of the conspiracy, and to effect its illegal objects, the defendant, and others known and unknown to the Grand Jury, committed the overt acts set forth in Count One of this Indictment, which are fully incorporated by reference.

(In violation of Title 18, United States Code, Section 2332a(a).)

<u>COUNT FIVE</u>

(Conspiracy to Murder United States Employees)

1. The allegations contained in Count One are repeated.

2. From in or about 1989 until the date of the filing of this Indictment, in the Eastern District of Virginia, the Southern District of New York, and elsewhere, the defendant, ZACARIAS MOUSSAOUI, a/k/a "Shaqil," a/k/a "Abu Khalid al Sahrawi," and other members and associates of al Qaeda and others known and unknown to the Grand Jury, unlawfully, wilfully and knowingly combined, conspired, confederated and agreed to kill officers and employees of the United States and agencies and branches thereof, while such officers and employees were engaged in, and on account of, the performance of their official duties, and persons assisting such employees in the performance of their duties, in violation of Section 1114 of Title 18, United States Code, including members of the Department of Defense stationed at the Pentagon.

<u>Overt Acts</u>

3. In furtherance of the conspiracy, and to effect its illegal objects, the defendant, and others known and unknown to the Grand Jury, committed the overt acts set forth in Count One of this Indictment, which are fully incorporated by reference.

(In violation of Title 18, United States Code, Sections 1114 and 1117.)

<u>COUNT SIX</u>

(Conspiracy to Destroy Property of the United States)

1. The allegations contained in Count One are repeated.

2. From in or about 1989 until the date of the filing of this Indictment, in the Eastern District of Virginia, the Southern District of New York, and elsewhere, the defendant, ZACARIAS MOUSSAOUI, a/k/a "Shaqil," a/k/a "Abu Khalid al Sahrawi," and other members and associates of al Qaeda and others known and unknown to the Grand Jury, unlawfully, wilfully and knowingly combined, conspired, confederated and agreed to maliciously damage and destroy, by means of fire and explosives, buildings, vehicles, and other real and personal property used in interstate and foreign commerce and in activities affecting interstate and foreign commerce, and buildings, vehicles, and other personal and real property in whole and in part owned and possessed by, and leased to, the United States and its departments and

(continued)

Exhibit 11-2 (continued)

agencies, and as a result of such conduct directly and proximately caused the deaths of thousands of persons on September 11, 2001, including hundreds of public safety officers performing duties as a direct and proximate result of the said damage and destruction.

<u>Overt Acts</u>

3. In furtherance of the conspiracy, and to effect its illegal objects, the defendant, and others known and unknown to the Grand Jury, committed the overt acts set forth in Count One of this Indictment, which are fully incorporated by reference.

(In violation of Title 18, United States Code, Sections 844(f), (i), and (n).)

_____
FOREPERSON

_____
MICHAEL CHERTOFF

ASSISTANT ATTORNEY GENERAL

_____
PAUL J. McNULTY

UNITED STATES ATTORNEY EASTERN DISTRICT OF VIRGINIA

_____
MARY JO WHITE

UNITED STATES ATTORNEY SOUTHERN DISTRICT OF NEW YORK

PUBLICATION DATE:

January 15, 2002

DATE:

20020115

Source: http://www.justice.gov/ag/moussaouiindictment.htm

Finally, remember that terrorists are subject to all the "traditional" penal laws of the states and nation. Terrorists that steal can be prosecuted for larceny and those that kill can be prosecuted for murder. States also have terrorism laws, similar to the federal laws discussed below.

CRIMES AGAINST THE ENVIRONMENT

With the modernization of the United States has come a threat to the environment. The air and water that people depend upon for sustenance have become polluted. Many species of flora and fauna have been lost, and many more are threatened.

Modernization threatens the environment in several ways. In the process of "developing" land, habitats are lost. Also, the use of dangerous chemicals and toxins has become commonplace. In many industries, toxic by-products of manufacturing are common. Toxic wastes and substances pose use, transportation, and disposal problems. The release of dangerous substances into the air or into water endangers public health and safety. It is estimated that air pollution kills 14,000 people annually and that 100,000 workers die annually from exposure to toxins.[56] The world's increased population aggravates the problem. Greater numbers of people place greater stress on natural systems. Resources are depleted faster and nature's cleansing process becomes strained and less effective.

While regulating for the environment has grown considerably in recent decades, the first major federal environmental law was the Refuse Act of 1899, a law that prohibits, with criminal penalties, dumping refuse into waterways.[57] It continues in effect today. Today there is a large body of environmental law that, to some extent, addresses many of the Nation's environmental problems. The federal government's policy is to create and maintain conditions in which man and nature can exist in productive harmony. Both the federal and state governments play a role in regulating the environment, although the federal government has the larger part currently. The federal government's role in regulating the environment dates back to at least 1899, when Congress enacted a statute making it a crime to discharge pollutants into navigable waters.

Several federal administrative agencies are charged with overseeing the enforcement and administration of environmental laws, including the Environmental Protection Agency, Coast Guard, Department of the Interior, Occupational Health and Safety Commission, and Department of Justice. Federal law provides for administrative, civil, and criminal sanctions on environmental law violators.

There are two classes of environmental laws. One class of laws is intended to further the public health and safety. The Clean Air Act, the Clean Water Act, and similar statutes are examples of this type of environmental regulation. A second class of laws is intended to protect the environment itself, for its aesthetic, recreational, and other values. The Endangered Species Act is an example of a conservation law. Of course, many laws serve both objectives.

Until recently, environmental offenses were not usually treated as criminal; rather, they were viewed as civil or administrative infractions. The federal government relied almost exclusively on administrative and civil processes to enforce environmental laws. Fines were the most common penalty sought by the government against offenders.

The belief that environmental violations are serious and should be prosecuted as criminal offenses is a recent development. For example, one of the most notorious environmental cases was that of the Love Canal neighborhood in Niagara Falls, New York, where it was discovered in 1978 that the improper disposal of toxins was causing death and illness to local residents. An entire community was forced to relocate to escape the danger—yet not one person was prosecuted in the Love Canal case.

The fear of another Love Canal—or an accident like the one involving Union Carbide in Bhopal, India, where 2,000 people were killed and 200,000 people were injured—and the dangers posed by other environmental wrongs led Congress to strengthen environmental laws. The measures included added criminal sanctions. Relying on civil remedies alone had proved ineffective. Individuals were not being held accountable, and corporations found it more cost-effective to violate the law and pay any fines than to comply with the law.

Therefore, although most violations continue to be handled through civil and administrative proceedings, the number of environmental criminal cases is increasing. Of the 500 largest corporations in the United States, one-fourth have been convicted of an environmental crime or have been subject to civil penalties for violating environmental laws.[58] The Department of Justice has a special division charged with prosecuting environmental law crimes.

Unlike at common law, today business entities, such as corporations, may be charged with crimes. Fines and dissolution of a corporation are examples of the penalties that may be imposed. Charging corporations for environmental violations is common. Of course, individuals may also be charged with violating environmental laws, and corporate employees may be charged for actions taken on behalf of a corporation. It is not a defense for an employee to claim that he or she was following a supervisor's directive, nor may it be a defense for the supervisor to claim that he or she is innocent because he or she delegated performance of the act to an employee.

Some environmental crimes are strict liability. Others, and of course those that can be punished with jail time, require some mens rea, usually a knowing violation.

Several federal environmental laws contain criminal sanctions. The most significant of these laws are the Clean Water Act; the Clean Air Act; the Comprehensive Environmental Response, Compensation, and Liability Act; the Resource Conservation and Recovery Act; the Occupational Safety and Health Act; the Toxic Substances Control Act; the Federal Insecticide, Fungicide, and Rodenticide Act; the Emergency Planning and Community Right-to-Know Act; and the Endangered Species Act. All statutes are examples of regulation for the public health, except for the final statute, which is a conservation law. These laws provide for administrative and civil remedies and procedures, in addition to criminal sanctions.

Clean Water Act

The Clean Water Act (CWA)[59] regulates the discharge of pollutants into the nation's navigable waters. The CWA establishes a scheme of permits and reporting. The contamination of water with a pollutant, without a permit or exceeding the limits of a permit, is criminal under the Clean Water Act.

Both negligent and knowing acts are criminalized and may be punished with fines and imprisonment. A knowing act is punished more severely than a negligent act. Offenders who have acted negligently may be sentenced to one year in prison, whereas knowing offenders may be sentenced to three years in prison.[60] Fines may also be imposed for both, in addition to any civil remedies.

Also, the CWA contains a "knowing endangerment" provision. If a person violates the CWA with knowledge that the violation "places another person in imminent danger of death or serious bodily injury," the offender may be sentenced to up to 15 years in prison, and significant fines may be imposed.

Finally, false reporting under the Act is criminal and may be punished by up to two years in prison, in addition to a fine.

Clean Air Act

The goal of the Clean Air Act (CAA) is to preserve air quality. It does this by regulating emissions of dangerous substances into the air.

Similar to the CWA in its criminal aspects, the CAA criminalized negligent and knowing violations of its mandates, punishing the latter more severely.[61] Further, it contains knowing endangerment and false reporting provisions.

Comprehensive Environmental Response, Compensation, and Liability Act

The Comprehensive Environmental Response, Compensation and Liability Act (CERCLA) is commonly known as *Superfund*. The purpose of CERCLA is to identify and clean up existing hazardous waste sites.

Any person who knowingly falsifies or destroys any required record or who fails to report a spill of hazardous materials may be punished with fines and imprisonment.[62]

Resource Conservation and Recovery Act

The Resource Conservation and Recovery Act (RCRA) is similar to CERCLA in that they regulate the same subject matter: hazardous materials. However, CERCLA is an after-the-fact regulation intended to clean up existing sites, whereas RCRA is intended to regulate the day-to-day use, storage, transportation, handling, and disposal of hazardous materials.

There are no negligent violations under RCRA; rather, the mens rea for conviction of its prohibitions is knowledge. For example, the knowing transportation of hazardous waste to an unlicensed facility; the knowing treatment, storage, or disposal of hazardous waste without a permit; and the knowing violation of a permit are criminal and may be punished with both imprisonment and fines. As with the CWA and the CAA, knowingly endangering another enhances the punishment for a violation of RCRA.[63]

Occupational Safety and Health Act

The Occupational Safety and Health Act (OSHA) regulates the work environment of the American worker. The objective of the law is to create safe working conditions. There is a plethora of regulations enforcing this mandate.

Any employer who causes the death of an employee as a result of noncompliance with OSHA may be prosecuted and sentenced to imprisonment and a fine. Of course, the employer may also be liable under other criminal laws, such as negligent manslaughter.

Additionally, OSHA requires employers to notify their employees of potential exposure to dangerous chemicals and to provide information and resources to protect the employees. Failure to notify employees of this risk is a criminal omission under OSHA. False reporting is also a crime under this statute.

Toxic Substances Control Act

The Toxic Substances Control Act (TSCA) is the most comprehensive federal law concerning dangerous substances. The Environmental Protection Agency (EPA) is delegated considerable authority under the TSCA to regulate the sale, manufacture, development, processing, distribution, and disposal of toxic substances. Under the TSCA, the EPA is empowered to ban, or otherwise control, the production and distribution of chemicals. Asbestos and radon are examples of chemicals that the EPA has heavily regulated under the TSCA.

Any person who knowingly or willfully violates the TSCA concerning the manufacture, testing, or distribution of a chemical may be punished with both a fine and imprisonment. Also, false reporting, failing to maintain records, and failing to submit records as required by law are criminal acts under the TSCA.[64]

Federal Insecticide, Fungicide, and Rodenticide Act

Chemicals that are lethal to pests may also be lethal or at least harmful to humans. In addition to being inhaled, pesticides find their way into human drinking water and food.

The Federal Insecticide, Fungicide, and Rodenticide Act (FIFRA) delegates to the EPA the task of regulating the manufacture, sale, distribution, and use of these chemicals. Some chemicals are forbidden; there are limits on the use of others. There are labeling and reporting requirements.

Knowing violations of any of FIFRA's requirements are criminal and may be punished with fines and imprisonment.[65]

Emergency Planning and Community Right-to-Know Act

Bhopal, India; Chernobyl; and closer to home, Three Mile Island—all three are reminders that accidents happen, or that the actions of one person, such as a terrorist, can cause a tragedy of enormous proportion. In both the Chernobyl and Bhopal incidents, there was no planning or preparation for an accident.

The purpose of the Emergency Planning and Community Right-to-Know Act is to better prepare the community in which a facility is sited for disaster and to inform the community about emissions of hazardous substances by the facility. The Act requires facilities that use or produce chemicals to report both accidental and routine releases of substances into the air or water. Further, facilities are required to provide local officials (e.g., hospitals) with information about the chemicals used.

Knowing or willful failure to give notice of a release may be punished by both imprisonment and a fine.

Endangered Species Act

The Endangered Species Act (ESA)[66] and the Marine Mammal Protection Act represent a different form of environmental law from those discussed so far. The purpose of these laws is not to protect the public health; rather, the intent is to preserve the integrity of the environment itself.

The ESA establishes a program of conservation of threatened and endangered species of plants and animals and the habitats where they are found. The law is coadministered by the Departments of Interior, Commerce, Agriculture, and Justice.

The ESA prohibits the sale, taking, possession, importation, and exportation of endangered species and the products of those species. Violations of the law are punishable by both fines and imprisonment.

Marine Mammal Protection Act

Similar to the ESA, the Marine Mammal Protection Act (MMPA)[67] is intended to protect and conserve marine mammals. The taking of such creatures without a permit by a U.S. flag vessel while on the high seas is a crime. The taking, possession, and trade of animals protected under the law is prohibited within the United States unless a permit has been obtained. Fines and imprisonment may be imposed on violators.

These are but a few of the federal environmental laws. Also, many states have similar laws. In some instances, the states have been delegated the authority to enforce federal law. Environmental laws affect every person, not just businesses that use or trade in hazardous materials.

Because of overpopulation, high-density urbanization, industrialization, resource exploitation, and technological advances, every person has a duty to be environmentally aware, and the laws of the nation impose environmental obligations on the individual. The proper disposal of trash, car batteries, and motor oil, and the regulation of hunting and fishing, are examples of environmental laws that affect the daily lives of members of the public.

Web Links

The Internal Revenue Service's website contains information on tax law, compliance and filing (including updated forms that may be downloaded), tax statistics, and other information. *http://www.irs.ustreas.gov*

Key Terms

breachs of the peace	fighting words	subornation of perjury
bribery	perjury	tax evasion
clear and present danger	prostitution	tax fraud
contempt		

Review Questions

1. Andy approaches Roberta, who is standing on a street corner, and offers her $50 for sex. Roberta, an undercover vice officer, arrests Andy. What crime should he be charged with?

2. Is there a constitutional right to engage in homosexual conduct between mature, consenting adults?

3. When may a state regulate material that is thought to be sexually repulsive? What constitutional provision hinders governments from regulating such expression?

4. What are fighting words? Are they protected by the First Amendment?

5. Is proof that a driver's blood-alcohol level exceeded the statutory maximum the only way to prove that a driver was under the influence? Is it a valid defense for driver-defendants to claim that they could drive safely, even though their blood-alcohol level exceeded the amount allowed by statute?

6. What are the elements of Continuing Criminal Enterprise, and who is the statute aimed at?

7. What are the basic elements of bribery? The Model Penal Code recognizes two types of bribery. Name the two.

8. Distinguish criminal contempt from civil contempt. Do the same for direct contempt and indirect contempt.

9. Is this statement true? "Perjury is a law that applies only to judicial proceedings." Explain your answer.

10. What are the elements of indecent exposure?

11. What are the elements of treason?

12. Identify two ways that the Patriot Act of 2001 expanded the authority of federal officials to address terrorism.

Problems & Critical Thinking Exercises

1. Are the following statutes constitutional? Explain, if not.

   Statute One: Loitering
   Any person who loiters in a place in an unusual manner for longer than 15 minutes and reasonably causes a person to be concerned for their safety must identify himself to police when requested. Any person who refuses to identify himself under these circumstances or takes flight when approached by a police officer is guilty of loitering.

   Statute Two: Loitering
   Any person who continually loiters in public parks without apparent employment or who lives off the handouts of others is guilty of loitering.

2. State law prohibits "hardcore pornography." Among the many prohibitions of the law is a provision making it a felony to possess or sell materials that are known to depict bestiality (sex between a human and an animal). Sam, a local adult bookstore owner, sold to Herb a magazine entitled *Wild on the Farm*. The magazine was sealed, and its contents were not visible. The magazine was delivered to Sam in error, part of a large shipment of magazines and books.

   During a raid on Sam's establishment, the local police discovered the sales ticket reflecting Herb's purchase, his name, and his address. The police then obtained a search warrant for Herb's home and found the magazine during their search. Sam and Herb have both been charged with violating the state's obscenity law. Should they be convicted? Explain your answer.

3. Do you believe that acts that harm no one, but that most members of society find immoral, should be criminalized? Explain your position.

4. How has bribery been changed since it has become a statutory crime?

5–7. Classify each of the following as direct or indirect contempt and civil or criminal contempt.

5. During a personal injury trial, Noah told the judge to "kiss my ass" and then threw an apple, striking the judge in the head.

6. During a union dispute, a judge ordered striking employees back to work. They refused to comply with the order and the judge ordered that each employee pay $50 per day until he or she returned to work.

7. Jon received a court order to tear down a fence he had constructed. The order was served by a sheriff. Immediately after the sheriff handed the order to him, Jon screamed, "Forget that idiot judge, I'm not tearing down the fence!" Jon never removed the fence, and the judge had him arrested and ordered him to remain in jail until he agreed to comply with the order.

8. Consider and discuss this statement:

Possession and use of drugs or alcohol should not be a crime. The only dangers presented from these substances arise when a person works, drives, or conducts some activity that requires the full use of the senses, while under their influence. Criminal statutes should be narrow and proscribe only the harm sought to be prevented. No harm is created by use in controlled environments, such as in the home. Accordingly, statutes should only proscribe engaging in certain undertakings while under the influence of alcohol or drugs.

9. Do you believe terrorists should be considered criminals (and handled by the criminal justice system) or combatants (and handled by the military)? Does it matter if the accused is a U.S. citizen?

Endnotes

1. Model Penal Code § 251.2(1).
2. Model Penal Code § 251.2(5).
3. 18 U.S.C. § 2421.
4. *Powell v. Georgia,* 270 Ga. 327, 510 S.E.2d 18 (1998).
5. 501 U.S. 560 (1991).
6. Model Penal Code § 251.1.
7. 18 U.S.C. § 1461.
8. Anderson, "Mapplethorpe Photos on Trial," *A.B.A. J.* 28 (Dec. 1990).
9. There are other limits on First Amendment freedoms. Some of these are discussed in Chapter 13, in the constitutional defenses section. For more on the First Amendment, see Daniel E. Hall and John P. Feldmeier, *Constitutional Values: Governmental Powers and Individual Liberties,* chs 10 and 11 (Upper Saddle River, NJ: Pearson Prentice Hall, 2009).
10. 378 U.S. 184 [1964]).
11. 354 U.S. 476 (1957).

12. *Manual Enterprises, Inc. v. Day*, 370 U.S. 478 (1962) (opinion by Justice Harlan).
13. 413 U.S. 15 (1973).
14. 50 Am. Jur. 2d *Lewdness, Indecency, etc.* 7 (1970).
15. See *Roth v. United States*, 354 U.S. 476, 487, n. 20 (1957).
16. *United States v. Guglielmi*, 819 F. 2d 451 (4th Cir. 1987).
17. See *New York v. Ferber*, 458 U.S. 747 (1982).
18. See Capitol News Co. v. Metropolitan Government, 562 S.W.2d 430 (Tenn. 1978).
19. 494 U.S. 103 (1990).
20. *Stanley v. Georgia*, 394 U.S. 557 (1969).
21. Model Penal Code § 251.4.
22. 143 *Cong. Rec.* E1633 (Sept. 3, 1997).
23. Timothy Zick, "Congress, The Internet, and The Intractable Pornography Problem: The Child Online Protection Act of 1998," 32 *Creighton L. Rev.* 1147 (1999).
24. 110 Stat. 56.
25. 521 U.S. 844 (1997).
26. 47 U.S.C. § 231.
27. *Ashcroft v. ACLU* (2002).
28. 969 F. Supp. 160 (S.D. N.Y. 1997).
29. 553 U.S. 285 (2008).
30. Model Penal Code § 250.1.
31. *Champlinsky v. New Hampshire*, 315 U.S. 568 (1942).
32. *Brandenburg v. Ohio*, 395 U.S. 444 (1969).
33. See Chapter 8 on personal status as an act.
34. 307 U.S. 174 (1939).
35. 445 U.S. 55 (1980).
36. 26 U.S.C. § 5801 *et seq*
37. 18 U.S.C. sec. 921.
38. Id.
39. Model Penal Code § 2.01(4).
40. *Robinson v. California*, 370 U.S. 660 (1962).
41. 21 U.S.C. § 848
42. *United States v. Brantley*, 733 F.2d 1429 (11th Cir. 1984).
43. 21 U.S.C. § 848(e).
44. 21 U.S.C. § 853(a).
45. Kenneth Johnson, "The Constitutionality of Drug Paraphernalia Laws," 81 *Columbia L. Rev.* 581 (1981).

46. *Posters 'N' Things, Ltd. v. United States*, 511 U.S. 513 (1994).
47. Model Penal Code § 224.8.
48. 26 U.S.C. § 7201 *et seq.*
49. Model Penal Code § 3.04(2)(a)(i).
50. 18 U.S.C. § 2381.
51. *See* 70 Am. Jur. 2d 70.
52. 18 U.S.C. § 2384.
53. 18 U.S.C. § 2389.
54. 18 U.S.C. § 792, *et seq.*, and 50 U.S.C. § 783.
55. See Oklahoma Department of Health, *Summary of Reportable Injuries in Oklahoma: Oklahoma City Bombing Injuries*, http://web.archive.org/web/20080110063748/ http://www.health.state.ok.us/PROGRAM/injury/Summary/bomb/OKCbomb.htm, retrieved January 10, 2011.
56. Michael Norton, Federal Environmental Criminal Law Enforcement in the 1990's 1 (ALI-ABA, C868, 1993).
57. 33 USC § 407.
58. Id.
59. 33 U.S.C. § 1319(a).
60. 33 U.S.C. § 1319(c).
61. 42 U.S.C. § 7413.
62. 42 U.S.C. § 9603.
63. 42 U.S.C. § 6928.
64. 15 U.S.C. §§ 2614–15.
65. 7 U.S.C. § 136i–1(d).
66. 16 U.S.C. §§ 1531–1543.
67. 16 U.S.C. §§ 1361–1384, 1401–7.

CHAPTER 12

PARTIES AND INCHOATE OFFENSES

Chapter Outline

Parties to Crimes
Inchoate Crimes
    Attempt
    Conspiracy
    Solicitation

Chapter Objectives

After completing this chapter, you should be able to:

- identify and describe the roles of the various participants to crimes in both common law and contemporary legal terms.
- identify the various participants to crimes in given fact scenarios.
- explain relative culpability of the participants to a crime.
- explain the culpability for unsuccessful attempts to commit a crime.
- identify the elements of, and contract, attempt, conspiracy, and solicitation.
- apply attempt, conspiracy, and solicitation to fact scenarios.
- identify the material facts and legal issues in one-half of the cases you read, and describe the court's analyses and conclusions in the cases.

PARTIES TO CRIMES

Not all crimes are committed by only one person. Not all planned crimes are completed. This chapter examines the two topics of group criminal responsibility and uncompleted crimes. Those who participate in a crime are referred to as *parties*. Uncompleted crimes are referred to as *inchoate crimes*.

At common law, there were four parties to crimes: principals in the first degree; principals in the second degree; accessories before the fact; and accessories after the fact.

A **principal** in the first degree is the participant who actually committed the proscribed act. For example, three people (A, B, and C) agree to rob a grocery store. A enters the store, points a gun at a checker, and demands that money be placed in a bag. A is a principal in the first degree.

A principal in the second degree is a party who aids, counsels, assists, or encourages the principal in the first degree during commission of the crime. A party must be present during a crime to be a principal in the second degree. However, constructive presence is sufficient. Whenever a party is physically absent from the location of the crime, but aids from a distance, that party is a principal in the second degree. So, if B, from our hypothetical case, waits in the getaway car outside the store, B is a principal in the second degree. First-degree and second-degree principals are punished equally. Principals in the second degree are also referred to as *accomplices*, as are accessories before the fact.

Anyone who aids, counsels, encourages, or assists in the preparation of a crime, but is not physically present during the crime, is an **accessory** before the fact. If C, an expert in bank security, assisted in planning the robbery, then C is an accessory before the fact. The primary distinction between a principal in the second degree and an accessory before the fact is the lack of presence during the crime of an accessory before the fact.

At common law, accessories could not be convicted until the principals were convicted. In addition, procedural rules made it more difficult to convict accessories than principals. These rules are no longer the law. Statutes commonly group principals in the first and second degree together with accessories before the fact and punish all equally.

The mens rea of an accomplice (before and during a crime) is usually intentional (specific) in common-law terms, or knowing or purposeful in Model Penal Code language. Negligent and reckless acts do not make a person a principal in the second degree or an accessory.

Accessories after the fact continue to be treated differently. A person is an accessory after the fact if (1) aid, comfort, or shelter is provided to a criminal (2) with the purpose of assisting the criminal in avoiding arrest or prosecution (3) after the crime is committed (4) and the accessory was not present during commission of the crime. D is an accessory after the fact, if A and B flee to D's house and D hides A and B from the police. It is possible to be an accessory both before and after the fact. Hence, if C were to hide A and B from the police, C would be an accessory both before and after the fact. Accessories after the fact are not punished as severely as the other three classifications of parties (Exhibit 12–1).

principal

■ A person directly involved with committing a crime, as opposed to an accessory.

accessory

■ A person who helps to commit a crime without being present. An accessory before the fact is a person who, without being present, encourages, orders, or helps another to commit a crime. An accessory after the fact is a person who finds out that a crime has been committed and helps to conceal the crime or the criminal.

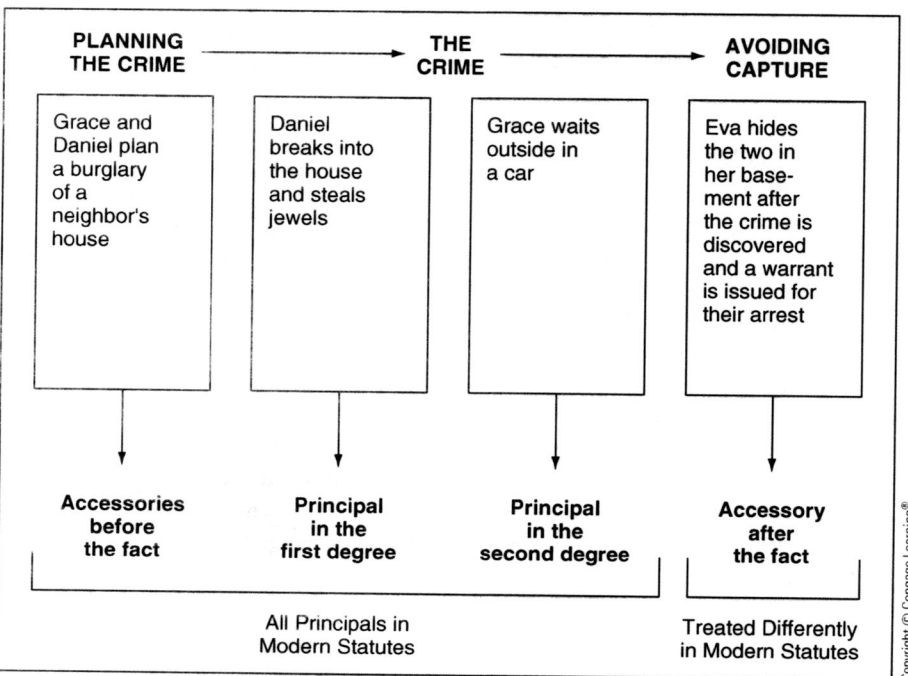

Exhibit 12-1 PARTIES TO A BURGLARY

The mental state required to prove that a person was an accessory after the fact is twofold: It must be shown first that the defendant was aware of the person's criminal status (scienter) and second that the defendant intended to hinder attempts to arrest or prosecute the criminal.

INCHOATE CRIMES

Not all planned crimes are completed. Because of the danger posed by substantial planning, accompanied by an intent to carry out a plan, some uncompleted crimes may be punished.

By punishing inchoate acts, the deterrent purpose of the criminal justice system is furthered. If the rule were otherwise, law enforcement officials would have no incentive to intervene in a criminal enterprise before it is completed. By punishing attempt, conspiracy, and solicitation, an officer may prevent a planned criminal act from occurring without risking losing a criminal conviction.

Attempt

The reasons planned crimes are not always successful are numerous. In some instances, law enforcement intervention prevents completion of a crime. If a police officer stops Penny from shooting Tom moments before she commits the act, should she be free from criminal liability because she was not successful? The law answers that question in the negative, calling such uncompleted crimes *attempt*.

Attempt was not a crime at early common law; however, attempt cases do appear later in English common law. The first cases began to appear in the late 1700s and early 1800s.[1] Many of the early cases have been traced to an English court that is no longer in existence, the Star Chamber. Today, attempt is recognized in the United States by all states.

The purpose of attempt laws is to deter people from planning to commit crimes; to punish those who intended to commit a crime, but were unsuccessful; and to encourage law enforcement officers to prevent unlawful activity. The last may appear obvious; however, if it were not for making attempts illegal, police would have an incentive to permit illegal acts, so as to be able to punish the wrongdoer.

There are essentially three elements to all attempts. One, the defendant must intend to commit a crime. Two, the defendant must act in furtherance of that intent. Three, the crime is not completed.

First, the mens rea element: The defendant must intend to take some act that amounts to a crime; in common-law language, specific intent, and under the Model Penal Code, knowingly or purposefully. Some statutes specifically identify what crime must be intended, whereas others simply refer to an intent to commit any felony. In any event, the accused must intend to commit some specific crime, such as murder, rape, or theft.

The second element, the actus reus of attempt, can be problematic. The problem revolves around this question: how close to completion of the intended crime must a defendant come to be guilty of attempt? It is well established that thoughts alone do not establish a crime; mere preparation without anything further does not amount to the crime of attempt. The failing student who sits at home and contemplates how to "do in" his or her criminal law instructor commits no crime. It is not until the student goes further that he or she can be liable for attempt.

Various tests are used to determine if an act is close enough to completion to permit an attempt conviction. The four commonly used tests are proximity, res ipsa loquitur, probable desistance, and the Model Penal Code's "substantial steps" test.

The *proximity test* examines what acts have been taken and what acts are left to be taken to complete the crime. Justice Holmes said that there "must be a dangerous proximity to success."[2]

The *res ipsa loquitur test* (also called the *unequivocality test*) looks at crimes individually and finds an act, a certain point in time, which indicates that the defendant has "no other purpose than the commission of that specific crime."[3] For example, most courts have held that once a defendant hires another to commit a crime, attempt has been committed. The step of hiring the person who will complete the crime crosses the line between mere preparation and illegal act.

The third test, *probable desistance,* focuses on the likelihood that the defendant would have followed through with the crime had the opportunity existed. The foundation of the theory is that all people may plan illegal acts at some time in life, but that there is a point where most stop. Any person who passes this line of demarcation has exhibited that the crime would have been completed, had the situation permitted. Critics have attacked this test, claiming that the determination of such a line, if it exists, is arbitrary.

attempt

■ An effort to commit a crime that goes beyond preparation and that proceeds far enough to make the person who did it guilty of an "attempt crime." For example, if a person fires a shot at another in a failed effort at murder, the person is guilty of *attempted murder.*

The Model Penal Code uses a *substantial step* to completion test.[4] That is, one is guilty of attempt if substantial steps have been taken toward commission of a crime. The Code specifically states that the conduct in question must "strongly corroborate" the actor's criminal purpose. The Code goes further and lists acts that may constitute attempts, provided that they "strongly corroborate" an intent to commit a crime. That list includes:

1. Lying in wait or searching for the intended victim.
2. Enticing or seeking to entice the intended victim to go to the place where the crime will be committed.
3. Investigating the location where the crime is to be committed.
4. Unlawfully entering a structure where the crime is to be committed.
5. Possession of materials necessary to complete the crime, provided that the tools are specially designed for the commission of the crime.
6. Possession, collection, or fabrication of materials to be used in the crime, near the scene of the crime, when the materials serve no lawful purpose.
7. Soliciting someone to commit a crime.

Keep in mind that different results are possible if these tests are applied to the same facts. In the *Murray* case, discussed later in this chapter, the line between preparation and attempt is examined. Do you agree with the court?

Regardless of which test is applied, if a defendant has a change of heart and does not complete the crime, even after crossing the line, abandonment may be a valid defense.

Of course, the abandonment must be voluntary. Generally, any reason that causes a defendant to desist, other than the defendant's independent decision not to complete the crime, falls outside the defense. A criminal who chooses not to rob a store because a police officer arrives at the scene moments before the planned act was to occur is not entitled to the defense of abandonment.

Two other defenses that arise in the context of attempt are legal and factual impossibility. **Legal impossibility** refers to the situation when a defendant believes that his or her acts are illegal when they are not.

If defendants commit an act while believing it illegal when it is actually lawful, they are not liable. The law of attempt does not punish one for attempting to do a lawful thing, even if the person had an evil mind.

Factual impossibility refers to situations when people attempt to commit a crime, but it is impossible to do so. For example, John breaks into his friend's school locker to steal property, but discovers that the locker is empty. Distraught by the situation, John decides to relax by smoking marijuana. Unknown to John, the cigarette contains no marijuana or other illegal drug. John has made two factual errors. In both instances John could be convicted because factual impossibility is not a defense. This rule is justified by the fact that the defendant possessed the required mens rea and took all the acts necessary to commit the offense. The crime was not fully completed only because of an extraneous fact unknown to the defendant.

legal impossibility

■ A person who is unable to commit a crime because of legal impossibility cannot be convicted of a crime he or she intends or attempts.

In the *Haines* case, a defendant appealed his conviction for attempted murder. He alleged that because of factual improbability, he did not take a "substantial step" toward completing a murder.

The Indiana Court of Appeals rejected factual impossibility (leaving open the issue of inherent factual impossibility) as a defense and rejected the factual assertion that AIDS cannot be transmitted through spitting and throwing blood on a person. Further, the court found that the acts of spitting and throwing blood on a person by a person with AIDS are substantial steps toward the commission of murder, thereby supporting an attempted murder conviction.

Conspiracy

In 2013 Gilberto Valle was convicted of conspiracy. But this was not an ordinary conspiracy case. Valle was a husband, father of an infant, and New York City police officer when arrested. He also became widely known as Cannibal Cop. Valle was convicted of conspiracy to kidnap. The plans included rape, torture, and eating women and children. One of the intended victims was Valle's wife. Fearing for her life after discovering the plot, she reported him to authorities.

Another intended victim was the daughter of one of Valle's co-conspirators, Michael Van Hise. Van Hise wrote to a third co-conspirator that he was preserving his 3-year-old stepdaughter until she was old enough to rape and hang to death, prompting one of his co-conspirators to write that the plan was "hot" and asked to be involved if "that would be turn-on" for Van Hise. Van Hise also offered his nieces as potential victims. The visioning and planning for the crimes occurred primarily, but not exclusively, online. Valle and his co-conspirators were charged - and convicted in federal court with conspiracy to commit kidnapping and Valle was also charged with misusing the National Crime Information Center, a federal law enforcement database, to obtain information about his intended victims. Gilberto Valle Guilty: "Cannibal Cop" Guilty of Conspiring to Kidnap and Eat Women. Huffington Post. August 12. 2013.

Conspiracy is (1) an agreement (2) between two or more persons (3) to commit an unlawful act or a lawful act in an unlawful manner. The agreement is the actus reus of the crime, and the intent to commit an unlawful act or a lawful act in an unlawful manner is the mens rea.

In some jurisdictions, the agreement alone satisfies the actus reus. In others, some act must be taken in furtherance of the objective of the agreement. Although at least one jurisdiction requires the conspirators to take "substantial steps" to be liable for conspiracy, most require less; often proof of an "overt act" will sustain a conviction. Hence, although mere preparation is not sufficient to impose liability for attempt, it is sufficient in many jurisdictions to prove conspiracy.

In the case of Valle, the so-called Cannibal Cop, prosecutors asserted that he committed the overt acts required by federal law to establish conspiracy by (1) discussing the crimes with others; (2) accessing and researching restricted law enforcement databases

conspiracy

■ A crime that may be committed when two or more persons agree to do something unlawful (or to do something lawful by unlawful means). The -agreement can be inferred from the persons' actions.

to identify victims; (3) traveling to meet one potential victim; (4) researching how to drug and abduct women leading to the creation of a document entitled "Abducting and Cooking [victim]: A Blueprint," and (5) communicating, by e-mail and instant messaging, his co-conspirators about "kidnapping, cooking and eating body parts" of the victims with detailed plans for two intended victims.[5]

Naturally, a conspiracy requires more than one person who must join in the agreement. One limitation on this rule is the **concert of action rule (Wharton's Rule)**. Under this rule, two people cannot be charged with conspiracy when the underlying offense itself requires two people. For example, gambling is a crime that requires the acts of at least two people. Wharton's Rule prohibits convictions of both gambling and conspiracy. Adultery and incest are other examples. This is not true of murder, as murder can be committed by one person. Wharton's Rule is limited, however, to two people. So if three people agree to gamble, a conviction of gambling and conspiracy to commit gambling is permitted.

> **concert of action rule**
>
> ■ The rule that, unless a statute specifies otherwise, it is not a conspiracy for two persons to agree to commit a crime if the definition of the crime itself requires the participation of two or more persons. Also called *Wharton Rule* and *concerted action rule*.

The mens rea of conspiracy has two aspects. First, conspirators must have an intent to enter into an agreement. Second, conspirators must possess a specific intent to commit some unlawful objective. That objective must be to commit an unlawful act or a lawful act in an unlawful manner. The language of conspiracy speaks of doing unlawful acts, not necessarily criminal. This is important because some acts, when taken by an individual, may lead to civil, but not criminal, liability. However, when the same acts are taken by a group, the law of conspiracy makes them criminal. This is common in the area of fraud.

The mens rea requirement of conspiracy is strict. Contrary to the general rule, mistake of law and fact are often accepted defenses. It is a defense for a party to have been under the mistaken belief that the group's actions and objectives were legal. This is because the conspiracy must be corrupt; the parties must have had an evil purpose for their union.

What if a party withdraws from the conspiracy while it is ongoing? As a general rule, withdrawal is not a defense, because the crime was complete when the parties entered into the agreement. However, if the jurisdiction requires an agreement plus an overt act or substantial steps, and the withdrawal is made before those acts occur, there is no criminal liability on behalf of the withdrawn party. To determine when withdrawal occurred, courts look to the defendants' actions. Withdrawal is effective at the time the acts would have conveyed to a reasonable person, standing in a co-conspirator's shoes, that they were abandoning the conspiracy. Additionally, the withdrawal must occur within a time that permits the other parties to abandon the objective. A last-second withdrawal, when it is too late to stop the wheels from turning, is not a defense. The Model Penal Code recognizes voluntary withdrawal as an affirmative defense.[6]

A few procedural issues are unique to conspiracy. As a whole, these rules favor prosecution. First, conspiracy is considered a crime, independent of any crime that is the objective of the conspiracy. If Amy and Ashley conspire to murder Elsa, they have committed two offenses: murder and conspiracy to murder. It is not a violation of the Fifth Amendment's double jeopardy prohibition to punish both crimes (cumulative punishment). Conspiracy to commit a crime and the commission of that crime do not merge into one. This is why conspiracy can be inchoate; it can be charged in cases where the objective is not met. If Amy and Ashley are not successful in their murderous plot, they are still liable for conspiracy to murder. One exception to the general rule of cumulative punishments is Wharton's Rule, discussed earlier.

Prosecutors must show an agreement between two or more parties to prove conspiracy. This creates some difficulties at trial. One difficulty concerns whether alleged co-conspirators should be tried together or separately. Because the United States Supreme Court has approved trial of all parties either at the location where the agreement was entered into or at any location where an act in furtherance of the conspiracy occurred, defendants are usually tried together.[7] It is possible for a defendant to be tried in a location where he or she has never been, and some argue that this practice is unconstitutional. In addition, critics argue that trying defendants together creates an increased likelihood of conviction because a form of "guilt by association" occurs in jurors' minds.

Another procedural irregularity is the **co-conspirator hearsay rule**. **Hearsay** is an out-of-court statement. Although hearsay evidence is normally inadmissible at trial, the co-conspirator exception permits the statements of one party that are made out of court to be admitted. The rule is limited to statements made during planning and commission of the conspiracy; statements made after it is completed are inadmissible.

Because two people (or more) are required to have a conspiracy, if only two people are charged, and one is acquitted, then the other cannot be punished. For example, Edgar and Robert are charged and tried together for conspiring to rob a bank. If the jury acquits one, the other must also be acquitted. At least two people must be convicted. So, if a group of people are charged, and the jury acquits all but two, the convictions stand.

Finally, be aware that many statutes deal with conspiracies, even though they are not named so. You have already examined two federal conspiracy statutes, the Racketeer Influenced and Corrupt Organizations Act and Continuing Criminal Enterprise. In recent years there has been a rise in the number of conspiracy filings. This is largely the result of RICO and related statutes and because of the procedural advantages that prosecutors have, as discussed earlier.

Solicitation

You have already encountered **solicitation** in the discussion of prostitution. But solicitation is much broader than attempting to engage someone in prostitution. Solicitation is the (1) encouraging, requesting, or commanding (2) of another (3) to commit a crime.

Solicitation is a specific-intent crime: The person must intend to convince another to commit an offense. Although the crime may be prostitution, it can be any crime in most jurisdictions. A few states limit the pool to felonies. The actus reus of the crime is the solicitation.

The crime is different from attempt, because the solicitation itself is a crime, and no act to further the crime need be taken. Of course, if Gwen asks Tracy to kill Jeff, and the deed is completed, then Gwen is an accessory before the fact of murder, as well as a solicitor.

co-conspirator's rule
■ The principle that statements by a member of a proven conspiracy may be used as evidence against any of the members of the conspiracy.

hearsay
■ A statement about what someone else said (or wrote or otherwise communicated). *Hearsay evidence* is evidence, concerning what someone said outside of a court proceeding, that is -offered in the proceeding to prove the truth of what was said. The *hearsay rule* bars the admission of hearsay as evidence to *prove the hearsay's truth* unless allowed by a hearsay exception.

solicitation
■ Asking for; enticing; strongly requesting. This may be a crime if the thing being urged is a crime.

> **Web Links**
>
> **GPO Gate**
>
> The U.S. Government Printing Office maintains a site with information of all three branches of the federal government. This includes the U.S. Code, Federal Register, and Code of Federal Regulations, among others. Direct access to the GPO site is at *http://www.gpoaccess.gov/index.html*

Key Terms

accessory
attempt
co-conspirator hearsay rule
concert of action rule

conspiracy
hearsay
legal impossibility
principal

solicitation
Wharton's Rule

Review Questions

1. Distinguish a principal in the first degree from a principal in the second degree. Which is punished more severely?
2. A person who helps principals prepare to commit a crime but is not present during the commission, is called what?
3. Has Jan committed attempted murder if she decides to kill her sister and mentally works out the details of when, how, and where?
4. What are the elements of conspiracy?
5. What is hearsay? What is the co-conspirator hearsay rule?
6. What is meant by the phrase "inchoate crimes?"
7. What is the difference between solicitation and attempt?

Problems & Critical Thinking Exercises

1-3. Use the following facts to answer problems 1 through 3: Abel and Baker were inmates sharing a cell in state prison. During their stay, they planned a convenience store robbery for after their release. They decided which store to rob, when they would rob it, and what method they would use. Having frequented the store on many occasions, Abel knew that the store had a safe and that the employees did not have access to its contents. Neither Abel nor Baker had any experience with breaking into safes and decided to seek help.

Accordingly, they sought out "Nitro," a fellow inmate who was a known explosives expert. They requested his assistance and promised to pay him one-third of the total recovery. He agreed. However, he would be able only to teach the two how to gain entry to the safe, because he was not scheduled for release until after the day they had planned for the robbery. He added that he owned a house in the area and that it would be available for them to use as a "hide-out until the heat was off."

The two were released as planned and drove to the town where the store was located. As instructed by Nitro, the two went to a store and purchased the materials necessary to construct an explosive, which was to be used to gain entry to the safe. That evening, Abel and Baker went to the convenience store with their homemade explosive. They left the car they were traveling in and went to the rear of the store to gain entry through a back door. However, as they entered the alley behind the store, they encountered a police officer. The officer, suspicious of them, examined their bag and discovered the bomb. Abel and Baker escaped from the officer and stayed in Nitro's house for 3 days before being discovered and arrested.

1. What crimes has Abel committed?
2. What crimes has Baker committed?
3. What crimes has Nitro committed?
4. John and Tyrone have a fight in a bar. Tyrone returns home, climbs into bed, and suffers a fatal heart attack. John, still angry from the earlier fight, climbs through a window into Tyrone's room and shoots Tyrone twice in the head. Has John committed a murder? Attempted murder? Explain your answer.

Endnotes

1. See *Rex v. Scofield,* Cald. 397 (1784) and *Rex v. Higgins,* 2 East 5 (1801).
2. *Hyde v. United States,* 225 U.S. 347 (1912).
3. Turner, "Attempts to Commit Crimes," 5 *Cambridge L.J.* 230, 236 (1934).
4. Model Penal Code § 5.01.
5. These elements are a composition of the overt acts that could be found in M. Bowman, *NYPD 'Cannibal Cop' Guilty of Kidnapping Conspiracy,* March 12, 2013, Lawyers.com found at http://blogs.lawyers.com/2013/03/nypd-cannibal-cop-guilty/ and FBI Press Release, *Manhattan U.S. Attorney Announces Arrest of New York City Police Officer for Kidnapping Conspiracy and Illegally Accessing Federal Law Enforcement Database,* October 25, 2012.
6. Model Penal Code § 5.03.
7. *Hyde v. United States,* 225 U.S. 347 (1912).

CHAPTER 13

FACTUAL AND STATUTORY DEFENSES

Chapter Outline

"Defense" Defined
Affirmative Defenses
Insanity
    M'Naghten
    Irresistible Impulse
    Durham
    The Model Penal Code Test
    Guilty But Mentally Ill (GBMI)
    Procedures of the Insanity Defense
    Disposition of the Criminally Insane
    Insanity at the Time of Trial
Duress and Necessity
Use-of-Force Defenses
    Self-Defense
    Defense of Others
    Defense of Property and Habitation
    Imperfect Self-Defense
    Arrests
Infancy
Intoxication
Mistake
Entrapment
Alibi and Consent
Statutes of Limitation

Chapter Objectives

After completing this chapter you should be able to:

- define, recite the elements of, and apply to factual scenarios common factual defenses to criminal accusations, such as alibi.
- define, recite the elements of, and apply to factual scenarios common statutory defenses to criminal accusations, such as the insanity defense.
- critically discuss these defenses.
- identify the material facts and legal issues in one-half of the cases you read and describe the court's analyses and conclusions in these cases.

"DEFENSE" DEFINED

Criminal defendants usually claim that they are innocent of the charges against them. A defendant's reason for asserting that he is innocent is called a *defense*. Defenses can be factual: "I didn't do it!" They can also be legal: "I did it, but the case was filed after the statute of limitation had run." Many defenses have been developed under the common law; however, many others have been created by legislation. Finally, some defenses find their origin in the constitutions of the states and federal government. Some defenses are complete (perfect); that is, if they are successful, the defendant goes free. Other defenses are partial; the defendant avoids liability on one charge but may be convicted of a lesser offense.

This chapter examines several factual and statutory defenses. Chapter 14 discusses constitutional defenses.

AFFIRMATIVE DEFENSES

There is a special class of defenses known as **affirmative defenses.** Affirmative defenses go beyond a simple denial; they raise special or new issues that, if proven, can result in an acquittal or lesser liability. Defenses that raise the question of a defendant's mental state to commit a crime (e.g., insanity and intoxication), whether justification or excuse existed to commit the crime (e.g., self-defense), and alibi fall into the affirmative defenses class.

As a general rule, criminal defendants may sit passively during trial, as the prosecution bears the burden of proving the government's allegations. In all instances, **burden of proof** refers to two burdens, the burden of production and the burden of persuasion. Because it is not practical to require prosecutors to prove that every defendant was sane, was not intoxicated, or did not have justification to use force, the burdens for affirmative defenses are different than for other defenses. First, defendants have the duty of raising all affirmative defenses. In some cases, this means that defendants must inform the prosecutor of their intention to raise the defense early in the process. At trial this means that defendants must produce some evidence to support the defense. This is known as the **burden of production.**

After defendants have met the burden of production, the **burden of persuasion** then must be met. There is a split among the states; some require the defendant to carry this burden, whereas others require it of the prosecution. If defendants have the burden, they must convince the fact finder that the defense is true. Defendants must prove this by a preponderance of evidence. In jurisdictions that require prosecutors to disprove an affirmative defense, there is again a split as to the standard of proof required. Some require proof by a preponderance, and others require proof beyond a reasonable doubt.

Some of the defenses covered in this chapter are affirmative defenses. It is necessary to research local law to determine which procedure is followed in a particular jurisdiction and what defenses are considered "affirmative".

affirmative defense

■ A defense that is more than a simple denial of the charges. It raises a new matter that may result in an acquittal or a reduction of liability. It is a defense that must be affirmatively raised, often before trial or it is lost.

burden of proof

■ The requirement that to win a point or have an issue decided in your favor in a lawsuit, you must show that the weight of evidence is on your side rather than "in the balance" on that question.

burden of going forward (production)

■ The requirement that one side in a lawsuit produce evidence on a particular issue or risk losing on that issue.

burden of persuasion

■ The requirement that to win a point or have an issue decided in your favor in a lawsuit you must show that the weight of evidence is on your side, rather than "in the balance" on that question.

INSANITY

Few aspects of criminal law have received as much public attention as the insanity defense. The defense has also been the subject of considerable scholarly research and discussion. Some critics charge that the defense should not be available. Others criticize not the availability of such a defense but the particular tests employed to determine sanity. Despite its critics, insanity is recognized by nearly all jurisdictions as a defense. At least four states—Montana, Kansas, Utah, and Idaho—have abolished the insanity defense.[1] In 1994, the United States Supreme Court denied certiorari in a case challenging the abolition of the defense as violative of due process.

In reality, insanity is a mens rea defense. If a defendant was insane at the time of the crime, it is unlikely that the requisite mens rea existed. It is generally held that one who is insane is incapable of forming a rational purpose or intent. In fact, in most jurisdictions defendants may put on evidence to establish that insanity prevented the requisite mens rea from being formed. This is the defense of **diminished capacity.** It is a direct attack on the mens rea element of the crime, separate from the defense of insanity. If successful, the result could be conviction of a lesser, general-intent crime. However, a few states have made defendants choose between the insanity defense and the assertion of lack of mens rea due to insanity.

The theory underlying the defense of insanity is that no purpose of criminal law is served by subjecting insane persons to the criminal justice system. Because they have no control over their behavior, they cannot be deterred from similar future behavior. Similarly, no general deterrence will occur, as others suffering from a mental or physical disease of the mind are not likely to be deterred. The one purpose that may be served, incapacitation, is inappropriate if the defendants no longer suffer from a mental disease, or if the disease is now controlled. If the defendants continue to be dangerous, there is no need to use the criminal justice system to remove them from society, because this can be accomplished using civil commitment.

Something that must be remembered is that criminal law has its own definition of insanity. Other areas of law (e.g., civil commitment) use different tests, as do other professions (e.g., psychiatry). Each jurisdiction is free to use whatever test it wishes to determine insanity. Three tests are used to determine sanity in the criminal law context: M'Naghten; irresistible impulse; and the Model Penal Code. A fourth test, the Durham, is no longer used in any jurisdiction but is mentioned because of its historical significance.

M'Naghten

In 1843 Daniel M'Naghten was tried for killing the British prime minister's secretary. M'Naghten was laboring under the paranoid delusion that the prime minister was planning to kill him, and he killed the minister's secretary, believing him to be the prime minister. The jury found M'Naghten not guilty by reason of insanity.[2] The decision created controversy, and the House of Lords asked the justice of the Queens Bench to state what the standards for acquittal on the grounds of insanity were.[3] Those standards were attached to the decision and set forth the following standard, known as the **M'Naghten rule.**

---

diminished capacity

▪ The principle that having a certain recognized form of *diminished mental capacity* while committing a crime should lead to the imposition of a lesser punishment or to lowering the degree of the crime.

M'Naghten rule

▪ A principle employed in some jurisdictions for determining whether criminal defendants had the capacity to form criminal intent at the time they committed the crime of which they are accused. The M'Naghten rule is also referred to as the M'Naghten test or the right-wrong test.

1. At the time that the act was committed
2. the defendant was suffering from a defect of reason, from a disease of the mind, that caused
3. the defendant to not know
    a. the nature and quality of the act taken or
    b. that the act was wrong.

The M'Naghten, or right-wrong, test is that used by most jurisdictions today. First, the defendant must have suffered from a disease of the mind at the time the act occurred. *Disease of the mind* is not clearly defined, but it appears that any condition that causes one of the two events from the third part of the test satisfies this element. That is, any disease of the mind that causes a defendant to not know the quality of an act or that an act is wrong is sufficient. In at least one case, extremely low intelligence was found adequate.[4]

The phrase "the defendant must not know the nature and quality of the act" simply means that the defendant did not understand the consequences of his or her physical act. The drafters of the Model Penal Code gave the following illustration: A man who squeezes his wife's neck, believing it to be a lemon, does not know the nature and quality of his actions.[5]

What is meant by "wrong," as used in the M'Naghten test? Courts have defined it two ways. One asks whether the defendant knew that the act was legally wrong, and the other asks whether the defendant knew that the act was morally wrong.

Irresistible Impulse

Under the M'Naghten test, defendants who knew that their actions were wrong, but could not control their behavior because of a disease of the mind, are not insane. This has led a few jurisdictions, which follow M'Naghten, to supplement the rule. These states continue to follow the basic rule but add that defendants are not guilty by reason of insanity if a disease of the mind caused the defendants to be unable to control their behavior. This is true even if the defendants understood the nature and quality of the act or knew that the behavior was wrong. This is known as **irresistible impulse.**

Irresistible impulse tests can be found in American cases as far back as 1863.[6] Of course, the largest problem with implementing the irresistible impulse test is distinguishing acts that can be resisted from those that cannot.

Durham

In 1871 the New Hampshire Supreme Court rejected the M'Naghten test and held that a defendant was not guilty because of insanity if the crime was the "product of mental disease." No other jurisdictions followed New Hampshire's lead until 1954, when the District of Columbia Court of Appeals handed down *Durham v. United States,* 214 F.2d 862 (D.C. Cir. 1954). Generally, the **Durham rule** requires an acquittal if defendants would not have committed the crime if they had not been suffering from a mental disease or mental defect.

irresistible impulse
■ The loss of control due to insanity that is so great that a person cannot stop from committing a crime.

Durham rule
■ The principle, used in *Durham v. U.S.* (214 F.2d. 862 (1954)), that defendants are not guilty of a crime because of insanity if they were "suffering from a disease or defective mental condition at the time of the act and there was a causal connection between the condition and the act."

Durham was overturned in 1972 by the District of Columbia Court of Appeals in favor of a modified version of the Model Penal Code test.[7] Today, Durham is not used by any jurisdiction.

The Model Penal Code Test

The Model Penal Code contains a definition of insanity similar to, but broader than, the M'Naghten and irresistible impulse tests. This test is also referred to as the *substantial capacity test*. The relevant section of the Code reads[8]:

> A person is not responsible for criminal conduct if at the time of such conduct as a result of mental disease or defect he lacks substantial capacity either to appreciate the criminality [wrongfulness] of his conduct or to conform his conduct to the requirements of law.

The Code is similar to M'Naghten in that it requires that mental disease or defect impair a defendant's ability to appreciate the wrongfulness of his or her act. The final line, "conform his conduct to the requirements of law," incorporates the irresistible impulse concept.

The Code's approach differs from the M'Naghten and irresistible impulse test in two important regards: First, the Code requires only substantial impairment, whereas M'Naghten requires total impairment of the ability to know the nature or wrongfulness of the act. Second, the Code uses the term *appreciate,* rather than *know*. The drafters of the Code clearly intended more than knowledge, and, as such, evidence concerning the defendant's personality and emotional state are relevant.

The Model Penal Code test has been adopted by a few jurisdictions. The federal courts used the test until Congress enacted a statute that established a test similar to the M'Naghten test.[9] That statute places the burden of proving insanity, by clear and convincing evidence, on the defendant.

Guilty But Mentally Ill (GBMI)

In 1981 John Hinckley attempted to assassinate President Ronald Reagan. The president was seriously wounded and his press secretary, James Brady, suffered permanent brain injury. It was later learned that Hinckley committed the act to impress a movie actress he had never met. At trial, Hinckley was found not guilty by reason of insanity. There was both public and legislative backlash to the decision and to the insanity defense. As a result, legislators throughout the nation moved to abolish or limit the scope of the insanity defense. Today, four states—Idaho, Montana, Utah, and Kansas—have abolished the defense altogether.[10]

Rather than abolishing the defense, other states sought to limit or alter its impact. One such measure was the establishment of the Guilty But Mentally Ill (GBMI) verdict. Pennsylvania's GBMI statute reads, in part, that a "person who timely offers a defense of insanity in accordance with the Rules of Criminal Procedure may be found 'guilty but mentally ill' at trial if the trier of facts finds, beyond a reasonable doubt, that the person is guilty of an offense, was mentally ill at the time of the commission of the offense and was not legally insane at the time of the commission of the offense."[11] As you can see, the GBMI verdict is a finding of mental illness at the time of the crime, but not insanity as defined by the applicable legal test. Unlike a defendant who is not guilty by reason of insanity, a defendant who is GBMI is both punished and treated. The defendant is sentenced as any other offender for the crime, but in addition the state provides mental health treatment.

Procedures of the Insanity Defense

Insanity is an affirmative defense. In the federal system and in many states, defendants must provide notice to the court and government that insanity will be used as a defense at trial. These statutes usually require that the notice be filed a certain number of days before trial. This notice provides the prosecution with an opportunity to prepare to rebut the defense prior to trial.

In most instances, lay testimony is not adequate to prove insanity; psychiatric examination of defendants is necessary. The judge presiding over the case will appoint a psychiatrist or psychologist, who will conduct the exam and make the findings available to the judge. Often defendants wish to have a psychiatrist of their own choosing perform an examination. This is not a problem if the defendant can afford to pay for the service. In the case of indigent defendants who desire an independent mental examination, statutes often provide reimbursement from the government for independent mental examinations up to a stated maximum. In the federal system, trial courts may approve up to $1,000 in defense-related services. Defendants who seek reimbursement for greater expenses must receive approval from the chief judge of the circuit.[12]

As with all affirmative defenses, the defendant bears the burden of production at trial. Generally, the defendant must present enough evidence to create some doubt of sanity. The states are split on the issue of persuasion. Some require that the prosecution disprove the insanity claim, usually beyond a reasonable doubt. In other jurisdictions the defendant bears the burden of persuasion, usually by preponderance of the evidence. One exception is federal law, which requires the defendant to prove insanity by the higher standard—clear and convincing evidence.[13]

Disposition of the Criminally Insane

Contrary to popular belief, those adjudged insane by a criminal proceeding are not immediately and automatically released. In most jurisdictions, after a defendant has been determined "not guilty by reason of insanity," the court (the jury in a few states) must make a determination of whether the person continues to be dangerous. If so, commitment is to be ordered. If the defendant is determined not to be dangerous, then release follows. A few jurisdictions have followed the Model Penal Code approach,[14] which requires automatic commitment following a finding of not guilty by reason of insanity. This is the rule in the federal system.[15]

In theory, those committed have a right to be treated for their mental disease. In fact, due to lack of funds, security concerns, and overcrowding problems in facilities, adequate treatment is often not provided.

Once a committed person is no longer a danger, release is granted. The determination of dangerousness is left to the judge, not hospital administrators or mental health professionals—an often-criticized practice. Patients, doctors, government officials, and even the judge can begin the process of release. Some states provide for periodic reviews of the patient's status in order to determine the propriety of release. The relevant federal statute reads, in part:[16]

> When the director of the facility in which an acquitted person is hospitalized . . . determines that the person has recovered from his mental disease or defect to such an extent that his release, or his conditional release under a prescribed regimen of medical, psychiatric, or psychological care or treatment, would no longer create a substantial risk of bodily injury to another person or serious damage to property of another, he shall promptly file a certificate to that effect with the clerk of the court that ordered the commitment . . . The court shall order a discharge of the acquitted person or, on the motion of the attorney for the government or on its own motion, shall hold a hearing [to determine if the patient is dangerous].

At that hearing, the defendant has the burden of proving by clear and convincing evidence that a risk to people or property is not created by release.

Finally, some states have a "guilty but mentally ill" verdict. Juries may return such a verdict when the defendant's illness does not rise to the level of negating culpability but treatment should be provided in addition to incarceration (see Exhibit 13–1).

Insanity at the Time of Trial

The United States Supreme Court has held that a defendant who is insane at the time of trial may not be tried.[20] The Court found that the Due Process Clauses of the Fifth and Fourteenth Amendments require that defendants be able to assist in their defense and understand the proceeding against them.

The test for determining insanity in this context is different from that discussed earlier. Insanity exists when defendants lack the capacity to understand the proceedings or assist in their defense. This simply means that defendants must be rational, possess the ability to testify coherently, and be able to meaningfully discuss their cases with their

Exhibit 13–1 INSANITY AND CRIMINAL PROCEDURE

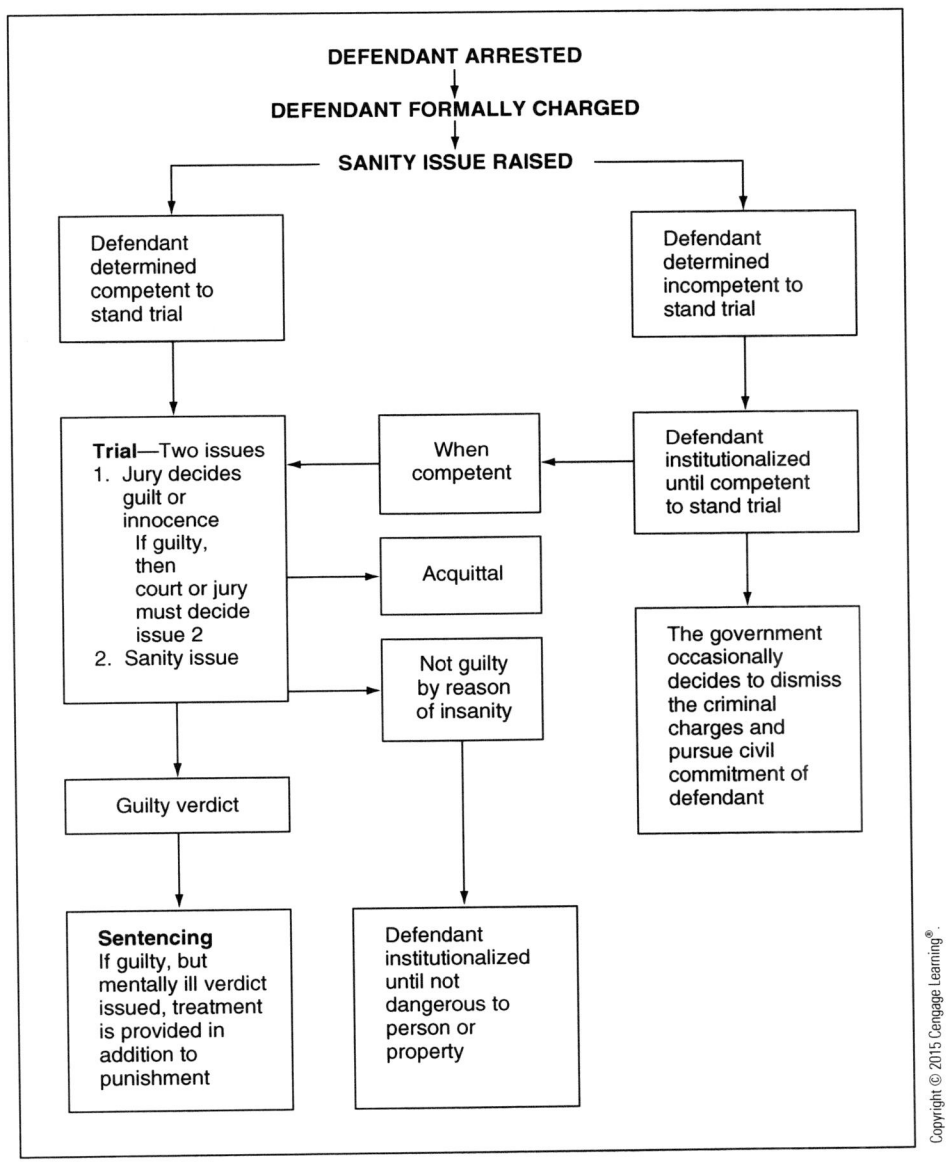

lawyers. The burden of establishing incompetence is placed on the defendant in many jurisdictions. While this procedure comports with due process, requiring the defendant to establish incompetence by clear and convincing evidence does not. In *Cooper v. Oklahoma* (1996),[21] the Supreme Court held that the burden of proof can be placed on the defendant but that the standard of proof cannot exceed preponderance of evidence.

If defendants are unable to stand trial because they are insane, they are usually committed until they are competent. Many statutes have mandatory commitment of defendants determined incompetent to stand trial. However, indefinite confinement is unconstitutional, based solely upon a finding of incompetence to stand trial. Generally, the Supreme Court has held that a lengthy (18 months or longer) detention (awaiting competence to stand trial) is tantamount to punishment and violative of the Due Process Clause.[22] In such cases, there must be a separate finding of dangerousness to continue to hold such persons.

A mistrial is to be declared in the event that a defendant becomes incompetent during a trial, and defendants who are sane at trial but become insane before sentencing should be sentenced to a psychiatric facility.

Last, the Supreme Court has held that a person who has become insane after being sentenced to death may not be executed until his or her sanity is regained.[23] The constitutional basis of the Court's decision was the Eighth Amendment's prohibition of cruel and unusual punishment. Thurgood Marshall penned, "It is no less abhorrent today than it has been for centuries to exact in penance the life of one whose mental illness prevents him from comprehending the reasons for the penalty or its implications."[24] Similarly, the Court has held that mentally retarded individuals may not be executed.[25]

Although not a defense, the issue of insanity during imprisonment and at the time of release is important. See Chapter 9 for a discussion of civil commitment of sex offenders and the dangerously mentally ill after release from prison.

DURESS AND NECESSITY

On September 5, 2012, the manager of a bank in Los Angeles, California, arrived at work shortly before opening, went to the vault and filled a bag with cash, proceeded to the back door, and threw the bag into the street, where two people were waiting and absconded with the money. Did the manager commit a crime? No. The night before the robbery, she was kidnapped by the two robbers. The morning of the robbery, they strapped a device to her chest, telling her that it was a bomb and that they would detonate it if she didn't comply with their directions. The device was removed by police and proved not be a bomb.[26]

Although the elements of theft may be satisfied, the manager acted under **duress**, a legal defense. To prove duress, one must show (1) that he or she was threatened (2) and that the threat caused a reasonable belief (3) that the only way of avoiding serious personal injury or death to oneself or others (4) was to commit the crime. Duress was recognized at common law and continues to be a statutory defense today.

First, it must be shown that a threat was made. Second, the threat must create a reasonable fear of immediate serious bodily harm or death. This fear must be reasonable; that is, even if the person making the threat had no intention of following through, the defense is still valid if a reasonable person would have thought the threat was real. Hence, even if bank robber never intended to kill Terry, she has the defense of duress. Terry need not be the one threatened for her to be able to claim duress. So, if bank robber threatened

duress

■ Unlawful pressure on what a person would not otherwise have done. It includes force, threats of violence, physical restraint, etc.

to kill a customer unless Terry complied, Terry could claim duress. The fear must not only be reasonable, but it must also be of serious bodily injury or death. If bank robber exclaims, "Put the money in the bag or I'll smack you across the face," the threatened danger is not sufficient to support the defense of duress. In addition, the threat of harm must be imminent or immediate. Threats of future harms are not adequate duress.

One limitation that is recognized nearly everywhere is that murder is not justified by duress. This rule is criticized, rightfully so, because it does not account for those situations where taking one life may save many more.

It is no defense to a crime to claim that one was only carrying out the orders of a superior, such as an employer or military superior. This issue was addressed in *United States v. Calley.*

The Court mentioned that the order's illegality was "apparent upon even cursory evaluation by a man of ordinary sense and understanding." What if an order appears to be legal and the person who follows it has a reasonable belief of its legality? In such cases, the defense of duress does applies.[27]

Necessity is similar to duress. However, whereas duress is created by human pressures, necessity comes about by natural forces. When people are confronted with two choices, both causing harm, they choose the lesser harm. If they do, they may have the defense of necessity to the act taken. For example, a person may be justified in breaking into someone's cabin to avoid freezing to death. Or a captain of a ship may be justified in a trespassory use of another's dock, if setting ashore is necessary to save the ship and its passengers.

Necessity is a broad and amorphous concept. As a general proposition, it applies anytime a person is confronted with the task of choosing between two or more evils. The harm avoided need not be bodily injury; it can also be harm to property. Of course, choosing property over life is never justified. Finally, if an alternative existed that involved less harm than the chosen act, the defense is invalid.

Duress and necessity are complete defenses. When valid, they result in acquittal of all related charges.

necessity
- Often refers to a situation that requires an action that would otherwise be illegal or expose a person to tort liability.

USE-OF-FORCE DEFENSES

A homicide on February 26, 2012, in Florida focused the Nation's attention on several criminal justice problems, including race, the role of citizens in preventing and responding to crime, and the law of self-defense. George Zimmerman, a Hispanic 28-year-old community watch leader, shot and killed Treyvon Martin, a 17-year-old African American male. Zimmerman was charged with Martin's homicide, Zimmerman asserted self-defense.[28]

On the night of the shooting, Martin was visiting with his father and his father's fiancée. While watching television, Martin left the home to walk to a convenience store. Martin trespassed through Zimmerman's neighborhood during his walk. Zimmerman observed Martin in the neighborhood during Martin's return from the store. Finding his presence suspicious, Zimmerman followed him, called the police, is alleged to have ignored a suggestion to discontinue the pursuit by the police dispatcher, and confronted and shot Martin. Zimmerman was charged with second degree murder, tried by jury, and acquitted.

Claims that Zimmerman had a racial motivation for pursuing Martin contributed to making the incident a national cause célèbre. As it too often the case, there was a media frenzy and a prejudicial rush to judgement. Of the many social and legal questions that the Treyvon Martin homicide raised, one concerns the nature of self-defense. The defense varies between the states.

All states permit the use physical force against others in specific circumstances. Self-defense, defense of others, defense of property, and use of force to make arrests fall into this area. Self-defense, defense of others, and defense of property, when successful, are complete defenses. Imperfect self-defense (including defense of another) does not lead to acquittal; however, it does reduce murder to manslaughter.

Self-Defense

self-defense

■ Physical force used against a person who is threatening the use of physical force or using physical force.

To prove **self-defense,** it must be shown that the actor (1) was confronted with an unprovoked, (2) immediate threat of bodily harm, (3) that force was necessary to avoid the harm, (4) and that the amount of force used was reasonable.

One who initiates an attack on another cannot claim self-defense, as a general proposition. There are two exceptions to this rule. First, if attackers are met with excessive force in return, they may defend themselves. For example, Mike attacks Norm with his fists, and in defense Norm uses a deadly weapon. In such a circumstance, Mike may also use deadly force to protect himself. Second, if an attacker withdraws from the attack and is pursued by the intended victim, then he or she may claim self-defense. Suppose Randy attacks Sue with an intent to sexually assault her. After he grabs her, she displays a gun, and he runs. If Sue follows after him, intending to cause him harm, then he would be privileged to use force to defend himself.

battered woman syndrome

■ Continuing abuse of a woman by a spouse or lover, and the resulting physical or psychological harm.

The threat of harm must be immediate in most jurisdictions. Threat of future harm does not justify using force against another. To satisfy this requirement, the harm must be one that will occur unless force is used, and no other means of avoiding the harm exists. However, this principle is occasionally stretched. For example, some jurisdictions have permitted a jury to be instructed on the **battered woman syndrome** defense. Under this defense, a woman who is constantly abused by her husband may be justified in using force at a time when she is not strictly in "immediate danger." The theory is that women in such circumstances have two choices: either wait for their husbands to kill them or strike first in a form of offensive self-defense. Critics of this defense contend that because other remedies are available, such as leaving the husband and obtaining a court order restraining him from bothering her, there is no immediate danger.

Finally, the force used to defend oneself must be reasonable. It would be unreasonable to knife a person who is attempting to slap one's hand. Deadly force may be used to defend against an attack that threatens serious bodily injury or death. Deadly force may not be used to defend against other attacks.

Retreat, Castle, and Stand-Your-Ground

Many states require that a person retreat from an attack, if possible, before using deadly force. This is known as the **retreat to the wall doctrine** or simply the **retreat doctrine.** But there are exceptions.

The first exception is when retreating poses a danger to the victim of the attack. Another is for police officers, who are not required to retreat when performing their lawful duties. The Model Penal Code has a retreat provision that recognizes these exceptions:

> The use of deadly force is not justifiable . . . [if] the actor knows that he can avoid the necessity of using such force without complete safety by retreating or by surrendering possession of a thing to a person asserting a claim of right thereto or by complying with a demand that he abstain from any action which he has no duty to take, except that (1) the actor is not obliged to retreat from his dwelling or place of work, unless he was the initial aggressor.[29]

The Code provides that public officials need not retreat during the performance of their duties. There is no duty to retreat rather than using nondeadly force.

Also, notice that the Code requires not only retreat, but that "thing[s]" be surrendered and one comply with another's demands before deadly force is used. Of course, one can later use civil law to recover unlawfully taken items or to recover for complying with a demand that caused damage. The aggressor will be liable both civilly and criminally for such unlawful demands.

Most states, for example, do not require one to retreat from his or her home. This is known as the **castle doctrine.** The castle doctrine dates to the old common law. Indeed the phrase "A man's home is his castle" is of ancient English origin. The castle doctrine reflects the idea that the home is a very special place, a venue that is inviolable by outsiders and where the residents can feel their safest and live free from intrusion.

There are different versions of the castle doctrine between the states where it is recognized. Castle doctrine statutes commonly include one or more of the following:

1. Repeal of the common law retreat doctrine for lawful residents of homes who use deadly force against an intruder into the home.
2. The creation of a presumption that intruders are a threat to life or limb.
3. Immunity from criminal and civil liability for residents of homes who use deadly force on intruders.

As to the first of these, there are common exceptions. For example, deadly force may not be used against people who have a lawful right to be on the premises. Police officers and family members are examples. This isn't to say that an ex-wife can't use deadly force against a homicidal ex-husband who happens to be a police officer. The statutes typically deny the castle doctrine defense to residents who use deadly force against individuals they should reasonably know are lawfully entering the premises.

retreat to the wall

■ The doctrine that before a person is entitled to use deadly force in self defense, he or she must attempt to withdraw from the encounter by giving as much ground as possible.

Castle Doctrine

■ An exception to the Retreat Doctrine, one has no obligation to retreat from his or her home before using deadly force to repel an intruder.

Another variation on the home element of the castle doctrine is the inclusion of more than homes in its grasp. For example, Ohio has extended the castle doctrine to include automobiles. The applicable statute provides that "Every person accused of an offense is presumed innocent until proven guilty beyond a reasonable doubt, and the burden of proof for all elements of the offense is upon the prosecution. The burden of going forward with the evidence of an affirmative defense, and the burden of proof, by a preponderance of the evidence, for an affirmative defense, is upon the accused."[30]

stand-your-ground

■ A law that enables a person to use deadly force to repel an attack without first retreating.

A minority, but growing number of states, have so-called **stand-your-ground** laws.[31] Florida, the location of the Zimmerman shooting of Martin, is such a state. Stand-your-ground laws are essentially the extension of the castle doctrine to public spaces. A victim of an attack that threatens life or limb in any space, not just the home or car, does not have a duty to retreat, even if a safe retreat is available. Florida's law provides, in part:

> (3) A person who is not engaged in an unlawful activity and who is attacked in any other place where he or she has a right to be has no duty to retreat and has the right to stand his or her ground and meet force with force, including deadly force if he or she reasonably believes it is necessary to do so to prevent death or great bodily harm to himself or herself or another or to prevent the commission of a forcible felony.

As the second dimension, reasonable force, states vary between requiring the use of deadly force to be objectively reasonable to creating a presumption of reasonable fear of life or limb by intruders in the home. The difference between the two is procedural. If the former, the law permits the use of deadly force without retreat but the person who used the force may bear the burden of proving to the jury that her fear was reasonable. If the latter, the law presumes the fear was reasonable and the burden falls to the state to prove it was unreasonable. Florida shifts the burden to the state to prove that the fear was unreasonable:

> (1) A person is presumed to have held a reasonable fear of imminent peril of death or great bodily harm to himself or herself or another when using defensive force that is intended or likely to cause death or great bodily harm to another if:
>
> (a) The person against whom the defensive force was used was in the process of unlawfully and forcefully entering, or had unlawfully and forcibly entered, a dwelling, residence, or occupied vehicle, or if that person had removed or was attempting to remove another against that person's will from the dwelling, residence, or occupied vehicle; and
>
> (b) The person who uses defensive force knew or had reason to believe that an unlawful and forcible entry or unlawful and forcible act was occurring or had occurred.
>
> * * *
>
> (4) A person who unlawfully and by force enters or attempts to enter a person's dwelling, residence, or occupied vehicle is presumed to be doing so with the intent to commit an unlawful act involving force or violence.[32]

The third dimension of most castle doctrine statutes is the creation of civil liability for individuals who use deadly force in a manner recognized by the statutes. Of course, liability may be found if the person using force is found to have acted outside the protection of the castle doctrine statute, e.g., used force unreasonably.

United States' law of self-defense has evolved considerably since the old common law and the variation between the states is considerable. See Exhibit 13–2 for a continuum of the right to use deadly force as a form of self-defense.

Exhibit 13–2 DEADLY FORCE CONTINUUM

Least Protection		Self-Defense		Greatest Protection
Retreat to Wall	Castle Doctrine	Castle Doctrine Plus	Castle Doctrine Enhanced	Stand-Your-Ground
Duty to retreat, even in the home, before using deadly Force	Deadly Force may be used by residents of homes against intruders without first retreating. Person using deadly force may have to prove it was reasonable.	The use of deadly force by the resident of a home is presumed reasonable, unless the victim had fight to enter premises.	Castle Doctrine is extended to cars or other venues.	Deadly Force may be used to repel an attacker in any location without first retreating, so long as reasonable attacker threatens life or limb.

Defense of Others

It is also a justified use of force to defend another. The rules are similar to that of self-defense: There must be a threat of immediate danger to the other person; the perception of threat must be reasonable; the amount of force used must be reasonable; and deadly force may be used only to repel a deadly attack.

At common law, one was privileged to defend only those with whom a special relationship existed, such as parent and child. Today, most jurisdictions permit any person to use force to protect another.

What happens when a person uses force to defend another who is *not* privileged to use force? For example, Perry is an undercover police officer attempting to arrest Norm, who is resisting. Randa observes what is happening and comes to Norm's defense, believing that Norm was being unlawfully attacked. There is a split of authority concerning this problem. Some jurisdictions limit the authority of the defender to use force to the privilege held by the person being attacked. Because Norm was not privileged to use force against the police officer, Randa is guilty of assault. Other states, however, use an objective test. Under such a test, if a reasonable person standing in Randa's shoes would have believed that force was justified, then he or she would be acquitted.

Defense of Property and Habitation

At common law and by legislative enactment today, one may use force to defend property. As with defending oneself, only reasonable force may be used. Because property is not as valuable as life, deadly force may not be used to protect property. Thus, one must allow another to take or destroy property before killing to defend it. No force is reasonable if other methods of protecting the property were available. So, if one has ample time to seek assistance from the police or the courts, force would be unreasonable. In contrast, if an enemy appears at one's house and begins to destroy a car in the driveway, force would be permitted to protect the vehicle. Actors must have a reasonable belief that their property is in danger of trespass or destruction and that the force used was necessary to defend the property.

The basic rules concerning defense of property also apply to defense of habitation: One must have a reasonable belief that the property is threatened; only reasonable force may be used to protect the property; and other non-violent remedies must be utilized before resorting to force. However, one difference between dwellings and other property is that deadly force may be used, under some circumstances, to protect one's home.

In early common law, the security of the home was as important as life itself. Therefore, people were permitted to use deadly force against any forcible intruder after warning the person not to enter. Today the rule has been narrowed, and statutes now commonly require that the occupant must believe that the intruder intends to commit a felony once inside before deadly force may be used.

The Model Penal Code allows the use of deadly force if either (1) the intruder is attempting to take the dwelling (with no legal claim to do so) or (2) the intruder is there to commit a crime (arson, burglary, theft) and has threatened deadly force or poses a substantial risk to those inside.[33]

This provision of the Code incorporates a self-defense concept. Remember, the rules of self-defense apply in the home also. So, any time a person's life (or another's) is threatened, deadly force may be used.

Some people choose to protect their property with manmade devices, such as electric fences and spring guns. Others have used natural protection, such as dogs and snakes. Whichever is used, the rules are the same. If the device employs nondeadly force, it is likely to be lawful. An electric fence that does not have sufficient electric current to kill is a justified use of force.

However, the result is often different when one uses deadly force. There are two perspectives on the use of deadly traps to protect property. One permits the use of deadly force so long as those who set the trap would have been permitted to use such force themselves, if they had been present. So, if a murderer gains entry to a house and is killed by a spring gun, the occupant is not criminally liable because he or she would have been privileged to use deadly force against the murderer. The second perspective, adopted by the drafters of the Model Penal Code, rejects the use of deadly traps in all instances.[34] This position is sound, as deadly traps do not discriminate between the dangerous and the nondangerous. The occupant who sets such a trap is simply lucky if the intruder is a criminal and not a firefighter responding to a blaze in the home.

Imperfect Self-Defense

The so-called imperfect self-defense is actually a mens rea defense. It applies to situations when people cannot make a successful self-defense (or defense of another) claim, but because they lacked malice aforethought (or purpose), the crime should not be murder but, rather, manslaughter. The defense applies only to homicides and is not recognized everywhere.

As stated, a person must have a reasonable belief that he or another is in danger of serious bodily injury or death before deadly force may be used. What if a person possesses a good-faith but unreasonable belief? Self-defense is unavailable, but because there is no malicious intent, purpose, or malice aforethought (depending on the jurisdiction's definition of murder), the crime is reduced to manslaughter. The defense is available in a second situation: whenever people who initiates an attack using nondeadly force later justifiably the use deadly force to defend themselves.

Arrests

Sometimes it is necessary for law enforcement officers to use force to execute their duties and to defend themselves. When a police officer uses force in defense of another's attack, the rules of self-defense that you have already learned apply. In addition, because the use of force is an integral part of law enforcement, it is often justified. However, a person making an arrest does not have an unlimited right to use force against an arrestee. This section examines a person's right to resist an unlawful arrest, the so-called citizen's arrest, and arrests by law enforcement officers.

Resisting Unlawful Arrests

In some states, people may use force to resist an unlawful arrest. The amount of force is usually limited to nondeadly, although some jurisdictions permit one to use deadly force. Of course, if a person uses force against a lawful arrest, he or she is fully liable for whatever crime results (assault, battery, or murder), as well as for resisting a lawful arrest.

The rule permitting force to resist an unlawful arrest evolved during a time when arrestees were detained for long periods before appearing before a court, jail conditions were extremely poor, and no civil remedies existed for unlawful arrests. In light of these harsh facts, public policy was best served by permitting people to resist unlawful arrests.

Today, many jurisdictions have adopted an approach closer to the Model Penal Code's, which prohibits any resistance to an arrest by a law enforcement officer. This is the sensible approach, as the reasons for permitting resistance no longer exist: Arrestees must be promptly brought before judges and released if there is no probable cause. When available, bail is set immediately. Also, federal law now permits civil suits against law enforcement officers for violation of a person's civil rights. Prohibiting resistance advances two important public policy objectives: First, it fosters obedience to police, and, second, it reduces violence.

Arrests by Law Enforcement Officers

A law enforcement officer is privileged to use reasonable force to apprehend criminals and to prevent those incarcerated from escaping. At common law, police could use all but deadly force to arrest misdemeanants and deadly force to arrest felons. This latter rule was justified by the fact that all felons were put to death at early common law.

In 1974 a Memphis, Tennessee, police officer shot and killed a 15-year-old male who was fleeing a burglary. The boy had stolen 40 dollars. The family of the deceased boy sued the police department in federal court for violating his constitutional rights. The case ended up before the United States Supreme Court.

In *Tennessee v. Garner*, 471 U.S. 1 (1985), the Court held that the use of deadly force by a police officer is a "seizure" under the Fourth Amendment. Accordingly, the test used to determine whether the use of deadly force is proper is the Fourth Amendment's test: reasonability. The Court then held that the use of deadly force is reasonable only when the person fleeing is a dangerous felon. This finding invalidated the laws of many states that permitted the use of deadly force to stop all fleeing felons, including those who posed no threat to life or limb, such as thieves, extortionists, and those who tendered bad checks. The Court did not state what standard must be applied in cases of nondeadly force. Some courts applied a due process standard, others the Fourth Amendment's reasonableness standard.

In 1989 the Court handed down *Graham v. Connor*, 490 U.S. 386 (1989) in which the standard was set for all preconviction seizures, deadly and nondeadly. Through that decision, the Court held that all seizures are to be evaluated under the Fourth Amendment objective reasonableness standard. Specifically the Court held that courts must review challenged use of force from the perspective of a reasonable officer at the time the force was applied.

High-speed police chases have received considerable public attention in recent years because they pose a threat not only to the police officer and the person fleeing, but to the general public. Whether *Garner* applied to these chases was not known until 2007.

Finally, note that police officers are often put into positions where they must defend themselves, such as during an arrest. The same rules discussed earlier concerning self-defense apply in these situations, with one exception: Police officers are not required to retreat. Thus, if a police officer is involved in an arrest that involves escalating violence, the police officer may have to use deadly force to defend against the criminal's attack.

Arrests by Citizens

At common law, private citizens were privileged to arrest those who committed a felony or misdemeanor (which amounted to a breach of the peace) in their presence. Some jurisdictions have retained this rule, and others have changed it by statute.

In jurisdictions that have changed the rule, it is common to permit so-called citizens' arrests any time probable cause exists to believe that the person has committed a felony. In most jurisdictions a citizen may not arrest a misdemeanant unless the person making the arrest witnessed the crime. Even in such cases, only certain misdemeanors may lead to such an arrest.

The reason for these rules is to provide citizens who make such arrests with immunity from civil and criminal prosecution. However, the citizen must be privileged to make the arrest and, even when privileged, a reasonable amount of force must be used.

In some jurisdictions, a private person making an arrest may use deadly force only when the person is in fact a felon. The jurisdictions employing this rule are split: Some permit the use of deadly force by private citizens to arrest for any felony and others only for specific felonies (e.g., murder and rape). These jurisdictions are similar in one important regard. The person against whom the deadly force is used must have *in fact* committed the crime. A reasonable, but incorrect, belief that the person has committed a crime is not a defense. So, if Pat kills Sam while attempting to arrest Sam for a crime he did not commit, Pat is liable for manslaughter, even though she had a reasonable belief that he committed the crime. Some states have followed the Model Penal Code approach, which prohibits the use of deadly force by private persons in all circumstances.[35]

The results are different if a private person is assisting a law enforcement officer. In fact, many states have statutes that require citizens to assist police officers upon order. In such cases, the private party is privileged to use whatever force is reasonable. In addition, a private person responding to a police officer's order to assist in an arrest is privileged, even if the police officer was exceeding his or her authority and had no cause to make the arrest. In such instances, the police officer may be liable for both his or her own actions and the actions of the private party summoned. Of course, there are limits to the rule. For example, a private person who obeys a police officer's order to strike an already apprehended and subdued criminal would not be privileged.

INFANCY

At common law, it was a complete defense to a charge that the accused was a child under the age of seven at the time the crime was committed. It was irrebuttably presumed that children under seven were incapable of forming the requisite mens rea to commit a crime. A rebuttable presumption of incapacity existed for those between 7 and 14 years of age. The presumption could be overcome for those between 7 and 14 if the prosecution could prove that the defendant understood that the criminal act was wrong.

Few minors are charged with crimes today. This is the result of the advent of the juvenile court systems in the United States. Currently each state has a juvenile court system that deals with juvenile delinquency and neglected children.

Statutes vary, but it is common for juvenile courts to possess exclusive jurisdiction over criminal behavior of juveniles. However, some states give concurrent jurisdiction to criminal courts and juvenile courts. If concurrent, the juvenile court usually must waive jurisdiction before the criminal court can hear the case. Determining who is a juvenile also differs, with some jurisdictions utilizing a method similar to the common law (irrebuttable and rebuttable presumptions) and others simply setting an age cutoff, such as 14 or 16.

The purpose of the juvenile justice system differs from that of the criminal justice system. Whereas criminal law has punishment as one of its major purposes, the purpose of the juvenile system is not to punish but to reform the delinquent child.

INTOXICATION

In this context, *intoxication* refers to all situations in which a person's mental or physical abilities are impaired by drugs or alcohol. It is generally said that voluntary intoxication is a defense if it has the effect of negating the required mens rea. In common-law language, this means that if intoxication prevents a defendant from being able to form a specific intent, then the crime is reduced to a similar general-intent crime. For the crime of murder, intoxication is a defense if it prevents the defendant from forming the premeditation, deliberation, or purposeful element. In such cases, the charge is reduced from first-degree to second-degree murder. Not all states recognize voluntary intoxication as a defense. The question whether a defendant has a due process right to have an intoxication defense heard by a jury was answered in the negative by the Supreme Court in the 1996 case *Montana v. Engelhoff*.[36] The Court's rationale for rejecting the right focused on the scientific ambiguity of the impact of intoxication on mens rea and the lack of consensus among the states in recognizing the defense.

In the rare case of involuntary intoxication in jurisdictions that permit the defense, the defendant is relieved of liability entirely. To be successful with such a claim, the defendant is required to show that the intoxication had the same effect as insanity. In jurisdictions using the M'Naghten test for insanity, a defendant is required to prove that the intoxication prevented him or her from knowing right from wrong.

MISTAKE

People may be mistaken in two ways. First, one may believe that some act is legal when it is not. This is a mistake of law. Second, a person may not understand all the facts of a given situation. This is a mistake of fact. As a general proposition, mistake of fact is a defense, and mistake of law is not. However, many exceptions to each rule have been developed. A few of these exceptions are noted here.

Mistake of fact is a defense whenever it negates the mens rea aspect of a crime. For example, an intent to steal another's property is an element of theft. If an attorney picks up a briefcase believing it to be his or hers when it is actually someone else's, it is not theft. The mistake negates the intent to steal. To be valid, mistakes must be made honestly and in good faith.

Although honest mistakes of fact usually constitute a defense, there are exceptions. One exception is obvious: strict liability crimes, as there is no requirement of mens rea to negate.

In some instances, an honest but unreasonable mistake of fact may not eliminate culpability entirely; however, it may reduce the crime. The imperfect self-defense previously discussed falls into this category.

We have all heard, if not quipped, "Ignorance of the law is no excuse." As a general rule, this statement is true. There are two situations in which a person can make a mistake of law. The first occurs when an individual is unaware that his or her actions are prohibited by statute: "I didn't know it was against the law not to file a tax return!" The second occurs when a person takes an act, under the color of a legal right and in good faith, only to find out later that the act was illegal. For example, a landlord may have a reasonable, but mistaken, belief that she has a right to take possessions from a tenant's house to satisfy a delinquent rent debt.

For the most part, unawareness that an act is illegal is not a defense. The law presumes that everyone knows what is legal and what is not. Mistakes that fall into the second group act to negate mens rea and are more likely to be successful. The landlord in the example would not be guilty of larceny because of the mistake. Another example of such a defense is when a person has a reasonable, but mistaken, belief that he or she has the authority to take a person into custody. Therefore, officers who arrest people in good faith, but without probable cause, are not guilty of kidnapping or criminal confinement.

Another exception to the rule that mistake of law is no defense exists when a person relies on statutes, judicial opinions, or certain administrative decisions that later turn out to be wrong. The rule is sound for two reasons. First, as a matter of public policy, it is not wise to prosecute people for acting in conformity with the law. The result would be individual interpretation of all laws and disregard for those statutes, regulations, or judicial decisions believed incorrect. Second, as a matter of due process, it appears that no notice has been provided that compliance with the law will be punished.

Finally, one defense that is not accepted is reliance on the advice of counsel. If a lawyer advises a client that a particular act is legal when it is not, the client will be liable for the crime if the act is taken.

ENTRAPMENT

To what extent should police officers be permitted to encourage someone to commit a crime? This question underlies the defense of **entrapment.** Entrapment occurs when law enforcement officers encourage a person to commit a crime with the intent of arresting and prosecuting that person for the commission of that crime.

Perjury traps are another form of entrapment. Perjury traps are committed by prosecutors whenever they inquire of a witness as to matters that are tangential or peripheral to an investigation in order to catch the witness in perjury.[37]

Entrapment is a defense of recent development, although all states and the federal government recognize some form of the defense today. There is no constitutional basis for the entrapment defense, so each jurisdiction is free to structure the defense in any

entrapment
■ The act of government officials (usually police) or agents inducing a person to commit a crime that the person would not have committed without the inducement.

manner. Of course, a state may also do away with the defense, although none have done so. This is a sound policy decision, as most people would agree that there must be some limit on police conduct. However, where the line should be drawn is debated. Currently two tests are used to determine whether a defendant was entrapped: the subjective and objective tests.

The test used in the federal system and most widely used by the states is the subjective test. The test attempts to distinguish between those who are predisposed to commit crime from those who are not. The test is subjective; the defendant's mental state at the time of the encouragement is imperative. A defendant is predisposed if he or she is ready to commit the crime and is only awaiting the opportunity. The Supreme Court has said that the subjective test is designed to draw a line between the "unwary innocent and the unwary criminal."[38]

Under the subjective approach, evidence of the defendant's criminal record may be relevant to show predisposition. For example, drug convictions may evidence a predisposition to enter into future drug purchases or sales.

The second method of determining whether a person was entrapped is objective. The Model Penal Code[39] adopts this approach, as do a minority of states. The objective approach does not focus on the particular defendant's predisposition, but asks whether the police conduct creates a "substantial risk that an offense will be committed by persons other than those who are ready to commit it."[40]

The defendant's actual state of mind is not relevant to this inquiry, and, accordingly, evidence of a defendant's criminal history is irrelevant. Under this approach, defendants may be acquitted even though they were predisposed to commit the crime. Suppose a police officer offers a prostitute $150,000 for sex. The prostitute would have agreed had the officer offered $50. Using the subjective approach, the prostitute would be convicted because she was predisposed to engage in prostitution. However, in jurisdictions using the objective test, she may have been entrapped, as women who do not normally sell sex might be encouraged to do so for $150,000.

In many states entrapment may not be used to defend against crimes involving violence to people, such as battery and murder. The Model Penal Code also takes this view.

ALIBI AND CONSENT

alibi

▪ (Latin) "Elsewhere"; the claim that at the time a crime was committed a person was somewhere else. [pronounce: al-eh-bi]

Alibi and consent are two factual defenses. An **alibi** is a claim by a defendant that he or she was not present at the scene of the crime at the time it was committed. Whenever defendants assert an alibi, they are simply refuting the government's factual claims. Alibi is an affirmative defense, and defendants are usually required to give the government notice of the alibi claim prior to trial. Alibi notice laws have been approved by the Supreme Court.[41] Of course, the government must prove the elements of the crime (e.g., presence at the crime) beyond a reasonable doubt. This means that the defendant bears no burden in an alibi defense.

Victim **consent** is a defense to some crimes, such as rape or larceny. That is, if a person consents to sex or to give you his property, there is no crime. Consent is, however, not a defense to many crimes, such as statutory rape, incest, child molestation, battery, and murder.

consent
■ Voluntary and active agreement.

STATUTES OF LIMITATION

Many crimes must be prosecuted within a specified time after being committed. A **statute of limitation** sets the time limit. If prosecution is initiated after the applicable statute has expired, the defendant is entitled to a dismissal.

Statutes vary in length; and serious crimes, such as murder, have no limitation. Generally, the higher the crime in the jurisdiction's classification system, the longer the statute. Statutes begin running when the crime occurs; however, statutes may be tolled in some situations. *Tolling* refers to stopping the clock. The time during which a defendant is a fugitive is commonly tolled. For example, assume that the limitation on felony assault is 6 years. The assault was committed on June 1, 2009. Normally, prosecution would have to be started by June 1, 2015. However, if the defendant was fugitive from June 1, 2009, to June 1, 2010, then the statute would be tolled, and the new date of limitation would be June 1, 2016. There is no limit to how long a tolling period may run.

In 2005, a defendant in New York was tried for the second time for one of a series of rapes he committed in 1970s. He became known as the Silver Springs rapist at the time of the attacks. His first trial had occurred 33 years earlier. It concluded with a hung jury, after which he fled the jurisdiction. This tolled the clock on the statute of limitation. While he was a fugitive, incriminating DNA evidence was recovered and DNA science developed into a reliable prosecution tool. He was eventually discovered and apprehended when he applied to purchase a gun in Georgia. He was extradited from Georgia to New York, where his DNA sample was collected. His sample not only connected him to the rapes in New York but to rapes in other states where DNA evidence existed. He was convicted at his second trial. Interestingly, the case caught the public's attention and was a catalyst to a change in statute of limitations law in New York. Today, there is no limitation in rape cases.[42]

statute of limitation
■ Federal and state statutes prescribing the maximum period of time during which various types of civil actions and criminal prosecutions can be brought after the occurrence of the injury or the offense.

At common law there were no statutes of limitations, and they do not appear to have a constitutional underpinning. They are purely legislative creations. This being so, legislatures are free to alter or abolish statutes of limitation. If there is no limitation fixed, prosecution may occur any time after the crime.

Sometimes a prosecution for a serious crime may begin after the statute on a lesser included crime has expired. For example, battery is a lesser included crime of aggravated battery. Assume that aggravated battery has a 6-year statute and battery 3 years. In most jurisdictions, a prosecutor may not circumvent the 3-year statute by charging aggravated battery and including the lesser battery offense in the information or indictment. After the time has run out on the lesser offense, but not on the more serious offense, the defendant is either convicted of the greater offense or acquitted, but can no longer be convicted on the lesser offense. However, at least one jurisdiction does not follow this rule.[43]

> **Web Links**
>
> **International and Comparative Law**
>
> Several sites contain government, law, and justice information from many nations and international organizations from around the globe.
>
> At *http://www.lawresearch.com* you will find both United States and foreign government legal information. Hieros Gamos claims to have descriptions and laws from all the nations of the world. It is an excellent site full of text and graphics. The URL is *http://www.hg.org/index.html*
>
> Constitutions of nations can be found in the following locations:
>
> *http://confinder.richmond.edu/*
>
> *http://www.findlaw.com/01topics/06constitutional/03forconst/index.html*

Key Terms

affirmative defenses	consent	necessity
alibi	diminished capacity	retreat to the wall doctrine /
battered woman syndrome	duress	retreat doctrine
burden of persuasion	Durham rule	self-defense
burden of production	entrapment	stand-your-ground
burden of proof	irresistible impulse	statute of limitation
castle doctrine	M'Naghten rule	

Review Questions

1. What are affirmative defenses? How do affirmative defenses differ from other defenses?
2. What are the elements of the M'Naghten test for insanity? Irresistible impulse? Model Penal Code?
3. What must be proven to support a claim of self-defense?
4. What is the retreat doctrine?
5. What is imperfect self-defense? When is it applicable?
6. When may a law enforcement officer use deadly force to stop a fleeing suspect?
7. What is entrapment? What are the two tests used to determine if a defendant was entrapped?
8. May an insane defendant be tried? If not, what standard is used to determine whether the defendant is insane?
9. What is a statute of limitations?
10. Distinguish legal from factual impossibility, and state whether a person is criminally culpable in both circumstances.

Problems & Critical Thinking Exercises

1. Should law enforcement be permitted to encourage children to engage in criminal activity with the purpose of arresting and prosecuting the child? Should law enforcement be permitted to use family and friend relationships to induce another to engage in criminal activity with the purpose of arresting and prosecuting the family member or friend? How about preying on another's drug or alcohol addiction?

2. Ira stabbed his good friend, inflicting a fatal wound. At trial, a psychiatrist testified that Ira could not control his behavior, as he has a brain tumor that causes him to act violently. The doctor also testified that the condition did not impair Ira's ability to know what he was doing or that it was wrong. Assume that the jury believes the psychiatrist's explanation. Would Ira be convicted in a jurisdiction that uses the M'Naghten test? The irresistible impulse test? The Model Penal Code?

3. Jane was attacked by an unknown man. She was able to free herself and ran to a nearby house, with the man chasing close behind. She screamed and knocked at the door of the house. The occupants of the house opened the door, and she requested refuge. The occupant refused, but Jane forced her way into the house. To gain entry, Jane had to strike the occupant. Once inside, she used the telephone to contact the police, who responded within minutes. At the insistence of the occupants of the house, Jane has been charged with trespass and battery. Does she have a defense?

4. Gary and Gene were both drinking at a bar. Gary became angered after Gene asked Gary's wife to dance. Gary walked up to Gene and struck him in the face. Gene fell to the floor, and as he was returning to his feet Gary hit him again. In response, Gene took a knife out of his pocket and attacked Gary with it. Gary then shot Gene with a gun he had hidden in his coat. The injury proved fatal. What crime has Gary committed?

Endnotes

1. See Henry F. Fradella, "From Insanity to Beyond Diminished Capacity: Mental Illness and Criminal Excuse in the Post-Clark Era," 18 U. *Fla. J. L. & Pub. Pol'y* 7, 28 (2007); and Samuel J. Brakel, "Searching for the Therapy in Therapeutic Jurisprudence," 33 *New Eng. J. on Crim. & Civ. Confinement* 455, fn82 (2007).
2. *M'Naghten's Case,* 8 Eng. Rep. 718 (H.L. 1843).
3. LaFave & Scott, *Criminal Law* § 4.2A(a)(Hornbook Series, St. Paul: West, 1986).
4. *State v. Johnson,* 290 N.W. 159 (Wis. 1940).
5. Model Penal Code, Tent. Draft 4, at 156.
6. LaFave & Scott at § 4.2(d).
7. *United States v. Brawner,* 471 F.2d 969 (D.C. Cir. 1972).
8. Model Penal Code § 4.01(1).
9. 18 U.S.C. § 17.
10. Justine A. Dunlap, "What's Competence Got To Do With It: The Right Not To Be Acquitted by Reason of Insanity," 50 *Okla. L. Rev.* 495 (1997).
11. 18 Pa. C.S.A. § 314.
12. 18 U.S.C. § 3006A(e)(3).
13. 18 U.S.C. § 17.
14. Model Penal Code § 4.08.
15. 18 U.S.C. § 4243(a).
16. 18 U.S.C. § 4243(f).
17. Angela Paulsen, Limiting the Scope of State Power to Confine Insanity Acquittees: *Foucha v. Louisiana, 28 Tulsa L.J,* 537 (1993).
18. Callahan, L., Steadman, H., McGreevy, M., Robbins, P. (1991) "The Volume and Characteristics of Insanity Defense Pleas: An Eight-State Study," *Bulletin of the American Academy of Psychiatry and the Law,* 19(4): 331–338.
19. Conner, K. (2006) Factors in a Successful Use of the Insanity Defense, *Internet Journal of Criminology.*
20. *Dusky v. United States,* 362 U.S. 402 (1960).
21. 517 U.S. 348.
22. *Jackson v. Indiana,* 406 U.S. 715 (1972).
23. *Ford v. Wainwright,* 477 U.S. 399 (1986).
24. *Id.* at 417.
25. *Atkins v. Virginia,* 122 S. Ct. 2242 (2002).

26. Winton, R., Quinones, S., Blankstein, A., Bank robbers use bomb to coerce East L.A. bank manager, *Los Angeles Times,* September 5, 2012, found at http://articles.latimes.com/2012/sep/05/local/la-me-bank-bomb-20120906
27. *See* LaFave & Scott at § 5.3(g).
28. See New York Times: Times Topics at www.nytimes.com and search for Treyvon Martin.
29. Model Penal Code § 3.04(2)(b)(ii).
30. O.R.C. §2901.05.
31. There are 21 states with stand-your-ground laws, according to the National Conference of State Legislatures; found on May 10, 2013, at http://www.ncsl.org/issues-research/justice/self-defense-and-stand-your-ground.aspx
32. Fla. Stat. §776.012.
33. Model Penal Code § 3.06(d).
34. Model Penal Code § 3.06(5).
35. Model Penal Code § 3.07(2)(b)(ii).
36. 518 U.S. 37 (1996).
37. *See Vermont v. Tonzola,* 621 A.2d 243 (Vt. 1993).
38. *Sherman v. United States*, 356 U.S. 369 (1958).
39. Model Penal Code § 2.13.
40. Model Penal Code § 2.13(2).
41. *Williams v. Florida*, 399 U.S. 78 (1970).
42. Sources: Emily Jane Goodman, "State Removes Statute of Limitations for Rape Cases," *Gotham Gazette: New York City News and Policy,* June 2006; Fox News, November 10, 2005, and Julia Preston, "After Thirty-Two Years, Clothing Yields A DNA Key to Dozens of Rapes," *New York Times*, New York Region, April 27, 2005.
43. 21 Am. Jur. 2d 225 (1990); *State v. Borucki,* 505 A.2d 89 (Me. 1986).

CHAPTER 14

CONSTITUTIONAL DEFENSES

Chapter Outline

Introduction
Double Jeopardy
Self-Incrimination and Immunity
Due Process and Equal Protection
Vagueness and Overbreadth
Analyzing Constitutional Claims
Ex Post Facto and Bills of Attainder
First Amendment and Religion
First Amendment and Speech
Privacy and Other Unenumerated Rights
Privileges and Immunities

Chapter Objectives

After completing this chapter, you should be able to:

- identify and describe specific rights discussed in the chapter, such as freedom from double jeopardy, to speak, to practice one's religion, from the establishment of a religion by the government, to privacy, to be treated equally, and to substantive and procedural due process.
- identify and explain the landmark Supreme Court cases featured in the chapter.
- apply the basic principles learned in the chapter to fact scenarios.
- identify the material facts and legal issues in two-thirds of the cases you read, and describe the court's analyses and conclusions in these cases.

INTRODUCTION

By its nature, a constitutional right is also a constitutional defense. After all, a right is something that may be asserted by person without suffering reprisal from the government. Inherently, a right stands as a limit on government. So, when a government interferes with speech, one defense may be the protection of speech itself. A variety of defenses arise from rights secured by the U.S. Constitution. Most of these rights are found in the first nine, as well as the Thirteenth, Fourteenth, and Fifteenth Amendments. You have already learned a few of these, such as the First Amendment's protection of expression. In addition, many rights that are procedural, such as the right to a speedy trial, are discussed later. A few critical defenses have been chosen for discussion in this chapter. The big dogs of criminal procedure, the Fourth, Fifth, and Sixth Amendments, are not examined in this chapter because they receive considerable attention in the chapters that follow.

Be aware that each state has its own constitution, which may provide greater protection than the U.S. Constitution. During this discussion you may want to refer to the U.S. Constitution, which is reprinted as Appendix A of this text.

DOUBLE JEOPARDY

The Fifth Amendment to the U.S. Constitution provides that "no person shall be subject for the same offense to be twice put in jeopardy of life or limb." The principle of not punishing someone twice for the same act can be found as far back as Blackstone's *Commentaries* in the 1700s.[1] The **Double Jeopardy Clause** applies only to criminal proceedings.

double jeopardy clause

▪ A second prosecution by the same government against the same person for the same crime (or for a lesser included offense) once the first prosecution is totally finished and decided. This is prohibited by the U.S. Constitution.

There are actually two prohibitions in the Double Jeopardy Clause. The clause prevents: (1) a second prosecution for the same offense and (2) a second punishment for the same offense.

Often the legal question in double jeopardy cases is whether a prior "jeopardy" occurred. It is generally held that a person has been put in jeopardy once a plea of guilty has been entered and accepted by a court. An unapproved plea will not suffice, and a subsequent prosecution will not be prohibited by the Double Jeopardy Clause. In jury trials, jeopardy attaches once a jury has been selected and sworn. States treat bench trials differently, although the prevailing view is that jeopardy attaches when the first witness has been sworn.

Once jeopardy attaches, the defendant may not be tried again. However, there are a few exceptions. A defendant may be retried if the first trial was terminated by a properly declared mistrial. Mistrials may be declared for a variety of reasons. Death of the trial judge or one of the participating attorneys would likely result in a mistrial. If a witness blurts out an answer to a question before the judge has an opportunity to sustain an objection to the question, and the answer is extremely prejudicial, a mistrial may be declared. The causes of a mistrial are endless. Note that the mistrial must be proper. That is, if an appellate court later determines that a mistrial should not have been declared, the defendant has been put into jeopardy. It is always proper to retry a defendant whose prior trial was declared a mistrial upon the defendant's motion. If a defendant objects to a government motion for a mistrial, there must be a "manifest necessity" (darn good reason) for the mistrial.[2]

It is also not a violation of the Fifth Amendment to prosecute a defendant who was previously charged but whose charges were dismissed prior to jeopardy attaching. Additionally, if a defendant appeals a conviction and prevails, the defendant may be retried, unless the appellate court finds that insufficient evidence exists to retry the defendant. However, if defendants are acquitted on a serious charge and convicted on a lesser and then prevail on appeal, they may be retried only on the lesser. It is violative of the Fifth Amendment to retry the defendant on the more serious offense. Whether a defendant may be retried following government appeals has been an issue in many cases. Clearly, the government may not win a new trial following an acquittal. However, a conviction may be reinstated by an appellate court if a trial court's order setting aside the conviction is found invalid.[3] But an appellate court may not order a new trial where the trial judge entered a judgement of acquittal following a hung jury.[4] The outcomes in this area of law are dependent upon what judgement is first entered by the trial court. If it is a conviction, then an appellate court may tamper with trial judge reversals of convictions. If it is an acquittal, then double jeopardy bars acting further against the accused.

The Supreme Court has also held that double jeopardy does not bar correcting a sentence on appeal or rehearing because such a procedure is not retrial of an "offense." However, the outcome may be different if resentencing results in the application of the death penalty.[5]

The Fifth Amendment only forbids retrial for the same offense. Determining whether two acts constitute the same offense is not always an easy task. Two offenses are the same unless one requires proof of a fact that the other does not.[6] This is the "same evidence test." The civil law concept of collateral estoppel, or the preclusion of relitigating the same issue, applies in criminal cases as well. The Supreme Court first announced this in *Ashe v. Swenson*.

The Double Jeopardy Clause is fully applicable to the states through the Fourteenth Amendment. However, the clause does not prevent second punishments for the same offense by different sovereigns. For example, a person who robs a federally insured bank may be prosecuted by both the state where the bank resides and the United States. This is true even though the offenses arise from the same acts. Although the Double Jeopardy Clause does not prohibit two sovereigns from prosecuting for the same offense, many states prohibit this by statute. In practice, and sometimes by policy, most prosecutors do not pursue a defendant who has been previously prosecuted in another jurisdiction for the same crime. The Model Penal Code incorporates this approach in certain circumstances.[7] Municipalities are not independent beings; they owe their existence not to the Constitution of the United States, but to a state. Accordingly, prosecutions by cities are treated as being brought by the state, and it is a violation of the Double Jeopardy Clause for a state and city to punish one for the same offense.

SELF-INCRIMINATION AND IMMUNITY

The Fifth Amendment also states that no person "shall be compelled in any criminal case to be a witness against himself." The following passage explains why the framers of the Constitution included a privilege against self-incrimination.

> Perhaps the best-known provision of the Fifth Amendment is the clause against forced "self-incrimination," whose origin goes back to England where persons accused of crimes before ecclesiastical courts were forced to take an ex officio oath. That is, they had to swear to answer all questions even if the questions did not apply to the case at trial. This requirement was later adopted by the Court of Star Chamber. One of the victims of the Court was a printer and book distributor named John Lilburne, charged in 1637 with treason for importing books "that promoted Puritan dissent." Lilburne told his accusers, "I am not willing to answer to you any more of these questions because I see you go about by this examination to ensnare me. For seeing the things for which I am imprisoned cannot be proved against me, you will get other material out of my examination; and therefore if you will not ask me about the thing laid to my charge, I shall answer no more. . . . I think by the law of the land, that I may stand upon my just defense." Lilburne was convicted, fined, whipped, pilloried, gagged, and imprisoned until he agreed to take the oath. . . .
>
> One notorious instance of forced self-incrimination in the American colonies occurred in the Salem witch trials. In 1692, Giles Corey, an elderly Massachusetts farmer, was accused of witchcraft. He knew whether he pleaded guilty or not guilty he would be convicted and executed and his property confiscated. So to assure that his heirs inherited his property, he refused to plead and thus could not be convicted. The judges ordered him strapped to a table, and stones were loaded upon his chest to force the plea out of him. Corey's final words were "more weight." Then his chest caved in.[8]

John Bradshaw, John Lilburne's attorney, stated it best when he said that "It is contrary to the laws of God, nature and the kingdom for any man to be his own accuser."

Generally, the Fifth Amendment prohibits the government from compelling people to testify when incrimination is possible. Most people have heard of "pleading the Fifth." However, if immunity from prosecution is granted to a witness, he or she may be compelled to testify. If a witness refuses to testify because of the fear of self-incrimination, the government may offer the witness immunity from prosecution so that the testimony may be compelled. There are two types of immunity: transactional and derivative use.

Transactional immunity shields witnesses from prosecution for all offenses related to their testimony. For example, if a witness testifies concerning a robbery, the government may not prosecute the witness for that robbery, even though the government may have evidence of guilt independent of the witness's testimony. Transactional immunity gives more protection to the witness than is required by the Constitution, so when it is granted, a witness may be ordered to testify.

transactional immunity
■ Freedom from prosecution for all crimes related to the compelled testimony, so long as the witness tells the truth.

The minimum immunity that must be provided a witness to overcome a Fifth Amendment claim is derivative **use immunity.** This prohibits the government from using the witness's testimony or any evidence derived from that testimony to prosecute the witness. However, all evidence that is independently obtained may be used against the witness.

Use immunity only prohibits the government from using the witness's testimony against him or her. Statutes that provide only for use immunity are unconstitutional, as derivative use is the minimum protection required by the Fifth Amendment.

States vary in how immunity is granted. Some permit the prosecutor to give the immunity; others require both the request of the prosecutor and the approval of the trial judge.

A person may also waive the Fifth Amendment privilege against self-incrimination. Generally, once a person testifies freely, the privilege is waived as to the subject discussed during the same proceeding. A witness (or defendant) may not testify selectively concerning a subject. It is often said that testifying to a fact waives to the details. This principle prevents witnesses from testifying only to the information beneficial to one party and then refusing to testify further, even though they may have omitted important facts. However, witness may not be compelled to testify if there is a chance of incriminating themselves beyond the original testimony.

The fact that a witness may waive the Fifth Amendment privilege against self-incrimination on one occasion does not mean it is waived forever. First, a defendant (or witness) may speak to the police during the investigative stage and later refuse to testify at trial, provided such testimony may be incriminating. Second, it is generally held that a person who testifies before a grand jury without claiming the Fifth does not waive the right to raise the defense at trial. Third, even within the same proceeding a person may invoke the Fifth Amendment privilege against self-incrimination if the two hearings are separate and distinct. For example, a defendant may testify at a suppression hearing without waiving the privilege not to testify at trial.

Finally, the Fifth Amendment applies to all proceedings, whether civil, criminal, or administrative.[9] Therefore, a person called to testify in a civil proceeding may invoke the Fifth Amendment's privilege and refuse to testify.

use immunity

■ Freedom from prosecution based on the compelled testimony and on anything the government learns from following up on the testimony.

DUE PROCESS AND EQUAL PROTECTION

The Fifth Amendment to the U.S. Constitution prohibits the government from depriving a person of life, liberty, or property without due process of law. This amendment acts to constrain the power of the federal government. You have previously learned that the Fourteenth Amendment has similar language and constrains the power of state governments.

The Fourteenth Amendment expressly requires the states to extend equal protection of the laws to the people. There is no express equal protection clause in the Fifth Amendment, but the Supreme Court has found it to be implied in the Due Process Clause. Equal protection concerns classifications and discrimination.

Discrimination is not inherently evil. Students discriminate between professors, possibly due to grading policy or teaching skill, when deciding what courses to enroll in. Governments also discriminate and make classifications, most of which are sensible and acceptable. For example, those who commit homicides are divided into groups: murderers, manslaughterers, and those who are excused or justified in killing. When classifications are based upon meaningful criteria (e.g., mens rea), the law is valid. However, our society has decided that certain classifications are improper and violative of equal protection. A classification between those who exercise a constitutional right and those who do not, if it results in prosecution or increased punishment for the former, is unconstitutional. Classifications based on race, religion, gender, and other immutable conditions are suspect and possibly violative of equal protection.

These clauses are important to criminal law and particularly to criminal procedure. Due process requires the government to treat people fairly; therefore, whenever a law or other governmental action appears to be unfair, there is a due process issue. In a sense, due process is a safety net, protecting the individual when another specific constitutional provision does not.

Due process has two aspects, substantive and procedural. The protection of privacy discussed later in this chapter is an example of substantive due process. On the procedural side, due process is the constitutional source of the **principle of legality**, which requires that criminal laws (and punishments) be written and enacted before an act may be punished. This is a notice concept. It would be unfair to announce that an act is illegal, or increase its punishment, after that act has been committed. You will learn later in this chapter that overly broad or vague laws may be violative of due process.

Through the Fourteenth Amendment's Due Process Clause, most of the provisions of the Bill of Rights, which initially applied only against the federal government, have been extended to the states. Today, the Fourth Amendment's right to be free from unreasonable searches and seizures, the Fifth Amendment's right to be free from self-incrimination, the Sixth Amendment's right to counsel at critical stages of criminal adjudications, and the Eighth Amendment's prohibition of cruel and unusual punishment are among the many rights that are now available to defendants in state courts.

In some instances, due process or equal protection increases the scope of a right found in the Bill of Rights. For example, the Sixth Amendment's right to counsel is limited to the critical stages of criminal proceedings. Appeals are not critical stages, and therefore the Sixth Amendment does not mandate counsel. But the Supreme Court has held that if a state provides for felony appeals by right, then the Equal Protection Clause requires that indigent defendants receive appointed counsel. To hold otherwise would unfairly discriminate against the indigent.[10]

principle of legality

■ The procedural side of due process, which requires that criminal laws (and punishments) be written and enacted before an act may be punished.

Although the Fourteenth Amendment is the source of the incorporation of most of the Bill of Rights, its importance extends further. Any time an issue of fairness surfaces, due process should be examined. If the issue concerns one of improper classifications, equal protection law should be considered. The Supreme Court stated of substantive due process:

> The inescapable fact is that adjudication of substantive due process claims may call upon the Court in interpreting the Constitution to exercise that same capacity which by tradition courts always have exercised: reasoned judgment. Its boundaries are not susceptible of expression as a simple rule. That does not mean we are free to invalidate state policy choices with which we disagree: yet neither does it permit us to shrink from the duties of our office. As Justice Harlan observed: "Due process has not been reduced to any formula: its content cannot be determined by reference to any code. The best that can be said is that through the course of this Court's decisions it has represented the balance which our Nation, built upon postulates of respect for liberty of the individual, has struck between that liberty and the demands of organized society."

VAGUENESS AND OVERBREADTH

The Due Process Clauses of the Fifth and Fourteenth Amendments to the U.S. Constitution are the foundation of the void-for-vagueness and overbreadth doctrines.

A statute is void for **vagueness** whenever "men of common intelligence must necessarily guess at its meaning and differ as to its application."[11] As to the meaning of a statute, confusion among lower courts, resulting in varying interpretations, is evidence of vagueness.[12] The Supreme Court has held that uncertain statutes do not provide notice of what conduct is forbidden and are violative of due process. The Court has also found statutes that permit arbitrary or discriminatory enforcement void. That is, if the police or courts are given unlimited authority to decide who will be prosecuted, the statute is invalid.

It is under the void-for-vagueness doctrine that many vagrancy laws have been attacked. If not for the doctrine, legislatures could draft statutes so that nearly everyone would be engaged in criminal activity at one time or another, and police and prosecutors would have the unfettered discretion to decide who to arrest and prosecute.

A closely related doctrine is **overbreadth.** A statute is overbroad if it includes within its grasp not only unprotected activity but also activity protected by the Constitution. For example, in one case a city ordinance made it illegal for "one or more persons to assemble" on a sidewalk and conduct themselves in an annoying manner. The United States Supreme Court found that the law was unconstitutional not only because it made unprotected activity illegal (fighting words or riotous activity) but also because it included activity that is protected by the First Amendment's free assembly and association provisions.[13] It is possible for a statute to be clear and precise (not vague) but overbroad.

vagueness doctrine

■ The rule that a criminal law may be unconstitutional if it does not clearly say what is required or prohibited, what punishment may be imposed, or what persons may be affected. A law that violates due process of law in this way is *void for vagueness*.

overbreadth doctrine

■ A law will be declared void for *overbreadth* if it attempts to punish speech or conduct that is protected by the Constitution and if it is impossible to eliminate the unconstitutional part of the law without invalidating the whole law.

ANALYZING CONSTITUTIONAL CLAIMS

The United States Supreme Court has developed standards of judicial review for claims that constitutional rights are violated. The first standard is generally known as strict scrutiny. A court applies the strict scrutiny test in one of two circumstances: (1) when the government burdens a fundamental right; and (2) when the government groups people into suspect classes.

As the first of the two, nearly all the rights found in the Constitution are "fundamental," and as such, laws that limit or set them aside are tested by the strict scrutiny test. Remember these standards as you read about the rights—e.g., speech, religion—discussed in this chapter. For the second condition to apply, the government must classify people by race, national origin, or religion.

Laws or actions that burden a fundament right or have a suspect classification are invalid unless the government can demonstrate *compelling governmental interest*. The government must also show that the law is narrowly tailored to achieve its objectives; that is, it is not overly broad.

Laws that don't encroach upon individual rights and don't classify along suspect lines are tested under an easier standard. They are valid if *rationally related to a legitimate government objective*. There is a third standard that applies to classifications based upon sex and when certain rights are at issue. This standard falls between strict scrutiny and rational relationship: Laws are valid if they are *substantially related to a legitimate governmental objective*. Most—but not all—laws tested under strict scrutiny fail and most laws—but not all—survive review under the rational relationship test.

EX POST FACTO AND BILLS OF ATTAINDER

Article I of the U.S. Constitution prohibits the state and federal governments from enacting both ex post facto laws and bills of attainder.

An **ex post facto law** is one that (1) makes an act illegal after the act was taken, (2) increases the punishment or severity of a crime after it occurred, and (3) changes the procedural rules so as to increase the chances of conviction after the crime occurs. In short, a government may not make criminal law retroactive, if doing so is detrimental to the defendant. However, changes that benefit a defendant may be applied retroactively. So, if a legislature increases the prosecution's burden of proof after a defendant has committed a crime, but before trial, the legislature may make the change applicable to the defendant. The clause advances the notice theory (due process) and prevents malicious legislative action from being taken against a particular person.

A **bill of attainder** is a legislative act punishing a person without a judicial trial. This provision reinforces the concept of separation of powers. It is the duty of the legislative branch to make the laws, and it is the duty of the judicial branch to determine who has violated those laws. Alexander Hamilton, in support of the prohibition of bills of attainder, wrote:

---

ex post facto law

■ (Latin) After the fact. An *ex post facto* law is one that retroactively attempts to make an action a crime that was not a crime at the time it was done, or a law that attempts to reduce a person's rights based on a past act that was not subject to the law when it was done.

bill of attainder

■ A legislative act pronouncing a person guilty (usually of treason) without a trial and sentencing the person to death and attainder. This is now prohibited by the U.S. Constitution.

Nothing is more common than for a free people, in times of heat and violence, to gratify momentary passions by letting into the government principles and precedents which afterwards prove fatal to themselves. Of this kind is the doctrine of disqualification, disfranchisement, and banishment by acts of the legislature. The dangerous consequences of this power are manifest. If the legislature can disfranchise any number of citizens at pleasure by general descriptions, it may soon confine all the votes to a small number of partisans, and establish an aristocracy or an oligarchy; if it may banish at discretion all those whom particular circumstances render obnoxious, without hearing or trial, no man can be safe, nor know when he may be the innocent victim of a prevailing faction. The name of liberty applied to such a government would be a mockery of common sense.[14]

In a few instances, however, Congress may act in a judicial role. Congress may punish those who disrupt its functions for contempt. In addition, Congress is authorized by the Constitution to conduct impeachment hearings of the president, federal judges, and other federal officers and to discipline its own members.

FIRST AMENDMENT AND RELIGION

The First Amendment contains many protections, including freedom of the press; freedom to choose and practice a religion; freedom of speech; and freedom to peaceably assemble. Although the First Amendment is directly applicable only against the national government, the Fourteenth Amendment extends its prohibitions to the states. The Amendment reads:

> Congress shall make no law respecting an establishment of religion, or prohibiting the free exercise thereof; or abridging the freedom of speech, or of the press; or the right of the people peaceably to assemble, and to petition the government for a redress of grievances.

Concerning freedom of religion, the First Amendment states that "Congress shall make no law respecting an establishment of religion, or prohibiting the free exercise thereof." The Free Exercise Clause is of the most importance in criminal law. The freedom to believe is, of course, absolute. Any law prohibiting a certain religious belief is void. However, the Supreme Court has held that some religious practices may be regulated.

To determine whether a specific religious act may be criminalized, the governmental interest in regulating the behavior is balanced against the First Amendment infringement. If the governmental interest is greater than the infringement, then a state may regulate the conduct. For example, it has been held that the Mormon practice of polygamy may be regulated.[15] Also, a parent who depends upon prayer to save a dying child may be charged with manslaughter for failing to seek competent medical care. In this instance the state's interest in protecting the child's life outweighs the parent's interest in practicing his or her religion in such a manner.

On the other side, the California Supreme Court disallowed the conviction of a member of the Native American Church for possession of peyote, a drug made from cactus. The court found that peyote was an important part of worship in the Native American Church, and, as such, California's interest in regulating the use of the drug was outweighed by the drug's religious significance.[16] Note that the United States Supreme Court took the opposite view concerning the use of peyote in *Department of Human Resources v. Smith*, 494 U.S. 872 (1990), wherein the Court stated that

> [T]he right of free exercise does not relieve an individual of the obligation to comply with a valid and neutral law of general applicability on the ground that the law proscribes (or prescribes) conduct that his religion prescribes (or proscribes).

Note further that Congress reacted to this decision by exempting the use of peyote by Native Americans from the Controlled Substance Act. In the *Hialeah* case, the Supreme Court invalidated several ordinances that prohibited the adherents of Santeria from sacrificing animals as part of their religious rites.

Smith can be distinguished from *Hialeah* because *Smith* involved a law of general applicability. That is, use of the drugs, including peyote, was generally prohibited to everyone. Clearly, the laws were not enacted solely to regulate religious worship. However, in the *Hialeah* case, the Court determined that the regulation was intended to target the Santeria's religious practices. Congress and the White House responded to the Supreme Court's decisions voiding religious practices that are prohibited by laws of general applicability. First, Native American use of peyote as a religious ritual was specifically exempted from The Controlled Substance Act. Second, the Religious Freedom Restoration Act was enacted.[17] Through this statute, courts are required to apply the strict scrutiny test when applying statutes of generally applicability to religious practices. So, a government must demonstrate both a compelling reason and that there is no less restrictive way to accomplish the governmental objective. The new standard was applied in the following 2006 case.

Determining whether an act is a genuine exercise of religious beliefs is not always easy. The practices of one religion may appear unusual, or even bizarre, to another. But this is not determinative. The *Hodges* case both illustrates the sensitivity with which our society treats religion and stands as an example of an activity that is not a religion, although the opinion does not contain the latter finding, for reasons you will see.

How does a court distinguish between fraudulent and bona fide religious practices? First, it must be determined that the defendant is asserting a religious belief, not a personal or philosophical belief. Several factors are considered. How well established is the religion in the world? If a defendant is the only adherent, or one of only a few followers, of a religion, it is less likely to be deemed legitimate. How old is the religion? For how long has the defendant practiced the religion? What is the nature of the practice in question? How important is the practice to the religion? Once it is determined that a religious practice is being regulated by the State, then the State's interest in regulating the defendant's conduct must be weighed against the defendant's First Amendment interest. If the State's interest is compelling, then the conduct may be regulated.

FIRST AMENDMENT AND SPEECH

The First Amendment also protects speech. Refer to the text of the First Amendment, which provides that "Congress shall make no law . . . abridging the freedom of speech." In spite of the plain language of this clause, several words mean something different than what is plain. First, the clause limits the authority of Congress, but in reality it limits all three branches of the federal government. Because the Amendment has been incorporated, state and local governments are prohibited from abridging free speech as well. Second, the term speech is used. Regardless, the Supreme Court has held that more than the spoken word is protected. All forms of expression, nonverbal, artistic, written, and visual, are protected by the Free Speech Clause. Third, as is true of all the amendments, there are exceptions – even though not recognized by the text of the Amendment. As you already learned, any law that burdens speech must be narrowly tailored and it must be supported by a compelling governmental interest. Underlying the First Amendment's protection of speech is the philosophical belief that a free market of ideas will advance both democracy and a society's development. The price of free market speech is the protection of provocative, annoying, offensive, and insulting speech.

You have already learned that fighting words and those words that create a clear and present danger or the likelihood of imminent lawlessness may be regulated because the government has a compelling interest in preventing these dangers. Although the lawlessness and clear and present danger exceptions commonly refer to violence, there are examples of speech that may be prohibited because it creates a likelihood of imminent non-violent lawlessness. Encouraging jurors to not follow the law during deliberations is an example. The Julien Heicklin case illustrates the line between protected speech and jury tampering.

Slanderous and libelous statements also fall outside the protection of the First Amendment. Fighting words, obscenity, some threats, and slanderous and libelous words are all content-based doctrines; that is, the substance of what is being said is regulated. There is a huge body of First Amendment free speech law. The application of the First Amendment to regulations of obscenity and the Internet are discussed in Chapter 11. You may want to refresh yourself with the content of that chapter before continuing. See Exhibit 14–1 for an illustration of the limits of free expression.

In some instances, a state may regulate speech, not because of its content, but by its time, place, and manner of being expressed. Here, a balancing of interests is conducted: does the government's interest in enforcing the statute outweigh the First Amendment interest? For example, it is unlawful to stand in the middle of the street to make a speech. The interest in maintaining a safe, consistent flow of traffic outweighs the First Amendment interest. However, the result would be different if a state attempted to prohibit all speeches made in a public place. Such a statute would be overbroad, as it includes not only activity that the state may regulate (standing in traffic), but also lawful activity. Commercial speech is also protected by the First Amendment, but is subject to greater control than other speech, particularly political speech.

Not only is the actual spoken word protected: Expression of ideas through acts is also protected, although to a lesser degree than pure speech. Picketing is an example of protected expression, as is flag burning.

First Amendment free exercise of speech claims also arise in the context of hate crime legislation. Such legislation either makes it illegal to express prejudicial opinions or enhances the penalty for a crime that is motivated by prejudice. The former is unconstitutional. As to the latter, most states enhance the penalties for crimes such as trespass, assault, battery, and harassment if the motive of the crime was the victim's race, religion, color, or other characteristic.

Two Supreme Court opinions, only one year apart, set the limits of hate crime laws. Both are excerpted here. In the first, the Court held an ordinance unconstitutional. In the second, the Court upheld the law.

Exhibit 14–1 THE LIMITS OF FIRST AMENDMENT FREE SPEECH

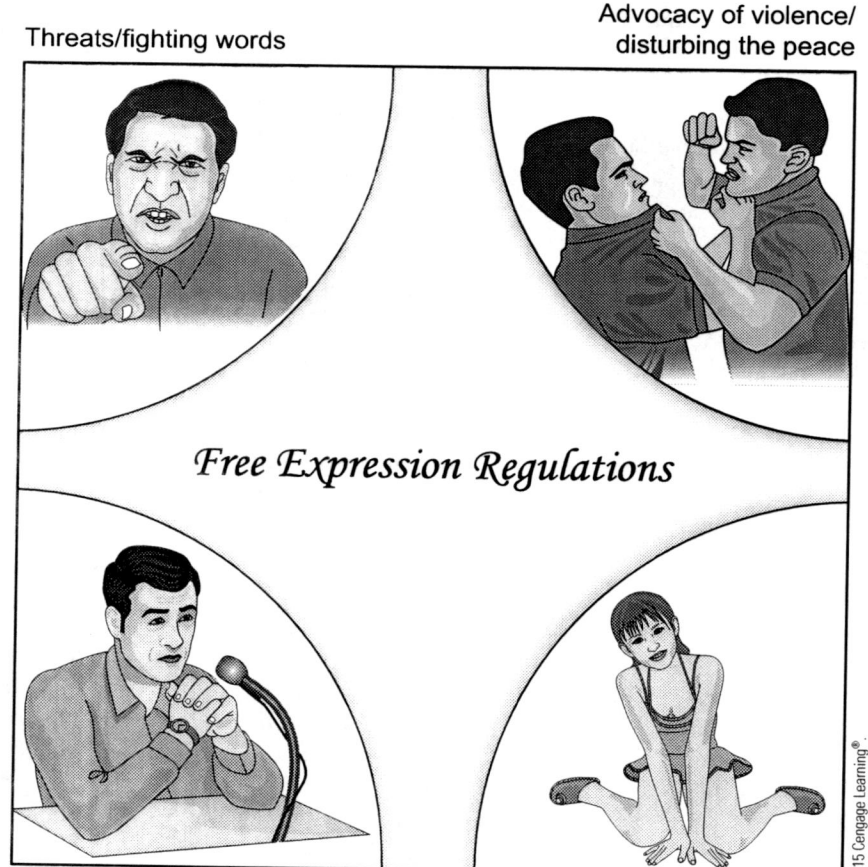

R.A.V. and *Mitchell* establish that while bigoted expressions themselves may not be prohibited (legislation aimed at content), bigotry as a motive may be considered at sentencing to enhance a penalty (legislation aimed at the motive of content). The Court pointed out in *R.A.V.* that the conduct itself could be punished under content neutral laws, such as open burning. Such laws apply to all outside burning, not just those that are the product of a (racial) opinion or belief. The Court upheld the sentence enhancement in *Mitchell* because it didn't criminalize the motive. Instead, a content neutral behavior was criminalized. Because of the long history of allowing motives of all sorts to be considered at sentencing, the law was upheld.

Subsequently, in a 2003 decision, *Virginia v. Black*, the Supreme Court upheld a Virginia statute that criminalized cross burning. The Supreme Court did not overrule *R.A.V.* Rather, it distinguished the Virginia statute from the challenged law in *R.A.V.* The distinguishing characteristic was Virginia's requirement that the burning occur with an intent to intimidate. There was no such element in the challenged law in *R.A.V.* The Court analogized intimidating cross burning to threatening speech, which it had previously determined could be regulated.[18]

PRIVACY AND OTHER UNENUMERATED RIGHTS

Unlike some state constitutions, the U.S. Constitution does not expressly protect privacy. Many of the expressly stated rights in the Bill of Rights protect privacy, such as the Fourth Amendment, which has been interpreted as applying to searches that encroach upon a person's reasonable expectation to privacy.

The issue is whether the Constitution protects privacy to a greater extent than through its express provisions. Stated another way, is there an independent and inherent privacy right in the Constitution? If so, what is the textual source of that right?

The Supreme Court answered the former question affirmatively in 1965 in *Griswold v. Connecticut*.[19] In that case, a Connecticut statute that prohibited the use of contraceptives, even by married couples, was held unconstitutional as invasive of a right to privacy.

As to the second issue, the source of the right, the Court found that the right to privacy grows out of the First, Fourth, Fifth, Ninth, and Fourteenth Amendments. Justice Douglas, writing for the Court, found the right to privacy to be a "penumbra" of these expressly protected rights. The Court stressed that the First Amendment's right to association protected the marriage relationship and that the intimate subject sought to be regulated was especially protected. The Court stated that

> [Prior case law] suggests that specific guarantees in the Bill of Rights have penumbras, formed by emanations from those guarantees that help give them life and substance.... Various guarantees create zones of privacy. The right of association contained in the penumbra of the First Amendment is one, as we have seen. The Third Amendment in its prohibition against the quartering of soldiers "in any house" in time of peace without

the consent of the owner is another facet of that privacy. The Fourth Amendment explicitly affirms the "right of the people to be secure in their persons, houses, papers, and effects, against unreasonable searches and seizures." The Fifth Amendment in its Self-Incrimination Clause enables the citizens to create a zone of privacy which government may not force him to surrender to his detriment. The Ninth Amendment provides: "The enumeration in the Constitution, of certain rights, shall not be construed to deny or disparage others retained by the people." . . .

The present case, then, concerns a relationship lying within the zone of privacy created by several fundamental constitutional guarantees. . . .

We deal with a right to privacy older than the Bill of Rights—older than our political parties, older than our school system. Marriage is a coming together for better or worse, hopefully enduring, and intimate to the degree of being sacred. It is an association that promotes a way of life, not causes; a harmony in living, not political faiths; a bilateral loyalty, not commercial or social projects. Yet it is an association for as noble a purpose as any involved in our prior decisions.

Note that Justice Douglas found that the right to privacy was a penumbra of other fundamental, express rights. He did not find the right to privacy to be an independent constitutional right. This is because he believed that the Fourteenth Amendment was intended to extend the rights found in the Bill of Rights to the states, but that it was not intended to create independent rights. This principle is known as *total incorporation.*

Privacy has also been an issue in abortion cases. Abortion cases are complicated by a competing interest that did not exist in *Griswold,* that is, the interest of the state in protecting the fetus. In 1973 the Supreme Court handed down the landmark decision of *Roe v. Wade,* in which the Court declared that the right to privacy protects a woman's right to elect to abort a fetus in some situations.[20]

Specifically, the Court adopted a trimester analysis wherein the state's authority to regulate abortion increases as the pregnancy lengthens. During the first trimester, states could not regulate abortion procedures. During the second trimester, states could regulate abortions insofar as necessary to protect the health and life of the woman. Finally, states could protect the fetus during the third trimester, including proscribing abortion, except in cases in which abortion was necessary to protect the life or health of the mother. The Court decided that governmental interest in protecting fetuses during the third trimester was compelling because fetuses are viable at that time.

The trial court found Roe's right to privacy in the Ninth Amendment, but the Supreme Court refused to rely on the Ninth Amendment alone. Rather, the Court found the right to privacy to stem from the Fourteenth, Ninth, and other amendments.

The *Roe v. Wade* decision was the subject of intense political and legal controversy during the 1980s and 1990s. Certiorari was sought in several abortion-related cases during this period; so-called right-to-life groups believed that, with a more conservative Court than had existed since the *Roe v. Wade* decision issued, the chances of reversing the decision were good. The Court granted certiorari in several abortion-related cases, but the cardinal principle announced in *Roe v. Wade* was reaffirmed again and again: The decision whether to abort a fetus is, in some circumstances, so private and intimate that it is protected by the Constitution from governmental intrusion. This situation occurred in *Casey v. Planned Parenthood*, wherein the Court also rejected the trimester analysis.

Although the Court reaffirmed the right to privacy in the abortion context, it also rejected the trimester analysis in favor of an "undue interference" test. That is, a regulation is invalid if it unduly interferes with a woman's choice. Also, the Court reaffirmed the *Roe* holding that until a fetus is viable outside of the mother's womb, a state may not prohibit its abortion. Further, even after viability, abortion is permitted to save the life or health of the mother.

The Court examined the Pennsylvania statute and concluded that:

1. Requiring information concerning abortions and abortion procedures to be distributed to patients before the procedure is performed is not unduly burdensome.
2. Mandating 24-hour waiting periods between receipt of the information and performance of the procedure is not unduly burdensome.
3. Requiring parental consent (with a judicial bypass) by minor girls is not unduly burdensome.
4. Requiring spousal notification by married women is unduly burdensome, and therefore, invalid.[21]

The right to privacy applies outside the abortion context as well. For example, as the Court stated in *Casey*, the right to engage in an interracial marriage is also protected by the Fourteenth Amendment.[22] In *Eisenstadt v. Baird*,[23] the Supreme Court invalidated a statute that prohibited the sale and distribution of contraceptives to unmarried persons. The Court stated in that opinion, "If the right of privacy means anything, it is the right of the individual, married or single, to be free from unwarranted governmental intrusion into matter so fundamentally affecting a person as the decision whether to bear or beget a child."

These are a few examples of how the power of the state to regulate conduct is limited by the right to privacy. Today, courts are likely to rely on the Fourteenth Amendment as the source of the right to privacy. Arguably, the privacy right has its roots in other amendments as well, such as the Ninth Amendment, which declares that the enumeration in the Constitution of certain rights shall not be construed as denying or disparaging others retained by the people. Although this amendment appears to be an independent source of rights, probably with natural rights origins, it has received little attention by the courts, and standing alone has never been relied upon by the Supreme Court to establish an unenumerated right.

The Supreme Court refused to extend the right to privacy to include a right for consenting adults to engage in "deviate sexual" behavior in its 1986 decision *Bowers v. Hardwick*,[24] where it upheld a Georgia statute that criminalized sodomy. But the Court reversed itself seven years later in *Lawrence v. Texas*[25] (see Chapter 11 for more on this subject).

PRIVILEGES AND IMMUNITIES

Article IV, sec. 2 commands that "The Citizens of each State shall be entitled to all Privileges and Immunities of Citizens in the several States." The purpose of the clause is to prevent states from discriminating against citizens of other states. The clause applies only to the most fundamental of rights, and even then a state may overcome the prohibition if it can demonstrate a compelling reason.

Once a viable source of individual rights, the reach of clause has been severely limited by the Supreme Court, which has increasingly turned to the Fourteenth Amendment's Due Process Clause to protect unenumerated rights. One of the few rights protected by the Privileges and Immunities Clause is the right to travel freely between the states. The right to travel abroad is subject to reasonable restrictions and regulations[26] because of national security and foreign affairs concerns.

The Fourteenth Amendment contains a sister clause that forbids states from abridging the privileges or immunities of citizens of the United States. While the Fourth Amendment's Privileges and Immunities Clause forbids states from discriminating against each other's citizens, the Fourteenth Amendment's Privileges or Immunities Clause forbids the states from abridging any person, local or not, from exercising federally secured rights.

Any time a statute conflicts with a constitutionally protected activity, the statute will fail unless the government has a compelling interest. The defenses discussed in this chapter are only a few of the many constitutional defenses. Most, but not all, criminal constitutional defenses appear in the Bill of Rights.

Nor does this chapter exhaust all the nonconstitutional defenses that may be asserted. Do not forget that each state is free to design its criminal law in any manner it wishes, so long as its design is consonant with the U.S. Constitution. The most common factual, legislative, and constitutional substantive law defenses have been discussed. Many procedural defenses are examined in later chapters of this text.

Web Links

Comparative Criminal Justice

At the World Factbook of Criminal Justice Systems, you will find descriptions of the legal and criminal justice systems of many nations of the world. http://bjs.ojp.usdoj.gov/content/pub/html/wfcj.cfm

The United States Department of Justice's National Institute of Justice and Bureau of Justice Statistics both offer some comparative justice information. *http://www.ojp.usdoj.gov/nij/* and *http://www.ojp.usdoj.gov/bjs/*

Key Terms

bill of attainder
Double Jeopardy Clause
ex post facto law
overbreadth
principle of legality
transactional immunity
use immunity
vagueness

Review Questions

1. Differentiate overbreadth from vagueness. Give an example of each.
2. Differentiate a bill of attainder from an ex post facto law.
3. May racially derogatory statements be made criminal? May racial motives be used to enhance the punishment for crimes such as assault and battery?
4. Is a right to privacy specifically expressed in the U.S. Constitution?
5. Through what amendment are rights incorporated and applied against the states?
6. May religious beliefs be regulated by the state? May religious practices be regulated by the state?
7. Which of the following is protected by the First Amendment's Free Speech Clause?
    a. A public flag burning in protest of a recently enacted law.
    b. An advertisement for potato chips found on a billboard.
    c. The placing of a hand over one's heart while the national anthem is played.

Problems & Critical Thinking Exercises

1. Senator Bob Kerry of Nebraska was initially outraged by the *Texas v. Johnson* flag-burning decision. However, he later stated, "I was surprised to discover . . . [that the decision was] reasonable, understandable and consistent with those values which I believe have made America wonderful." Do you agree with Senator Kerry? Explain your position.
2. State law requires that all children between the ages of 5 and 16 years attend an approved school. Defendants have been charged with violating the

statute, as they do not permit their children to attend school. The defendants are Mennonites and claim that it would violate their First Amendment right to freely exercise their religion. The defendants teach their children in a manner consistent with their religious teachings. Should they be convicted?

3. Do you believe that a person should be subjected to two prosecutions, by different sovereigns, for the same offense? Consider specifically the prosecution of the Los Angeles police officers who arrested and beat Rodney King. They were acquitted of assault and battery in state court. Federal civil rights charges were brought in apparent reaction to the acquittal. In your opinion, is this proper? Support your answer.

4. Do you believe that the federal Constitution implicitly protects privacy? Support your conclusion. If so, name one right not mentioned in this text that you believe is protected.

Endnotes

1. David S. Rudstein, "Brief History of the Fifth Amendment Guarantee Against Double Jeopardy," 14 *Wm & Mary Bill of Rts. J.* 193, 204 (2005).
2. *Arizona v. Washington*, 434 U.S. 497 (1978).
3. *United States v. Dreitzler*, 577 F.2d 539 (9th Cir. 1978).
4. *United States v. Martin Linen Supply Co.*, 430 U.S. 564 (1977).
5. *See Monge v. California*, 524 U.S. 721 (1998).
6. *Blockburger v. United States*, 284 U.S. 299 (1932).
7. Model Penal Code § 1.10.
8. Passage taken from a 1991 calendar prepared by the Commission on the Bicentennial of the United States Constitution, Washington, D.C.
9. *Pillsbury v. Conboy*, 459 U.S. 248 (1983).
10. *Douglas v. California*, 372 U.S. 353 (1963).
11. *Connally v. General Construction Co.*, 269 U.S. 385 (1926).
12. *United States v. Cardiff*, 344 U.S. 174 (1952).
13. *Coates v. Cincinnati*, 402 U.S. 611 (1971).
14. See *United States v. Brown*, 381 U.S. at 444 (quoting John C. Hamilton, *History of the Republic of the United States* 34 (1859), who is *quoting* Alexander Hamilton).
15. *Reynolds v. United States*, 98 U.S. 145 (1878).
16. *People v. Woody*, 61 Cal. 2d 716, 394 P.2d 813 (1965).
17. 42 U.S. sec. 2000bb.
18. 538 U.S. 343 (2003).
19. 381 U.S. 479 (1965). The Supreme Court noted in *Roe v. Wade*, 410 U.S. 113 (1973), that the right to privacy may have been recognized by the Court as early as 1891, in *Union Pacific Railroad v. Botsford*, 141 U.S. 250 (1891), in which it held that a plaintiff in a tort action could not be compelled to submit to a medical examination because it would have been an invasion of privacy.

20. 410 U.S. 113 (1973).
21. *See also Webster v. Reproductive Health Services*, 492 U.S. 490 (1989).
22. *Loving v. Virginia*, 388 U.S. 1 (1967).
23. 405 U.S. 438 (1972).
24. 478 U.S. 186 (1986).
25. 539 U.S. 558 (2003).
26. *Zemel v. Rusk*, 381 U.S. 1 (1965).

GLOSSARY

accessory A person who helps to commit a crime without being present. An accessory before the fact is a person who, without being present, encourages, orders, or helps another to commit a crime. An accessory after the fact is a person who finds out that a crime has been committed and helps to conceal the crime or the criminal.

actus reus (Latin) An act. For example, an *actus reus* is a "wrongful deed" (such as killing a person) which, if done with mens rea, a "guilty mind" (such as *malice aforethought*), is a crime (such as *first-degree* murder).

admission A voluntary statement that a fact or a state of events is true.

adversary system The system of law in the United States. The judge acts as the referee between opposite sides (between two individuals, between the state and an individual, etc.) rather than acting as the person who also makes the state's case or independently seeks out evidence.

affirmative defense A defense that is more than a simple denial of the charges. It raises a new matter that may result in an acquittal or a reduction of liability. It is a defense that must be affirmatively raised, often before trial or it is lost.

aggravating circumstances Actions or occurrences that increase the seriousness of a crime, but are not part of the legal definition of that crime.

alibi (Latin) "Elsewhere"; the claim that at the time a crime was committed a person was somewhere else. [pronounce: al-eh-bi]

appellate court A higher court that can hear appeals from a lower court.

arraignment The hearing at which a defendant is brought before a judge to hear the charges and to enter a plea (guilty, not guilty, etc.).

arrest The official taking of a person to answer criminal charges. This involves at least temporarily depriving the person of liberty and may involve the use of force. An arrest is usually made by a police officer with a warrant or for a crime committed in the officer's presence.

arson The malicious and unlawful burning of a building.

assault An intentional threat, show of force, or movement that could reasonably make a person feel in danger of physical attack or harmful physical contact. It can be a crime or tort.

attempt An effort to commit a crime that goes beyond preparation and that proceeds far enough to make the person who did it guilty of an "attempt crime." For example, if a person fires a shot at another in a failed effort at murder, the person is guilty of *attempted murder*.

bail The money or property given as security for a defendant's appearance in court. The money, often in the form of a bail bond, may be lost if the defendant released does not appear in court.

battered woman syndrome Continuing abuse of a woman by a spouse or lover, and the resulting physical or psychological harm.

battery An intentional, unconsented to, physical contact by one person (or an object controlled by that person) with another person. It can be a crime or a tort.

beyond a reasonable doubt The level of proof required to convict a person of a crime. Precise definitions vary, but moral certainty and firm belief are both used. Beyond a reasonable doubt is not absolute certainty. This is the highest level of proof required in any type of trial.

bill of attainder A legislative act pronouncing a person guilty (usually of treason) without a trial and sentencing the person to death and attainder. This is now prohibited by the U.S. Constitution.

bill of particulars A detailed, formal, written statement of charges or claims by a plaintiff or the prosecutor (given upon the defendant's formal request to the court for more detailed information).

Bill of Rights The first 10 amendments (changes or additions) to the U.S. Constitution.

breach of the peace A vague term for any illegal public disturbance; sometimes refers to the offense known as "disorderly conduct." It is defined and treated differently in different states.

bribery The offering, giving, receiving, or soliciting of anything of value in order to influence the actions of a public official.

brief A written document filed with a court through which a party presents a legal claim, legal theory, supporting authorities, and requests some form of relief.

burden of going forward (production) The requirement that one side in a lawsuit produce evidence on a particular issue or risk losing on that issue.

burden of persuasion The requirement that to win a point or have an issue decided in your favor in a lawsuit you must show that the weight of evidence is on your side, rather than "in the balance" on that question.

burden of proof The requirement that to win a point or have an issue decided in your favor in a lawsuit, you must show that the weight of evidence is on your side rather than "in the balance" on that question.

burglary Unlawfully entering the house of another person with the intention of committing a felony (usually theft).

castle doctrine An exception to the Retreat Doctrine, one has no obligation to retreat from his or her home before using deadly force to repel an intruder.

certiorari (Latin) "To make sure." A request for certiorari (or "cert." for short) is like an appeal, but one that the higher court is not required to take for decision. It is literally a writ from the higher court asking the lower court for the record of the case.

chain of custody The chronological list of those in continuous possession of a specific physical object. A person who presents physical evidence (such as a gun used in a crime) at a trial must account for its possession from time of receipt to time of trial in order for the evidence to be "admitted" by the judge. It must thus be shown that the *chain of custody* was unbroken.

challenge for cause A formal objection to the qualifications of a prospective juror or jurors.

civil liberties Political liberties guaranteed by the Constitution and, in particular, by the Bill of Rights, especially the First Amendment.

clear and present danger A test of whether or not speech may be restricted or punished. It may be if it will probably lead to violence soon or if it threatens a serious, immediate weakening of national safety and security.

co-conspirator's rule The principle that statements by a member of a proven conspiracy may be used as evidence against any of the members of the conspiracy.

common law The legal system that originated in England and is composed of case law and statutes that grow and change, influenced by ever-changing custom and tradition.

commutation of sentence Changing a criminal punishment to one less severe

compensatory damages Damages awarded for the actual loss suffered by a plaintiff.

complaint A *criminal complaint* is a formal document that charges a person with a crime.

concert of action rule The rule that, unless a statute specifies otherwise, it is not a conspiracy for two persons to agree to commit a crime if the definition of the crime itself requires the participation of two or more persons. Also called *Wharton Rule* and *concerted action rule*.

concurrent jurisdiction Two or more jurisdictions or courts possessing authority over the same matter.

concurrent sentences Prison terms that run at the same time.

confession A voluntary statement by a person that he or she is guilty of a crime.

consecutive sentences An additional prison term given to a person who is already convicted of a crime; the additional term is to be served after the previous one is finished.

consent Voluntary and active agreement.

conspiracy A crime that may be committed when two or more persons agree to do something unlawful (or to do something lawful by unlawful means). The agreement can be inferred from the persons' actions.

constructive Inferred, implied, or presumed from the circumstances.

contempt A willful disobeying of a judge's command or official court order. Contempt can be *direct* (within the judge's notice) or *indirect* (outside the court and punishable only after proved to the judge). It can also be *civil contempt* (disobeying a court order in favor of an opponent) or *criminal contempt.*

contract An agreement that affects or creates legal relationships between two or more persons. To be a *contract,* an agreement must involve at least one promise, consideration, persons legally capable of making binding agreements, and a reasonable certainty about the meaning of the terms.

conversion Any act that deprives an owner of property without that owner's permission and without just cause.

corporate liability The liability of a corporation for the acts of its directors, officers, shareholders, agents, and employees.

corpus delicti (Latin) "The body of the crime." The material substance upon which a crime has been committed; for example, a dead body (in the crime of murder) or a house burned down (in the crime of arson).

court of general jurisdiction Another term for trial court; that is, a court having jurisdiction to try all classes of civil and criminal cases except those that can be heard only by a court of limited jurisdiction.

court of limited jurisdiction A court whose jurisdiction is limited to civil cases of a certain type, or that involve a limited amount of money, or whose jurisdiction in criminal cases is confined to petty offenses and preliminary hearings.

court of record Generally, another term for trial court.

criminal law The branch of the law that specifies what conduct constitutes crime and establishes appropriate punishments for such conduct.

criminal procedure The rules of procedure by which criminal prosecutions are governed.

culpable Blamable; at fault. A person who has done a wrongful act (whether criminal or civil) is described as "culpable."

damages Money that a court orders paid to a person who has suffered damage (a loss or harm) by the person who caused the injury (the violation of the person's rights).

deadly weapon Any instrument likely to cause serious bodily harm under the circumstances of its actual use. Such things as a fan belt used to choke a man and a fire used to burn an occupied house have been called *deadly weapons* by courts.

deposition The process of taking a witness's sworn out-of-court testimony. The questioning is usually done by a lawyer, and the lawyer from the other side is given a chance to attend and participate.

detainer A warrant or court order to keep a person in custody when that person might otherwise be released. This is often used to make sure a person will serve a sentence or attend a trial in one state at the end of a prison term in another state or in a federal prison.

deter To discourage; to prevent from acting.

determinate sentence An exact penalty set by law.

diminished capacity The principle that having a certain recognized form of *diminished mental capacity* while committing a crime should lead to the imposition of a lesser punishment or to lowering the degree of the crime.

discovery The formal and informal exchange of information between the prosecution and the defense.

discretion The power to act within general guidelines, rules, or laws, but without either specific rules to follow or the need to completely explain or justify each decision or action.

DNA printing Comparing body tissue samples (such as blood, skin, hair, or semen) to see if the genetic materials match. The process is used to identify criminals by comparing their DNA with that found at a crime scene, and it is used to identify a child's parent. Most states allow its use as evidence.

double jeopardy A second prosecution by the same government against the same person for the same crime (or for a lesser included offense) once the first prosecution is totally finished and decided. This is prohibited by the U.S. Constitution.

due process The *due process* clauses of the Fifth and Fourteenth Amendments to the U.S. Constitution require that no persons be deprived of life, liberty, or property without having notice and a real chance to present their side in a legal dispute.

duress Unlawful pressure on what a person would not otherwise have done. It includes force, threats of violence, physical restraint, etc.

Durham rule The principle, used in *Durham v. U.S.* (214 F.2d. 862 (1954)), that defendants are not guilty of a crime because of insanity if they were "suffering from a disease or defective mental condition at the time of the act and there was a causal connection between the condition and the act."

element A basic part. For example, some of the *elements* of a cause of action for battery are an intentional, unwanted physical contact. Each of these things ("intentional," "unwanted," etc.) is one "element."

embezzlement The fraudulent and secret taking of money or property by a person who has been trusted with it. This usually applies to an employee's taking money and covering it up by faking business records or account books.

entrapment The act of government officials (usually police) or agents inducing a person to commit a crime that the person would not have committed without the inducement.

ex post facto law (Latin) After the fact. An *ex post facto* law is one that retroactively attempts to make an action a crime that was not a crime at the time it was done, or a law that attempts to reduce a person's rights based on a past act that was not subject to the law when it was done.

exclusionary rule "The exclusionary rule" often means the rule that illegally gathered evidence may not be used in a criminal trial. The rule has several exceptions, such as when the evidence is used to impeach a defendant's testimony and when the evidence was gathered in a good-faith belief that the process was legal.

exhaustion of remedies A person must usually take all reasonable steps to get satisfaction from a state or federal government before seeking judicial relief.

exigent circumstances A situation where law enforcement officers must act so quickly to prevent the destruction of evidence, the successful flight of a suspect, or serious injury or death to any person, that there isn't time to obtain a warrant. Warrantless searches that occur when exigent circumstances exist are valid.

extortion To compel, force, or coerce; for example, to get a confession by depriving a person of food and water. To get something by illegal threats of harm to person, property, or reputation. The process is called *extortion*.

extradition One country (or state) giving up a person to a second country (or state) when the second requests the person for a trial on a criminal charge or for punishment after a trial.

false imprisonment The unlawful restraint by one person of the physical liberty of another.

false pretenses A lie told to cheat another person out of his or her money or property. It is a crime in most states, though the precise definition varies.

federalism A system of political organization with several different levels of government (for example, city, state, and national) coexisting in the same area, with the lower levels having some independent powers.

felony-murder rule The principle that if a person (even accidentally) kills another while committing a felony, then the killing is murder.

fighting words Speech that is not protected by the First Amendment to the U.S. Constitution because it is likely to cause violence by the person to whom the words are spoken.

final judgement (order) The last action of a court; the one upon which an appeal can be based.

first-degree murder The highest form of homicide. The killing of another person with malice and premeditation, cruelty, or done during the commission of a major felony is typically murder in the first degree.

foreseeable The degree to which the consequences of an action *should* have been anticipated, recognized, and considered beforehand. *Not* hindsight.

forfeiture A deprivation of money, property, or rights, without compensation, as a consequence of a default or the commission of a crime.

forgery Making a fake document (or altering a real one) with intent to commit a fraud.

fruit of the poisonous tree doctrine The rule that evidence gathered as a *result* of evidence gained in an illegal search or questioning cannot be used against the person searched or questioned even if the later evidence was gathered lawfully.

general intent The desire to commit a prohibited act but not the outcome of that act.

grand jury Persons who receive complaints and accusations of crime, hear preliminary evidence on the complaining side, and make formal accusations or indictments.

habitual offender statutes Laws that may apply to a person who has been convicted of as few as two prior crimes (often violent or drug-related crimes) and that greatly increase the penalties for each succeeding crime.

halfway house A facility in which persons recently discharged from a rehabilitation center or prison live for a time and are given support and assistance in readjusting to society at large.

harmless error A trivial mistake made by a judge in the procedures used at trial, or in making legal rulings during the trial.

hearsay A statement about what someone else said (or wrote or otherwise communicated). *Hearsay evidence* is evidence, concerning what someone said outside of a court proceeding, that is offered in the proceeding to prove the truth of what was said. The *hearsay rule* bars the admission of hearsay as evidence to *prove the hearsay's truth* unless allowed by a hearsay exception.

hung jury   A jury that cannot reach a verdict (decision) because of disagreement among jurors.

identity theft   The act of assuming another person's identity by fraud.

in limine   (Latin) "At the beginning"; preliminary. A motion in limine is a (usually pretrial) request that prejudicial information be excluded as trial evidence.

independent source   The general rule that if new evidence can be traced to a source completely apart from the illegally gathered evidence that first led to the new evidence, it may be used by the government in a criminal trial.

indeterminate sentence   A sentence having a minimum and maximum, with the decision of how long the criminal will serve depending on the criminal's behavior in prison and other things.

indictment   A sworn, written accusation of a crime, made against a person by a prosecutor to a *grand jury*.

inevitable discovery rule   The principle that even if criminal evidence is gathered by unconstitutional methods, the evidence may be admissible if it definitely would have come to light anyway.

inference   A fact (or proposition) that is *probably* true because a true fact (or proposition) leads you to believe that the inferred fact (or proposition) is also true.

inferior court   A court with special, limited responsibilities, such as a probate court.

information   A formal accusation of a crime made by a proper public official such as a prosecuting attorney.

injunction   A judge's order to a person to do or to refrain from doing a particular thing.

intentional   Determination to do a certain thing.

interlocutory appeal   The *Interlocutory Appeals* Act (28 U.S.C. 1292 (1948)) is a federal law that provides for an appeal while a trial is going on if the trial judge states in writing: (1) A legal question has come up that directly affects the trial. (2) There are major questions as to how that point of law should be resolved. (3) The case would proceed better if the appeals court answers the question.

interpret   Studying a document *and* surrounding circumstances to decide the document's meaning.

interrogation   Questioning by police, especially of a person suspected or accused of a crime. A *custodial interrogation* involves a restraint of freedom, so it requires a *Miranda* warning. A routine *investigatory interrogation* involves no restraint and no accusation of a crime.

intervening cause   A cause of an accident or other injury that will remove the blame from the wrongdoer who originally set events in motion.

irresistible impulse   The loss of control due to insanity that is so great that a person cannot stop from committing a crime.

JNOV   A request by a defendant convicted by a jury for the court to set aside the verdict as unsupported by the evidence.

judicial review   A higher court's examination of a lower court's decision.

jurisdiction   The geographical area within which a court (or a public official) has the right and power to operate. Or the persons about whom and the subject matters about which a court has the right and power to make decisions that are legally binding.

kidnapping   Taking away and holding a person illegally, usually against the person's will or by force.

knowingly   With full knowledge and intentionally; willfully.

larceny   Stealing of any kind. Some types of larceny are specific crimes, such as larceny by trick or grand larceny.

legal cause   The proximate cause of an injury; probable cause; cause that the law deems sufficient.

legal impossibility   A person who is unable to commit a crime because of legal impossibility cannot be convicted of a crime he or she intends or attempts.

legislative history   The background documents and records of hearings related to the enactment of a bill.

lineup   A group of persons, placed side by side in a line, shown to a witness of a crime to see if the witness will identify the person suspected of committing the crime. A *lineup* should not be staged so that it is suggestive of one person.

M'Naghten rule   A principle employed in some jurisdictions for determining whether criminal defendants had the capacity to form criminal intent at the time they committed the crime of which they are accused. The M'Naghten rule is also referred to as the M'Naghten test or the right-wrong test.

malicious (criminal) mischief   The criminal offense of intentionally destroying another person's property.

manslaughter   A crime, less severe than murder, involving the wrongful but nonmalicious killing of another person.

mayhem The crime of violently, maliciously, and intentionally giving someone a serious permanent wound. In some states, a type of aggravated assault. Once, the crime of permanently wounding another (as by dismemberment) to deprive the person of fighting ability.

mens rea (Latin) A state of mind that produces a crime.

merger of offenses When a person is charged with two crimes (based on exactly the same acts), one of which is a lesser included offense of the other. The lesser crime *merges* because, under the prohibition against double jeopardy, the person may be tried for only one crime.

mitigating circumstances Facts that provide no justification or excuse for an action, but that can lower the amount of moral blame and thus lower the criminal penalty or civil damages for the action.

Model Penal Code A proposed criminal code prepared jointly by the Commission on Uniform State Laws and the American Law Institute.

motion A request that a judge make a ruling or take some other action.

motive The reason why a person does something.

National Crime Information Center Computerized records of criminals, warrants, stolen vehicles, etc.

necessity Often refers to a situation that requires an action that would otherwise be illegal or expose a person to tort liability.

negligence Under the MPC, a defendant acts negligently when the resulting harm or material element of a crime occurs because of the defendant has taken a substantial and unjustifiable risk, even if the risk is not perceived, so long as the risk involves a gross deviation from the standard of conduct that a law-abiding person would observe.

nolle prosequi (Latin) The ending of a criminal case because the prosecutor decides or agrees to stop prosecuting. When this happens, the case is "nolled," "nollied," or "nol. prossed."

objection A claim that an action by your adversary in a lawsuit (such as the use of a particular piece of evidence) is improper, unfair, or illegal, and you are asking the judge for a ruling on the point.

omission Failing to do something that should be done.

ordinance A local or city law, rule, or regulation.

overbreadth doctrine A law will be declared void for *overbreadth* if it attempts to punish speech or conduct that is protected by the Constitution and if it is impossible to eliminate the unconstitutional part of the law without invalidating the whole law.

pardon A president's or governor's release of a person from punishment for a crime.

parole Early release from prison or jail. Parole is usually granted with conditions such as requiring the parolee to refrain from communicating with the victim of the crime that led to the confinement and remaining free of criminality while on parole. If the conditions of parole are violated, parole may be revoked and the parolee may be returned to confinement to complete the original sentence.

peremptory challenge The automatic elimination of a potential juror by one side before trial without needing to state the reason for the elimination.

perjury Lying while under oath, especially in a court proceeding. It is a crime.

plain view doctrine The rule that if police officers see or come across something while acting lawfully, that item may be used as evidence in a criminal trial even if the police did not have a search warrant.

plea bargain (plea agreement) Negotiations between a prosecutor and a criminal defendant's lawyer, in the attempt to resolve a criminal case without trial.

plea The *defendant's* formal answer to a criminal charge. The defendant says: "guilty," "not guilty," or "nolo contendere" (no contest).

police power The government's right and power to set up and enforce laws to provide for the safety, health, and general welfare of the people.

polling the jury Individually asking each member of a jury what his or her decision is. Polling is done by the judge, at the defendant's request, immediately after the verdict.

precedent Prior decisions of the same court, or a higher court, that a judge must follow in deciding a subsequent case presenting similar facts and the same legal problem, even though different parties are involved and many years have elapsed.

preliminary hearing The first court proceeding on a criminal charge, in federal courts and many state courts, by a magistrate or a judge to decide whether there is enough evidence for the government to continue with the case and to require the defendant to post bail or be held for trial.

presumption A presumption *of law* is an automatic assumption required by law that whenever a certain set of facts shows up, a court must automatically draw certain legal conclusions.

principal A person directly involved with committing a crime, as opposed to an accessory.

principle of legality The procedural side of due process, which requires that criminal laws (and punishments) be written and enacted before an act may be punished.

probable cause The U.S. Constitutional requirement that law enforcement officers present sufficient facts to convince a judge to issue a search warrant or an arrest *warrant*, and the requirement that no warrant should be issued unless it is more likely than not that the objects sought will be found in the place to be searched or that a crime has been committed by the person to be arrested.

prostitution A person offering her (in most states, his or her) body for sexual purposes in exchange for money. A crime in most states.

provocation An act by one person that triggers a reaction of rage in a second person. *Provocation* may reduce the severity of a crime.

proximate cause The "legal cause" of an accident or other injury (which may have several actual causes). The *proximate cause* of an injury is not necessarily the closest thing in time or space to the injury, and not necessarily the event that set things in motion, because "proximate cause" is a legal, not a physical concept.

punitive damages Damages that are awarded over and above compensatory damages or actual damages because of the wanton, reckless, or malicious nature of the wrong done by the plaintiff.

purposely Intentionally; knowingly.

quash Overthrow; annul; completely do away with. *Quash* usually refers to a court stopping a subpoena, an order, or an indictment.

racketeer influenced and corrupt organizations act (19 U.S.C. 1961). A broadly applied 1970 federal law that creates certain "racketeering offenses" that include participation in various criminal schemes and conspiracies, and that allows government seizure of property acquired in violation of the act.

rape The crime of imposing sexual intercourse by force or otherwise without legally valid consent.

receiving stolen property The criminal offense of getting or concealing property known to be stolen by another.

recklessness Indifference to consequences; indifference to the safety and rights of others. Recklessness implies conduct amounting to more than ordinary negligence.

record on appeal A formal, written account of a case, containing the complete formal history of all actions taken, papers filed, rulings made, opinions written, etc.

regulation Law created by governmental administrative agencies.

reprieve Holding off on enforcing a criminal sentence for a period of time after the sentence has been handed down.

retreat to the wall The doctrine that before a person is entitled to use deadly force in self defense, he or she must attempt to withdraw from the encounter by giving as much ground as possible.

revocation hearing The due process hearing required before the government can revoke a privilege it has previously granted.

robbery The illegal taking of property from the person of another by using force or threat of force.

rules of court Rules promulgated by the court, governing procedure or practice before it.

scienter (Latin) Knowingly; with guilty knowledge. [pronounce: si-*en*-ter]

second-degree murder Murder without premeditation.

self-defense Physical force used against a person who is threatening the use of physical force or using physical force.

separation of powers Division of the federal government (and state governments) into legislative (lawmaking), judicial (law interpreting), and executive (law carrying out) branches.

shield laws A state law that prohibits use of most evidence of a rape (or other sexual crime) victim's past sexual conduct at trial.

showup A pretrial Identification procedure in which only one suspect and a witness are brought together.

sidebar An in-court discussion among lawyers and the judge that is out of the hearing of witnesses and the jury. Sidebar conferences are usually *on* the record.

sodomy A general word for an "unnatural" sex act or the crime committed by such act. While the definition varies, *sodomy* can include oral sex, anal sex, homosexual sex, or sex with animals.

solicitation Asking for; enticing; strongly requesting. This may be a crime if the thing being urged is a crime.

sovereign immunity The government's freedom from being sued. In many cases, the U.S. government has waived immunity by a statute such as the Federal Tort Claims Act; states have similar laws.

specific intent An intent to commit the exact crime charged or the precise outcome of the act, not merely an intent to commit the act without an intention to cause the outcome.

stalking The crime of repeatedly following, threatening, or harassing another person in ways that lead to a legitimate fear of physical harm. Some states define *stalking* more broadly as any conduct with no legitimate purpose that seriously upsets a targeted person, especially conduct in violation of a protective order.

standing A person's right to bring (start) or join a lawsuit or to raise a particular issue because he or she is directly affected by the issues raised.

stand-your-ground A law that enables a person to use deadly force to repel an attack without first retreating.

stare decisis (Latin) The doctrine that judicial decisions stand as precedents for cases arising in the future.

statute A law passed by a legislature.

statute of limitation Federal and state statutes prescribing the maximum period of time during which various types of civil actions and criminal prosecutions can be brought after the occurrence of the injury or the offense.

statutory construction Guidelines employed by judges in the interpretation of statutes that have developed and evolved over hundreds of years.

statutory rape The crime of having sexual intercourse with a person under a certain state-set age, regardless of consent.

strict liability crimes Crimes or offenses in which mens rea or criminal intent is not an element. Such offenses include regulatory crimes, petty offenses, and infractions.

strict liability Guilt of a criminal offense even if you had no criminal intention (mens rea).

subornation of perjury The crime of asking or forcing another person to lie under oath.

suspended sentence A sentence (usually "jail time") that the judge allows the convicted person to avoid serving (usually if the person continues on good behavior, completes community service, etc.).

tax evasion The deliberate nonpayment or underpayment of taxes that are legally due. Criminal tax evasion has higher fines than civil fraud and the possibility of a prison sentence upon the showing of "willfulness."

tax fraud The deliberate nonpayment or underpayment of taxes that are legally due.

terrorism The definition of terrorism is the subject to ongoing debate. However, one federal statute defines it as activities that involve violence or acts dangerous to human life that are violations of law and appear to be intended to intimate or coerce a civilian population, to influence a policy of government by intimidation or coercion, or to affect the conduct of government through mass destruction, assassination, or kidnapping. 18 U.S.C. §2331.

tort A civil (as opposed to a criminal) wrong, other than a breach of contract.

transactional immunity Freedom from prosecution for all crimes related to the compelled testimony, so long as the witness tells the truth.

transferred intent The principle that if an unintended illegal act results from the intent to commit a crime, that act is also a crime.

trial court A court that hears and determines a case initially, as opposed to an appellate court; a court of general jurisdiction.

use immunity Freedom from prosecution based on the compelled testimony and on anything the government learns from following up on the testimony.

vagueness doctrine The rule that a criminal law may be unconstitutional if it does not clearly say what is required or prohibited, what punishment may be imposed, or what persons may be affected. A law that violates due process of law in this way is *void for vagueness*.

vicarious liability Legal responsibility for the acts of another person because of some relationship with that person.

victim impact statement At the time of sentencing, a statement made to the court concerning the effect the crime has had on the victim or on the victim's family.

voir dire examination (French) "To see, to say"; "to state the truth." The preliminary in-court questioning of a prospective witness (or juror) to determine competency to testify (or suitability to decide a case). [pronounce: vwahr deer]

INDEX

Note: page numbers followed by e indicate exhibits

A

ABA. *See* American Bar Association
abortion, 251–252
absolute immunity, 67, 68
accessories, 299–300
accomplices, 299
accusatorial system, 56–57
acquired immunodeficiency syndrome (AIDS), 201
acquitted crimes, 178, 305, 328
actus reus
    assumption of duty, 182
    causation, 183–185
    creating danger, 183
    defined, 177
    duty by contract, 182
    duty by relationship, 181–182
    duty imposed by statute, 180–181
    omissions as, 180
    overview, 177
    personal status as, 178–179
    possession as, 179–180
    statements as, 178
    thoughts as, 178
    voluntariness, 177–178
    "year-and-a-day rule," 185–186
        concurrence, 186
administration of government, crimes against
    bribery, 267–268
    contempt, 271
    obstruction of justice, 270
    perjury, 266–267
    tax crimes, 268–270
administrative law, 41–46
adversarial system, 56–57
defined, 56
advocacy of unlawful conduct, 258–259
affirmative defenses, 309
agencies, 41–2, 46
aggravated assault and battery, 208–209
aggravating circumstances, 144
AIDS (acquired immunodeficiency syndrome), 201
Alabama v. Shelton, 122
alcohol crimes, 263–264
alcohol treatment programs, 264
alibis, 328
Alien and Seditions Acts, 272
Allen charge, 129
ambiguous language canon, 170e
American Bar Association (ABA) ethics, 27
American Library Association v. Pataki, 256
Antiterrorism and Effective Death Penalty Act (1996), 273
appeal, 9–10, 152–154
appellate courts, 9–13
    defined, 9
appreciable, in gap in time, 198
apprehension of imminent battery, 207–208
arraignment, 101–102
    defined, 101
arrests
    by citizens, 324–325
    defining, 89
    Fourth Amendment, 324
    during hot pursuits, 110
    by law enforcement officers, 324
    overview, 89, 323
    resisting unlawful, 323
arson, 226–227
asportation, 229, 230
    of the victim, 216
assault and battery, 207–209
    defined, 207
assistant United States attorneys (AUSAs), 60
assumption of duty, 182
Atkins v. Virginia, 142
attempt, 300–302
    defined, 301
attempted battery, 208
AUSAs (assistant United States attorneys), 60

B

bail, 89, 93, 94
Barker v. Wingo, 120, 121
Barron ex rel. Tiernan v. Mayor of Baltimore, 73
battered woman syndrome defense, 318
battery, defined, 207. *See also* assault and battery
Baze v. Rees, 141
beyond a reasonable doubt, 119
bifurcated procedures, 151
bill of attainder, 342–343
bill of particulars, 103
Bill of Rights, 23
    incorporation and, 76e
bills of attainder, 342–343
blackmail, 238
blood testing, 150
BMW v. Gore, 18
bonds, 93–94

363

booking, 89
Booth v. Maryland, 137
Bowers v. Hardwick, 350
Brady doctrine, 105
Brady Handgun Violence Prevention Act (1993), 262
Brady v. Maryland, 105
breach of the peace, defined, 258
bribery, 267–268
    defined, 267
briefing, 36–37
briefs, 9
Brown v. Allen, 155
Bullcoming v. New Mexico, 118
Bundy, Ted, 99
burden of going forward, 309
burden of persuasion, 309
burden of production, 309
burden of proof, 119–120, 309
Bureau of Justice Statistics, 245
burglary, 227–228
    defined, 227
    example of, 228e
    parties to a, 300e
by right, defined, 154

C

CAA (Clean Air Act), 291
Callins v. Collins, 140–141
canons of statutory construction, 170e
capital punishment, 16, 139–142
captions, 20e
case names/titles, 19
Casey v. Planned Parenthood of Southeastern Pennsylvania, 349
castle doctrine, 319–321
castration, 209, 214–215
causation, 183–185
cause in fact, 183
caveat emptor, 232–233
CCE (Continuing Criminal Enterprise), 265–266
CERCLA (Comprehensive Environmental Response, Compensation and Liability Act), 291
certiorari, 10
C.F.R. (Code of Federal Regulations), 42
challenge for cause, 125

checks, fraudulent, 234
Child Online Protection Act (1991), 256
Child Pornography Prevention Act (CPPA), 256
children, sex crimes against, 212–214
citizen v. citizen, 19
citizens' arrests, 324–325
civil law, 15–21
civil liberties, 22
civil rights crimes, 219–220
Clean Air Act (CAA), 291
Clean Water Act (CWA), 290–29
clear and present danger, 259
closing arguments, 128
co-conspirator hearsay rule, 305
cocaine, 137, 138
Code of Federal Regulations (C.F.R.), 42
collateral estoppel, 337
commitment, 214–215
common law, 33–41, 49e, 163–164
    and homicide, 194–195
    and mens rea, 163–164
    overview, 33–41
Commonwealth v. Hughes, 216
Communications Decency Act (1996), 218, 256
community service, 148
compensatory damages, 17
complaints, 89, 90–93e
    defined, 89
Comprehensive Environmental Response, Compensation and Liability Act (CERCLA), 291
Comprehensive Forfeiture Act (1984), 266
Computer Abuse Amendments Act (1994), 244
computer crimes, 243–244
Computer Fraud and Abuse Act (1986), 243
concert of action rule, 304
concurrence, 186
concurrent jurisdiction, 3, 4e
concurrent sentencing, 145
concurring opinions, 37
Confrontation Clause, 117–118
consecutive sentencing, 145
consent, 329
conservation laws, 289, 290–291
consolidated theft statutes, 238–239

conspiracy, 303–305
    defined, 303
constitution, dates in history of, 48e
constitutional aspects of criminal procedure
    defined, 73
    exclusionary rule, 77–78
    expansion of rights, 77
    fruit of the poisonous tree doctrine, 78–79
    incorporation, 73–76
    "New Federalism," 81–83
    overview, 73
    standing, 80–81
constitutional claims, analyzing, 342
constitutional defenses
    bills of attainder, 342–343
    constitutional claims, analyzing, 342
    double jeopardy, 336–337
    due process, 40, 57–58, 339–341
    equal protection, 339–341
    ex post facto law, 342
    First Amendment and religion, 343–344
    immunity, 338–339
    overbreadth doctrine, 341
    privacy, 365, 366–367
    self-incrimination, 338–339
    and speech, 345–347, 346e
    vagueness doctrine, 341
constitutional interpretation, 77
constitutional law, 47–48
constitutionality presumption canon, 170e
constitutionalization, 81
Constitutions, 49e
constructive intent, 165–166
constructive possession, 230, 236
contemporaneous objections, 78
contempt, 271
    defined, 271
Continuing Criminal Enterprise (CCE), 265–266
contraception, 251–252
contract, 16, 17
conversion, 231
cooling-off period, 203
Cooper v. Oklahoma, 315
cooperative federalism, 2, 4
coram nobis, 129

Corey, Giles, 338
corporal/physical punishment, 142
corporate liability, 171–173
corpus delicti, 206–207
counsel. *See also* right to counsel
    effective assistance of, 123–124
    indigency, 122–123
    no right to, 123e
    right to self-representation, 124
    scope of right, 124–125
County of Riverside v. McLaughlin, 93, 95
court rules, 46–47, 49e
    Model Penal Code, 47
    ordinances, 6, 12, 41
    statutory law, 41
court system, 8–13
courts of general jurisdiction, 12
courts of limited jurisdiction, 12
courts of record, 12
CPPA (Child Pornography Prevention Act), 256
Crawford v. Washington, 117
crime clock, 194e
crime control, due process compared to, 58e
crimes. *See* administration of government, crimes against; environment, crimes against; names of specific crimes; person, crimes against; property and habitation, crimes against; public, crimes against; public morality, crimes against; public order, crimes against; sovereignty and security, crimes against
criminal complaints, 90e
criminal enterprises, 265–266
criminal law
    authority of government to regulate behavior, 21–24
    compared to civil law, 15–21, 16e
    compared to criminal procedure, 32
    ethics and, 27
    purposes of punishing violators, 24–27
    sources of administrative law, 41–46
criminal mischief, 241–242
criminal procedure
    basic process, 97–98e
    compared to criminal law, 15–21, 16e, 32
    defined, 56
criminal records, 104
cross-examination, 117–119
culpability, 21
curtilage, 226
custody requirement, habeas corpus, 156–157
CWA (Clean Water Act), 290–291
cyberstalking, 218–219

D

damages, 17
danger, creating, 183
de novo, 12
deadly force continuum, 321e
deadly weapon doctrine, 199, 201
death certificate, of Timothy McVeigh, 273, 274e
death, determination of, 205
Death With Dignity Act (1997), 206
defendants
    confrontation and cross-examination, 117–119
    counsel, 121–123
    jury trial, 115–116
    presumption of innocence/burden of proof, 119–120, 309
    public trial, 116
    to self-representation, 124
    speedy trial, 120–121
defense appeals, 153–154
defense attorneys, 50–51
    ethics and, 63–64
    overview, 63
defense cases, 127–128
defense of others, 203, 321
defense of property and habitation 322
defenses
    affirmative, 309
    alibis, 328
    consent, 329
    constitutional bills of attainder
        double jeopardy, 336–337
        due process, 40, 57–58, 339–341
        equal protection, 339–341
        ex post facto law, 342
        First Amendment, 249, 345
        immunity, 338–339
        overbreadth doctrine, 341
        privacy, 347–350
        self-incrimination, 338–339
        vagueness doctrine, 341
    constitutional claims, analyzing, 342
    defined, 309
    duress, 316–317
    entrapment, 327–328
    ethics of, 50–51
    infancy, 325–326
    insanity
        disposition of criminally insane, 313–314
        Durham rule, 311–312
        guilty but mentally ill, 312–313
        irresistible impulse, 311
        M'Naghten test, 310–311
        Model Penal Code test, 312
        overview, 310
        procedures of, 313, 315e
        at time of trial, 314–316
    intoxication, 326
    mistake, 326–327
    necessity, 317
    statutes of limitation, 329
    use-of-force
        arrests, 323
        defense of others, 321
        defense of property and habitation, 322
        imperfect self-defense, 203, 323
        self-defense, 318
deferred sentencing, 265
definite sentencing, 144
deliberate homicide, 198
Department of Homeland Security (DHS), 275
Department of Human Resources v. Smith, 344
Depo-Provera, 215
depositions, defined, 105
derivative evidence, 79, 80, 340
destruction of property, 241–242
detainers, 109–111
    defined, 110
detention, 94–95
deter, defined, 25
determinate sentencing, 143
    defined, 143
deterrence, 25
deviate sexual conduct, 250–251

DHS (Department of Homeland Security), 275
diminished capacity defense, 310
direct contempt, 271
directed verdict, 127
discovery
  bill of particulars, 103
  Brady doctrine, 105
  criminal record of defendant, 104
  defined, 102
  depositions, 105
  documents and tangible objects, 104
  freedom of information laws, 106
  overview, 88, 89, 102–103
  reciprocal discovery, 106
  scientific reports and tests, 104
  statements of defendant, 103–104
  statements of witnesses/Jencks Act, 104–105
discretion
  defined, 61
  law enforcement officers, 59
  prosecutors, 61–62
disease of the mind, 310, 311
disposition of criminally insane, 313–314
District of Columbia v. Heller, 261
disturbing peace, 258
diversion. *See* suspended imposition of sentence
documents, 104
Double Jeopardy Clause, 336–337
  defined, 336
Douglas v. California, 154
drug crimes, 264–265
drug treatment programs, 150
drunk driving, 122–123, 204, 264
dual federalism, 4
Due Process Clauses
  defined, 40
  determining insanity, 314–316
  and equal protection, 339–341
  models, 57–58, 58e
  principle of legality, 35–40, 340
duress, 316–317
  defined, 316
Durham rule, 311
Durham v. United States, 311–312
duty, 180–182
dwellings, 226

E

Eighth Amendment, 94
Eisenstadt v. Baird, 349
elements, 174–175, 193
embezzlement, 231–232
Emergency Planning and Community Right-to-Know Act, 292
Endangered Species Act (ESA), 289, 290, 293
entrapment, defined, 327–328
environment, crimes against
  Clean Air Act (CAA), 291
  Clean Water Act (CWA), 290–291
  Comprehensive Environmental Response, Compensation and Liability Act (CERCLA), 291
  Emergency Planning and Community Right-to-Know Act, 292
  Endangered Species Act (ESA), 289, 293
  Federal Insecticide, Fungicide, and Rodenticide Act (FIFRA), 229
  Marine Mammal Protection Act (MMPA), 293
  Occupational Safety and Health Act (OSHA), 291–292
  overview, 289–290
  Resource Conservation and Recovery Act (RCRA), 291
  Toxic Substances Control Act (TSCA), 292
equal protection, 339–341
ESA (Endangered Species Act), 293
espionage, 272–273
Estes v. Texas, 116
ethics
  defense attorneys, 50–51, 63–64
  judges, 63
  law enforcement officers, 59–60
  lawyer competency and prosecutors, 62–63
evidence, 6, 27, 78–79
ex post facto law, 342–343
excessive bail, 94
exclusionary rule, 77–78
  defined, 77
  in practice, 77–78
executive branch, 6, 7e
exhaustion of remedies doctrine, 156

expansion of rights, 77
exploitation, 293
  child, 213
extortion, 238
extradition, 109–111
  defined, 109
Exxon Shipping Co. v. Baker, 18
eyewitness identification, 505–508

F

factual guilt, 57
factual impossibility, 201, 302, 303
false imprisonment, 217
false pretenses, 232–233
Faretta v. California, 124
Fed. R. Crim. P 5(f), 103
Fed. R. Crim. P6, 108
Fed. R. Crim. P13, 105
Fed. R. Crim. P 14(a) (1) (A), 103
Fed. R. Crim. P.19, 107
Federal Counterfeit Access Device and Computer Fraud and Abuse Act (1984), 243
federal court structure, 13e
federal government, described, 2
Federal Insecticide, Fungicide, and Rodenticide Act (FIFRA), 292
federal judicial circuits, 11e
Federal Kidnapping Act, 216, 217
federal law enforcement agencies, 59
Federal Sentencing Guidelines, 145–146
Federal Tort Claims Act (FTCA), 68
Federal Wiretap Act, 486
federalism, 2–6
  defined, 2
Federalist Papers, 14
felony-murder doctrine, 195–197
felony-murder rule, 195
fences, 236
field sobriety tests, 264
FIFRA (Federal Insecticide, Fungicide, and Rodenticide Act), 292
Fifteenth Amendment, 48
Fifth Amendment, 61–62, 74, 76e, 77
fighting words, 258
final orders, 153
fines, 148–149, 168, 235, 266, 289, 290–291
firearms, 260–263

licensing, 263
possession, 261–262
registration, 263
sale and transfer laws, 261–262
use laws, 262–263
First Amendment
and assembling, 76e
and religion, 343–344
and speech, 252, 345–347
first-degree murder, 197, 198, 199
defined, 197
FISA (Foreign Intelligence Surveillance Act of 1978), 273
FOIA (Freedom of Information Act), 106
Foreign Intelligence Surveillance Act of 1978 (FISA), 273
foreseeability, 166, 167, 183
defined, 183
forfeiture, 149–150, 235
forgery, 235
formal charges
grand juries, 96–99, 97–98e
indictment, 96, 99–101, 100e
information, 96, 101
overview, 96
Fourteenth Amendment, 48e, 339–341, 343
Privileges and Immunities Clause, 350
Fourth Amendment
privacy, 347, 348
fraudulent checks, 234
Free Exercise Clause, 343
Free Speech Coalition, 256–257
freedom, 21
Freedom of Information Act (FOIA), 106
freedom of information laws, 106
Frisbie v. Collins, 110
fruit of the poisonous tree doctrine, 78–80
defined, 79
exceptions, 79–80
FTCA (Federal Tort Claims Act), 68
fundamental fairness, 74
Furman v. Georgia, 139

G

GBMI (Guilty But Mentally Ill) verdict, 312–313

general deterrence, 25
general intent, 164–166
Gideon v. Wainwright, 122
Gonzales v. Raich, 5–6
government. *See* administration of government, crimes against
Graham v. Connor, 324
Graham v. Florida, 143
grand juries, 96–99, 97–98e
defined, 96
indictments and, 96, 99–101, 100e
procedures of, 96, 99
purpose of, 96
subpoenas, 97–98e
grand larceny, 229
Gregg v. Georgia, 140
Griswold v. Connecticut, 347
Guilty But Mentally Ill (GBMI) verdict, 312–313
Gun Control Act (1968), 261–262
Gun-Free Zone Act (1990), 5

H

habeas corpus, 154–157
defined, 154
habitation, 226, 227, 322. *See also* property and habitation, crimes against
habitual offender statutes, 151
defined, 151
halfway houses, 151
Hamilton, Alexander, 342
hard labor, 142
Harmelin v. Michigan, 143
harmless errors, 470, 153
hate crimes, 219–220
hearings
preliminary, 95–96
revocation, 123e, 147–148
sentencing, 177e, 208, 315e
hearsay, 117, 305
heat-of-passion manslaughter, 202
hierarchical federalism, 4–5
Hinckley, John, 312
H.J. Inc. v. Northwestern Bell Telephone Co., 235
Holbrook v. Flynn, 120
Homeland Security Act, 275, 277–278
homicide, 193–207

and common law, 194–197
communicable diseases and, 201
corpus delicti, 206–207
deadly weapon doctrine, 199, 201
first-degree murder, 197, 198, 199
life and death determination, 205
manslaughter, 202
Model Penal Code approach to, 204–205
overview, 193, 194
provocation and, 202–203
second-degree murder, 197, 198, 199
statutory approaches to AIDS, 201
suicide, 205–206
hung jury, 129

I

IACP (International Association of Chiefs of Police), 59
identity theft, 239–240
defined, 239
immunity
absolute, 67
constitutional defenses, 338–339, 339–341
privileges and, 350
self-incrimination and, 338–339
imperfect self-defense, 203, 323
in limine, 108–109, 127
In State Farm v. Campbell, 18
incapacitation, 25
incarceration, 25, 142–143, 168, 209
incest, 212
inchoate crimes
attempt, 300–302
conspiracy, 303–305
overview, 300
solicitation, 250, 305
incitement of unlawful conduct, 258–259
incorporation, 73–77
Bill of Rights and, 76e
defined, 73
process, 75e
indecent exposure, 252
indefinite sentencing, 144
independent content approach, 74
independent sources, 79
indeterminate sentencing, 143

indictment
  of 20th hijacker in Sept. 11, 278–288
  defined, 96
  waiver of, 100e
indigency, 122
indirect contempt, 271
inevitable discovery rule, 80
infamous crimes, 99
infancy, 325–326
inferences, 175
inferior courts, 10, 12
information, 96, 101
initial appearance, 93, 96
injunctions, 172
insanity defense
  disposition of criminally insane, 313–314
  Durham rule, 311–312
  guilty but mentally ill, 312–313
  irresistible impulse, 311
  M'Naghten test, 310–311
  Model Penal Code test, 312
  overview, 310
  procedures of, 313, 315e
  at time of trial, 314–316
intent
  constructive, 165–166
  to do serious bodily harm, 199, 201
  general, 164–166
  specific, 164–166
  transferred, 167
intentional tort, 17
interlocutory appeals, 153
International Association of Chiefs of Police (IACP), 59
Internet, regulating, 255–257
interpret, 14
Interstate Agreement on Detainers, 110
intervening causes, 184
intoxication, 326
investigation, 88
involuntary intoxication, 326
involuntary manslaughter, 197, 204
irrebuttable presumptions, 176, 264
irresistible impulse, 311

J

Jake's Law, 111
Jencks Act, 104–105
JNOV (judgment notwithstanding the verdict), 129–130
  defined, 129
Johnson v. Zerbst, 122
Jones v. United States, 5
judgement of acquittal, 57, 337
judges, 63
  ethics, 63
judgment notwithstanding the verdict (JNOV), 129–130
judgment of acquittal, 127
judicial branch, 7e, 13–15
judicial court, 11e
judicial opinions, 36–37
judicial review, 14–15
jurisdiction, 3, 4e
jury deliberations, 128–129
Jury Information, 129
jury selection, 125
jury trials, 115–116
juvenile justice system, 326

K

Kanka, Megan, 214
Kansas v. Ventris, 79
Keeler v. Superior Court, 38–39
Kennedy v. Louisiana, 141
Kevorkian, Jack, 206
"knowing endangerment" provision, 291
kidnapping, 216–217
  defined, 216
knowingly acting, 174

L

larceny, 229–231
  defined, 229
larceny by trick, 233
law enforcement officers
  arrests by, 59
  discretion, 59
  ethics, 59–60
  overview, 59
legal assistants, 349–350
legal cause, 183–184
legal guilt, 57
legal impossibility, 302
legal system
  comparing civil law and criminal law, 15–21
  duties and powers of judicial branch, 13–15
  federalism, 2–6
  separation of powers, 6–8
  structure of court system, 8–13
legality, principle of, 35–40
legislative branch, 6, 7e, 41, 78
legislative contempt, 271
legislative history, 169
legislative prerogative canon, 170e
lewdness, 252
liability
  of governments and officials, 67–68
  strict, 17, 167–168
  vicarious, 171
licensing of firearms, 263
life, determination of, 205
Lilburne, John, 338
Logan Act, 273
Love Canal case, 289–290

M

Magna Carta, 115, 120, 125
mail fraud, 234
malice, 226
malicious mischief, 241
malpractice, 17
malum in se, 166–167, 197
malum prohibitum, 166–167, 197
manifest necessity, 337
manslaughter
  defined, 202
  imperfect self-defense and defense of others, 203
  involuntary, 197, 204
  misdemeanor, 197
  overview, 202
  provocation, 202–203
Mapp v. Ohio, 77
Mapplethorpe, Robert, 253
Marbury v. Madison, 15
Marine Mammal Protection Act (MMPA), 293
marital rape exception, 209–210
marriage, 251–252

Marshall, Thurgood, 15, 39, 43, 316
Martin, Treyvon, 317–318
materiality, 233, 267
mayhem, 209
McCleskey v. Kemp, 141
mens rea
  and common law, 163–164
    constructive intent, 165–166
    general intent, 164–166
    malum in se, 166–167
    malum prohibitum, 166–167
    overview, 163–164
    specific intent, 164–166
    transferred intent, 167
  current approaches to, 173–175
  defined, 163
  motive, 176, 177e
  proving, 175–176
  strict liability, 17, 167–169
  vicarious liability, 171
mental illness, 312–313, 316
merger of offenses, 193
Miller v. California, 253
minors, 208, 209, 254, 255, 256, 257, 264
Miranda v. Arizona, 77
misdemeanor manslaughter, 197
mistakes, 326–327
mistrials, 336–337
mitigating circumstances, 144
MMPA (Marine Mammal Protection Act), 293
M'Naghten test, 310–311
  defined, rule of, 310
Model Code of Professional Responsibility, 27, 50, 62, 65
Model Penal Code, 49e
  approach to homicide, 204–205
  consolidation of theft offenses, 238–239
  corporate liability, 171
  elements and, 185, 193
  insanity defense, 313
  mens rea under, 173e
  overview, 47
  and states of mind, 172–173
Model Penal Code and Commentaries. *See* Model Penal Code
modernization, 289
molestation, child, 211, 212, 214

Montana v. Engelhoff, 326
morality. *See* public morality, crimes against
motion practice
  defined, 99
  motion for change of venue, 107–108
  motion for continuance, 109
  motion for severance, 108
  motion in limine, 108–109
  motion to dismiss/quash, 99, 101, 107
  motion to suppress, 107
  types of, 109
motive, 176, 177e
  defined, 176
  mens rea v. motive, 176, 177e
murder. *See* homicide
mutuality, 202

N

NALA (National Association of Legal Assistants), 27, 65
narrow construction canon, 170e
National Association of Legal Assistants (NALA), 27, 65
National Crime Information Center (NCIC), 244, 303
National Federation of Paralegal Associations, 27
National Firearms Act, 261, 263
National Instant Background Check System (NICS), 262
National Institute of Justice, 245, 351
national jurisdiction, 4e
NCIC (National Crime Information Center), 244
necessity, 317
negligence, 17, 174
negligent homicide, 199, 201, 204
negligent tort, 17
"New Federalism," 81–83
NICS (National Instant Background Check System), 262
no right to counsel, 123e, 135–136
nolle prosequi, 61
nolo contendere, 101, 102
nonforcible rape, 210–211
notice, 36

nulla poena sine lege, 36
nullum crimen sine lege, 36

O

objections, 127
objective intent, 175
obscenity, 252–255
obstruction of justice, 270
Occupational Safety and Health Act (OSHA), 291–292
omissions, 180
  defined, 180
opening statements, 126
order. *See* public order, crimes against
ordinances, 41, 49e
Osborne v. Ohio, 254
OSHA (Occupational Safety and Health Act), 291–292
others, defense of, 203, 321
overbreadth doctrine, 341
Oyler v. Boles, 62

P

panhandling, 259–260
Papachristou v. City of Jacksonville, 259
parental kidnapping, 217
Parental Kidnapping Prevention Act (1980), 217
parole, 145
participants
  defense attorneys, 63–64
  judges, 63
  law enforcement officers, 59–60
  legal assistants, 65
  liability of, 67–68
  prosecutors, 60–63
  victims, 65–66
parties to crimes, 299, 300e
Patriot Act, 273, 275
peace, disturbing, 258
The People of the State of New York v. citizen, 19
People v. Warner-Lambert Co., 172, 185
peremptory challenges, 573
perjury, 266–267
  defined, 266
perjury traps, 327

person, crimes against
　assault and battery, 208–209
　civil rights crimes, 219–220
　false imprisonment, 217
　hate crimes, 219–220
　homicide, 193–207
　　and common law, 194–198
　　communicable diseases and, 201
　　corpus delicti, 206–207
　　deadly weapon doctrine, 199, 201
　　first-degree murder, 197, 198, 199
　　life and death determination, 205, 143–144
　　manslaughter, 197, 202, 204
　　Model Penal Code approach to, 204–205
　　overview, 193, 194
　　provocation and, 202–203
　　second-degree murder, 197, 198, 199
　　statutory approaches to AIDS, 201
　　suicide, 205–206
　kidnapping, 216–217
　mayhem, 209
　sex crimes
　castration, 214–215
　against children, 212–214
　commitment, 214–215
　incest, 212
　rape, 209–211
　rape shield laws, 66, 211–212
　sodomy, 211
　stalking, 217–219
　studying, 193
personal recognizance, 94
personal status, 178–179
Phillip Morris U.S.A. v. Williams, 18
pimps, 250
plain meaning canon, 170e
plea agreements, 101
plea bargaining, 101
plea, defined, 101
police power, 5
polling the jury, 129
possession
　as actus reus, 179–180
　of drug paraphernalia, 266
　of handguns, 261
postconviction remedies, 152

Posters 'N' Things, Ltd. v. United States, 266
Powell v. Alabama, 122
Powell v. Georgia, 251
precedents, 33
preliminary hearings, 95–96
　defined, 95
premeditated homicide, 198
present, as part of a factual statement, 233
presentence investigation, 65, 88e, 135–136
preservation requirements, 153
presumption of innocence, 309, 119–120
presumptions, 176
presumptive sentencing, 144
pretrial conferences, 109
pretrial process
　arraignment, 101–102
　arrests, 89
　complaints, 89, 90–92e
　detention, 94–95
　discovery
　　bill of particulars, 103
　　Brady doctrine, 105
　　criminal record of defendant, 104
　　depositions, 105
　　documents and tangible objects, 104
　　freedom of information laws, 106
　　and investigation, 88
　　overview, 88
　　reciprocal discovery, 106
　　scientific reports and tests, 104
　　statements of defendant, 103–104
　　statements of witnesses/Jencks Act, 104–105
　extradition and detainers, 109–111
　formal charges
　　grand juries, 96–99, 97–98e
　　indictment, 96, 99–101, 100e
　　information, 96, 101
　　overview, 96
　initial appearance, 93, 96
　motion practice, 106–109
　preliminary hearings, 95–96
　pretrial conferences, 109
　release, 93–94
　removal, 111
　right to counsel, 123e

scientific identification, blood testing, 104
primary evidence, 78–79
principals, 299
principle of legality, 35–40, 340
Printz v. United States, 5
privacy, 347–350
Privacy Act (1986), 106
private retribution, 26
privileges, 350
probable desistance test, 301
probation, 265, 146–148
property and habitation, crimes against
　arson, 226–227
　burglary, 227–228
　defense of, 322
　theft crimes, 229–244
　computer crimes, 243–244
　consolidated theft statutes, 238–239
　destruction of property, 241–242
　embezzlement, 231–232
　extortion, 238
　false pretenses, 232–233
　forgery, 235
　fraudulent checks, 234
　identity theft, 239–240
　larceny, 229–231
　mail fraud, 234
　Model Penal Code consolidation of, 240–241
　overview, 229
　racketeering, 234–235
　receiving stolen property, 236
　robbery, 236–238
property bonds, 93, 94
prosecution appeals, 153–154
prosecution's case in chief, 126–127
prosecutors, 60–61
　discretion, 61–62
　ethics, 62–63
prostitution, 250
prove the matter asserted, 117
provocation, 202–203
　defined, 202
proximate cause, 183, 185
proximity test, 301
psychiatrists, 313
public, crimes against
　administration of government
　bribery, 267–268

contempt, 271
obstruction of justice, 270
perjury, 266–267
tax crimes, 268–270
defined, 249
environment
Clean Air Act (CAA), 291
Clean Water Act (CWA), 290–291
Comprehensive Environmental Response, Compensation and Liability Act (CERCLA), 291
Emergency Planning and Community Right-to-Know Act, 292
Endangered Species Act (ESA), 293
Federal Insecticide, Fungicide, and Rodenticide Act (FIFRA), 292
Marine Mammal Protection Act (MMPA), 293
Occupational Safety and Health Act (OSHA), 291–292
overview, 289–290
Resource Conservation and Recovery Act (RCRA), 291
Toxic Substances Control Act (TSCA), 292
public morality
deviate sexual conduct, 250–251
indecent exposure, 252
lewdness, 252
obscenity, 252–255
prostitution, 250
regulating Internet, 255–257,
solicitation, 250, 305
public order
conduct, 258–259
disturbing peace, 258
drug and alcohol crimes, 263–265
incitement/advocacy of unlawful, 258–259
involving firearms, 260–263
overview, 257
riot and unlawful assembly, 257–258
threats, 259
vagrancy and panhandling, 259–260
sovereignty and security
espionage, 272–273
sedition, 272–273
terrorism, 273–288

treason, 272
public defenders, 63
public morality, crimes against
deviate sexual conduct, 250–251
indecent exposure, 252
lewdness, 252
obscenity, 252–255
prostitution, 250
regulating Internet, 255–257
solicitation, 250, 305
public offenses, 39, 168
public order, crimes against
alcohol crimes, 263–264
disturbing peace, 258
drug crimes
overview, 264–265
possession of drug paraphernalia, 266
RICO and CCE, 265–266
incitement/advocacy of unlawful conduct, 258–259
involving firearms, 260–263
panhandling, 259–260
riot, 257–258
threats, 259
unlawful assembly, 257–258
vagrancy, 259–260
public retribution, 26
public trials, 116
punishment
forms of, 139
purpose of, 24–27
punitive damages, 17
purposely acting, 174

Q

qualified immunity, 68
quash, 99, 101, 107
quasi-judicial acts, 67, 68

R

race, 125–126
Racketeer Influenced and Corrupt Organizations Act (RICO), 234–235, 265–266, 149
rap sheets, 136
rape, 209–211

defined, 209
rape shield laws, 66, 211–212
R.A.V. v. City of St. Paul, 361–362, 347
RCRA (Resource Conservation and Recovery Act), 291
rebuttable presumptions, 176, 326, 94
rebuttals, 128
receiving stolen property, 236
recidivism, 151
reciprocal discovery, 106
recklessness, 174
record, 9
record on appeal, 9
registration of firearms, 263
regulations, 42, 49e
regulatory offenses, 168
rehabilitation, 26
relationship, duty by, 181–182
release, types of, 93–94
religion, 343–344
Religious Freedom Restoration Act, 344
remand, 10
removal, 111
Reno v. ACLU, 256
res ipsa loquitur test, 301
resisting unlawful arrests, 323
Resource Conservation and Recovery Act (RCRA), 291
restitution, 148, 66
retreat to the wall doctrine, 319
retribution, 26–27
revocation hearings, 118, 147–148
defined, 147
Richardson v. United States, 237
RICO (Racketeer Influenced and Corrupt Organizations Act), 234–235, 265–266
right to counsel
appeals, 9–13, 154
chart, 76e
habeas corpus, 157
and Seventh Circuit Court of Appeals, 135
right to self-representation, 124
riots, 257–258
robbery, 236–238
defined, 236
Robinson v. California, 178
Roe v. Wade, 205, 348–349
Rogers v. Tennessee, 186

Roth v. United States, 253
rules of court, 46–47. *See also* court rules

S

Salinas v. Texas, 127
same evidence test, 337
The Scarlet Letter, 143
scienter, 164
scientific reports and tests, 104
scope of review, habeas corpus, 155
scope of right, 124–125
searches and seizures
    Fourth Amendment
        overview, 348
        privacy, 347–348
second-degree murder, 197, 198, 199
    defined, 198
security. *See* sovereignty and security, crimes against
sedition, 272–273
seduction, child, 214
selective incorporation doctrine, 74
self-defense
    defined, 318
    imperfect, 203, 323
    overview, 318
self-incrimination, 338–339
sentencing
    alternatives, 150–151
    capital punishment, 139–142
    community service, 148
    concurrent and consecutive, 145
    corporal/physical punishment, 142
    definite and indefinite, 144
    Federal Guidelines, 145–146
    fines, 148–149
    forfeiture, 149–150, 235
    habitual offender statutes, 151
    hearings, 136–137
    incarceration, 142–143
    indeterminate and determinate, 143
    overview, 135
    parole, 145
    presentence investigation/no right to counsel, 135–136
    presumptive, 144
    probation and revocation, 146–148
    proving facts for, 138–139
    punishing acquitted crimes, 137–138
    restitution, 148
    shaming, 143
    suspended imposition of sentence, 265, 144
separation of powers, 6–8, 7e
    defined, 6
series, defined, 266
Seventh Circuit Court of Appeals, 135
sex crimes
    castration, 214–215
    against children, 212–214
    commitment, 214–215
    incest, 212
    Megan's Laws, 214–215
    rape, 209–211
    rape shield laws, 211–212
    sodomy, 211
shaming, 143
shield laws, 211–212
shock treatment, 150
sidebars, 2, 127
Simmons v. United States, 80
sine qua non test, 183
SIS (suspended imposition of sentence), 265, 144
Sixth Amendment
    confrontation and cross-examination, 117–118
    defense attorneys, 63, 64
    effective assistance of counsel, 123–124
    jury trials, 115–116, 120e
    Seventh Circuit Court of Appeals, 135
60 minutes program, 206
sodomy, 211
solicitation, 250, 305
    child, 214
    defined, 305
solitary confinement, 142
sources of criminal law, 32–51, 49e
    administrative law, 41–46
    common law, 33–41
    constitutional law, 47–48
    court rules, 46–47
    Model Penal Code, 47
    ordinances, 41
    statutory law, 41
sovereign immunity, 68
sovereignty and security, crimes against
    espionage, 272–273
    sedition, 272–273
    terrorism, 273–288
    treason, 272
specific deterrence, 25
specific intent, 164–166
speech, 272, 345–347, 346e
Speedy Trial Act (1974), 121
speedy trials, 120–121
split sentences, 146
spoofing, 218
stalking, 217–218
    defined, 218
stand-your-ground laws, 320
standards of proof, 399e
standby counsel, 124
standing, defined, 80–81
stare decisis, 33
state constitutions, 6, 48, 81–83
state court structure, 13e
state jurisdiction, 4e
state trial courts, 9
State v. Snowden, 198
statements, 178
    of defendant, 103–104
    of witnesses, 104–105
states of mind, 173–174
statutes, 6–7, 49e
    approaches to homicide, 198
        AIDS, 201, 303
        deadly weapon doctrine, 199, 201
        first-degree murder, 197, 198, 199
        second-degree murder, 197, 198, 199
    defined, 6
    duty imposed by, 180–181
    of limitation, 329
statutory construction, 169
statutory law, 41
statutory rape, 210–211
stolen property, receiving, 236
strict liability, 17, 167–169
    and statutory construction, 169–171
strict liability crimes, 168–169
    defined, 168
strict liability tort, 17
strict scrutiny test, 342, 344
subjective intent, 175
subornation of perjury, 267
subpoenas, 97–98e
substantial capacity test, 312

substantial step to completion test, 302
suicide, 205–206
summons, 91–92e
Superfund, 291
Supremacy Clause, 3
surety bonds, 93
suspended imposition of sentence (SIS), 265, 144
suspended sentences, 146

T

tangible objects, 104
tax crimes, 268–270
tax evasion, defined, 269
tax fraud, defined, 269
Tennessee v. Garner, 324
Tenth Amendment, 2, 4, 76e
terrorism, 5, 273–288
theft crimes
    computer crimes, 243–244
    consolidated theft statutes, 238–239
    destruction of property, 241–242
    embezzlement, 231–232
    extortion, 238
    false pretenses, 232–233
    identity theft, 239–240
    larceny, 169, 174, 194e, 229–231
    Model Penal Code consolidation of, 240–241
    receiving stolen property, 236
    robbery, 236–238
Thirteenth Amendment, 48e
threats, 259
titles, 233
tolling, 329
tort, 17
tortfeasor, 17
total incorporation, 74, 348
total incorporation plus, 74
Touby v. United States, 43, 44–46
Toxic Substances Control Act (TSCA), 292
transactional immunity, 338
transfer laws, and guns, 261–262
transferred intent, 167
treason, 272
trial, 177e
    closing arguments, 128

courts, 8–9
defense case, 127–128
final instructions, 128
JNOV, 129–130
jury deliberations and verdict, 128–129
mistrials, 336–337
opening statements, 126
preliminary instructions, 126
prosecution's case in chief, 126–127
rebuttal, 128
rights of defendants
    confrontation and cross-examination, 117–119
    counsel, 121–125
    jury trial, 115–116
    presumption of innocence/burden of proof, 309, 119–120
    public trial, 116
    to self-representation, 124
    speedy trial, 120–121
voir dire, 125–126
TSCA (Toxic Substances Control Act), 292
Twenty-seventh Amendment, 48e

U

undercover officers, 321
unequivocality test, 301
Uniform Controlled Substance Act, 264
Uniform Interstate Criminal Extradition Act, 109
Union Carbide, 290
United States, legal system of
    comparing civil law and criminal law, 15–21
    duties and powers of judicial branch, 13–15
    federalism, 2–6
    separation of powers, 6–8
    structure of court system, 8–13
United States v. Booker, 139, 146
United States v. Comstock, 6
United States v. Grimaud, 43–44
United States v. Jackson, 116
United States v. James Daniel Good Real Property, 149
United States v. Lewis, 261

United States v. Miller, 260
United States v. Morrison, 5
United States v. Watts, 137
United States v. Williams, 257
United States v. Windsor, 252
Uniting and Strengthening America by Providing Appropriate Tools Required to Intercept and Obstruct Terrorism Act of 2001, 273, 275
unlawful arrests, resisting, 323
unlawful assembly, 257–258
unlawful disclosure, 269, 270
U.S.C. codes. *See also* endnotes
    18 U.S.C. § 875(c), 218, 251
    47 U.S.C. § 223(a)(1)(A), 218, 219
use immunity, 339
use-of-force defenses
    arrests
        by citizens, 324–325
        by law enforcement officers, 324
        resisting unlawful arrests, 323
    defense of others, 203, 321
    defense of property and habitation, 322
    imperfect self-defense, 203, 323
    overview, 317–318
    self-defense, 318
uttering, 235

V

vagrancy, 259–260
vagueness doctrine, 341
Valle, Gilberto, 303–304
Van de Kamp v. Goldstein, 67
Van Hise, Michael, 303
vehicular homicide, 204
verdict, 193, 312–313, 314, 315e, 57, 116, 128–129. *See also* specific types
vicarious liability, 171
    corporate liability as, 171–173
    defined, 171
vicarious sexual gratification, 213–214
victim assistance organizations, 66
victim compensation programs, 66
victim impact statements, 66, 136–137
"victimless" crimes, 249
victims, 65–66
Victims' Bill of Rights, 66

violators, punishing, 24–27
Violent Crime Control and Law
    Enforcement Act (1994), 262
Virginia v. Black, 347
voir dire, 125–126
voluntariness, 177–178

W

waiver of indictment, 100e
Washington v. Glucksberg, 206
weapons of mass destruction, 278
Web site information
    American Bar Association, 187
    attorney listings, 111
    case laws, 51
    for comparative law, 330
    for courts, 28
    for crime data, 245
    for criminal justice, 351
    for famous trials, 130
    government printing office, 306
    for international law, 330, 69
    IRS, 293
    for legislative information, 220
    metasearching the WWW, 84
    for prosecutors, 28
    punishment, 157
    sentencing, 157
    for tax laws, 293
    Washburn Law School, 220
    www.findlaw.com, 51
Wharton's Rule, 304
Wilkins, Cole Allen, 195, 196
willful homicide, 198
Williams v. Illinois, 118, 149
withdrawal, 304
World Factbook of Criminal Justice
    Systems, 351

Y

"year-and-a-day rule"
    concurrence, 186
    overview, 185–186

Z

Zimmerman, George, 317–318